HELLO, WORLD!

To Mr Bone and our friends from the Carthy Foundation, with the gratitude of our participants...

and my best wishes

Jacques Hébert

Montréal

August 10, 2005

Talonbooks

BY THE SAME AUTHOR

I Accuse the Assassins of Coffin (Éditions du Jour)	Montreal 1964
The Temple on the River, roman (Harvest House)	Montreal 1967
Two Innocents in Red China–co-written with Pierre Elliott Trudeau (Oxford University Press)	Toronto 1968
The World is Round (McClelland & Stewart)	Toronto 1976
Have Them Build a Tower Together (McClelland & Stewart)	Toronto 1979
The Great Building-Bee–co-written with Maurice F. Strong (General Publishing)	Don Mills 1980
The Coffin Affair (General Publishing)	Don Mills 1981
21 Days– One Man's Fight for Canada's Youth (Optimum Publishing)	Montreal 1986
Travelling in Tropical Countries (Hurtig Publishers)	Edmonton 1986
Yemen–An Invitation to a Voyage in Arabia Felix (Heritage Publishing)	Montreal 1989

In French

Autour des trois Amériques (Beauchemin)	Montreal 1948
Autour de l'Afrique (Fides)	Montreal 1950
Aïcha l'Africaine, contes (Fides)	Montreal 1950
Aventures autour du monde (Fides)	Montreal 1952
Nouvelle aventure en Afrique (Fides)	Montreal 1953
Coffin était innocent (Éditions de l'Homme)	Montreal 1958
Scandale à Bordeaux (Éditions de l'Homme)	Montreal 1959
Deux innocents en Chine rouge–en collaboration avec Pierre Elliott Trudeau (Éditions de l'Homme)	Montreal 1960
J'accuse les assassins de Coffin (Éditions du Jour)	Montreal 1963
Trois jours en prison (Club du Livre du Québec)	Montreal 1965
Les Écoeurants, roman (Éditions du Jour)	Montreal 1966
Ah ! mes Aïeux ! (Éditions du Jour)	Montreal 1968
Obscénité et Liberté (Éditions du Jour)	Montreal 1970
Blablabla du bout du monde (Éditions du Jour)	Montreal 1971
La terre est ronde (Fides)	Montreal 1976
Faites-leur bâtir une tour ensemble (Éditions Héritage)	Montreal 1979
L'Affaire Coffin (Domino)	Montreal 1980
Le Grand Branle-bas–en collaboration avec Maurice-F. Strong (Les Quinze)	Montréal 1980
La jeunesse des années 80 : état d'urgence (Éditions Héritage)	Montreal 1982
Voyager en pays tropical (Boréal Express)	Montreal 1984
Trois semaines dans le hall du Sénat (Éditions de l'Homme)	Montreal 1986
Yémen–Invitation au voyage en Arabie heureuse (Éditions Héritage)	Montreal 1989
Deux innocents dans un igloo (Héritage Jeunesse)	Montreal 1990
Deux innocents au Mexique (Héritage Jeunesse)	Montreal 1990
Deux innocents au Guatemala (Héritage Jeunesse)	Montreal 1990
Deux innocents en Amérique centrale (Héritage Jeunesse)	Montreal 1991
Bonjour, le monde! (Éditions Robert Davies)	Montreal 1996

In German

Jemen—Einladung zu einer Reise nach Arabia felix(Azal Publishing)	Ottawa 1989

Jacques Hébert

HELLO, WORLD!

On Canada, the World and Youth

Translated by Jean-Paul Murray

Preface by Michael Oliver

Talonbooks / Robert Davies Publishing
VANCOUVER, MONTREAL, TORONTO, PARIS

ISBN 1-895854-60-1

Cover design by Yvan Adam

Royalties from this book will be entirely donated to Canada World Youth

This book may be ordered in Canada from

General Distribution Services

☎ 1-800-387-0141 / 1-800-387- 0172 🖷 1-416-445-5967;

in the U.S.A., from Associated Publishers Group,
1501 County Hospital Road, Nashville, TN 37218
dial toll free 1-800-327-5113;

In the U.K., from Drake International Services,
Market House, Market Place, Deddington, Oxford OX15 OSF, ☎/🖷 01869 338-240

or call the publishers:
Robert Davies Publishing, toll-free throughout North America:

1-800-481-2440, 🖷 1-888-RDAVIES
or
Talonbooks, ☎ 1-604-444-4889 🖷 1-604-444-4119

e-mail: rdppub@vir.com

Visit our Internet website,
where our full updated catalogue is available:

http://www.rdppub.com

This book was typeset in American Garamond 11 on 13 points.

The publishers take this opportunity to thank the
Canada Council and the Ministère de la Culture
du Québec for their continuing support of publishing.

TO PIERRE ELLIOTT TRUDEAU, A NOBLE AND LOYAL FRIEND, WITHOUT WHOM CANADA WORLD YOUTH WOULD HAVE NEVER EXISTED

(Without me either, by the way!)

CONTENTS

PART III: Hello, World!

Preface

What kind of young women and men do we need to cope with the twenty-first century? They'll have to face change—a changing environment, changing relationships among people, changing concepts of career and vocation. But above all, they should be confident that they can induce *change. Will they have to be profoundly different? I doubt it. It isn't a question of setting aside the hallowed virtues of tradition—integrity, truthfulness, courage and the rest. The person who is right for the third millennium will need to be alert to new meanings for these qualities rather than on the hunt for new values.*

Context is crucial. Recognizing how similar we are to one another, and yet how important our differences are—things that make each of us special—is a kind of understanding best gained through experience. The most careful reading of the growing literature on multiculturalism, or on identity and authenticity, risks producing surface, unincorporated knowledge unless it's matched by real-life encounters, dialogue and sharing.

The more we can gain perspective by entering a little into other people's lives, rather than peering at them, the more likely we are to substitute understanding, and perhaps some affection, for fear and hate. We are painfully beginning to realize that a secure future for any of us must be based on common security *and common understanding.*

Jacques Hébert began early to see things through others' eyes. Being transplanted from Québec to Prince Edward Island, to be educated in another language, meant a change in perspective that differed only in degree from the shifts in outlook that he later was able to make when he met people in Latin America, Africa or China. He came to believe how exciting and transforming *it was to be within another culture, even if briefly. Founding and leading Canada World Youth was only one of the ways Jacques found to express this conviction, but what a great choice it was!*

I admit I had forgotten much about the early hand-to-mouth days of Canada World Youth. Jacques' account in Part I of this book inflates, with typical generosity, the spear-carrier role I played; but I do remember that fateful interview with the Secretary of State for External Affairs, Mitchell Sharp, when all our funding was in jeopardy, and the feeling of triumph after it. It also brought back the midnight telephone calls when, Jacques being off in some obscure corner of the world, it fell to me to track down the President of CIDA, Paul Gérin-Lajoie, to get him to intervene personally to release a blocked cheque in time for a whole contingent of participants to board the morning plane for Senegal. Hectic days indeed! But with Jacques, they were always fun. Memories are always punctuated by bursts of laughter and lightened by the perpetual twinkle in Jacques' eye.

It was fun—but it was so much more. Jacques Hébert found a way to let thousands of young people partake in his vision of shared development. Imagine having the audacity to believe that Canada should become the conscience of rich countries and the catalyst of North-South dialogue, and then getting huge cohorts of young people to live their faith in that vision, a vision that they had made their own. Read Part II, and find out how transformations were made. What I like about these accounts of individual experience brought together by Jacques Hébert is the gradual accumulation of insights: there are no instantaneous conversions, no blinding lights. There is just growing comprehension of how rich one can be even in material poverty, and yet how vital it is to eliminate that poverty; how many distortions are made in the evaluation of others and, reciprocally, how many mistakes others make in their judgements.

When they were young, most of my children went each summer to the French language Camp Minogami. One of the activities they described to me involved clambering over barriers, climbing obstacles, running, leaping and trying, not to be first, but just to complete the course, to do it well and enjoy it. The activity was called "Hébertisme!" What better name I thought, and from then on it became in my mind "Jacques Hébertisme."

Canada World Youth was and is "Jacques Hébertisme" and much more. I know you'll enjoy reading about it in the pages that follow.

Michael Oliver

Preamble[1]

There should be a law to protect the masses against autobiographies, memoirs and other ramblings, which can only interest authors and their moms. Unless you're Stendhal, Neruda or Churchill.

What nerve to talk about your scarlet fever to people who couldn't care less! To write dreadful things such as: "I'm a dyed-in-the-wool Montrealer born on Saint-Denis Street, at the corner of Sherbrooke (That takes some doing!). My father was a doctor and my mother was beautiful. My earliest recollections go back to the nasty scarlet fever I'd had as a child, etc."

There should definitely be a law!

I've immunized myself against the autobiographical virus because the past bores me dreadfully: I can't change it, whereas the present moment, as luminous and vibrant as a South-Seas bird , fascinates and astounds me. At this very instant, I cherish the precious and fleeting seconds, as my pen (*Pilot Fineliner*) glides over the paper with the infinite smoothness of sand in an hourglass. (Soft-boiled egg: three minutes.)

We're masters of the present. We can give it wings and let it fly away like a swallow crossing the sky without leaving a trace. Or seize it by the hand and let it carry us towards grace.

The most exhilarating moments I've had over the last twenty-five years I owe to Canada World Youth's young participants, to the warmhearted conversations we had, in the shade of a mango tree somewhere on the island of Sumatra, inside a flimsy straw hut in Mali, around a fire in the frigid Andes. In Vancouver, Vegreville, Toronto, Île Perrot, Saint-Georges-de-Beauce, Halifax and, very recently, in a humble Prince-Edward Island village. Exquisite moments. The only ones from my albeit event-ridden past which I can still recall effortlessly.

Seated Indian-style on warm sand or a braided palm-leaf mat, there I am surrounded by a dozen boys and girls from every corner of Canada and from every corner of our host country. Together, they've already shared unique human experiences, months of strenuous work in the most extreme climates; they're no longer the same, they'll never again be the same. This can be seen in their intense gaze, and heard in their serious conversations about the future of the world, not usually the main concern of youth their age. (This doesn't mean there's no time for laughter, quite the contrary!)

---

1 From the Latin *praeambulare* (*prae*, meaning forward, and *ambulare*, meaning to go).

Alas! there's always a wise guy from Newfoundland or a tall blond Vancouver girl to ask the dreaded question, the only one I never feel like answering:

"Won't you please tell us how all this began? Who *gave you the idea* for Canada World Youth?"

When I'm lucky, the question comes at the end of the session, when we make our farewells:

"Oh! what a shame the question wasn't asked earlier! I'd need over an hour to answer it properly ... I'm already late, another group awaits me a hundred kilometres away ... You understand? But the next time we meet, I promise to tell you everything!"

Saved by the bell!

At times, however, a particularly clever participant raises the question at the right moment. I hesitate, shilly-shally and babble before this group of boys and girls whom I love, and wouldn't want to disappoint. Their large inquisitive eyes literally terrify me. They expect a beautiful story, a darned "message," bloody hell! As if I were Gandhi ... or Baden-Powell!

I sometimes manage to weasel out of it with a joke:

"One day, I was alone under an old maple atop Mont Saint-Hilaire. I was daydreaming while chewing on a blade of grass; suddenly, an angel appeared: 'Jacques,' he said in a firm yet gentle voice, 'you must found ...'"

My tiny audience breaks into laughter and, generally, doesn't press me further.

The reason I'm loathe to answer such a typical question is that I'd have to plumb the depths of my recollections, something I despise above all. I have no memory, no archives, that would be awful!

And yet, I've promised a hundred times that "when we meet again, I'll relate everything."

In the first part of this book, I've finally resigned myself to keeping that promise.

* * *

Over the years, my numerous meetings with Canada World Youth participants were always brief, too brief. With one exception.

In 1985, during International Youth Year, Canada World Youth launched a special program that was original and daring, and directed to youths having *already* participated in the regular program, in eleven Third World countries. Half the project would take place in Zaïre, the other in Canada.

I then decided to follow this new undertaking very closely: I'd take part in the training camp with the eighteen Canadian participants, get to know them a little, join them in the backwater towns of Western Kasaï, where the reconstruction of two rundown hospitals awaited them and, finally, meet them again in Canada where, with the help of their Zaïrian friends, they'd share their experiences with tens of thousands of Canadians, from Halifax to Vancouver.

A wonderful love story I'll relate in the second part of this book.Or, more precisely, that participants will relate.

* * *

I love books as much as I love countries, those vast illustrated books. I've read all countries of the world, ten times more often than once, except Mongolia (maybe!) and no doubt a few odds and ends like Tonga and Suriname. I haven't had my fill yet, and have trouble resisting the appeal of a still-undiscovered corner of the world ("Suriname, here I come!"). I experience the joy of a child as soon as the doors of mystery are opened. Joy gives way to rapture when I discover an unknown jewel like rugged Yemen, or proud and melancholy Albania, a sorry witness to the great stupidity of the twentieth century.

My principal trips took place between the ages of twenty-two and thirty, when I crossed the Americas, Africa and Asia from one end to the other. Afterwards, family commitments and the demands of various occupations prevented trips of more than a few weeks a year, and rarely more than a month.

Following the creation of Canada World Youth, in 1971, I often had to go on missions to the four corners of the Third World to urge countries to join the movement, negotiate protocols of agreement and, eventually, spend a day or two with participants in some small village in Peru, Togo, or the Philippines. The only trips that have really interested me since, and to which I've devoted Christmas holidays for nearly twenty-five years.

On returning from each mission, I write a report for the board of directors, staff and a few of Canada World Youth's friends. I try to recreate my privileged encounters with participants, as well as provide suggestions that might improve the program from one year to the next.

I'm aware that reports are rarely read and almost never to the end. I've therefore devised a technique: instead of being run-of-the-mill, my reports take the shape of a travel diary reamed with anecdotes, at times poignant, at times comical. The reader might allow himself to be taken in ... and thereby swallow the rest, for fear of missing an exciting moment or funny incident!

In all, these mission reports must exceed a thousand pages ... forever buried in Canada World Youth's archives. I'll quote a few excerpts from them in the third part of this book to, as it were, once again salute a dozen countries of the world.

PART ONE

"Next Time, I'll Tell You Everything!"

Discovering the world can provide human judgement with wonderful enlightenment. We're all constrained and gathered up within ourselves, and see no further than the end of our nose. When asked where he was from, Socrates answered not "from Athens," but "from the world."

Montaigne

The world is so full of a number of things, I'm sure we should all be as happy as kings.

Robert Louis Stevenson

1.
An Unusual Layman Among the Jesuits

I've finally discovered what I want to be later:
a little boy.

Joseph Heller

Hervé Benoist speaking to a young scout at the Lac Simon camp.

Friendship has always been very important to me. Since childhood, I'd dreamed of having tons of friends, true and lifelong friends some day.

At thirteen, long after the scarlet fever, I enrolled in Montreal's Collège Sainte-Marie, to study in the *éléments latins* class (the equivalent of first-year high school), as it was called in the good old days when we still had an education system. With the Jesuit Fathers, who it was said needed fourteen years schooling—*following* the baccalaureate—to become full-fledged members of their order. (They occasionally didn't hesitate to remind us!) This impressed me to no end. Fourteen years! More than my age!

I rather liked the Jesuits, save when they poisoned us with their bloody notions of a Catholic and French *Laurentie*! Or when they included Salazar and Franco, the two "good" Catholic dictators of the day, in discussions about great men. They even considered that dunce Mussolini to be a swell guy, due to the concordat with the pope, and the blasted Pontine Marshes, which he'd ostensibly drained with a teaspoon!

What rescued me from this oppressive predicament were a wonderful layman who worked at the college, Hervé Benoist, as well as an unusual Jesuit, Father Thomas Migneault: huge, intelligent, astonishing, unconventional, cheerful, a tad crazy, perhaps a saint.

When we'd run into Father Migneault in the halls of the college, he'd grab us by the shoulders and shake us rather vigorously. His large cheerful grey eyes would overwhelm us with manly affection, as he trotted out some incredible tirade: "Son, the country needs you! Son, you must become a man! *Esto vir*! Strong and brave. Steadfast and dependable. Dedicated and straightforward. Resourceful and competent. *Esto vir*! A leader! Tell me son, you want to become a leader, don't you?"

Naturally, we'd say yes without quite understanding the meaning of those curious remarks.

At lunch time, in the dining hall, while we ate pork and beans saturated with fat, washed down with sugar-laden ginger ale, Father Migneault gave us endless and rousing speeches, not on Ignatius Loyola's noble virtues but, rather, on those of raw vegetables. Without raw fruits and vegetables, we'd apparently all be done for!

Other times, he waged war on mumblers. A topic on which he could talk forever. "AR-TI-CU-LATE! AR-TI-CU-LATE! AR-TI-CU-LATE!" he'd tirelessly shout at us. One day, he brought a woman into the college—how dreadful! She was plump and, though from France, named MacDonald. She taught diction by using small rubber balls she'd have us put in our mouths: two at first, then four, and even six ... Mumblers were given quite a ride!

Students, though non-boarders, were forbidden from going to movie theatres, those lairs of the devil. Many had been caught at the *Imperial* or *Loews* exit by some cassock-wearing monitor trying to gild his heavenly crown by being on the lookout, often when the weather was Siberian. Miscreants thereby earned numerous stiff blows of a strap on each hand, something more humiliating than painful.

Contrary to his colleagues, Father Migneault believed in the cinema and had trouble accepting that teenagers—future leaders!—were denied access to it. He knew everybody who was somebody in Montreal, including Alexandre de Sèvres, the chairman of France-Film and owner of the Saint-Denis movie theatre. He managed to convince him to show a film, free of charge, to all students at the college on given Saturday mornings. As a result, I saw my first film, *Michel Strogoff*, starring the amazing Harry Baur, thanks to Father Migneault ... and fell in love with the superb Anabella, star of *L'Appel du silence*. In fact, the beautiful French actress enraptured all students at the college, without exception, for a long time.

The incredible Father Migneault had numerous other obsessions, including physical fitness, outdoor living, Quebec's flora and fauna, initiation to all the arts and, of course, individual achievement and character building. All this lead him to create the Collège Sainte-Marie scout troop, with the requisite co-operation of Hervé Benoist, a layman in his thirties, an exceptional educator as well.

From the outset, this man would have an effect on the young scouts that was more profound, more lasting even than that of his friend and accomplice, Father Migneault. He was one of the college's rare lay teachers, a Franco-Manitoban, more or less an architect, a great humanist and universal spirit who taught English and math to earn a living. But his true vocation was leading the scout troop—which would become unique.

Hervé Benoist was the kind of master everybody wants to meet at least once in a lifetime. And I had the singular delight of getting to know him by the time I was thirteen. No man has influenced me more. Without him, I'm absolutely certain that Canada World Youth would have never seen the light of day. I therefore have to talk about him somewhat ...

And so, I belonged to this unique scout troop, so unique in fact that other scouts were rather wary of us at the time, perhaps even envious. They'd jokingly refer to us as "Benoist's Scouts!"

Scouting was only an excuse to this exceptional master. Without rejecting its fundamental principles, he'd changed many of its methods. Instead of wasting our time teaching us to "tie knots," (something we'd learned anyway) he'd inspire us about the arts, especially music, and about science, every science. At a time when science was more or less held as suspect by the Jesuits, Sulpicians, etc., Hervé Benoist had transformed our old scout quarters, located in the Collège Sainte Marie's dusty and dark basement, into a genuine laboratory, where awful explosions happened occasionally, thereby contributing to our troubling reputation: a lab used for chemistry, physics, radiophony, biology, astronomy, etc. There was also a darkroom for photo enthusiasts and, in every corner, tiny and ingenious devices that Hervé Benoist had fashioned with his large and nimble fingers, to help us understand the mysteries of Hertzian waves, the internal combustion engine, or the wonder of constellations.

With his splendid round handwriting, Hervé Benoist had even written an *atomic theory* manual, illustrated with a hundred-or-so wonderful colour drawings. In 1936! A treasure we venerated all the more since there was only one copy. When we'd been "good scouts," according to his own definition, we'd earn the distinguished privilege of borrowing the famous green notebook for a few days ... and a few nights during which we'd feverishly transcribe large portions.

It mustn't, however, be assumed we were a gang of serious little chaps, only preoccupied with arts and sciences. On the contrary, we were jovial fellows, given to the occasional outrageous prank. (Isn't that right, Gilles Lefebvre?). How I laughed, and what fun I had in those days!

While other scouts brayed the boring songs of the *Éclaireurs de France*, we'd sing the most beautiful French folklore ballads, in four part harmony, or else some Mozart or Mendelssohn. Whereas other scouts wore rather insignificant badges, we were allowed to sport a single one on a sleeve of our sky-blue shirts: the universally recognized Royal Life Saving Society badge.

In summer, we'd go wilderness camping in the Laurentians on the shores of splendid Lac Simon. Our excursions took on the appearance of genuine expeditions, on foot in the midst of the forest, or long perilous journeys in birch-bark canoes (made by local natives) on remote lakes and rivers.

Does any of this really concern Canada World Youth? Any more than my scarlet fever? It's with these peculiar scouts that I learned, among other things, about the virtues of group living, of exchanges between boys (girls would come later) who often had nothing in common, of solid friendships which were nonetheless created, some of which still endure: Gabriel Phaneuf, Jean-Louis Roux, and a few others still. It's said a man is wealthy if, towards the end of his life, he's managed to maintain two or three real friendships. By that token, I'm a filthy millionaire!

Although Father Thomas Migneault was prefect at the Collège Sainte-Marie, to the scouts he was first and foremost the troop's chaplain, Hervé Benoist's powerful ally. Before anyone else, this rather strange Jesuit had understood that the clergy's hegemony over our education system wouldn't last forever. With the help of prominent secular personalities, including a few wealthy businessmen, he'd taken part in a top-secret plot: the founding of the first secular school in Quebec, a *lycée* whose principal would naturally be Hervé Benoist, and we the scouts its first students. Distinguished intellectuals had accepted, under a cloak of secrecy for the time being, to teach at this future school, including André Laurendeau, his father Arthur, a famous musicologist, etc.

When the Jesuit Provincial got wind of the story, the very naive and very wonderful Father Migneault found himself exiled overnight to the Jesuit College in Edmonton, Alberta. The *lycée* was dead.

Comprising nearly eighty students, the scout troop had weathered this catastrophe as best it could. To the school's Jesuits, we were a "state within the state." They were obsessed by this, save in the rarest of cases. How could they tolerate that Hervé Benoist, a mere layman who hadn't gone through fourteen years of schooling to become one, continue to have such a powerful hold on so many students?

And so, when school resumed in September 1938, nobody, save the scouts, was really surprised to learn that Hervé Benoist no longer taught at the college and was, therefore, no longer the troop's scoutmaster. He'd moved to the Canadian Officer Training Corps, a school for students wanting to become infantry officers.

Hervé Benoist *knew* we'd soon be at war. Contrary to popular opinion in Quebec, poisoned by nationalist elites with *Le Devoir* in the lead, he'd understood that freedom and democracy would be at stake in the eventual conflict.

He'd say to his *guys*: "One of these days, whether you like it or not, you'll have to go to war. At least go as officers."

In becoming captain and quartermaster at the Canadian Officer Training Corps, Hervé Benoist would continue to help his former scouts by encouraging them to become officers.

When Canada joined the Allies by declaring war on the Axis, the government urged students to stay in school until they earned diplomas, on condition they follow night courses at the Canadian Officer Training Corps, and take part in military camps at Farnham during summer holidays.

Many of "Benoist's Scouts" became officers. As for me, I finished university with the rank of infantry lieutenant and, like my graduating classmates, was getting ready to transfer from the reserve to the regular army. I'm still amazed I contemplated that prospect so serenely, while nearly all of Quebec's intelligentsia denounced the "dirty war" that "British imperialism had dragged us into."

For example, beginning in 1941, the great majority of francophone Quebeckers was convinced that Pétain was the man of the hour, and that De Gaulle was a rebel if not a traitor. That's what I read in *Le Devoir* and elsewhere, that's what university professors told us, some even claiming that Nazi concentration camps were outright allied-propaganda fabrications. Thank goodness there was a Captain Benoist, in the old Canadian Officer Training Corps building on Sherbrooke Street, at the corner of Berri, who thought differently.

Be that as it may, I didn't take part in that war: it ended a few weeks before I was to join the regular army.

But let's return to that first day of school in September 1938, which was particularly painful for the Collège Sainte-Marie's eighty or so scouts: one year after losing the irreplaceable Father Migneault, they were being deprived of their beloved Hervé Benoist. Rightly or wrongly, they believed the Jesuits had ruthlessly dismissed him from the school because they could no longer tolerate the amazing influence of this layman on students in general, and scouts in particular.

Outraged by what appeared to be the century's greatest injustice, "Benoist's Scouts," resigned as a unit from the "new" troop, and decided to continue meeting surreptitiously which, of course, had been forbidden under threat of immediate expulsion from the college.

The threat added to the excitement of the situation. We found secluded premises on Saint-Hubert Street, behind the large house of Louis Dupire, sub-editor of *Le Devoir* at the time, three of whose sons were "Benoist's Scouts." We gained access to it through shadowy Saint-Christophe Lane, not a popular haunt of Jesuit spies.

Ten years later, when nearly all of us were at university, we'd still meet once a week, and spend the better part of our holidays together, going on trips that were becoming longer, whether walking, biking or paddling birch-bark canoes.

Each year we'd hold a grand party to celebrate friendship on August 8, the birthday of our beloved Hervé Benoist. The last one was held in 1979, on his eightieth birthday.

Group living, camaraderie, friendship, a Spartan lifestyle, travelling: Canada World Youth, Katimavik ...

2.
"You'll Discover Freedom!" My Father Told Me.

We must learn to live together as brothers, or else we'll die together like idiots.
Martin Luther King

Dalton Hall at Saint Dunstan's College in Charlottetown, Prince Edward Island.

Backwards in time. Once again, let's tear another shred from my recollections that may concern Canada World Youth, and the answer requested by those wide-eyed participants ...

In 1939, I was a pimply and daydreaming teenager, thrilled by anything besides Latin and Greek, who'd flunked his *méthode* exams (the equivalent of third-year high school). Horrors! My father, like all fathers at the time, couldn't accept that his son, moreover his eldest son, had failed a year. Unthinkable! The usual solution: change schools. Like all fathers at the time, mine wanted me to learn English. That's why he packed me off on the double to a small college in Charlottetown, Prince-Edward Island: Saint-Dunstan's College, Catholic of course, but administered by secular priests so different from the Jesuits I had to wonder if they belonged to the same faith. A punishment? Not at all. A quarter century earlier, my grandfather had also sent his son to study at this college located at the ends of the earth. "You'll see," my father had told me, "you'll like Saint Dunstan's. You'll discover freedom there." Words filled with mystery for a sixteen-year-old French Canadian who didn't speak a word of English, who really believed the province of Quebec was the centre of the universe, that we had "a mission in America," and that the *English* were nearly all scoundrels.

In early September 1939, my parents drove me to Montreal's sinister Bonaventure train station, with an enormous trunk containing all that was needed to survive on that unknown island for ten months.

A lengthy journey to Moncton, New Brunswick, which seemed a very strange place to me. From there, another train took me to Cape Tormentine. I then transferred onto a boat, an imposing craft that had nothing in common with the Lévis ferries, the only boats I knew. I have no recollection of the time needed to cross the Northumberland Strait, on rough seas. But I recall the island's red-earth cliffs. "If the earth is red, this must be a different country!" Another train for the final leg: Borden-Charlottetown. In fact, the train stopped three kilometres from the capital, in the middle of a field where the college was located.

A student, anglophone of course, waited beside the railway to greet me and help carry my enormous trunk. The first real *Anglais* I'd ever met. I didn't understand a word he said, but he smiled and, with numerous gestures, joked about the weight of my darned trunk. So I told myself that, if other *Anglais* were as friendly, everything would be all right. But at the bottom of my heart, like a bird in a trap, stirred a feverish anxiety ... As a boarder, I expected to live in an enormous and solemn dormitory with a hundred or so students, as was the practice in Quebec boarding schools. But no! Since I was in the Freshman class, which roughly corresponds to the *belles-lettres* class, I was entitled to a room in Dalton Hall, a lovely red-brick house, the colour of the island's soil. I shared my room with a hearty fellow, a giant really, who was a star of the football team and the son of a farmer: Larry Landrigan.

Should I live a thousand years, I'll never forget that boy who was two or three years older than me, always a little rough, as though to conceal his sensitivity, and who treated me more or less as his son. My first *English* friend quickly informed me he was *Irish*. Naturally, we used signs to communicate at first. At Canada World Youth, this is called "non-verbal communication." Really!

During the first weeks, first months even, I went from one "culture shock" to another, to use today's jargon. I no longer understood anything! I was questioning all Quebec values (known as French-Canadian back then), our wonderful "historic mission," all the nonsense expounded by Canon Groulx and my *Laurentian* Jesuits. And I thanked the heavens for having *flunked* my *méthode*, which allowed me, at sixteen years of age, to open myself to the world and learn to love others, the *Anglais* in this case. From then on, I was forever lost to the "independence" cause, for which so many of my companions would waste megatons of energy.

"You'll discover freedom there," my father, who always spoke with a degree of pomposity, had told me. But, in essence, how right he was!

Of course, Collège Sainte-Marie, a day school, had nothing in common with the Dark-Age prisons then known as the Séminaire de Lévis, the Collège de Sainte-Anne-de-la-Pocatière, the Séminaire de Trois-Rivières, where a throng of cassocked prison guards relentlessly spied on students, day and night, even following them into the washrooms, due to "sins of the flesh."

However, authorities at the moderate Collège Sainte-Marie forced us to go to confession at least once a month, and sign a *confession note*, without which our monthly report cards would be withheld.

Each student had to have a spiritual advisor who'd speak to him mostly about purity, as though there aren't more important virtues. We always related the old joke about the spiritual advisor who always began his interviews in the same way: "And so, my son, how goes your purity?" A student was said to have answered: "And how's yours, father?"

I experienced a significant "culture shock" in Charlottetown, finally meeting priests who never talked about purity, who seemed at ease with themselves, Catholic surely, but athletic, relaxed, cheerful, almost friends.

Was daily mass compulsory? Perhaps not. It was expected of young people, all of them devout Catholics, to attend; but if they didn't really feel like it on a given morning, they could sleep in. A student—not a teacher!—was put in charge of taking down the names of those absent from the chapel, automatically considered as "sick." A student on each floor at Dalton Hall was responsible for bringing a copious English-style breakfast to his "sick" schoolmates: oat porridge, eggs, bacon, toast, coffee, etc. The attendant on my floor was my own roommate, Larry Landrigan, a very devout Catholic, but filled with solicitude for his often "ailing" young French Canadian. When I'd missed church three days in a row, he began to gripe: "Now come on Jacques, are you laughing in my face? Do you think I'm your slave? Breakfast in bed, cut it out!" But he'd still bring it to me the next day, until I became really ashamed of abusing the freedom this college offered on a silver platter—or a wicker basket!—and resumed going to church. Not because of the priests, who controlled nothing, but because of my old buddy Larry. "You'll discover freedom ..."

The Jesuits at Collège Sainte-Marie had taught us that "going out with girls" wasn't proper. This would disturb studies; and, especially, women, who were instruments of the devil, could only lead to sin, the worst of all as it happens. Another "serene truth" we accepted without protesting too much.

Things were different at Saint-Dunstan's. These complacent priests must have belonged to another religion: they considered it normal that sixteen-year-old boys wanted to date girls their age!

One week after classes began, something occurred that seemed inconceivable to me, but which was already an old tradition at Saint Dunstan's. All boys at the college, sixteen and older, were invited to tea with girls from Charlottetown's Catholic convent. The tea biscuits had been lovingly made by these girls who were our age, as dreadfully shy as we were, and with whom we'd initiate innocent flirts. The college rector and the convent's mother superior no doubt told themselves that, since boys had to "go out with girls," it was preferable for this to be done "among Catholics." Oh! it was amusing to see them both laughing, while nibbling their biscuits: "Look," the rector must have said to the mother superior, "Look at how John and Suzannah seem to get along! Don't they make a darned nice couple? ..." I somewhat hesitate to admit it, but this clever scheme didn't prevent me from falling in love with the alluring Josephine, a Protestant, of German extraction to boot. Alas! she was frivolous and *deceiving* me with Robert Cliche[1]. He was two years older than me, and incredibly charming: "He speaks English like Charles Boyer ..." cooed Josephine, who granted me her discreet favours when Robert was otherwise occupied. I thought I was suffering ...

The Jesuits had convinced me that, if French Canadians were poor, it was because they justifiably placed spiritual values above everything, whereas the *Anglais*, those filthy materialists, had *enriched* themselves at our expense. I believed this as well, along with everybody else: when you're fifteen, and when they have fourteen years of schooling behind them, on top of their classical studies ...

At Saint Dunstan's, the *Anglais*, mostly Irish or Scottish in fact, were poor. Only the eight French Canadians could be considered rich! For example, my friend Larry Landrigan owned, in all, two pairs of pants, one for weekdays, one for Sundays, two white shirts, two pairs of socks, a patched sweater, three times nothing. His football uniform was a discreet gift from the rector, since he was one of the college's best players, and very important when confronting Mount Allison's imposing team. He served mass every morning and thereby managed to earn thirty-five cents a week ... while, every Monday, my father sent me a dollar, a small fortune. In Charlottetown, going to the movies cost twenty-five cents. Therefore fifty cents when I brought Josephine along, which didn't happen every week due to that bloody Cliche! The entrance fee at the Knights of Columbus hall, where we went to dance on certain Saturday nights: ten cents! And when we'd won somebody's heart, an occasion deserving a chocolate sundae, the best ones were ten cents at the swanky *Old Spain*. With one dollar a week, I was rich. I was having a grand time while Larry Landrigan slogged away at philosophy in our tiny room. Between two football games. His parents were as poor

1 We were eight French Canadians from Quebec at Saint Dunstans's that year, including the wonderful Robert Cliche, who was later to become leader of the New Democratic Party in Quebec and chairman of the renowned Cliche Commission.

as church mice, since growing potatoes didn't pay much during those years. He didn't envy me: he thought it normal for me to be rich, since I was French Canadian. Oh! yes, another "culture shock!"

I had my first apprenticeship of freedom at this humble college—from 1939 to 1941—where students were trusted, and where, as a result, nothing was totally forbidden.

I also learned at Saint Dunstan's that we discover everything about ourselves and others when confronted by a different culture and other values. *There you have it!*

One day, many years later, I was in Charlottetown, chairing a public hearing of the Applebaum-Hébert Committee.[1] In a moment of enthusiasm, I told the tiny and astonished audience: "It's here in your city, at Saint Dunstan's, that I learned about freedom!" And, driving the point still further, I might have added: "This is perhaps where Canada World Youth was born!"

---

1 The Federal Cultural Policy Review Committee was created by the Trudeau government and published a report in November 1982.

3. The Third World in His Heart.

My country is the world,
and my brothers, all men.
Thomas Paine

In Saïgon with Dr. Jean Phaneuf, the *Jeep*, and two charming Vietnamese women (October, 1950).

Following two happy years among the *Anglais*, I had to return to Montreal to register at the École des hautes études commerciales, of all places. I felt no attraction to business and still less to accounting. But since I wanted to be neither a doctor, like my father, nor a lawyer or Jesuit, I'd chosen that school because it numbered many of the day's intellectual leaders: Victor Barbeau, Édouard Montpetit, Esdras Minville.

During my university days, I continued to explore every last corner of Quebec, still in the company of the old "Benoist's Scouts." Now convinced that Larry Landrigans awaited me everywhere, I pressed my explorations on to the United States, and to the West, right up to the Rockies.

In 1945, I obtained a business degree—big deal!—but before settling down, I wanted to travel to the ends of the earth, to see how other people lived. The simplest way was to begin with Latin America; I was basically without means, and that continent seemed the most accessible and least costly to visit, since it could be travelled by car. Well, almost ...

June 1946: accompanied by three friends, in a small 1931 *Chevrolet* whose best days were behind it, I set out to discover all those wonderful countries whose very names had filled me with dreams since childhood: Mexico, Guatemala, Panama, Ecuador, Peru, Brazil ...

A rough fourteen-month journey on the so-called "Pan-American" highway, large sections of which were still missing. To help us subsist, I wrote a weekly article about our adventures for a large Montreal newspaper named *La Patrie du dimanche* ... which paid $10 an article! We didn't eat much during those months, but the *tortillas* and bananas were nourishing and not very costly. I related that first great adventure of my life elsewhere.[1] In the manner of Canada World Youth participants, I'd at least claim the following: "I'd profoundly changed by the time I returned. I knew I'd never be the same again!" I'd forever hold Latin America in my heart ... [2]

Following a year in Canada, needed to recover my health and restore my finances (speeches, articles, book), I decided to set my sights on Africa[3]. In 1948, practically the whole continent was under colonial occupation ... whose virtues I'd therefore observe first-hand!

I found a good travelling companion, Jacques Dupire, without difficulty among "Benoist's Scouts." We landed in Algiers along with another *Chevrolet*—rather decrepit, unfortunately, already a wreck—which we had to abandon a few months later

1 *Autour des trois Amériques*, Beauchemin, Montréal, 1948.

2 I borrowed this expression from a letter sent to me by Stéphane Lamer, a Canada World Youth participant, when he returned from Somalia in 1985. At the end of his deeply moving letter, he wrote: "Thank you for having put the Third World in my heart forever." Stephen has worked on development projects in many countries (Azerbaijan, Burkina Faso and Zaïre). He now works in Burundi, and bears the impressive title of director of humanitarian activities for the United Nations in Burundi.

3 *Autour de l'Afrique*, Fides, Montreal, 1950.

in the middle of the Sahara. With great sorrow. But since we'd decided to do the tour of Africa, there was no question of turning back. The goal was to cross the continent from Algiers to Capetown and from Capetown to Cairo. A more difficult trip than the first one, since we had to depend on local transportation: old trucks, rickety buses, third-class train fares, river barges, etc. By the end of a year, however, we had Africa in our hearts forever.

1950: Asia[1], an extensive trip around the world with Jean Phaneuf, another of "Benoist's Scouts." The colonial system was already beginning to splinter all over. India and all former British *possessions*, save Hong Kong, had gained independence or were about to. The French were slower off the blocks, as it were, hanging on to *their* Indochina, but only with the energy of despair. One thing must be said: my trip accounts were very popular in Quebec. To such an extent that Gérard Filion, then publisher of *Le Devoir*, perhaps in the hope of increasing his paper's scanty circulation, had managed to entice me ... by paying $17.50 for each of the *daily* articles I promised to send during one year. Painstaking business since, before relating your adventures, you still have to experience them.

It's no doubt because I was a little older, or more "sensitized" as we'd say today, that Asia affected me more profoundly than the other two continents. I was beginning to understand the enormous challenges facing Asians in the area of development, which hadn't been the main concern of their former European masters. I was fascinated by the Third World, at a time when the term hadn't been invented. Does Canada World Youth have a few Asian roots? Most certainly.

1951. A terrific year, when I married a marvellous young woman, with whom I was madly in love. We dreamed of a little house in the country where a throng of children would blossom. But I couldn't think of this before Thérèse and I shared at least one of those extensive trips that had so profoundly marked me.

Since continents were beginning to get scarce, we decided to return to Africa[2] and tour it along a different and more difficult itinerary. We'd travel from Algiers to Dakar in a brand new *Jeep* station wagon, and then from Dakar to Addis Ababa, crossing Africa at its widest point, ending up in Port Sudan, on the Red Sea, before embarking for Europe and then home. Over ten months on the road ... and over 260 articles in *Le Devoir*! Those were heady days, and we witnessed the independence movement's first great disruptions, in Morocco and elsewhere.

Back home, somewhat in the manner of Canada World Youth participants, I gave "presentations." In fact, I gave nearly three hundred talks that year, complete with colour films and everything, sharing our thoughts on Africa with thousands of Canadians from Quebec, New Brunswick and Northern Ontario.

The years that followed don't really concern Canada World Youth. Fulfilling the dream of all journalists, I founded and managed a small and combative weekly

---

1 *Aventure autour du monde*, Fides, Montreal, 1952.
2 *Nouvelle aventure en Afrique*, Fides, Montreal, 1953.

newspaper[1] during the bitter years when the Duplessis regime, in the latter stages of decay, quite naturally had to be contested. I wrote and published a few books before concluding it was more exciting to publish others, all those young Quebec writers showing up out of everywhere and nowhere. Another dream fulfilled: my own publishing company, *Les Éditions du Jour*, which was to launch a hundred or so novelists and poets, print numerous controversial books including a few which, so I'm told, helped launch the Quiet Revolution.

During those years of intense activity, I kept a certain nostalgia for all those countries of Latin America and Asia that I held in my heart like a treasure, with the need to share it. I'd occasionally return, but those trips were brief and discouraged me, since they didn't help improve things at all in the hard-up Third World.

I gradually began to convince myself that Canada could, if it were so inclined, become the conscience of rich countries, the catalyst of North-South Dialogue. We had no colonial past to reproach ourselves (would aboriginals have agreed?), no desire to dominate; we weren't racist (history hadn't yet given us the opportunity!) and were (without deserving it) highly esteemed by both rich and poor countries. Weren't we, therefore, *predestined*, as it were, to play a major role in that North-South Dialogue, without which all mankind has no future? Whatever our government's good intentions, nothing would happen before Canadians were sensitized to international-development problems. But that was an imposing task, and what appeared most simple and definite was to begin with young people; to lay the groundwork for the future and world peace with them ... (A minor aspiration!)

In the mid-seventies, or perhaps at the beginning of 1971—I have no memory for dates, those tombstones of the past—I began to muse about a grand scheme that was still somewhat vague. I submitted my dreams, even the most extravagant ones, to the world's most critical audience, my five children and their friends who, during family meals, would be subjected to my endless ramblings: "Try to imagine a group of young people your age living in a small village of Ivory Coast for three or four months, with young inhabitants from that country with whom they'd have previously lived for four months in Canada. And, while over there, work with the people on community development, discover another culture and integrate into it as much as possible, understand the needs of those men and women, our most destitute brothers and sisters and, together, discover what each individual can do to change things."

The Canada World Youth concept was beginning to gel and would offer me no rest until it became a reality. And even afterwards ...

Of course, I'd taken into account the insightful comments and criticisms of my children and their friends[2]. However, I still needed to submit this wonderful and crazy

---

1 *Vrai*, Montreal, 1954 to 1959.

2 One of them, René Dagenais, took part in the pilot project with Tunisia in 1972-1973. The

idea to adults who were wiser and more experienced than me.

From the outset I was to find, among the *Anglais*, a prestigious and steadfast ally. I'd always harboured an intense admiration for Frank Scott that bordered on veneration. During the dark years of the Duplessis regime, when individual rights were being glaringly trampled, the first to man the barricades was always Frank Scott. Busy elsewhere, our great French-Canadian lawyers often left to Frank Scott the most difficult cases and the defense of freedom and justice, implicating Premier Duplessis himself: the Roncarelli and Guindon affairs, as well as countless others. This *Anglais*, the son of an Anglican archdeacon, was dean of McGill's law faculty; he was an authentic Quebecker, a bilingual Montrealer, with a soft spot for the Eastern Townships. He was idealistic, generous and, for a time, national chairman of the CCF, the New Democratic Party's ancestor. But even more than a socialist, he was a poet whose verse remains one of our literary treasures. As well, he'd translated the works of French Canadian poets into English, including those of my illustrious second cousin, Anne Hébert. Naturally, when the Civil Liberties Union was founded in 1963, he was there, with Pierre Trudeau, Gérard Pelletier, Jean Marchand, Pierre Dansereau, J.-Z.-Léon Patenaude and the others. When I was elected chairman of the union, he became its vice-chairman. The opposite would have been more reasonable, but Frank Scott wouldn't accept that the chairman of Quebec's Civil Liberties Union be an anglophone, even a perfectly bilingual one.

It may now be understood why I submitted the Canada World Youth concept to that exceptional man. How could I ever forget the day when I had lunch with Frank Scott at Montreal's Cercle Universitaire, then located in a beautiful old house on Sherbrooke Street, the birthplace of the marvellous Thérèse Casgrain? Feverish, enthusiastic, anxious, I described as best I could to Frank Scott a somewhat sketchy Canada World Youth, which still didn't have a name. He listened, no doubt with interest, without reacting very much. A typical *Anglais*! Following the meal, he stretched out his long and slender hand and squeezed my forearm: "Jacques, that's a worthy and beautiful idea. You can count on me."

From that very moment, I knew that Canada World Youth had seen the light of day.

"Whom do you propose for when we'll need another *Anglais*?" I asked Frank Scott.

"Michael Oliver, he replied, without a shadow of hesitation. You know, I'm gradually getting older. One day, Michael will have to replace me ..."

Michael Oliver was a younger version of Frank Scott. A Montrealer. Bilingual. Civil Liberties Union. Laurendeau-Dunton Commission. CCF. Third World. Though not a poet, he was an avid bird watcher, which boils down to the same.

Before dragooning Michael Oliver into service, in all fairness, I had to approach

---

following year, he participated in the first program with Cameroon. He was afterwards, for a five-year period, a pillar of Katimavik in the Atlantic region. I met up with him more recently in Pakistan, where he was co-ordinator of the Canada World Youth program, an organization he still works with at the Halifax regional office.

a French Canadian, as distinguished as Frank Scott if possible. Naturally, the man I invited to lunch at the Cercle Universitaire was Pierre Dansereau. Another exceptional personality, a wonderful humanist, a man of science, our first great ecologist, concerned about human rights and Third World problems, and generous with his time as soon as a worthy cause needed him. When coffee was served, he told me straight out that Canada World Youth would henceforth be one of his causes.

Two down! And then it was Michael Oliver's turn; for many years he'd play a prominent role with Canada World Youth. He became its president and, more important still, *its conscience*. Each time a board or staff member seemingly wanted to veer away from the broad objectives, Michael Oliver was there, vigilant, ready to listen but also protest and, finally, always able to convince.

I've forgotten the order in which I solicited the support of other prominent Canadians I'd invited to join the first board of directors. But I remember a lengthy dinner at the Cercle Universitaire where, for the first time, I'd gathered six or seven people. In addition to Frank Scott, Pierre Dansereau and Michael Oliver, I believe the party included Léon Dion, the Laval University political scientist, Rhéal Bérubé, our Acadian friend from Moncton, perhaps Gertrude Laing from Calgary, and Maurice Champagne, the prospective director general. I've surely forgotten some.

Following a very animated and enthusiastic discussion, I asked:

"So now what do we do?

"Well, we found!" exclaimed Frank Scott.

"Okay. But what do we found? A name's needed ...

"The matter pertains to Youth, to Canada, to the World," said someone. "Then how about *Canada Jeunesse Monde* or *Jeunesse Canada Monde*?

"How does it sound in English?

"Canada World Youth? *Pas mal du tout...*"

I wanted things to get going. Immediately. That very evening. I turned to Frank Scott, the only lawyer in the group:

"So, Mr. lawyer, tell us how we go about founding?

"If we're all agreed, it's a done deal. We'll draft a charter and regulations afterwards ...

"It's that simple?

"That's right! And so," says Frank Scott, "I move that Jacques Hébert become the first chairman of the board of directors.

"It's unanimous!"

I protested as a matter of form, but down deep, I was rather proud. And I proposed Frank Scott for vice-chairman ... as usual!

We'd done it! Canada World Youth had come into being. But we weren't out of the woods yet ...

As a non-governmental agency, Canada World Youth obviously needed financial support from the government. Each Third World country invited to participate would pay its share, but in all fairness, Canada's would have to be more substantial.

I knew nothing about federal politics, and even less about the intricate workings of its bureaucracy. Friends who were better informed assured me that the Secretary of State would be the most suitable department to fund such a program. The minister at the time was Gérard Pelletier, an old friend. Would this facilitate things? Yes and no, as we'll see.

On that question, I'd like to dispel a myth—with little hope of success. It's often been repeated that Canada World Youth received government support as *easily* as it did because the prime minister of the day, Pierre Elliott Trudeau, and the Secretary of State, Gérard Pelletier, were both my friends. It would've been more fitting to say that these two politicians had always been particularly sensitive to Third World problems and, as a result, couldn't reject out of hand a program whose objective was to alert young Canadians to those problems and, through them, our entire society. Whatever anyone thinks, nothing was *easy*, and precisely because Pierre Trudeau and Gérard Pelletier were my friends, they acted with the greatest circumspection to avoid being accused of complacency afterwards, although I'd draw no benefit from the organization in my capacity as volunteer chairman.

Oh! I'll always remember those long Sunday afternoon discussions with Gérard Pelletier in his beautiful house on Elm Street, week after week ... The objections he raised were mostly accurate, forcing me to clarify my thinking, so that, the next time, I could provide answers likely to convince him. Things no doubt would've gone more briskly had I not been an old friend. But he knew me too well, and was justifiably sceptical of my enthusiastic effusions, of my occasionally zany ideas, to which he'd been the first confidant during so many years. I was chafing with impatience from one Sunday to the next ... But Gérard Pelletier stood his ground because he was wise. How could I've reproached him for this since his very wisdom, which I'd so often benefited from, was one of the qualities I admired most in him? "Until next Sunday, then!"

He'd no doubt broach the question with his senior officials during the week, and their objections would fuel our next dominical meeting. Without saying it outright, I surmised that, in his heart of hearts, Gérard Pelletier wanted his department to take Canada World Youth under its wing and help prove the program deserved consideration, although it was unique in the world. But he wasn't a man to impose views to his officials: he wanted to convince them first.

One day, he phoned me from Ottawa: "I'm gathering my department heads next week at a hotel in the Laurentians. A working meeting. Come on down and take the time to explain your concept."

I was awfully intimidated by those tie-wearing bureaucrats, with their impressive black-leather briefcases. Powerful people no doubt, whom I was meeting for the first time, with a few rare exceptions.

One of them had frankly driven me round the bend: "The population of an African or Asian village," he told me, "will never allow a group of long-haired youths wearing patched jeans into its midst. They'll be rejected in less than three days! Can you imagine the diplomatic complications and yackety-yack ..."

I answered that I was relatively familiar with Third World countries, that I'd lived there without a glitch for nearly four years, that the hospitality of Malian or Thai villagers was so extraordinary that we couldn't even begin to imagine it, in our stingy Western societies.

The official stuck to his guns: "Let's admit, hypothetically, that your young

Canadians are not rejected ... Given the unhealthy climates and poor hygiene in those countries, malaria, cholera or typhus will wipe out all those fragile young Canadians. Unless they're devoured by lions! Can you imagine the scandal pouring out in the newspapers, the questions in the House, etc."

That I'd lived through four long journeys to those "unhealthy" lands didn't impress this timorous bureaucrat whom, no doubt, had never set foot in a single Third World village.

I finally told him, exasperated: "Since you don't believe me, there's only one way to settle this question. Let your department fund a tiny pilot project. For example, we could send three or four young Canadians to Africa, an equal number to Asia and Latin America, with the mission of living and working in a village for three or four months. If they don't survive, losses will still be limited."

I returned from the Laurentians profoundly saddened, without suspecting that the idea tossed to my counterpart with the black briefcase, in a moment of supreme impatience, would slowly gain ground.

A little while later, I was invited to a dinner honouring an African dignitary who was visiting Ottawa. This didn't concern Canada World Youth; rather, it no doubt pertained to my knowledge of the country of the guest in question. By coincidence, I was seated to the right of Jules Léger, who was then under-secretary of state, i.e., Gérard Pelletier's deputy minister. I knew this prince of bureaucrats by reputation and had shaken his hand once or twice, during some reception at the Canadian embassy in Paris, where he'd been ambassador for many years. One thing is certain, he wasn't a friend, at least not yet. The poor chap had to suffer my inevitable chatter about Canada World Youth during the entire dinner. Of the torrential kind! Once in awhile, Jules Léger managed to ask an always-intelligent question. He finally stopped me: "Don't insist. You've convinced me and I'll do my utmost to ensure its success ..." From a man as respected and distinguished as Jules Léger, that promise was filled with hope. I finally had a powerful ally among senior bureaucrats. More important still, Gérard Pelletier had a powerful ally, able to overcome the most tenacious bureaucratic resistance.

From then on, things happened quickly. Canada World Youth received an initial grant allowing it to carry out the mini-pilot project conceived somewhere in the Laurentians. Four teams consisting of four young Canadians were created: a co-ordinator (thirty years of age), a group leader (twenty-five years of age) and *two* participants aged between seventeen and twenty: one boy and one girl, one francophone, the other anglophone. The destination of teams: Tunisia, Cameroon, Mexico and Malaysia. Mission: to live three months in a village, integrate into it as well as possible, work with the inhabitants on small development projects and, *above all*, survive!

That's right! Our young people were greeted with open arms by the villagers, none died of cholera, nor was eaten by a lion. Proof had been given and Canada World Youth was becoming possible. In our internal vernacular, we referred to this as *Year Zero*.

By Year I, things were already getting more serious: a one-and-half-million dollar budget, nearly four hundred participants and young project leaders, divided into four countries where we'd had a first experience. From one year to the next, funds were increasing, the number of countries doubled, tripled, quadrupled, and the program ended up being offered to nearly five hundred Canadian youths a year, and to as many Third World youths. Alas! that number has never been exceeded. Quite the contrary: in 1985, Canada World Youth's budget began to melt away before our eyes. But times change, better days will eventually return ...

For his part, Jules Léger wanted *as many young people as possible* from Canada and developing countries to benefit from the unique experience offered by Canada World Youth. One day, at the end of Year II if memory serves, he told me confidentially: "You know I'm a friend of Canada World Youth, and proud that it depends on my department for funding. However, I have a suggestion: leave the Secretary of State as soon as possible, and associate yourself to CIDA[1]. This would be the most normal course, since your work effectively contributes to sensitizing youth and the general population to international-development problems. There's another more important reason: Canada World Youth must expand, the quicker the better. The Secretary of State, however, has a limited budget, and your present subsidy seems enormous to our bureaucrats. Whereas, with CIDA, the extra millions you'll need will only ever be a drop in the ocean! And especially, joining CIDA will allow you to distance yourself from politics somewhat. Ministers and deputy ministers change, as well as governments ..."

Needless to say that this astonishing advice, coming from the most skilled senior bureaucrat, the mandarin of mandarins, greatly impressed me. A few months later we "switched to CIDA," then headed by Paul Gérin-Lajoie, whom I knew rather well. Nonetheless, CIDA fell under the jurisdiction of External Affairs, which was uncharted territory to me.

It would be exaggerated to say that Cida greeted Canada World Youth with wild enthusiasm. Other non-governmental organizations it funded envied our relatively high subsidy and believed that, had we not existed, they could've divvied up our millions.

Things have greatly changed since. Canada World Youth is now a full partner within the large CIDA family. NGOs, as they're called in the business, have learned to understand and appreciate our program, to the extent they often recruit executives from the ranks of our former participants.

I've kept no bitterness about the suspicion in which we were held during those first years, when Canada World Youth was far from being the efficient and smooth-running organization we know today. Dreadful and tedious years I wouldn't want to relive! Since our program was unique in the world, we couldn't benefit from the experience of a similar organization. We had to improvise, risk experiences that didn't always turn out well, completely design a program so ambitious, demanding and intricate that, in theory at least, it appeared downright unrealistic and unworkable. Let's use our imagination a little ... Each group of Canadian participants, aged

---

1 Canadian International Development Agency.

seventeen to twenty, represents a cross-section of the population that's as near perfect as possible. An appropriate proportion of anglophones and francophones, mostly unilingual at first, an equal number of boys and girls, from all social classes: urban sophisticates, country dwellers from Newfoundland or Quebec's Beauce region, the unemployed, students, dropouts ... How could we expect groups of young people to live in harmony for seven or eight months, when their culture, background, values and language were so different? And to complicate things further, each group of young Canadians is, from the beginning, paired with an equal number of young people from the ends of the earth, bringing another culture, religion and language along with their baggage. Wouldn't such a cocktail ultimately blow up before the end of seven or eight months? All the more so, given the program demands a great deal from each participant: working hard on development projects, first for four months in a Canadian community, and then another four months in the harsh climate of Mali, Indonesia or Bolivia.

In theory, therefore, an impossible program. In practice, it works! Wonderfully. Since its creation in 1971, over twenty thousand participants and project leaders, half of them young Canadians, the other half youths from nearly fifty Third World countries[1], have given daily proof that Canada World Youth was possible ... and that mankind perhaps has a future!

In the wake of this triumphant effusion, let's come down to earth, and go back in time: it wouldn't be very forthright to skip the more troublesome parts. Therefore, I'll say it once more: Canada World Youth's first three years were *very* difficult. There weren't any scandals, since they would've been disclosed. But there were some missteps and blunders, as well as a few foolish acts; in short, something to justify the criticism of other more experienced NGOs, of bureaucrats, even that from the political realm.

During those first years, both CIDA and the Secretary of State considered Canada World Youth as a simple pilot project; its existence was therefore threatened every year. We were forced to live in constant anguish, ceaselessly renew negotiations with CIDA, and go through endless efforts.

Without having access to cabinet secrets (where we didn't only have friends), I knew that Canada World Youth was occasionally on the receiving end of more or less warranted criticism. The prime minister, Pierre Trudeau, certainly liked us and didn't conceal it. He only had to say the word to muzzle our opponents; but, contrary to a persistent myth, Pierre Trudeau was as loathe to brutally imposing his will to ministers, as Gérard Pelletier was to his bureaucrats. I received proof of this at the end of Year III ...

Each year, during the holiday season, abandoning my family and the Éditions du Jour to their fate, I'd visit our groups in a corner of the world, to experience the program for a few weeks, talk with participants at leisure, and negotiate next year's

---

1 A few Central and East European countries have been part of the program since 1994.

protocol of agreement with the authorities ... without really knowing there would be a next year!

On one such occasion, I was on the Ivory Coast when I got a phone call from Canada, something unexpected and inauspicious. At the other end of the line, was the director general at the time, Pierre Bourdon, completely discomfited, though he was usually the most collected of men: "You've just received a letter from the External Affairs minister," he informs me with a flat voice. He read me Mitchell Sharp's letter, congratulating us for Canada World Youth's good work over the years and yackety-yak. "But ..." CIDA will henceforth no longer be able to ensure our funding. "Sincerely ..."

I'd just understood that Pierre Trudeau, against his will I'm sure, had abandoned us to the good will of his minister. Moreover, he'd warned me: "You know I believe in Canada World Youth, but that's not the case for all ministers. And your being my friend really complicates things. Make sure you have support in cabinet. Sort things out yourself!" That night, in Abidjan, I bitterly regretted not having followed that advice. I didn't know Mitchell Sharp, the Foreign Affairs minister who was in charge of CIDA. He intimidated me to death! (He still does!) And so, I'd neglected him, like the others, to say the least.

Pierre Bourdon still had some news to tell me, or rather shout at me, since the line was so bad: "I hear that CIDA's president, Paul Gérin-Lajoie, is in Dakar on an official visit. I thought that, maybe ..."

Dear Pierre Bourdon! He didn't have to spell it out. In any event, since we had a program with Senegal, I had to pass through Dakar before returning to Canada. I quickly settled my business in Abidjan and, the very next day, was sipping a beer with Paul Gérin-Lajoie. Yes, he'd received a copy of the minister's letter. Yes, he did believe in Canada World Youth. Yes, he'd talk to the minister as soon as he returned to Ottawa.

All this reassured me somewhat, though not completely. Indeed, I knew that Paul Gérin-Lajoie was a sincere friend of Canada World Youth, that he defended it to the best of his ability; but what troubled me was that, to this day, he'd never seen its profoundly moving and wonderful reality. We had a program here in Senegal, alas! in the distant province of Casamance. I pleaded with the energy of a desperate man: "I'm convinced you believe in the Canada World Youth concept. However, please come to Casamance to see for yourself what really takes place. I swear you won't regret it ..."

Paul Gérin-Lajoie is a compassionate man; visibly moved by my distress, he was ready to head for Casamance, but his officials were unyielding. "Look at your trip schedule. It's ab-so-lute-ly impossible!"

I wasn't letting up: "But Paul, you have nearly nothing to do on your last day!

"What do you mean, nothing," replied one of his assistants, impatiently. "In the morning: the official inauguration of an important CIDA project. In the afternoon, the president *must* rest since he takes the plane for *Chile* that very evening!"

I continued to insist. Paul Gérin-Lajoie was beginning to give in: "What if we held the inauguration the previous day?" he suggested to his advisor.

"Absolutely out of the question: invitations have already gone out. What's more, there's no plane to Casamance."

I'd anticipated that possibility. Thanks to the complicity of friends at Senegal's

Youth Ministry, I knew the government was ready to put a small Twin Otter plane—a gift from Canada, moreover—at the CIDA president's disposal.

"So we'll head to Casamance," said Paul Gérin-Lajoie. "Too bad about the afternoon rest!"

He didn't suspect the wild greeting that awaited him. At the entrance to the village, where our young participants had been living for two months, villagers had erected a sort of triumphal arch in honour of Paul Gérin-Lajoie (and perhaps a little to mine, who knows?). Thousands of villagers formed a guard of honour. Flowers everywhere, flags, tom-toms beating furiously, a very, very Senegalese form of rejoicing.

As soon as a harbinger announces the arrival of Canadian visitors, musicians and dancers let loose, storming the entire street, raising an endless cloud of red dust.

Accompanied by a prefect clad in a ceremonial uniform, the village chief, magnificent in his blue boubou, and the Senegal Youth Minister's representative, Paul Gérin-Lajoie makes a solemn entrance walking amid the shrill cries of women and the cheers of a jubilant crowd. Never had the president of CIDA received such a welcome, even when he'd inaugurated roads, bridges or public buildings, in Senegal or elsewhere, that had perhaps cost millions to Canada.

The procession heads for the palm-leaf shelter, erected for the occasion. The prefect, mayor, ministerial representative, and finally, Paul Gérin-Lajoie, will make rousing speeches before the rallying crowd, where much is said about Canada World Youth's modest but very important activities in this country. "No doubt," says Paul Gérin-Lajoie, "Canada has brought you airplanes, motors and materials of all kinds in the past. But in the future, even more important than all this, will be to work *together* to develop your beautiful country." He highlights the example of Canada World Youth, which allows young people from Senegal and Canada to do precisely that: they work *together* to improve living conditions in this village. The applause punctuating each flight of oratory indicates that CIDA's efforts are very much appreciated, even in this remote village. As for Canada World Youth's contribution, it's clear that it has deeply touched the people. The Senegalese have fully understood the spirit which motivates us and which doesn't in the least resemble all previously known forms of aid. "What really touches us about your efforts," admits a Senegalese official, "is that, for the first time, Europeans (a term encompassing all Westerners) aren't only providing genuine and necessary aid, though modest in appearance. What really touches us is that Canadian youth are taking a real interest in our country and culture. They come to Senegal to broaden their horizons, just as our youth want to broaden theirs in Canada. In sharing the simple lifestyle of our villagers, they help convince our young people, attracted to large cities, that village life holds very important values, which Canadian boys and girls discover with obvious joy, though they could live more comfortably in Vancouver, Toronto or Montreal. Canada World Youth is a noble and grand idea, at the vanguard of what co-operation between your rich countries and our developing countries will have to be. Frankly, only a country like Canada could have imagined such an idea." I'm overcome with emotion, and thankful to the dancer who twirls before me, sheltering me beneath a thick blanket of dust ...

Following the speeches, the village's best dancers give us an extraordinary show during which one of them, camouflaged beneath an enormous palm-leaf costume, literally rolls before our eyes like a ball, without any part of his body ever showing. It was incredible.

Paul Gérin-Lajoie reluctantly tears himself away from the feast to visit our building site, a small youth centre, still without a roof. The sun is beating down, but the village chief insists on describing *each* room: "Here, the library, here the dance hall, here the small café ..." Our participants follow at a distance, somewhat intimidated but proud of the sudden importance taken on by this humble building they'll help erect, with the full measure of their strength. I couldn't help saying to Paul Gérin-Lajoie: "Isn't this the very illustration of your speech's theme: we now have to build *together*?" He doesn't even have time to answer, as he's dragged away by a group of women who've prepared a duck hotpot, a meal typical of this village.

The sole drawback to this enthusiastic hospitality: little time will be left for Paul Gérin-Lajoie to talk with Canadian and Senegalese participants. Nonetheless, he was greatly touched by what he saw and heard. He claims to be convinced that this new form of co-operation between Canada and developing countries is very effective and sincerely hopes it can evolve in the future.

My only regret is that those who question supporting Canada World Youth couldn't have been here today to experience this moving feast celebrating friendship between Canada and Senegal, in the brotherly warmth of this beautiful Senegalese village. They would've understood that the future of co-operation, and no doubt that of world peace, proceeds along the dusty road leading to the village of Kagnobon.

Inside the small Twin Otter that's tossed around by the wind and taking us back to Dakar, Paul Gérin-Lajoie tells me directly: "You were right, Jacques. It was worth the effort!"

I was sure of it, just as I'm sure that if, by a miracle, all Canadian ministers had the opportunity to experience such a moment only once, they'd beg Canada World Youth to increase its activities to the limit!

Some time later, I attended a meeting of the Commons External Affairs and National Defence Committee in Ottawa, where Paul Gérin-Lajoie was testifying. He obviously had to answer the sometimes-insidious questions about Canada World Youth asked by members from *all* parties. Ah! what wonderful confidence he had! What persuasiveness!

"I *was* in Casamance a few weeks ago," he says in essence, "and I saw with my own eyes what Canada World Youth participants have accomplished: they're finally giving a human face to our co-operation efforts in that country, etc."

I was delighted, but not without realizing that Canada World Youth's fate rested not with MPs nor even CIDA's president, but with a minister of the Trudeau government, the very important minister of External Affairs who'd written me the aforementioned letter.

I finally got a meeting with Mitchell Sharp: I'd be accompanied by Canada World Youth's vice-chairman, Michael Oliver, who'd just replaced Frank Scott.

On the agreed day, Michael and I met in an Ottawa hotel to meticulously prepare the script for this meeting on which Canada World Youth's very survival depended:

I'd aim for the heart, and he'd aim for the head. Well, why not! I was the *Frenchman* and he the *Anglais* ...

After inviting us to sit down, the minister voiced these icy words: "This time, the prime minister has asked *me* to decide." Good old Pierre Trudeau, he'd really let me down!

The script went as planned: Michael took care of the head, and I the heart. As during a Ping-Pong game, the minister turned his head to the left, to the right, Oliver, Hébert, Oliver, Hébert ... The minister was rather flabbergasted.

At the end, he spoke these historic words, whose exact sense I'd wait for Michael Oliver to explain: "Gentlemen, all I can say is that I'll reconsider my decision.

"What exactly does that mean," I asked Michael as we'd barely left the large and imposing office.

"It means we've won!" he exclaimed triumphantly. "Hurrah for us!"

Goodness me! Perhaps Mitchell Sharp wasn't such a bad guy!

"I believe we deserve a Cognac," Michael says, "And it's on me!"

We repaired to some small Ottawa bar where we raised our glasses to Canada World Youth, whose future we felt was assured for a thousand years.

Year IV (1975-1976). I was still chairman of Canada World Youth's board of directors, but had to devote most of my time to the Éditions du Jour. Novelists, poets, the Quiet Revolution, all of these were important as well. Raising my children, earning a living, paying the mortgage. And I admit, I had a certain passion for my job as publisher, a worthy profession if there is one. Each launching by a young author was a celebration for me, a joy I wanted to share with all of Quebec, all of Canada and, if possible, with the entire world, which nearly happened thanks to Marie-Claire Blais and a few others.

But Canada World Youth ... The future was ours, as long as we avoided major blunders. I nevertheless felt too remote from the action to be effective, too far from participants, whom I met hastily without ever having the time to get to know them, or understanding why Canada World Youth was such an important part of their lives. I spoke with the director general nearly every day, presided over the board of directors' four annual meetings, participated in the work of most committees, but felt *this was not enough*.

One day, I was in a plane flying over Canada's endless prairies, in the company of Gertrude Laing, an admirable woman from Calgary. She spoke wonderful French, had been a member of the famous Laurendeau-Dunton Commission, and was then Canada World Youth's vice-chairman.

We were in the clouds over Saskatchewan: "Gertrude, I have this crazy urge to forget about the Éditions du Jour and devote *all* my energy to Canada World Youth for a few years. What do you think? Of course, I'd need a modest salary, enough to ensure the livelihood of my wife and children. But if I became a sort of full-time president, I'd have no trouble raising three or four times my salary from the private sector."

Gertrude Laing didn't hesitate for a moment: she totally agreed. Wonderful! Farewell, dear Éditions du Jour.

Year IV was first earmarked by the arrival of a new director general, Pierre Dionne, still very young, though his severe and imposing beard made him look older. Hardly had he been selected that he learns the unusual news: the chairman of the board is to become president. Yes, he'll be accountable to the board of directors. No, he won't really have authority over the director general. But he'll be there, in person, every day. Like a pest!

I did enjoy some prestige with the organization of course. But I especially had no intention of abusing it and, on no account did I want to subvert Pierre Dionne's authority. I'd only handle cases the board of directors would assign me, including raising funds from large companies, an unspeakable drudgery! Perhaps government and press relations, negotiating protocols of agreement with foreign countries, etc.

Pierre Dionne had a good sense of humour. When asked, in confidence, about the nature of the authority relationship between us, he usually answered: "Jacques Hébert is governor general. I'm prime minister!" There was a lot of truth in that sally: I had no power, but a certain influence.

I spent some happy years with Pierre Dionne, without conflict, nor the hint of a problem. Together, we'd set up Canada World Youth in that dubious blockhouse in the Cité du Havre, the Labyrinthe, which had been the NFB's pavilion during Expo 67. An extraordinary building abandoned after the exposition, since it was deemed unusable. Canada World Youth spent seven years there, in strange and crazy spaces conceived for very specific purposes by the poets at the NFB.

With some difficulty, we'd managed to set up a youth hostel specifically intended for Canada World Youth groups, but also available to all the young people coming to us from the rest of Canada, the United States, Europe and elsewhere. A swimming pool, a cafeteria, a photo gallery, a large theatre or conference hall; in short, luxury! All this for $1 a year, payable to the Canadian Mortgage and Housing Corporation. The century's bargain!

Unfortunately, the energy crisis made the "century's bargain" increasingly expensive to maintain, as heating costs became prohibitive. I loved the old Labyrinthe with a passion, and the idea of perhaps leaving it some day broke my heart.

Enticed by new challenges, the director general, or "Prime Minister" Pierre Dionne, tendered his resignation. After seven years of excellent work. He was replaced on an interim basis by Ross Bannerman, an admirable and loyal team-mate, absolutely unique, loved by all the staff, not to mention participants, our favourite *Anglais* ... albeit *very* Scottish.

Then came André Legault, a more managerial director general no doubt, a feature which suited the demands of the time. Important administrative reforms were needed, difficult decisions, including that of leaving our beautiful Labyrinthe ... Afterwards, Canada World Youth settled in more conventional premises on Côte-des-Neiges Road, in front of the cemetery where I'll rest someday, later on, there's lots of time yet! After a few years, like those great families that have been ruined, and who discreetly move from elegant Westmount to the Notre-Dame-de-Grâce neighbourhood, before ending up in Saint-Henri, Canada World Youth set up shop on Notre-Dame Street, near Atwater, where it has remained to this day.

On occasion, Pierre Trudeau and I would like to share a Chinese meal, remember a few funny anecdotes from out trip to China ... and discuss current events.

One day, in the spring of 1983, at my house on Pru'dhomme Street, I'd ordered a few dishes we rather fancied from a restaurant famous for its Hunan cuisine. Suddenly, while sipping green tea, my friend tells me: "As you know, I must soon leave politics. Pelletier and Marchand have already gone ... and I'd like a few guys and girls who share our profound convictions to remain in Parliament. I want to appoint you to the Senate."

I was literally staggered.

"Out of the question," I replied, "Canada World Youth is my entire life!

"But one doesn't prevent the other," said Pierre Trudeau calmly. "Even as a senator, you'll be able to continue serving the movement. More effectively perhaps, since you'll be closer to government, parliamentarians, bureaucrats ..."

Well, then, why not?

Better than anyone, Pierre Trudeau knew that I'd carefully kept to the political sidelines, and never been active in a federal or provincial party. With the infinite consideration that characterizes him (most of the time!), he gently added: "I know, your not a Liberal. So I gather you'll want to sit as an independent. That doesn't bother me at all."

I hesitated a few seconds.

"In any event, I've always been taken for a Liberal, due to my compromising friendships. So, too bad, I'll become a Liberal!"

The Prime Minister of Canada smiled with a hint of mockery ...

Following an eight-year term as full-time president, I resigned from Canada World Youth's board of directors. To console me, a new position was created, that of founding president. For life! Like Papa Doc! I once again became a volunteer, would continue to sit on the board of directors, participate in the work of committees, even keep a small office on Côte-des-Neiges Road. My parliamentary activities would prevent me from devoting as much energy to Canada World Youth but, happily as it turned out, my presence was no longer as necessary. The organization was now running smoothly, and I had full confidence in the new director general, Jacques Jobin, a good administrator, who'd formerly served with CUSO in Burundi. He'd long held the Third World in his heart.

In 1992, after eight years, Jacques Jobin chose to leave Canada World Youth for greener pastures. Once again, the board of directors buckled down to the thankless and precarious task of finding a new director general. We called on an important firm specializing in seeking candidates for positions of that importance. We received over *three hundred* applications from across the country, some very impressive. After an exhaustive process and hours of discussions, the board chose Paul Shay, a thirty-five year-old young man.

One of the reasons for this choice was obviously Paul Shay's lengthy association to Canada World Youth: he'd been a participant with the Tunisian program in 1975. He afterwards attended university, without ever managing to tear himself away from Canada World Youth. In 1980, he was group leader with the program in Colombia, and then assumed various functions with the regional office in Ontario, before doing the same at the national headquarters in Montreal. In 1990, he became director of the research service.

In short, Canada World Youth's fifth director general came from within its own ranks.

* * *

Well, there you have it. That's it, dear participants with the large inquisitive eyes. I promised. It's done. I've told you everything. Or almost ...

PART TWO

Annik, Scott, Carole, Ian and the Others

Youth is mostly excessive in its judgements. It must be: much of this immoderation will soon be discarded, like fleece dangling from bushes on the roadside. If moderation were a virtue of the twenty-year old, he'd be shorn of it before reaching thirty, while dull and vapid conformism lurks around the corner.

Romain Rolland

Foreword

Up to now, unfortunately, I've spoken a good deal about myself, and especially periods of my life I felt concerned Canada World Youth and its origins. It's time to let the young participants speak for themselves; without them, everything would be limited to fine words and yackety-yak.

Over the last quarter century, I've had the opportunity of meeting hundreds, if not thousands, of participants from Canada and abroad. Encounters that were mostly too brief, although I have fond memories about some of them. Only once, in 1985, did I follow a group quite closely, to discuss at leisure with each of the eighteen participants, and meet them before, during and after the program. Nineteen eighty-five was International Youth Year, followed in 1986 by the International Year for Peace. To celebrate those two years, Canada World Youth, with the co-operation of Katimavik—then at the height of its glory—had devised a rather unusual program. It would involve eighteen young Canadians who'd *already* lived the Canada World Youth experience; it would take place, first in Zaïre, for three months, and then in Canada.

The eighteen participants will therefore talk to us about Zaïre, as well as their first trip to a Third World country. Their combined experience covers Mali, Togo, Bolivia, Costa Rica, Ecuador, Jamaica, the Dominican Republic, Bangladesh, India, Pakistan and Sri Lanka. A fascinating world tour on the horizon!

This two-fold experience would help them reach the first goal of this special program; namely, to share their thoughts, once they return from Zaïre, with as many Canadians as possible, in all regions of the country.

Why Zaïre? Well, why not? Zaïre is a vast and fabulous country, the enormous pulsating heart of sub-Saharan Africa. Considerable natural resources, a population comprising over two hundred ethnic groups, and as many languages, traditions and cultures. But, alas! a country grappling with massive development problems, which have now been exacerbated by the disintegration of political and social institutions, something that wasn't as obvious in 1985.

Besides, Canada World Youth had found a worthy counterpart in Zaïre, the Mama Mobutu Foundation, that was concerned with the problems of youth and development. Its president, Mama Mpinga, was an astonishing woman, with extraordinary energy.

In a first instance, Canadian and Zaïrian participants would go through a regular three-month program in two villages of Western Kasaï. Besides carrying out community development projects, (reconditioning two dilapidated hospitals, building cisterns for filtered water, etc.), Canadian and Zaïrian participants prepared audio-visual chronicles for future presentation throughout Canada, in schools, CEGEPs, social clubs, on radio and television, etc. From the outset, they could count on seven hundred firm bookings! This vast operation had been made possible thanks to the collaboration of Katimavik which, that year, had groups in more than three hundred communities, evenly distributed throughout the ten Canadian provinces, the Northwest and Yukon Territories.

On their return to Canada, divided into small groups of three (one Zaïrian and two Canadians) participants would be greeted by groups of their Katimavik counterparts, with whom they'd stay a few days to make their presentations in the immediate surroundings. Each team would then be greeted by another Katimavik group, and so on for six weeks, thereby sending a message of peace and universal co-operation to tens of thousands of Canadians.

Accordingly, it may be seen why I was closely involved, on an intermittent basis of course, in the special program with Zaïre, from beginning to end.

My first encounter with participants took place in September 1985, during their training camp in Saint-Liguori, Quebec. From the first glimpse, I understood these young people weren't ordinary participants: they *already* had the Third World in their hearts and, with a wonderful enthusiasm, were preparing to carry out a new and unprecedented mission that Canada World Youth had given them. I knew maybe two or three of them, but quickly felt at ease amid this group I was to adopt, as it were.

From Canada World Youth's very beginning, I've spent a few weeks during the Christmas holidays on a so-called "official" trip for the organization. That year, God be blessed! I was sent to Zaïre.

I left Montreal in the evening of December 20, 1985, and landed in Kinshasa, the capital of Zaïre, around midnighton December 22. A twenty-seven hour trip, half spent in the air, the other half languishing in airports. A six-hour time difference ...

Exhausted, bleary-eyed, almost in a trance, I shake hands with representatives from the Mama Mobutu foundation, who've come to greet me on the runway; I shake hands with the Canadian Ambassador, Mr. Ewan Nigel Hare, Adam Blackwell, also from the embassy[1]; I shake more hands, white ones, black ones, like a robot ...

On December 24, I hop the plane to Mbuji Mayi, the capital of Western Kasaï. I'm awaited by the Canadian project co-ordinator, Philippe Mougeot, already and old friend, a genuine institution at Canada World Youth, greatly loved by participants fortunate enough to have known him as a group leader or project co-ordinator, a passionate devotee of the type I like.

A two-hour road trip to Mwene Ditu, where we're greeted by one of the two participant groups. This is where I once again meet Pauline, Scott, Yvonne, Paul-André, and the others, not to mention Sylvie Thériault, the group leader. A wonderful and happy reunion. Shortly thereafter, we head to the village of Kalenda, where the other group lives, under the leadership of Daniel Renaud. We celebrate Christmas together: midnight mass, sumptuous meal, small-gift exchange, etc.

Whoa! Halt! Stop! That's enough. I promised at the outset to give participants

---

1 This young diplomat afterwards told me he was a former Canada World Youth participant (Sri Lanka, 1975-1976).

their say. And I'm again falling back into a minor shortcoming: I chatter, babble, relate, relate ... There is, of course, no shortage of things to relate; anecdotes touching enough to draw tears from the public, strange or funny incidents (not everyone has eaten ants with the governor of a Zaïrian province!). Well, that's it. Enough is enough. You'll get a glimpse of what happened in Mwene Ditu and Kalenda by reading the eighteen interviews that follow.

I spent twenty or so hours recording casual conversations with each participant. I'm presenting them in a jumble, live as it were, though each participant was given the opportunity of making corrections or deletions felt to be useful.

There you have it. I'm clamming up. And none too soon!

I. The Kalenda Group

Never doubt that a small group of thoughtful and committed citizens can change the world. Indeed it's the only thing that ever has.

Margaret Mead

1.
Michael Smith

From British Columbia to Sri Lanka

Michael Smith and his Kalenda friends.

Michael: I was born in Vancouver, British Columbia in 1962 and am now twenty-three years old. I was raised on the British Columbia coast, in Prince Rupert and Bella Coola, a native village. I went to grade school and high school in British Columbia, but haven't yet been to university. I have a diploma in industrial first aid though! In the middle of my last year in high school, I decided to take a year to travel around Canada and supported myself doing odd jobs here and there. I've also studied piano and taken singing lessons. After a year, I went back to finish high school. I didn't know what to do following graduation, nor which direction to head in. In short, I'm a typical Canadian youth! I really didn't know how I wanted to participate in society ... nor even if I wanted to participate at all! I was rather disillusioned by the way things were going in the world ...

J.H.: Like what?

Michael: All the poverty ... the world seemed to be filled with injustice, wars and waste. I was somewhat of an environmentalist at that point. I'd done a lot of camping with my parents and been on numerous backpacking expeditions. I was aware of pollution problems and all the chemicals we put in our food. So the condition of our world and the way we treat it disturbed me somewhat. One day, I heard about a youth program called Katimavik. I also wanted to learn French. I'd been frustrated with studying the language in high school: it's very difficult to learn in two or three hours a week.

J.H.: And British Columbia is perhaps not the best place to practice French ...

Michael: That's true. So I thought Katimavik would give me a chance to see the country and learn French. At that point, I didn't know about the program's other learning objectives. I basically wanted to see Canada, learn French, meet people and acquire work skills. I sent an application to Katimavik, was accepted and off I went. The three training programs, lasting three months each, took place in francophone regions, which was quite unusual.

J.H.: Unusual indeed! Normally, Katimavik participants live and work for three months in a francophone region. The two other training programs take place in anglophone provinces.

Michael: In any event, my group went to New Brunswick (the Charlo-Campbellton region), Ontario (the Penetanguishene-Lafontaine region) and, finally, northern Alberta (the Girouxville-Falher region near Peace River).

J.H.: Bilingual regions, at the very least.

Michael: Precisely. But I got to work and speak with French Canadians.

J.H.: So you finally learned French.

Michael: I got a good start and continued to improve afterwards. Learning a language is a never-ending process.

J.H.: How did you like Katimavik?

Michael: Well, Katimavik really gave me direction. Though it didn't give me any specific goals, it provided lots of ideas, especially about the environment and appropriate technology ... We also talked a lot about international relations and international politics. I began to understand the world somewhat, as well as my own country, naturally. Katimavik gave me lots of new ideas and work skills, which was all very interesting.

J. H.: What kind of work skills?

Michael: In New Brunswick, we worked in the forest renovating an old logging camp and building outhouses. We had no electricity, no running water, no telephone, no radio. We were very, very isolated. So group skills were extremely important. That's when I became interested in working with groups. I also learned carpentry and masonry skills. I drove a *skidoo* at a cross-county ski resort for awhile in Ontario; but my main job was being an occupational therapy facilitator at the Penetanguishene Psychiatric Hospital. This provided an excellent opportunity to learn and we were given lots of responsibility. And then, in Alberta, I did some typing at a small French elementary school, while also working on a farm. Following the Katimavik program, I went back to my Alberta host family to work on their farm.

J.H.: So you had a close relationship with your host family. Where did they live?

Michael: In a small rural community called Jean-Côté, near Peace River. The farmer I worked for was French Canadian. He had a huge farm where he raised cattle and Percheron draught horses. We did some logging with the horses. Very hard work but really super. At that point, I actually wanted to become a farmer, but decided I still had too many things to do before settling down. My boss offered me 160 acres of land if I'd stay and work with him. But I decided I wasn't ready to assume such a responsibility.

J.H.: How old were you?

Michael: Nineteen, I think. Nineteen or twenty.

J.H.: You were rather young! What did you do after this farming experience?

Michael: I went back home for Christmas and, shortly thereafter, was asked to attend a conference in Detroit, Michigan, called "Young Christians for Global Justice." That's when my eyes really opened to what was happening in the world. There were people from Argentina and the South Pacific, a woman from Peru, people from South Africa, coming to talk about the problems in their countries and regions. I then started working with the nuclear disarmament movement. On returning from the Detroit conference, I began building a network in the lower mainland of British Columbia, with the help of a friend, to get young people involved in disarmament issues. Oh! I almost forgot, I also worked as an actor for about five months, with two different theatre companies. I was beginning to think about a career in theatre and music. Especially since I was becoming rather dissatisfied with disarmament. I realized how important it was, but felt we were missing the point of militarism. We weren't attacking the root of the problem. So I told myself: "I need more experience and have to know a little more about what's happening in the world to put things in perspective." That's when I sent an application to Canada World Youth!

J.H.: Not a bad idea!

Michael: No! And I started the program a year later, almost exactly to the day. Half of it would take place in Ontario, the other in Sri Lanka. I remember the phone call from Canada World Youth ... I believe there was a postal strike and they'd had to phone me. It was the same with Katimavik: our annual postal strike! So I said "Okay!" And went right to the Atlas to find out where Sri Lanka was: I hadn't the faintest idea! In fact, my first choice had been Africa, then Asia, then Latin America. I got my second choice but, once there, realized it should have been first. Sri Lanka was perfect for many reasons. Very, very distant and very isolated. I probably wouldn't have felt like going there had I been travelling alone. And Sri Lanka is so beautiful. And interesting ...

J.H.: But before reaching wonderful Sri Lanka, you lived numerous months in Ontario with your group. Let's talk about this a little ...

Michael: We lived in a small town called Binbrook, in the county of Hamilton-Wentworth. It was their second year hosting a Canada World Youth group.

J.H.: A Sri Lankan group?

Michael: That's right.

J.H.: As you know, Canada World Youth's policy is to be in the same community for two years: the impact is much stronger ...

Michael: So there was a group of Binbrook families that were already very interested and, as a result, really interesting for us. I was fortunate to be billeted on a pork farm with a young family. There were two houses for the mother, father, two children and grandparents. That was particularly interesting for my Sri Lankan counterpart, Sunil Jayamaha. He was really short, which was quite significant since we were always together ... and I'm tall! Sunil was quite active in Sri Lanka's youth movement; I found this extremely interesting. Our host family (this was their second experience) was very active in the community. We worked on the pork farm together, as well as at the Binbrook Fairgrounds.

J.H.: You were already somewhat of a farmer yourself ...

Michael: It was absorbing nonetheless, since this was my first experience working on a pig farm and I learned a good deal. Our family, as I mentioned, was young, active and very interested in the program. To the point that, following our departure for Sri Lanka, they got together with other host families from the region, left their farms in the hands of others for a month—something unusually daring for farmers!—and visited *their* participants in Sri Lanka.

J.H.: Amazing! We'll return to this later. First, tell me a little about Sunil Jayamaha, your Sri Lankan counterpart.

Michael: Oh! my counterpart. Well, at first we had no language in common. He spoke neither English nor French, and I spoke no Singhalese. So we gradually learned a few words, a kind of minimum language; I didn't really get to know him until the end of the first four months, when we reached Sri Lanka. Only then were we able to communicate somewhat better and really get to know each other ... as well as get into a few major conflicts, which we had to smooth out quickly to keep moving forward. We realized we had enough ideas and experience in common to get along. So we became good friends.

J.H.: What was your first impression of Sri Lanka, the distant country whose location you'd had to look up in your atlas?

Michael: Sri Lanka! I'll never forget the first hour. When we got off the plane, we noticed a tall wire fence with a crowd of Sri Lankans pressed against it; they were yelling at us to throw them things. As agreed, our counterparts spent a few days with their families, which they hadn't seen in four months. So Canadians ended up alone, piled into a little van with a Sri Lankan driver. We drove through Colombo, the capital, at breakneck speed, passing in curves, which is typical in that country. I'd never seen anything like it. During my first half hour in Sri Lanka, I think I saw, smelled, touched and heard more strange things than in the first twenty years of my life! I was in a kind of euphoria for the first two days: thinking, walking around, listening, looking at things. My first impression was that Sri Lankan nature—its wildlife, trees and flowers—was extremely beautiful. I also noticed there was destruction everywhere brought about by the racial strife that erupted shortly before we arrived. Canada World Youth organizers in Montreal even wondered whether they should send us. I didn't really know what was happening at the time. And of course, I was struck by the standard of living: many places were dirty and people were hungry, an image typical of the Third World ... But I also noticed that people were chatting, laughing, smiling and telling jokes. It all seemed simple, so wonderfully simple. We had no luxuries, to say the least, living in the villages, with families, and in the Boys' Town where the orientation camp took place. But we had enough to meet our basic needs.

J.H.: Tell me a little about your host family.

Michael: I lived with two families. One month with the first, until the mother fell ill, and the remainder of my stay with another. Our small village, Arawawela, was in the central province of Kandi. Our work project consisted of building a playground for the village's tiny school. In Sri Lanka, a playground is just a flat space. It's difficult to find a piece of land that's level and cleared in the mountains, one that can be used for games, theatre performances and cultural events. My first host family was, by Sri Lankan standards, fairly wealthy. They had electricity, a solid roof, a fair-sized house. The father was a retired school principal. The family included a policeman and his wife, another son who'd worked in Saudi Arabia, his wife and child, and two other sons. One was a music teacher, the other a student. The family's overall income allowed it to live reasonably well.

J.H.: What about your second host family?

Michael: It was much poorer. The master of the house had died about two weeks before we arrived. This allowed us to observe the attitude of Sri Lankans towards life and death. But that's another story. Many children would come and go, being passed from one family to the other, since their parents had died following an accident or illness. My host family received a small subsidy to provide for my counterpart and me, so they had more than enough food. As a result, there were always lots of children around the house. One son worked in a ricefield, and the other on a construction site.

J.H.: Did you feel comfortable with that family?

Michael: They were very generous. I found it hard to accept that they deprived themselves to ensure my comfort, despite all my protests. They finally agreed to eat with me, at the same table. The children slept on the floor so I could have a bed. There were certain things I couldn't change, since they wanted me to be comfortable. I didn't take out my camera for the first months, since this would've reinforced their image of North Americans, of white people, an image that comes from movies like *Lady Chatterley's Lover*, *James Bond*, etc. An image even more distorted by tourists who come to Sri Lanka and are responsible for the rise in prostitution and drug trafficking. That's the image they have of white people. So I did my utmost to change that image and explain that I wanted to do things like they did, live like them, learn their lifestyle and experience it personally. They gradually began to understand this and started treating me like a normal family member ... to the point they'd lecture me if I came home too late at night! At first, I couldn't even go to the outhouse alone. Someone had to show me where it was, as well as explain how I should bathe! I caught on pretty quickly, but it was still rather humiliating. One night, I had to go to the bathroom while it was pouring rain. I told myself: "I'll go on my own!" No, no, no: someone absolutely had to go with me. Good thing, too, since I slipped on a hillside and landed in a pool of mud. Everyone had a good laugh: I was literally covered in mud! In short, I was completely accepted by the family.

J. H.: How did you communicate? Did they speak any English?

Michael: I actually picked up Singhalese fairly quickly and even learned to write it somewhat, thanks to a book.

J.H.: But it's a rather strange form of writing ...

Michael: Yes, but it's so beautiful! It's very round and filled with spirals. Furthermore, my counterpart, Sunil, would explain local customs, including less important ones, so I might avoid being embarrassed. For instance, you must only eat with the right hand. And when you're given a glass of water before a meal, you mustn't drink it: only touch it and then come to the table. Sunil gave me useful information about things like that. About attitudes as well. He understood my problems because of his Canadian experience; this meant a lot to our relationship. During our stay in Canada, I sometimes stretched the Canada World Youth rules a bit...

J.H.: Oh!

Michael: ...and snuck off with my counterpart to visit relatives in other parts of the country. I wanted to do as many things as possible with Sunil, and he did the same for me in Sri Lanka. It was very interesting. Even when I was really tired, he insisted I accompany him somewhere. I did the same for him in Canada ...

J.H.: Did you keep in touch with Sunil?

Michael: Yes, we write. But his English has deteriorated somewhat, so I'm trying to improve my Singhalese. At least enough to write a letter he can understand.

J.H.: You mentioned earlier that one of your Ontario host families called on you in Sri Lanka. Tell me more.

Michael: My host family—the pork farmers—spent all their savings on this trip to Sri Lanka.

J.H.: That's absolutely amazing, though it's happened a few times in Canada World Youth's history. How many people took part in the trip?

Michael: About a dozen. A small minibus filled with people.

J.H.: We might assume this was their first trip of the kind ...

Michael: Most had never travelled, especially not to a country like Sri Lanka. Some had been to the United States, even as far as Florida, or travelled somewhat in Canada, but none had been on such a long trip.

J.H.: And their purpose was really to visit *their* participants?

Michael: Yes, and to try to understand Sri Lanka better. Naturally, they realized there are limits to what can be done in a month; for example, they wouldn't be living with a family. But they visited every host family. Some of them actually left the group to stay overnight with one. My family from Binbrook, Ontario, came to our village and shared a meal with my Sri Lankan parents. They stayed for one day. They didn't spend much time at the beach, perhaps two or three days. I think they really wanted to find out more about this place, as well as see how the participants they'd known in Canada were living. They wanted to discover it a little more. It was a once-in-a-lifetime experience for most of them. I'm sure they'll never be able to do it again. Yet some of the Canadian farmers I talked to wanted to find a work project here, through CIDA or some other organization, if their skills could be useful to this country.

J.H.: This is rather new at Canada World Youth. But it's happening more frequently. Which highlights the impact participants are having on communities.

Michael: I think it's an important factor for many people too. Canadians are generally aware of what's happening in the world. Thanks to Canada World Youth, people are put into direct contact with problems, so they can understand them, which is very motivating. The news is always brief and provides a type of information; but it's very discouraging. It stops you dead and numbs you. But when you see things for yourself, and touch the people, you realize they're humans with the same basic values we have; you can begin to live with that reality. It then becomes an integral part of your life and no longer something external that you don't really understand and can't do anything about. Reality becomes easier to understand and accept.

J.H.: What's the most important thing you learned in Sri Lanka?

Michael: Well, as I just said, I believe the world became a part of me, so to speak. It's now an integral part of my life. However, most of the practical knowledge Canada World Youth helped me acquire came following the program. I gained experience, insight and a new motivation. Canada World Youth was really a starting point. I learned mainly by thinking about and expanding the ideas I'd just acquired.

J.H.: And after your stay in Sri Lanka ...

Michael: Following a Latin American experience, I decided to head to Fraser Valley College in British Columbia and do a transfer program to get into International Development Studies at the University of Toronto.

J.H.: A department that attracts many former participants ...

Michael: That's right. Many former Canada World Youth participants study there. After doing some research, I realized this was the best program I could find—a good mix of practical and theoretical knowledge. I'd therefore registered to study economics, political science, biology, French and another language; in a word, a wonderful array. Despite everything, I wasn't really sure this was what I wanted to do ... That's when I got the fateful phone call: I was asked whether I was interested in applying for the special program with Zaïre. I made up my mind in about twenty seconds. In fact, this was perfect since I'd already had experience in Latin America and Asia: by going to Africa, I'd be going full circle. I'd have some notions about each region, and perhaps specialize later. The timing was perfect. I'd obviously have to put off school for another year, but was already two or three years behind schedule. And practical experience is what I value most. So, yes sir, I decided to apply. My whole life was up in the air for a month, while I waited to find out if Canada World Youth would accept me. This project interested me in particular, since its goal was to inform Canadians about development, which is one of my major concerns.

J.H.: You were finally accepted. Shortly thereafter, you landed in Kinshasa, Zaïre's bustling capital. What was your first impression?

Michael: At first I felt intimidated by Zaire, by Africa ... I thought integrating would be difficult. I think I was really conscious of my "whiteness," I felt like a white "colonizer", which gave me a bit of a guilt trip.

J.H.: So tell me about Kalenda, the small village we're in.

Michael: Well, it's very isolated. I believe the standard of living is the lowest I've ever experienced.

J.H.: A village with thatched huts ...

Michael: Exactly. But they have a good well, though it's a lot of work to carry the water from it. The quality of nutrition is questionable. Though the land is very rich, people tend to sell the best products from their harvest. And yet, Zaïre is a wonderful country. Very rich. Everything can be found in this country filled with natural resources. Moreover, its land is fertile and provides good harvests ...

J.H.: But transportation is a problem ...

Michael: I think transportation is the root of all problems. The greatest obstacle is carrying produce from point to point.

J.H.: Now tell me, Michael, about the huge, dilapidated hospital you had to repair ...

Michael: The hospital consists of an enormous complex of buildings raised by the Belgians. Kalenda is a good example of what colonialism bequeathed to Africa, in rural regions where seventy-five to eighty per cent of the population lives. After Zaïre gained independence, the hospital was abandoned and then plundered during the five years of insurrection that began in 1960. Our work project involves rebuilding the roof on what's left of the hospital.

J.H.: The region is in dire need of a hospital ...

Michael: Indeed. Shortly after we arrived, over one hundred patients came to the hospital, thinking we were doctors. We then realized our goal wasn't to integrate into the village, but to rebuild the hospital.

J.H.: As a result, you had to make a special effort to go into the village and talk to the people.

Michael: Yes, and we lacked motivation at times. Moreover, the people were somewhat intimidated by our living as a group inside a wing of the huge hospital. They hesitated to visit us. There was a barrier between the village and hospital. I personally believe that this type of project can only be educational if participants live with families.

J.H.: I totally agree!

Michael: It's the ideal situation. We had to make quite an effort. Unfortunately, we only had nine weeks. It took a long time for villagers to accept us, as it did for us to get to know them. I don't know if you've been told the following story ... One night, a group of participants went hunting ... for termites! A group of villagers saw us ... and thought we were cannibals! In fact, whites from the region had once been involved in cannibalism. At one point, a man was ready to attack us with a machete! Fortunately, they thought of going over to our friends, the Zaïrian nuns: they awoke them instead of attacking us, since they were afraid of us cannibals.

J.H.: You hunted termites?

Michael: That's right, termites. You can only hunt them during the full moon, very late at night when the moon is high and radiates a lot of light. You make a small fire and dig a large hole between it and the termite nest. The smell of the fire—from palm wood—attracts the insects. They fall in the hole, you put them in your bucket and cook them the next day.

J.H.: Are they tasty?

Michael: Sure. We even ate them raw. You should try some!

J.H.: If your mother could only see you!

Michael: I ate too many ... and had diarrhea the next day!

J.H.: What do they taste like?

Michael: Somewhat like bread. Rather crunchy. Strangely enough, they aren't bad at all.

J.H.: So how did you learn to hunt termites?

Michael: We befriended Eelunga, a youth from the village; he invited us to come and see how it's done ...

J.H.: But why were the others afraid of you, since you were with a Zaïrian from the village?

Michael: Fergus, one of the Canadian participants, asked Eelunga if the villagers we'd met "had caught any" (termites). He asked the question in French: "Have they caught any?" The villagers understood: "Eelunga, catch them!" They quickly ran away!

J.H.: Did the incident have any repercussions on your integration into the village?

Michael: Not really. But it highlighted the various barriers we had to cross. As I said was the case in Sri Lanka, we had to struggle against the image of the rich, white colonizer who's come to teach them how to do things.

J.H.: Let's come back to your integration into the village ...

Michael: Sure. I've made a couple of friends I'll write to. We gradually integrated into the village. Now, after nine weeks, we have all kinds of contacts. We've been invited for boat rides on the river, as well as a thousand other things. We're getting to know the people. If we had another two, three or four weeks, or a little longer, we'd really succeed. It takes time.

J.H.: I agree ... And you had to prepare the audio-visual for your grand tour of Canada.

Michael: The grand tour of Canada, indeed ... This was our group's main concern from the first day. I'm extremely excited at the prospect and look forward to it. It'll be a new experience for me. Trying things, finding out if they work. Everything won't be settled before we start. I hope it'll be a process that gradually evolves.

J.H.: You'll once again have contact with Katimavik groups during the entire tour.

Michael: I think we'll have an impact, especially with Katimavik participants, the only groups we'll spend time with. I intend to include one or two Katimavik participants in my presentation, especially in the schools and communities. You naturally have time to chat when living with a Katimavik group. I think that's where our major impact will be. I'm not so sure about schools. I worked with schools when I returned from Sri Lanka and Latin America ...

J.H.: Next March, following the program, I presume you won't be expecting another phone call from Canada World Youth ...

Michael: That would be wonderful!

J.H.: Of course. But in case it doesn't happen, what will you do, Michael?

Michael: Well, I've changed my plans: I'm not going into International Development Studies. I want something a little more open and general. I plan on doing a year at Concordia University in Montreal. I'm interested in studying languages, not from a strictly linguistic standpoint, but more as a practical means of communication.

J.H.: I presume this includes French?

Michael: French, African languages and Spanish. Universal languages spoken by the majority of people in the world: French and Spanish. But there are also languages in Asia spoken by millions of people and a certain number of basic African languages. Besides learning these languages, I want to touch on sociology, history, political science, and so on. I'm not yet completely sure about the direction I want to head in. I also want to study overseas. And I have a few projects in mind: working with Katimavik and Canadian schools. I'd also like to work as a group leader with Canada World Youth.

J.H.: You already have quite a background ...

Michael: But I think I need a little break from Canada World Youth and Katimavik. I believe I should study more before becoming a group leader. I don't have enough time to do all these things.

J.H.: I can see that! Perhaps we'll meet again when you're a group leader somewhere in the world ...

Michael: Even before, I hope ...

Michael Smith's Comments on the Canadian Tour

Our grand tour of Canada took place during January and February 1986. We were nine participants divided into sub-groups of three and accompanied by the tour co-ordinator. Everyone piled into a van with three projectors, screens, portable stereos, maps, artifacts and luggage. Over a six-week period we travelled from Vancouver Island to Thunder Bay, Ontario. We went from British Columbia's spring-like weather, to a temperature of -49°C in Saskatchewan. We did audio-visual presentations on our Zaïrian experience in grade schools, high schools, colleges and universities, before women's groups, NGOs, Katimavik groups as well as groups of former Canada World Youth participants. And finally reached the general public through television, radio and newspapers.

The majority of our presentations were held in high schools, before very receptive students from grades ten, eleven and twelve. Students and teachers gave us a warm reception; many told us how much they needed this kind of presentation. The students seemed to like our style a lot: "This is the first time I've found history interesting! I could really get into sociology if that's how it is! You guys should be teachers!"

The tour was a remarkable experience for me. Working intensively with a group, learning how to express myself clearly and effectively, putting my ideas in order before discussing them with groups. It was also very interesting to find out what's happening in schools throughout the country.

Following the tour, we resumed our trek through the world, on paths leading through the jungles of societies. After camping for a few months, I'll finally have to get a more formal education. And, as my backpack fills with experiences and memories, so increases my vast family throughout the world, a really extended family that shares my sorrows and delights.

Michael Smith Ten Years After

Less than a year after the Zaïre program, Michael began studying international development at the University of Guelph. He also completed a masters degree in community economic development at New Hampshire College's Graduate School of Business. His thesis involved creating a workers' co-operative in Montreal's southwestern neighbourhoods with the help of local community groups. The Co-op's goal was to help severely marginalized young adults, aged eighteen to thirty, reintegrate socially and economically.

He left the reintegration program after three years to pursue interests in music and technology. He started with a diploma in computer-assisted sound design at Montreal's Musitechnic. *After completing the diploma, he taught at that college for a year and a half. During this time, he produced a multimedia performance with two other artists. The act includes contemporary dance, video, three-dimensional animation and multi-channel audio.*

Michael is presently working full-time at the research and development department of Softimage *in Montreal.*

2.
Josée Galipeau

From Quebec to Pakistan

Josée and her Pakistani counterpart.

Josée: I'm a country girl from Lac-Mégantic. There were eight children in my family, and we weren't rich. My father had to work nights, so I never really got to know him. But my mother was always around ... I didn't get very far with my education. I went to school until I was sixteen-years old, then decided I'd had enough and wanted to do something else. One of my friends had a job in Manitoba taking care of children. One day, she offered me her job. I accepted without hesitating and soon ended up in Manitoba.

J.H.: Did you speak any English?

Josée: Not a word. But I was determined to learn. Unfortunately, the lady for whom I worked was a Quebecker ... who refused to speak English to me! Not very practical. But with time, I finally was able to manage somewhat. When I returned to Lac-Mégantic, I finished my secondary education at a school for adults.

J.H.: And you heard about Canada World Youth one day ...

Josée: I went to the Canada Employment Office. I tried as best I could to get information, but nobody seemed to know about Canada World Youth. Someone told me it vaguely resembled Crossroads International, an organization about which I knew a little. In any event, the prospect interested me.

J.H.: Did you dream about going to a country in particular?

Josée: I'd mentioned a few countries on my application, but wholeheartedly agreed when I was offered Pakistan. Even after I was informed this was to be Canada World Youth's first experience with the country. I'd been warned the program would likely be difficult, as is the case for all new endeavours of the type. This didn't really worry me.

J.H.: In short, you were afraid of nothing!

Josée: That's it. I like adventure ... I once again ended up out West for the Canadian part of the program. In Prince Albert, Saskatchewan this time. We had a choice between numerous work projects, some of them with the Métis. I opted for a day-care centre, where I'd longed to work for some time.

J.H.: You and your counterpart lived with a host family ...

Josée: Our "parents" were really young: the father was maybe twenty-six or twenty-eight years old. He had two children. They owned a grocery store and we were able to discover that world somewhat. More importantly, we learned a lot about the métis and natives of Prince Albert, about whom I'd previously known nothing. I befriended a native and we talked at length about the problems of his people. I and other participants joined in ceremonies on the reserve. I really liked the Canadian part of the program because I learned a great deal about my country. My biggest problem was not knowing enough English. Fortunately, my Pakistani counterpart spoke the language very well, and I finally learned it thanks to her.

J.H.: So a girl from Pakistan taught you English in Canada ...

Josée: Unbelievable! I must say that, from the first day, I managed to understand her better than the other anglophone participants. She spoke more clearly, more slowly, and payed a lot of attention to me. We really had a wonderful relationship. She was a sweetheart!

J.H.: So you reached Pakistan one day and, as predicted, the program was hampered by our counterpart's inexperience.

Josée: What struck me is that they immediately separated the girls from the boys.

J.H.: Part of the custom in this fundamentally Muslim country. We couldn't impose our values to its people ...

Josée: For greater security, the boys were left in the city, while the girls were sent to the country!

J.H.: You discovered the separate world of Pakistani women, while the boys got to live in the more open world of men—closed to women, nonetheless. This must have provided interesting debriefings on your return!

Josée: Due to the lack of organization, I briefly lived with two Pakistani families, before ending up with a third. A very typical family with five children as well as a sister-in-law and her son. Space in the house was rather cramped! But this family was wonderful. Of course, there was the language problem and I constantly had to rely on my counterpart. We lived near the mosque, which means that we talked a lot about religion. My counterpart was very devout and would get up to pray in the middle of the night. But we never talked about politics. Pakistanis can't really say what they think about the subject, so we simply didn't mention it.

J.H.: What kind of work did you do?

Josée: Here again, organization was lacking. For example, at the beginning we worked in a public park, something women never do around here. Pakistani boys came to pester us until we realized women had no business working in a park. I was finally given work in a school for the physically handicapped. It was really sad to see those unfortunate children, some of whom suffered from muscular dystrophy. They had trouble standing up and, when they fell, couldn't get up without our help. We realized many of them didn't have long to live. They got attached to us, although we'd be leaving soon ... Verbal communication was difficult since the children only spoke Punjabi ... while we'd just been introduced to Urdu! But we had fun with them. At lunch time, all the children would pool food prepared by their parents, creating a buffet of really varied dishes. They helped one another a great deal.

J.H.: In a few words, what did you mostly retain from Pakistan?

Josée: A difficult question! When I was young, I always wondered why the world was divided into rich and poor. I didn't really find the answer I expected in Pakistan. At least, I got to ask myself what I could do to help poor countries. Even before the program, I'd been very "ecological" and avoided all waste. On my return, I read *Utopia or Else* by René Dumont, a book that helped me understand that the poor from the Third World pay for the waste of rich countries. I wanted to change things, not in another country but in mine. A little each day. A long-term project ...

J.H.: What's the first thing you did when you got back to Canada?

Josée: I registered into a nursing course. I'm still not sure whether this is my vocation, but I tell myself it will always come in handy, wherever I go, whatever I do. As well, since I have a lot of energy, I worked with disabled seniors and with children in a daycare centre. It was okay, but not enough. I guess I wanted to save the world!

J.H.: That's all there is: saving the world!

Josée: So, when Canada World Youth offered me the Zaïre program, I saw it as an opportunity to learn more. It would be easier this time, since French is spoken in that country. And what a pleasure it was to be with other former participants at the Saint-Liguori orientation camp. It was very easy to communicate, since we'd had similar experiences. Everyone had a thousand things to relate about one country or another. For example, André, who'd been to the Dominican Republic, had lots to say about the poverty of sugar-cane cutters ...

J.H.: And a few weeks later, you landed in the middle of Zaïre ...

Josée: When I first got to Kinshasa, I had a lot of trouble adapting to the Zaïrians; they're so different from Pakistanis. In Pakistan, for example, people never touch one another, girls never look a man in the eyes. Here, men and women continually call out to each other.

J.H.: Zaïrians are obviously more relaxed and approachable ...

Josée: In a way. They're more direct, more candid, whereas Pakistanis are, let's say, more reserved. Well! Let's stop comparing Africa and Asia! Here, in Kalenda, I immediately got along with the swarms of children. From the first day, I was surrounded by fifty or so of them. I even managed to get one to fall asleep in my arms. Thanks to the children, I was able to integrate into the community.

J.H.: I've noticed the children adore you.

Josée: Oh, yes! They all know my name. When I fetch water at the well, I hear them say all along the way: "Josée! Josée! Josée!" I do spend a lot of time with them. As soon I see one with torn pants, I run to get my needle and thread ... I'm a mother hen ...

J.H.: There's no shortage of little chickens in Kalenda!

Josée: The village women befriended me when they realized I really loved children, since they're the most important thing to them. When I walk by a hut, the woman immediately hands me her baby which I rock while we chat. We smile and gesticulate to one another, since these women don't speak French.

J.H.: How do the children here differ from ours?

Josée: Our children are too spoiled, they get everything they want. Zaïrian children are extremely ingenious because they have very little. I don't know if you've seen the small whistles they make. They cut old sardine cans, tie two *kalbas* pieces to them, and place a tiny ball inside. The result: a lovely whistle that works very well. They're ingenious and resourceful. They make all kinds of objects which they try to sell to make a little money. Brothers and sisters help, protect and are very fond of one another. Oh! and they're so beautiful! My best friend is called Ishiama. He's often with me at the hospital, and I regularly drop by to see him at his place in the village, where I'm always warmly received. The people are generally outside, in front of their huts. They often invite me to sit with them and treat me like a member of the family. If they're preparing a meal, they continue doing so as we chat. And immediately offer me some food when it's ready. The children join us, and we have a family meal. When they see me arrive, the children swarm about me, waiting for me to do something to amuse them. I taught them a song, *Frère Jacques*, with the bell ringer's gestures and all.

J.H.: What do you eat during those family meals?

Josée: *Fufu* and manioc leaves most of the time. Always the same thing. Only once did I eat chicken. Another time, peanuts with the shell, cooked in salt water, were all they could give me. So we ate peanuts the whole evening, under the moonlight.

J.H.: Did you get used to eating *fufu* and manioc leaves every day?

Josée: It's rather monotonous at first, but you get used to it. Not a very well-balanced diet. *Fufu* is made with corn flour and manioc. Corn is alright, but the nutritional value of manioc is relatively worthless. The leaves are more nutritious than the roots. The people also eat fruit. Bananas and pineapples grow all year round. The villagers have mangos in plentiful supply. They pick them at leisure, since the mango trees belong to everyone.

J.H.: But you don't spend all your time playing with the children and eating *fufu*...

Josée: I naturally helped rebuild the hospital. I'd work on the roof in the afternoon, in the blazing sun. There was also water duty: a ten-minute walk to the well ... and twenty minutes to return with our buckets! And we'd often have to wait in line with the *mamous*.

J.H.: So there's no running water in that large hospital?

Josée: No. We had to fetch water for cooking and doing the laundry. There's a place in the tall grasses where the women can bathe during the day.

J.H.: And the boys?

Josée: They'd go at night.

J.H.: Did participants have any health problems during your stay in Kalenda?

Josée: Very few. Right now, two or three have sore stomachs. They probably ate too much meat during the Christmas Eve dinner.

J.H.: Which I attended. A calf had been slaughtered for the occasion: it was obviously fresh ...

Josée: There was also some pork, about which people are justifiably wary. Our patients had to eat some ... And then there was fatigue and the emotion of soon having to leave our Kalenda friends ...

J.H.: It nonetheless was a nice Christmas Eve dinner.

Josée: With our Christmas tree made from a banana plant ... But today everyone is really saddened at the prospect of our imminent departure. Our friends from the village spent most of the day with us.

J.H.: And in a few weeks, the great Canadian tour. Are you all set?

Josée: Some members of my team prepared slide shows, while I worked on the oral presentation with Michael, Todd and Nkoy. A sort of play. It's very formal for ten minutes, almost boring, with tons of statistics about Zaïre. Suddenly, Todd emerges on the stage, completely breathless and making lots of noise. He's the late-arriving student who excuses himself and disturbs everyone. The formal presentation resumes, but Todd continually interrupts, saying he doesn't understand anything. The least word must be explained to him. "What do you mean by development? What's interdependence?" Etc. Michael pretends to think for a moment, and then strives to explain everything very clearly ... which ought to suit our Canadian audiences. We held a preview in Mwene Ditu. People said we were going too far, that our Canadian audiences would have trouble understanding our stories about bananas and multinationals. We therefore decided to simplify our play, even if it meant serving our bananas and multinationals to Katimavik groups, surely more likely to understand us. We pinned a lot of hope on Katimavik participants, with whom we'll spend more time since we'll be living with them.

J.H.: What part of Canada will get the privilege of seeing your great show, with or without the bananas?

Josée: The Atlantic provinces. Three weeks in English and three weeks in French. I hope we'll have an impact on the people, on the youth at least. The older ones already have their habits and prejudices ... Difficult to change. Whereas young people, such as Katimavik participants, will be more open. They'll have children some day and will provide them a better understanding of things. We're mutants ...

J.H.: What will you do after the tour?

Josée: My nursing degree. But I also want to take sociology courses, and get more involved in the international arena. Before Canada World Youth, I preferred not thinking about the misery of people, especially that of children. It really saddened me. Particularly at night ... I now realize each of us can do a small part to change the course of things and improve the world ...

J.H.: Together, dear Josée, we will change the world!

Josée: I'm sure of it!

Josée Galipeau's Comments on the Canadian Tour

The enormous amount of work that went into the Canadian tour helped us avoid just about all logistical problems. We were generally well received and I particularly enjoyed living with the Katimavik groups. It was like a microcosm of Canada, with the same barriers, the same imperfections, but with the same spirit.

I had some difficulty talking about Zaïre, a country I hadn't sufficiently lived in and explored. It was also difficult to keep up with Steven. Compared to him, my knowledge of international development was very limited.

I find international development interesting, but prefer it on a local, even family, level.

However, I hope our journey throughout Canada helped open the hearts of a few people, and explain that international development begins locally. Right here! Today!

Josée Galipeau Ten Years After

Following the Canadian tour, Josée and another participant, Pauline McKenna, worked in a summer camp for children suffering from cancer (Camp Trillium). The children lived with their brothers and sisters. A human experience which contributed to her career choice. When she returned home to Lac-Mégantic, she continued to work with children at the Coco-Soleil daycare centre, where she remains. She learned she couldn't change the world on her own and that teaching children would be more effective. The world would afterwards change on its own ...

Josée has had four children: Raïssa (eight years old), Hansé (six years old), Maïlé (five years old) and Youri (three years old). She's raising them in the country, in a hundred-year-old house surrounded by a vast garden. "I'm teaching all these tiny ones openness to the world," she says, "sharing, respect and acceptance of differences. But I'm especially teaching them to love ..."

3.
Todd Repushka

From Saskatchewan to India

Todd during his program in India (1985).

Todd: I was born in Regina, Saskatchewan. At the age of eleven, I moved to Ontario, and lived in Toronto and London for two-and-a-half years with my mother and sister. At fifteen, I moved back to Regina to live with my father; that's where I finished high school and went to university for a year. I then thought about studying at the College for Translators and Interpreters in Sudbury, Ontario.

J.H.: Did you already know a little French?

Todd: It was my major during first-year university.

J.H.: So you wanted to become a translator?

Todd: I thought I did. However, after one year at the College for Translators and Interpreters, I switched disciplines to study French for non-francophones, since I felt I didn't yet have a good grasp of the language. I found out about Canada World Youth during my French immersion from a student who'd gone to Bangladesh. She related her experience in class one day. I told myself: "Wow, sounds interesting!" And immediately sent an application. Shortly after the evaluation weekend in Ontario, I got a call from Canada World Youth: "Would you like to go to India?" I answered: "Give me a second to think it over!" And even before I realized what was happening ... I was off to India!

J.H.: Didn't your program start in Canada, in British Columbia?

Todd: Yes, originally. But organizers suddenly decided to do a reverse program, i.e., start in India.

J.H.: I remember now ... The reverse program ... Indian authorities felt their participants might not be safe in British Columbia at the time, because a small group of Sikhs was stirring things up. I think their fears were unfounded, but we must always respect our foreign counterpart's opinion. As a result, you were sent to India first. Cold ...

Todd: Not exactly. We had a two-and-a-half week orientation camp before departing. One advantage for Canadian participants was getting to know the host families with whom we and our counterparts would live for four months. So we kept them informed of our activities during our stay in India, allowing the families to become an even more integral part of the program.

J.H.: Tell me, Todd, what were your first impressions of India?

Todd: It was midnight and 30° C. The humidity, the smells, the commotion, so many things to see. It was hard to take it all in. We left New Delhi and headed to the state of Karnataka, where we lived in a village of three thousand people. I worked on a family farm: in the vineyard, rice paddy, *ragi* field and vegetable garden. I even washed the cows once a week. I also participated in the group project consisting of building a small community centre.

J.H.: Tell me about your host family.

Todd: It was really unique! It wasn't the usual extended family: only the father, mother and three children. The father wasn't wealthy by our standards, but relatively well off. He had quite a standing in the community. There were seven of us in the family, including my counterpart and me.

J.H.: You really felt you were part of the family?

Todd: Oh, yes!

J.H.: How did you call your parents?

Todd: Father, mother ... They did the same and referred to my counterpart and me as sons. They even took us to my mother's village to *show* us to the rest of the family! So we managed to integrate with the whole family. We established a really good relationship which continues by correspondence.

J.H.: Perhaps you'll call on them some day ...

Todd: I sure hope so!

J.H.: Tell me about your counterpart.

Todd: My brother.

J.H.: Your brother?

Todd: Yes, my little brother. He was from Bombay. A second-year student at Sydenham College in Bombay. He was with the National Cadet Corps. We hit it off very quickly, especially in India, though it took a little while to really get to know each other.

J.H.: Was he about your age?

Todd: No, he was seventeen and I was twenty-one.

J.H.: That's why you called him little brother ...

Todd: So to speak. I never felt like he was seventeen and I was twenty-one. At times, he gave the impression of being thirty ... and made me feel like seventeen! He gave me a lot of help in understanding the culture, traditions, as well as what you can and can't do. However, he was sometimes as astonished as me, since he came from another part of India. The food, language and clothing weren't the same. So it was a new experience for both of us.

J.H.: Did you get to know many villagers?

Todd: We lived in the village of Jakkur, but the work project was in Srirampur, three kilometres away. So we had contact with the other host families, the workers and the children. Especially the children. I love children!

J.H.: You mentioned your collective work project was three kilometres away. How did you get there?

Todd: By walking.

J.H.: In the blazing sun ...

Todd: We'd leave early in the morning and follow the railroad tracks. We'd all meet, walk on the rails and talk about what we'd done the night before. We'd come across women carrying water and farmers heading to their fields.

J.H.: What's the most important thing you learned in India?

Todd: I learned a lot and am continuing to learn. But the most significant thing India taught me was the wonderful closeness of the family and the importance of family ties. Things we take for granted in Canada. This really impressed me.

J.H.: Did you discover other values we've lost?

Todd: The importance of religion to their daily lives. My family was Hindu and I took part in the *pooja* with them.

J.H.: What's the *pooja*?

Todd: The prayer.

J.H.: Did you pick up a bit of Hindi?

Todd: A little. But the language we spoke in our village was Kannada, not Hindi. Although Hindi is the national language, it's barely spoken in the region. Only at the administrative level; even there, Kannada is used extensively.

J.H.: So you returned to Canada one day, for the second half of the program, which was to take place in British Columbia.

Todd: We were in Nelson, British Columbia, right in the Kootenay region, living with host families that Canadian participants already knew. Our work project was with the Early Childhood Education program; it was quite interesting since it actually comprised five work programs. We'd go from one to the other, working at the recently opened library, at a daycare centre, the Nelson Children's World, as assistant instructors at the grade school, with Taking Action For Special Kids, a program designed for children with particular needs, as well as with another daycare centre affiliated to the Nelson Daycare Family Society.

J.H.: How did your counterpart react to all this?

Todd: He took everything in stride. Even snow didn't really shock him. He'd already seen some in the mountains of India. He loved snow and loved skiing. He adapted as well as any Canadian, if not better.

J.H.: Given this was a reverse program, did the Canadians find it less interesting to return to Canada for the second part?

Todd: I felt it might be, but I was wrong. In fact, we discovered another region of our country, a new community, a new family. And I discovered all this with my counterpart ... I remember talking about it to other participants who were thinking of going home. I even wanted this part to last longer.

J.H.: What did you plan to do following the program?

Todd: My plans were very scattered! I'd thought of staying in British Columbia and earn some money to return to India or continue studying. I made up my mind after five days in Vancouver: "Well, at this point, I have to return home." I therefore went back to Regina and worked at a co-operative restaurant, and as activity director for pre- and elementary school children with Parks & Recreation. So, I didn't return to Vancouver, India, or school. Then, in September, Canada World Youth called me about the Zaïre program. I had no specific plans in mind and told myself: "Opportunity is knocking ... I'll open the door!" And, before I knew what was happening, ended up at the Saint-Liguori orientation camp ...

J.H.: ... with numerous participants who, like you, had gone through the program in one country or the other.

Todd: It was very exciting. The atmosphere was really charged and we were all eager to get into action.

J.H.: And get to Zaïre ...

Todd: Oh! Kinshasa... I felt at ease from the moment we reached the airport. There was a lot of warmth ... and I'm not only talking about the temperature! The people were extremely friendly and gracious, not to mention curious about seeing a group of twenty or so *Bandeles* (whites) driving through the city in a truck at 1:00 a.m. I was seated atop a pile of luggage with a few others in the back of a three-ton truck. Music from local bars filled the air, groups of strollers were chatting, laughing and greeting us with waves and shouts. I was astonished by their spirit of solidarity. This sense of security and solidarity amazed me. After a few days in Kinshasa, we headed to Kalenda, my "home away from home."

J.H.: A humble village of thatched huts ...

Todd: As well as impressive remnants from the colonial period. Huge abandoned buildings ...

J.H.: ... which you desperately tried to renovate!

Todd: Exactly, by replacing metal gutters on some hospital pavilions, for example, or completely renovating the doctor's residence: from replacing windowpanes and ceiling tiles, to repainting the interior and outside trim.

J.H.: How did you find group living?

Todd: Challenging! Especially when considering we had to work both on rebuilding the hospital and on presentations. We worked hard on audio-visual presentations. However, group living for three months ... I need a little solitude at times. But we were always with participants or villagers. It was very, very hard to get away. Except when going to the bathroom! I'd see the children and villagers mostly in the evening. We were somewhat separated from them when working at the hospital, while they attended to their business. When washing up after work, near the village well, we'd come across the women; there was no other water supply and this was their meeting place.

J.H.: So participants had the same daily chores as the women?

Todd: Precisely! Many of these women visited their sick relatives at the hospital. They quickly got to know us by name ... or nickname.

J.H.: You had a nickname?

Todd: They called me Mario or ... *Citoyen Mbuyi.*

J.H.: What does *Mybuyi* mean?

Todd: I think it means twin. I have a friend called Mbuyi here at the village medical centre. Perhaps that's why I was called Citoyen Mbuyi. I'd visit the centre to get to know the students, understand their lifestyle, and especially the point of view of young people.

J.H.: Was it easy to communicate with the people?

Todd: Very much so. The villagers were very warm; they'd offer us drinks and invite us to dance.

J.H.: Traditional dances?

Todd: Traditional as well as popular.

J.H.: Are you a good dancer?

Todd: I try!

J.H.: Few villagers speak French; was this a problem for you?

Todd: Not so much a problem as an opportunity to learn their language. I remember one evening sitting on the ground with people who spoke no French, save for "*Bonjour! Comment ça va?*" They taught me a little Tshiluba, the regional language, by mimicking animal sounds and using sign language.

J.H.: Your stay in Africa is coming to an end ... What's the most important thing it taught you?

Todd: Like India, Africa taught me the importance of the family. How solidarity, sharing and straightforward communication are transmitted from family to community. I learned about the joy and happiness that flow from a simple yet very fulfilling lifestyle. I also learned patience, which is needed to adapt to the local pace.

J.H.: Have your views on development changed?

Todd: I don't know if they've really changed. Perhaps they've expanded enough to allow me to put things in perspective. I learned about development-related problems from a practical standpoint, through agriculture, education, health, the economy, social structures ...

J.H.: This should help you communicate with hundreds or thousands of Canadians in the coming months.

Todd: The Canadian tour seems the most important part of the program. That's when we'll put our main goal into practice: sensitize Canadians, especially young Canadians, and convey our message. I'm no expert in development, but that's what I want people to understand. You don't have to be an expert, a professional or a bureaucrat: you can start at your own level, within your own community. You don't have to go to a foreign country and say: "Okay, here I am! I'm literally immersed in development issues." Anyhow, I'm very eager to begin the tour. I'm certain we'll manage to make people aware of Zaïre, Africa and development-related issues.

J.H.: What do you plan on doing after the Canadian tour?

Todd: I have an inkling. Before going to Zaïre, I was thinking about studying education. Since I really enjoy working with young children, I plan to study elementary education. I'd like to work in Canada, to share my knowledge of foreign countries, as well as abroad, to share our culture, lifestyle and education.

J.H.: It'll happen, Todd, if you really want it.

Todd Repushka's Comments on the Canadian Tour

"What comes to mind when you hear the word Africa?" This was the opening question of our presentations during our six-week tour of Western Canada. From Vancouver to Portage la Prairie, Canadians, young and old, gave the same basic answer: "Starvation, Apartheid, deserts, jungles, Tarzan ..." All good answers, though one thing was missing—people! People like themselves, with distinct cultures, religions, joys, sorrows, goals and achievements. Not only did audiences overlook the people, most also failed to recognize Africa as a continent and not a country.

Our goal of sensitizing Canadians to development issues, using Zaïre as an example, was a success. We were able to touch people of all ages and from all walks of life: students, teachers, community and church group members, and Katimavik participants with whom we'd lodged. We discussed, exchanged and shared ideas—often surprised at our similarities, and always celebrating our differences.

Following the six-week tour, I was left with a great desire to learn more about others—not only those from abroad, Canadians as well. I believe it's important to break down the barriers created by stereotypes and sensation. Looking beyond differences and seeking similarities is only a beginning. And the beginning is always a good place to start!

Todd Repushka Ten Years Later

Inspired by the Canadian tour, Todd studied language training. An avid francophile, he settled in Quebec, where he worked as an English teacher and co-ordinator of a linguistic exchange program. His need to work in an intercultural context brought him back to the fold at Canada World Youth. This time, as a project leader in programs with Rwanda and Togo (1990 and 1991).

Forever seeking adventure and new challenges, Todd once again went abroad at the beginning of 1993 (Poland). He taught future English teachers for two-and-a-half years at the Rzeszow College for Foreign Language Teachers. On returning from Poland, he moved to Quebec's Matapédia Valley, where he works as an itinerant English teacher at the elementary level. But he's already dreaming of new projects ...

4.
Susan Machum

From New Brunswick to Bolivia

"Life is wonderful!" Susan seems to be saying ...

Sue: My family lives on a farm in rural New Brunswick, just below Hampstead. My father raised pigs when I was young, but the farm is now just a hobby. My parents keep ducks and chickens and we grow vegetables and fruits for our own consumption. I have three brothers and one sister. I've finished my third year of sociology at Saint Thomas University in Fredericton, where I focused on women's issues as they pertain to development and religion. I also took Spanish, but put it aside for the moment since I'm trying to learn French. I'd stopped taking French in grade ten; studying it again is a real challenge.

J.H.: How did you get the idea of joining Canada World Youth?

Sue: Canada World Youth participants came to talk to my grade ten geography class at Saint John High School. I immediately jotted down the address of the Atlantic regional office. But I was only fifteen and too young to apply. So I forgot all about this. Later on, following my first year at university, two really good friends of mine took part in the program: Peter Thomas went to Jamaica, and Sally Dibblee went to Indonesia. They were getting ready to leave during the summer. I was working with Peter at a summer camp and remembered the participants who'd visited my class. But I wasn't seriously thinking about it. I was in second year at university and not really happy with studying since I was beginning to look at things in a broader perspective than my university friends. They were mostly interested in weekend parties. However, since I lived off campus, I began to realize the city around me had a lot more to offer than the campus. That's when I understood there was a kind of wall around the university, and that students didn't see what was happening beyond it. So I sent an application to Canada World Youth over the Christmas holidays. I soon got a letter saying it had, unfortunately, been rejected ... and thank you very much! I told myself: "Oh, well, too bad!" So I was getting ready to continue studying, but got a phone call from Canada World Youth in February: a participant had dropped out and I was being offered her spot, on condition, of course, I go for an interview in Moncton. It lasted the whole day. Finally, in mid-April, I learned I'd been chosen for the Bolivian program.

J.H.: Had you mentioned Latin America as your first choice?

Sue: Of course, since I was studying Spanish. I wanted to improve my fluency in the language and was really interested in working on a Latin American development project. The Canadian part of the program was in Nova Scotia and Prince Edward Island. I lived on a cattle farm in the Wallace-Pugwash region of Nova Scotia. My host family owned fifty head of cattle, something I found really interesting. Although my own parents have a small farm, I'd never really taken much interest in it. I'd leave the farm in the summer to do other things and was never there during planting season. So it was really nice living on a farm in the Maritimes: it allowed me to appreciate my parent's lifestyle a lot more.

J.H.: Tell me about your host family ...

Sue: I had a lot of fun with Eden and Marita McDonald. They were in their twenties and had a five-year old child, Shannon. We tended a small vegetable garden together. It was summer and the cattle were grazing. Besides gardening, we did minor chores like mending fences. It wasn't a major project.

J.H.: You still haven't said a word about your Bolivian counterpart ...

Sue: He was from Tomayapom, Bolivia ... and his name was Concepcion! But we called him Sandy in Canada. It was easier for the family. He was happy to be in Canada, but found it difficult having an outspoken female counterpart. I think he wasn't used to that kind of relationship! Moreover, he came here with preconceptions about what he'd learn and was disappointed things turned out otherwise. Many of the Bolivians in our group expected to study agriculture intensively, although the practice differs in both countries. He learned to drive a tractor, but there are no tractors where he lives.

J.H.: Bolivian participants had obviously been misinformed from the outset. Did you get along with Concepcion ... I mean Sandy?

Sue: Yes. We studied Spanish and English together and had interesting conversations about cultural differences. I stayed on his family's farm in Bolivia. Sandy had one sister and three brothers. They grew peaches and raised goats, which provided milk and cheese for sale in the market. They were relatively well off when compared to other families from the region.

J.H.: What impressed you most when you reached Bolivia?

Sue: I remember my first impressions: the land was extremely dry and cracked all over, with deep fissures running through it. I remember thinking these were the scars of unbridled exploitation. A barren and parched land. Another striking image: women with huge water buckets on their heads, babies on their backs and a gaggle of children tagging along. I remember the hundreds of women wearing multicolored dresses, washing their clothes at river's edge. I recall the smells of streets and markets. I spent my first day strolling, looking at everything and trying to absorb it. You get used to it later on, everything becomes a part of your environment ...

J.H.: I'm very surprised your host family was that of your counterpart. That's against Canada World Youth's policy.

Sue: About ten people in our program lived with their counterparts' families. The downside is that when my counterpart returned home, he resumed family and social obligations. He was, however, able to convey his feelings about me to his family, since we'd spent three months together. This rapidly allowed me to establish good relations with all family members. I really enjoyed living with them; we had really strong bonds by the time I left.

J.H.: What kind of work did you do during your stay?

Sue: I spent most of my time in the kitchen! And did a little work in the fields, helping with irrigation. I was a little resentful at first: I thought I was supposed to be participating in a program aimed at agriculture, but was spending a lot of time in the kitchen. I gradually realized I was playing a very important role within the family, that it really pertained to agriculture: I was at one extremity of the food chain! I thought I'd be working at the other end, but it turned out okay.

J.H.: Did you enjoy Bolivian food?

Sue: Oh, yes, I love *empanados*. What's interesting about Bolivia is that you must change your whole diet. Light meals are eaten in the morning and evening: bread and cheese or bread and coffee. Heavy meals take place at noon, which differs from our custom. But I quickly adapted. I'd go to bed very early, at about 7:00 p.m., and rise at about 7:00 or 8:00 a.m. Since we lived in a rural area, there were neither stores, nor places for people to meet, and no *plazas* to stroll around in the evening. The lifestyle pleased me nonetheless. At the midpoint of our stay, my counterpart and I went to visit his brother's family in Tarija. The parents and three children lived in a very small room that was ten feet square. There were three beds, a table, a stove. We stayed for three days in any event ...

J.H.: What about the language problem?

Sue: Well, you manage to convey your message somehow. But you have to accept not always being understood. You have to laugh about it! I actually was able to manage in Spanish but couldn't take part in as many discussions as I'd have liked to. For example, I didn't feel comfortable talking about politics. But I continued to study Spanish. I was able to polish what I already knew, which allowed me to learn even more.

J.H.: Did you learn anything about development and Third World problems during your stay in Bolivia?

Sue: Absolutely. I went back to university when I returned to Canada, which seemed the best way to expand on what I'd learned in Bolivia. I put my experience on paper. I became more interested in questions dealing with women and development in Bolivia, since I had a lot of contact with the women in my host family and with their lifestyle. One thing that struck me particularly was how religion is intimately linked to the daily life of Bolivians. I used to think that development should focus on personal growth instead of economic progress; I soon realized this wasn't possible. People can't have spiritual well-being if their economic needs aren't satisfied. They must first have food, clothing and the other necessities of life, like health care and education. All these are part of development; spiritual development can't occur without economic development. I began to understand this during the program. It's a huge field and I still have lots to learn!

J.H.: So you went back to university ... until Canada World Youth interrupted you once again!

Sue: That's it. I'd found a summer job when I finished university. That's when Norma Scott from the Atlantic regional office called. She wanted to know if I was interested in going to Zaïre. Of course I was ... but I was registered at university! So I drew up a list of the pros and cons of going to Zaïre. I'd intended to finish my undergraduate degree in 1986—I'd have to postpone this for another year. But I've always wanted to travel, and Canada World Youth offers countless opportunities to learn while travelling. Moreover, the program would allow me to learn French. And the list of pros kept getting longer than the list of cons. So I went to the interview feeling very confident. I really wanted to learn more about communication skills and see another part of the world, i.e. Africa, with Canada World Youth. I had to be ready to leave in a month. Besides, I was anglophone and had to go through a week of French immersion in Quebec City with the family of a participant, Carole Godin.

J.H.: You didn't speak a word of French at that point?

Sue: Not a word. I couldn't even say *Bonjour, comment ça va?* when I landed at Montreal's airport. I was able to speak a little with Sylvie, a participant who spoke Spanish. I spoke English with Carole, who's perfectly bilingual. This really helped me during my stay with her family. We worked on French grammar every day. We then had really great language classes at the Saint-Liguori orientation camp. It gave me some basics that would prove very useful in Zaïre.

J.H.: Yes, one day, Zaïre ...

Sue: I remember it was very hot when we got to Kinshasa. It was really late at night and the air was filled with the odour of charcoal fires. We were dead tired, but the airport was bustling with activity; political personalities and television cameras awaited us. We'd experienced nothing of the kind in Bolivia, and certainly hadn't expected such a welcome. Zaïrian participants were already asleep when we finally reached Niganda, the centre where we'd stay a few days. We awoke them, since we knew it's very important for Zaïrians to greet visitors properly. We spent the next few days visiting Kinshasa, exploring the markets, talking to people, especially to our counterparts. We talked at length to them about Canada and explained our intention of preparing an audio-visual presentation concerning Zaïre with them. They weren't too familiar with the techniques.

J.H.: After a week in Kinshasa, your group settled in Kalenda, somewhere in Western Kasaï.

Sue: Kalenda is very interesting with all its colonial relics. There are huge buildings constructed by the Belgians in the forties. Most of the structures are part of a huge hospital complex which opened in 1952. When Zaïre became independent in 1960, most doctors embarked for Belgium, leaving the hospital understaffed. It was finally abandoned during the turmoil that rocked the country between 1960 and 1966. The strangest section of the hospital is the one that was bombed: trees grow inside the buildings. It's fun to explore and you always find something new. Since we were to help rebuild the hospital, it was decided we'd live in a group right here, in one of the large houses abandoned by the Belgians. This had benefits and drawbacks. Belgians had built this section of Kalenda, *their* section, some distance from the old Zaïrian village, which considerably hampered the integration of both areas. That's still the case; we've realized an entire day can go by without our going to the village. The Belgians had managed to create two lifestyles in Kalenda, with no communication between them. The layout made it very difficult to get to know the villagers. Fortunately, we have a mama who cooks for us and helps us communicate with the Zaïrians. I remember she was very uncomfortable with us at first. And now ... she says she'll cry when we leave! Although we don't speak a word of Tshiluba, we manage to communicate with gestures and expressions. This gave us a good lesson in communication: learning to get a point across using gestures and drawings, and managing to talk about different things.

J.H.: And your work project was enormous!

Sue: Oh, yes! It's sheer magnitude was daunting. Before leaving Canada, we thought we'd be rebuilding the central and side pavilions of the Kalenda hospital. Unfortunately, construction materials arrived three weeks late, which delayed the start of the project accordingly. We used the time to do less-important things: cleaning the prospective doctor's residence, whitewashing walls, and fixing the maternity ward's leaking roof as best we could.

J.H.: Did you have any time to talk with the villagers ?

Sue: A little, though I found it difficult since my French is still shaky. We managed to integrate thanks to the presentations we did in schools concerning Canada. Besides, the village children are very open, they drop by the house; we chat and play cards.

J.H.: Did you get along with the Zaïrian nuns who work at the hospital?

Sue: They're totally dedicated to the hospital, which greatly benefits Kalenda and the region's development. They'd sometimes get up our nose, since they didn't like the way we dress ... for example, when our pagnes covered only three quarters of our legs! They'd pull them down to cover our ankles. It wasn't easy to accept.

J.H.: That's part of their tradition.

Sue: I found the directness of Zaïrians the most difficult thing to adjust to. They were very straightforward from the outset—I didn't even know them. It's part of the culture shock, something you have to get used to. At first, I had trouble not feeling singled out, until I realized Zaïrians spoke that way to everyone, not only me.

J.H.: So you dressed like the villagers.

Sue: Yes, and it pleased them. Pagnes are beautiful and brightly coloured skirts. They're very comfortable, easy to wash and dry quickly.

J.H.: Besides rebuilding the hospital, you obviously had to work on your presentations.

Sue: I put together sketches on different themes concerning development, such as colonialism and how it still affects Zaïre's economy. It's especially obvious in Kalenda: every day and everywhere, you see what Belgians left behind. The contrast between the straw-hut village and huge Belgian houses is striking. I feel it's important that our presentations be very *visual*. We'll have a much stronger impact in Canada if we manage to convey certain concepts visually. For example: that twenty per cent of the world's population consumes eighty per cent of its resources. When people hear the word development, they're taken aback, it seems too enormous, too vast, they don't want to approach it. And anyway, there are too many definitions of development. Nobody's ideas are particularly right or wrong. I hope we can at least convey that development can begin on a local level, within communities. There are many organizations in Canada, but we must develop our own communities before we can act globally. The multiplicity of media messages in our society desensitizes us to what we're seeing. Television images have lost their impact: Ethiopia, South Africa ... Only sensation sells. I really don't think Canadians are aware that other news sources are available. I feel I'm now more aware of development issues, but it's an on-going process. I'll have to keep working at it. This time, when I get back home, I really want to return to university and finish my sociology degree. I think travelling is very important to that discipline; it allows you to study the lifestyles of people. Moreover, coming into contact with numerous cultures will allow me to understand Canadian culture better. I'm thinking about doing a master's degree in sociology, at the University of Toronto perhaps. I don't yet know if I'll concentrate on issues related to women, development and religion. What's certain is I'll do things I like.

J.H.: Have you one final word?

Sue: The experience has been interesting and educational. But I may not have learned as many things as I'd expected. Nevertheless, what I did learn will help me become a better person.

Susan Machum's Comments on the Canadian Tour

It's only after thinking at length about it that I managed to appreciate the Canadian tour's success. As we moved from one community to the next, from one presentation to the other, we were too involved in the immediate action to realize the extent of our impact.

Miango, the Zaïrian participant, caught everybody off guard by greeting the audience in his language, Lingala. Students sometimes appeared panic stricken, as though wondering how they'd get through the next hour.

Before long, everybody would be laughing as girls tried on pagnes, and boys tried on bubus. People started to relax as our "goodie bag" made the rounds. Next was the audio-visual presentation, followed by a question period: we tried to provoke people regarding their positions and tried to establish parallels between life in Zaïre and Canada.

Attempting to explain the inconceivable is always a challenge. For example, how do you describe public transportation in Zaïre? It isn't like rush hour in Toronto (though some would argue otherwise). Finally, I depicted the situation by comparing it to a can of sardines stuffed with the contents of three or four other cans.

I particularly loved working with elementary school children. I loved to see them hopping between desks, carefully balancing math books on their heads, pretending they were carrying water. Their curiosity about the unknown is tremendous. They're willing to question everything and stretch the limits of their imagination, since they're not yet intimidated by social norms.

I did a presentation in my home community during the tour. The young girls (Brownies) marvelled at Miango's health. "He doesn't appear to be dying of starvation, he isn't scrawny! He's like us. His clothes are like a Canadian's. His hair's different though—it's not like mine!" (We then let children run their fingers through Miango's frizzy hair, so they could make personal contact.) "He can even speak a little English!" These are just a few of the comments I heard. I know we were able to make a lasting impression just by our presence.

Though it's impossible to measure our effect, we can be sure people will remember our brief visit. No doubt our presentation has faded from the minds of many people in our audiences, but we can never be sure when a given concept will resurface, or when an event will rekindle a memory.

The tour taught me a great deal. About myself, about my abilities. I believe I acquired a quiet self-confidence; I'm now able to present my ideas and experience by adapting them to an audience.

I'm sure only time will reveal the full compass of what I learned. I now have many new friends and often think about them. I've amassed countless memories ... that allow me to laugh in the most unexpected places!

I'll always be indebted to Canada World Youth for having given me this second chance.

Susan Machum Ten Years later

Following operation Zaïre, Sue played a very active role with Canada World Youth. She was a participant in the 1989 Co-op Program between Quebec and Costa Rica, group leader in the Ontario-Costa Rica program in 1990, group leader in the British Columbia-Uruguay Program, project supervisor in the Co-op Training Program between Nova Scotia and Central America, and program co-ordinator with the Environmental Leadership Program between Nova Scotia, Newfoundland and Costa Rica in 1993 and 1994.

Sue completed her bachelor's degree with honours in sociology at Saint Thomas University in 1987, and her master's degree in the same discipline at Dalhousie University, with the prestigious Isaak Walton Killian Scholarship, in 1992. She's worked in a variety of other areas, notably as communications officer for the Ecology Action Centre in Halifax in 1988 and 1989, and executive director for the Conservation Council of New Brunswick. After teaching sociology at the University of New Brunswick and Saint Thomas University in 1994, she started a doctorate with the Department of Sociology at the University of Edinburgh, Scotland, in the Fall of 1994, earning numerous fellowships (SSHRCC Doctoral Fellowship, the British Council's Overseas Research Student Award, and a New Brunswick Women's Doctoral Scholarship).

She's currently doing fieldwork concerning the work of farm wives in New Brunswick, while lecturing at the University of New Brunswick. In 1991, Susan married Dr. Michael Clow, a sociologist and associate professor at Saint Thomas University in Fredericton.

5.
André Charlebois

From Quebec to the Dominican Republic

André Charlebois in a dugout with Zaïrian friends from Kalenda.

André: I'm from Hull, Quebec, and was lucky enough to have been born into a relatively well-off family. My father has a good position with the government.

J.H.: In short, you're a petit-bourgeois!

André: That's right, a petit-bourgeois! I even attended a private high school, the Collège Saint-Alexandre, though I wasn't a model student. I wasn't exactly a delinquent, but I was unruly and did a lot of foolish things with my friends. I could've done a lot better given my ability. Following high school, I studied social sciences at the CEGEP, an institution that didn't motivate me very much and where I had trouble integrating. The classes often bored me. In fact, I wasn't really sure what I wanted to do with my life. That's when I decided to join Katimavik. While some of my friends remained in CEGEP and others headed to university, I set off on an adventure, without really knowing what I was in for, alone ...

J.H.: Alone? But Katimavik was filled with young people!

André: Other participants who'd also gone off on their own ... to live an interesting experience. Katimavik taught me a great deal and helped me discover Canada.

J.H.: What regions specifically?

André: At first, I discovered the Beauce. I'd only ever lived in the city and now had to spend three months working on a farm near a small village of three thousand people called Sainte-Claire. That's where I learned there were major cultural differences, even within our own country. After the Beauce, I headed to the other end of Canada, to the Esquimalt naval base on Vancouver Island. We experienced military life for three months. I had numerous reservations about the lifestyle, but realized it could offer an interesting career and provide an education. But I couldn't forget the army's drawbacks ... I afterwards spent three months with a Katimavik group in Peterborough, Ontario. An interesting city with numerous organizations involved in development, fighting acid rain and nuclear arms—such as Project Ploughshares. I taught French in a small immersion school, which prompted me to register at Trent University to study education. I was really enthralled by this discipline, but my motivation suffered a severe blow when I failed to obtain a grant for second-language teachers. In short, after Katimavik, I returned to Hull to finish CEGEP. It was more interesting, especially since I dabbled a little in theatre. I had a role in *Les fourberies de Scapin*! Although I didn't feel ready for university, I sent applications to various geography departments: I was simultaneously accepted by the University of Montreal, the University of Ottawa, and the University of Quebec in Montreal!

J.H.: Deciding was your only difficulty!

André: In the meantime, I'd met Jean Chatelain, a good friend who'd been a Canada World Youth participant in Indonesia. He told me: "If you want to travel, join Canada World Youth. It has a lot to offer and teach you." Two months later I found myself in an orientation camp in Quebec.

J.H.: With the Dominican Republic program I believe.

André: That's right. Needless to say I was in the dark about international development. I still am ... but much less so! Soon after the Dominicans arrived, the fourteen of us participants headed to Alma, moved in with host families and began the work projects.

J.H.: What was your counterpart's name?

André: José Demorici. His father was a fisherman and merchant. His family worked with the *Oficina de Desarollo de la Communidad*, Canada World Youth's counterpart in the Dominican Republic. So José had contacts, which likely helped him become a participant. That's often how it is in those countries.

J.H.: Tell me a little about José.

André: He was too easygoing, unfortunately, and completely oblivious to issues discussed at Canada World Youth, even those concerning the development of his country. He only understood that people were better off in North America, and only dreamed of one day emigrating to Canada or the United States. (In fact, he afterwards moved to Canada.) I was greatly disappointed by his lackadaisical attitude and indifference to the Dominican Republic, given that the country's future depends on its young people. This happily wasn't the case for the other Dominican participants, who were more open minded and determined to learn.

J.H.: So tell me about your host family in Alma.

André: Marjolaine and Jules Gaudreau! Jules was active in regional and municipal politics and Marjolaine was heavily involved in the women's movement. We had a wonderful relationship. All of us, including José, talked a great deal. José and I considered Jules and Marjolaine as our father and mother. They treated us as though we'd been their eighteen year-old sons. It was great. But we didn't see them as much as we'd have liked, since they were very busy ... as were José and I. Our work project dealt with community television. Everything was new, particularly to José: in a "developing" country like the Dominican Republic, he hardly had access to these kinds of things. Handling television equipment and working in a studio was an extraordinary experience for him. In his country, this experience is only available to professionals working at the national television network. I interviewed our co-ordinator, Philippe, to better inform Alma residents about Canada World Youth. This was my first interview and I was relatively nervous ... we explained the presence here of seven youths from every corner of Canada, and from a tiny country called the Dominican Republic. It was also to help encourage local youth to participate in our program.

J.H.: After Hull and the Beauce, you discovered another region of Quebec.

André: There's no end to discovering all the regions of Quebec, and Canada! It's so different from one place to the next. The language, the mentality. French is spoken in Hull and Lac Saint-Jean: the same language, though not the same idiom. At home, in Hull, people speak French and English; everyone is bilingual. No one speaks English in Lac Saint-Jean. I've found that Quebec culture has remained intact in this region, whereas it's lost some ground to English back in Hull. I got the same impression in the Beauce. To those people, Hull and Ottawa are far away and Parliament is something abstract on which they have no control. Yet there are many benefits to living in my region: employment, education, access to government, etc. We have everything.

J.H.: And one day, you landed in the Dominican Republic ...

André: When you get off the plane, you realize that absolutely everyone speaks Spanish. You understand nothing, you're no longer at home; suddenly, you're the stranger. You therefore have to observe and act like the people to avoid shocking them. In Santo Domingo, you must stop being a Quebecker and become a Dominican. To get to know people, you have to integrate into their society. That's what I think.

J.H.: What struck you besides this?

André: The poverty, underdevelopment, the small cabins, the tiny huts ... Our orientation camp was located in small village called Jarabacoa. We were plunged into the harsh reality of the countryside. To Canadians, poor people are street drunks, or those living in underprivileged neighbourhoods like Saint-Henri in Montreal. Over here, all of society is poor. It forces you to think ... After a short stay in Jarabacoa, we headed to *our* village, located even deeper in the mountains, near the Haitian border. It's called Loma de Cabrera and has about seven thousand inhabitants. We were given an official welcome at the community centre. Important speeches: "We wish to welcome these young Canadians. They've come as friends to work with us and learn about our country ... Our young Dominicans have already been welcomed as friends in Canada ... We hope you all have a very pleasant stay in Loma de Cabrera."

J.H.: Following the wonderful speeches, you had to deal with the reality of living with host families ...

André: As though by coincidence, my father was a local politician, like the one in the Beauce. But he didn't do much politicking since his party was in opposition. He took care of the city hall secretariat. A relatively well-off family that lived in a solid concrete house, with power and running water. It was great as far as comfort was concerned. Naturally, the bathroom and kitchen were outside, but that's where we did most of our living. Some people in the village were obviously very poor. I imagine steps were taken to lodge us in the best houses ...

J.H.: Due to your frail healths!

André: No doubt! My family knew everyone in the village. I was very quickly accepted, since I was the family's "Canadian son." The people liked us a lot, they invited us into their homes, we'd talk and get to know them. Were it only for this, the program would still be a success. What we experienced here is worth its weight in gold. Living with people is the only way to fully understand their culture. Besides, I feel that three months isn't enough. I'd have easily lived in that village for a year.

J.H.: What about your work project?

André: We worked at the agricultural technology centre. Unfortunately, it was located in Caotaco, eighteen kilometres from our village, which greatly complicated things. There are no phones here; you can't call people and say: "I'll be over in ten minutes!" As for transportation ... So you learn to be patient and set your clock to "Dominican" or "flexible" time. But things got to be interesting once we reached the centre. I tilled soil with the workers, using an ox-drawn plough. They had a very good irrigation system and made sincere efforts at development. But what struck me most about the Dominican Republic were the people, their outlook on life, their making do with what they have, which is often very little. The poorest among them invite you into their homes, offer you a chair and give you something to eat or drink. This profoundly touched me.

J.H.: What did you talk about?

André: Everything, and often about politics, since Dominicans are rather politicised. They understand their government system and are rather critical of it. The government often has to raise the price of certain basic staples to satisfy the demands of the IMF, the International Monetary Fund, and to increase its domestic revenue, to accelerate repayment of its foreign debt. The people get upset when this happens: students demonstrate in the capital and repercussions of this are felt throughout the regions. The government then mobilizes the army to prevent violence; people are killed. And an overabundance of imports creates many more problems for the country. Of course, a lot of sugar is exported, but barely a fifth of the land is cultivated. Another country forced into monoculture by multinationals—that of sugar in this case. The best land belongs to those who hold power: they keep it for sugar cane, housing developments, or the building of airports to bring in even more tourists. So a lot has to be imported, especially to satisfy the needs of a privileged elite.

J.H.: I thought the Dominicans produced most of their food.

André: To a certain degree. They produce rice, raise a lot of chickens and are generally well fed. But there is some undernourishment, as well as problems related to health, transportation and education; however, the situation doesn't compare to the extreme poverty found next door, in Haiti. While in the Dominican Republic, I realized the extent to which the world is in dire straits. Thousands of things need to be done and profound changes must be made on a global scale. Lip service is paid to nuclear disarmament, pollution, problems of developing countries, but the enormous machine keeps churning along, to the benefit of the few and the detriment of the great many. People are suffering. Too bad! Others keep getting richer at their expense. That's where I realized how incredibly lucky I am to be from a well-off background, to be healthy and able to reach my potential, which isn't the case for most young Dominicans. The flip side of the coin, of course, is that they've maintained the spiritual values we've lost ...

J.H.: Since you couldn't spend a year in your Dominican village, you finally returned home ...

André: I was becoming very interested in development problems. So I registered in International Development Studies at the University of Toronto. I had a few months before classes began and worked here and there to make some coin. Then, one day, Canada World Youth contacted me about the special program with Zaïre. I ran over to the interview and, one week later ... was told I'd been refused!

J.H.: You weren't good enough!

André: That's it, I wasn't good enough. Since university was about to start, I moved to Toronto, but returned to Hull to work a little more and accumulate lots of money! And, one day, the phone rang. It was Philippe Mougeot, the Zaïre project co-ordinator: "What are you up to these days, André? Still feel like going to Zaïre?" I was flabbergasted: "You're pulling my leg! You turned me down only two weeks ago. I nearly had a depression! I'm now starting to get over it and you're telling me we're leaving Friday ..." You can imagine my answer: "Okay, I'm in!" I'd obviously missed the orientation camp and had barely a few days to get my shots and visa, and bid my family farewell. In fact, I joined up with the group when it came to see you in the Senate. Remember?

J.H.: I do ... so, you'd replaced a participant who'd withdrawn ... unfortunately for him.

André: At first it was difficult to integrate into a group that already had three weeks of communal living under its belt. However, we were on an even footing when we reached Kalenda. We all had to adjust to an unknown country, a new situation. And settle in Kinshasa, the village we'd call home. A small village of about five hundred people, located a three-hour drive south of Mbuji-Mayi, the major centre of Western Kasaï. Our village had known its heyday when the University of Louvain, in Belgium, had built a huge hospital complex, the Formulac which, in French, means *Formation médicale de l'Université de Louvain au Congo*. The hospital was abandoned, for well-known reasons, and has fallen to ruins. Our job is to fix it up so at least one doctor can move into it. At present, there's no doctor in Kalenda, but lots of very sick people. Even in Mbuji-Mayi, there are only three doctors to serve 130,000 people.

J.H.: At least the Zaïrian nuns help out with the Kalenda hospital.

André: The nuns have nursing experience, but can't administer more complicated treatment for lack of equipment. There isn't even a device to sterilize surgical instruments in this enormous "hospital."

J.H.: Kalenda's destitution is hardly believable ...

André: Have you seen how people live in their tiny huts? With less than nothing. The average Canadian would say they're "camping" on a permanent basis ... People sleep on hut floors and are constantly exposed to all kinds of diseases due to poor hygiene, mosquitoes, malaria, tsetse flies, and a complete lack of medication. For example, they don't even know their water is contaminated, that it ought to be boiled. We should start by educating the women. They're less emancipated than in Canada, but hold the power within families: they educate the children, prepare meals, transport water from the wells, and do everything. So the women are the ones who ought to be taught to boil water.

J.H.: But you have to burn wood to boil water ...

André: Unfortunately! Which wastes wood. Deforestation occurs, wood becomes scarce and land arid. A vicious circle. All this is so complex! The colonial system bears a good part of the responsibility; the Belgians caused a great deal of damage to Zaïrian society. Before the Belgians arrived, Zaïrians were evolving at their pace. They may have appeared "underdeveloped" to Westerners but they were at least moving forward and evolving. The worst thing Belgians did was, not only take over the territory, but impose their culture and subject Zaïre to monoculture intended for export. Zairians were forced to give up their food crops, forget about self-sufficiency and buy Belgian goods, to the greater benefit of the Belgian economy. The Zaïrian standard of living was no doubt higher in the colonial era. But there was no justice. All the country's infrastructure lay in Belgian hands. When they departed, *nothing* was left. The doctors, engineers and administrators were all Belgian. When Zaïre gained independence, people realized that, over a period of fifty years, the Belgians had only allowed *six* Zaïrians to get a university education!

J.H.: Well. Tell me more about the Kalenda hospital.

André: One day, while we were working on renovations, 120 patients arrived without warning. They had the sleeping disease, an illness transmitted by the tsetse fly which can be deadly if not treated with inoculations. Though there's no doctor in the hospital, patients can at least expect to be treated by the Zaïrian nuns. The problem was *sheltering* these 120 patients in a hospital where every roof leaked—in the midst of the rainy season! The Belgian architects had built a beautiful hospital, but they weren't very good at building watertight roofs ... We finally managed, as best we could, to fix the roof of a pavilion to shelter these patients. A lot still needs to be done before this hospital is in full working order. We did our best. Following our departure, the Mama Mobutu foundation will continue exploring the possibility of making the Kalenda hospital completely functional. And getting at least one doctor for it!

J.H.: Do you get the feeling you did something useful?

André: I think so. But the work project wasn't everything. I also discovered Zaïre, the village, the people. It took some time and effort to venture into the village on my own and talk to the people. It was very easy with the children, they're so nice. Whenever they'd see me, they'd shout: "André, come over here!" And take me into the forest, show me what paths to follow and introduce me to their families. The other day, some children dragged me down to the river and gave me a ride in a dugout. Since I had to take some pictures for my slide show, I found a Zaïrian who was ready to help me explain to the people why I wanted to photograph them. They think you're a Martian if you aim a camera at them!

J.H.: And now, for the momentous question: what struck you most about Zaïre?

André: When talking about the Dominican Republic, I'd said it was the *people*. Well, here, in Zaïre, it's still the *people*. But the people here particularly impress because they work so hard. And have absolutely nothing. The farmer owns a simple wooden hoe he built himself. He has two arms and two legs. Everyday he works really hard in the field. At the end of the day, he returns to his hut to rest. You show up and he immediately offers you something to eat. He's worked all day, he's poor as a church mouse, owns nothing, but still offers something. A piece of manioc, anything, even though it's sometimes way beyond his means. In that respect, we have a great deal to learn from these people!

J.H.: You'll soon get to talk about all this, somewhere in Canada ...

André: In Quebec and Ontario. Our presentations are ready. What I'd like to tell Canadians is that there are other people on this planet, other countries to discover, other problems to consider besides our own. Explain to them that we must all participate, open our eyes, broaden our horizons, think globally, accept that the world goes beyond Ottawa or Hull, that there are a thousand things to discover. And tell them that a lot of people are suffering. Pain which touches me deeply. For example, I can't help thinking about those little girls in Kalenda who cry because they have sore stomachs brought on by some amoeba. I'll never forget that. So I have to convey this feeling to Canadians.

J.H.: I'm sure you'll manage to. And afterwards?

André: I'd like to continue. Michael and I are talking about what we might do together. With Katimavik groups for instance.

J.H.: A very receptive audience which, however, is short of resources ...

André: Exactly. Michael and I would like to submit a plan to Katimavik, offer it our experience, devise an information tour aimed at Katimavik participants ...

J.H.: And what will you do with the rest of your life?

André: You once told me that goals must be set. I agree. But, at the same time, I have a compulsive nature. When an opportunity arises, I feel like jumping at it. If I were asked to return to Zaïre and work on some co-operation project, I'd go without hesitating. I don't know if this is how I'll choose a career ... but I'll certainly have to keep studying. You must have a solid education to have influence, to affect the system's evolution, in Canada or elsewhere, to be in a position of power. For example, you're a senator and have a strategic position; you can incite people to action.

J.H.: I hope you're right, dearest André.

André: A decent education is needed to accede to a position like yours. I'm not denying the educational value of travelling. In fact, I'd like to discover all the countries in the world. But also tell myself: "I should settle down and do something with my life." And so much the better if this should include another trip. I fully realize that this is much easier for me than for someone else: I'm always able to find a job, earn money and travel. No problem!

J.H.: But you can't do this indefinitely ...

André: Of course not. That's why I'm seriously thinking about continuing to study after I return home. In that sense, my father has helped me a great deal. I have very understanding parents. They shouldn't worry about me: I'll get along quite well. But I know I'll have to study to reach my full potential ...

J.H.: And, one day, you'll be a senator!

André: I doubt it!

J.H.: It's the last thing I'd wish for you!

André Charlebois's Comments on the Canadian Tour

The tour was an extremely intense, educational and revealing experience.

Intense, since we made up to six presentations a day before the most diverse groups, over a six-week period.

Educational, because the tour allowed me to learn a great deal about development, verbal expression, and the means of explaining how people can help find solutions.

Revealing, given that I realized how much Canadians lack information about issues related to the development of the Third World and their own country.

Therefore I believe it's crucial that we sensitize Canadians, so they understand the role they can play to improve the world.

André Charlebois Ten Years Later

Following Operation Zaïre, André continued to work with young people, demonstrating a special interest in teaching languages and intercultural communication. He's taught French to Canada World Youth's anglophone and allophone participants on numerous occasions.

He's travelled on his own to Brazil to teach the language of Ducharme. On returning to Quebec, he worked throughout the province as a facilitator for the Mouvement Québécois des Chantiers. *Afterwards, Canada World Youth offered him a position as group leader with the Malawi program. From one contract to the next, he worked in Indonesia, Brazil, Honduras and Mexico.*

He recently gained prominence in the arts by playing the lead role in a feature-length film shot in Montreal and several European countries. He now lives in Montreal.

6.
Sara Whitehead

From Ontario to Sri Lanka

Sara Whitehead with her teammates, André and Lusamba, the Zaïrian participant, during the Canadian tour.

Sara: My name's Sara Whitehead. I was born in New York City, and only ten months old when my family moved to Hong Kong. My parents worked with the United Church and did research on the People's Republic of China. I lived in Hong Kong until I was nine years old when, in 1976, we moved to Toronto, where I've lived since.

J.H.: You went to high school there?

Sara: I'd just finished grade thirteen at the University of Toronto Schools when I began Canada World Youth.

J.H.: Did you have any idea about what you wanted to do with your life?

Sara: Not really. I'd decided to go to university, but not right away. I only had vague notions about what I wanted to study.

J.H.: How old were you?

Sara: Seventeen.

J.H.: Seventeen! It's ridiculous that our society expects people to choose a career path at seventeen.

Sara: That's definitely too young ...

J.H.: But not too young to be interested in Canada World Youth!

Sara: Not at all. I think it was the perfect age, though most other participants were older. It came at the right time for me. I was ready to leave the confined high school environment.

J.H.: You might be happy to know that I've always struggled to convince Canada World Youth's board of directors that participants be aged from seventeen to twenty. Others have often claimed that participants should be at least eighteen. And that the age limit be twenty-one or twenty-two. I disagreed. You're living proof that I may have been right! So who gave you the good idea to join Canada World Youth?

Sara: A friend of mine, Janet MacIntosh, had done the program with Indonesia about a year before I finished high school. She kindled my interest by telling me about her experience. I applied, went through the whole process and ended up in Sri Lanka.

J.H.: Was Asia your first choice?

Sara: It was. Probably because I'd lived in Hong Kong. I'd had some contact with Asian culture and wanted to return to that corner of the world.

J.H.: But where did the program start?

Sara: In Ontario. A small town called Millbrook, just south of Peterborough. It was great. Since I'm from a large city, spending three months on a dairy farm was very disorienting. I was doing physical work for the first time in my life. I learned a lot about agriculture.

J.H.: Tell me about your host family.

Sara: A young, rather traditional family. Two children, six and eight-years old. The family had lived in the region for over a century, which was a discovery to me. They were very nice and we really got along. I think that living with families, both in Ontario and Sri Lanka, was the best part of the program. It's from families that I learned the most.

J.H.: Who was your counterpart?

Sara: Her name was Mallika. She belonged to the National Youth Service Council, Canada World Youth's counterpart in Sri Lanka. She came from a small town. Her parents were shopkeepers who worked in the market. Mallika had finished high school but, as is the case for many young Sri Lankans, couldn't find work.

J.H.: The same holds for young Canadians!

Sara: Exactly!

J.H.: Did Mallika adapt easily?

Sara: I didn't notice anything at first, since I didn't know what she was like normally. But the Sri Lankans had a pretty rough time initially. They had to adjust to a lot of things at once. I think Mallika changed quite a bit.

J.H.: Among other things, she had to get used to you ...

Sara: Yes. That must have been tough, right? But we really got along. We were very lucky, and among the few who managed to hit it off easily.

J.H.: So after three months you left Ontario for Sri Lanka. It was your turn to experience a culture shock, I presume?

Sara: To a certain extent, though it didn't hit me all at once, likely because I'd already travelled and lived away from home. But this wasn't the case for everybody. We lived in a small village of about three hundred people. Rather isolated. The nearest bus stop was two miles away. But the location was beautiful, a dream really!

J.H.: The whole island is wonderful. It would be paradise were it not for racial conflicts ... Were you affected by this in any way?

Sara: Not directly. Two Tamil participants and one group leader stayed in Canada as refugees. We lived in a small and fairly isolated Sri Lankan village, located in an area that was completely Singhalese. Were it not for the newspapers, we wouldn't even have known there was trouble in the country.

J.H.: So what did you do in that lovely little village?

Sara: We lived with a family. Our work project consisted of enlarging an irrigation tank, to help increase the rice harvests. Our group worked with young villagers, which helped us get to know them. At first, it was difficult to work in the blazing sun. It was very hot and there wasn't any shade. This was hard physical labour: digging with a *mammoty* and carrying dirt up a hill. It was rather monotonous, but we got used to it. Besides, we only spent three days a week on that project. We devoted some time to other community work: fixing the road, cleaning the area around the village temple, cleaning the school, that kind of thing.

J.H.: How did you get along with your host family?

Sara: Very well, though we were never really close, due to language and cultural barriers. I felt comfortable with the family, but we couldn't have lengthy conversations. The best moments I had were helping the mother prepare meals in the kitchen.

J.H.: Did you like the food?

Sara: It was wonderful. Sri Lankan food is fantastic. Pretty spicy, but you get used to it.

J.H.: Did you have contact with other families or people in the village?

Sara: Mostly with families billeting other participants. It was easy ...

J.H.: But, as you said, there was the language barrier ...

Sara: That's right. Our Sri Lankan counterparts weren't very fluent in English, and our Singhalese was pretty basic. It's difficult to learn such a language properly in only three months, especially since its structure is so different. Language was a barrier, but there are so many other ways to communicate. We managed.

J.H.: What's the most important thing you learned in Sri Lanka?

Sara: Even more important than anything I learned about Sri Lanka, was what I learned about myself and Canada. Sri Lanka helped me gain a new perspective on my own background. Though I'll never fully understand Sri Lanka, I managed to get a better handle on Canada and re-evaluate my own values.

J.H.: Give me some examples.

Sara: North Americans are very goal-oriented ... The lifestyle, our attitude towards work ... All those materialist "values." When you've had the opportunity to live modestly, and feel at ease with this, returning to Canada gives you quite a shock, when you see how people live there.

J.H.: Did you change your lifestyle as a result?

Sara: I think so. For instance, I became more or less vegetarian when I returned: I'd lost the taste for meat.

J.H.: You ate no meat in Sri Lanka?

Sara: Maybe twice. Very little.

J.H.: Were there other changes, besides your conversion to vegetarianism?

Sara: Yes, though nothing very dramatic. I'd already taken some steps in the right direction, even before the program, thanks to the influence of my parents and surroundings. But Canada World Youth allowed me to understand a lot of things, and provided concrete experience. For example, the interdependence of nations is something very real and no longer an abstract notion to me.

J.H.: I take it your interest in international development broadened considerably.

Sara: Yes. I was deeply concerned about the issue even before the program; but have now acquired a profound motivation and yearning to study it further.

J.H.: What did you do when you returned home?

Sara: I got involved with a few NGOs and volunteered with Bridgehead Trading, an alternative business. For example, they import coffee from Nicaragua and tea from Sri Lanka directly from growers, thereby avoiding multinationals. I also worked at Canada World Youth's Toronto office over the summer, helping with pre-orientation weekends for participants. Finally, I geared my personal readings towards understanding more about what was happening around the world.

J.H.: Did you have any plans to study?

Sara: I wanted to attend university and study political science, economics and at least two languages.

J.H.: Two languages?

Sara: I wanted to study Chinese and improve my French. I still have several ideas, like studying international development, or political science and economics. Perhaps delve into environmental studies. I wasn't sure yet ... Then I heard about the Zaïre project ... After hesitating somewhat, I joined in. Finding myself with all these former participants was fascinating. They had clear ideas, knew where they were heading and had a lot of resolve. The positive side of the program is that the group provides varied resources; we had a lot to learn from one another.

J.H.: What was your first impression of Zaïre?

Sara: The first thing that struck me were its similarities to Sri Lanka. A superficial first impression: the heat, palm trees—traits common to all tropical countries.

J.H.: Did you adapt more easily than in Sri Lanka?

Sara: It was a lot easier. First, in terms of language. People spoke perfect French and, though mine was far from the greatest, I could speak it a lot better than Singhalese. The cultural differences aren't as broad. Zaïrians are much more straightforward and open. It's much easier to start a relationship with them than with Sri Lankans. Experience in another country likely helped us.

J.H.: I suppose you'll have some criticisms about living in groups, here in Kalenda, rather than with families. All the other participants did!

Sara: Strangely enough, I believe group living was one of our most successful experiences. From an educational standpoint, however, I think it has many drawbacks. It makes integrating into the community more difficult. We lived in a small colonial house built by the Belgians and were really isolated from the village. On one side are the hospital and old Belgian neighbourhood, on the other, the village. As a result, it took a lot of time and effort for us to get to know the villagers.

J.H.: Still, they must've realized you were rebuilding the hospital for the benefit of the community.

Sara: We did our best. But there were numerous technical problems: materials arrived late, and let's admit it, our group lacked construction expertise. So there were numerous reasons for us to be frustrated! We had difficulty believing in our own effectiveness ... But managed to fix up the doctor's house.

J.H.: Perhaps some doctor will be attracted to that lovely house as a result of your efforts and rush to Kalenda ... where a doctor is sorely needed.

Sara: I sure hope so. That would be terrific. And I really hope the Mama Mobutu Foundation maintains its interest in this hospital.

J.H.: Tell me more about Kalenda.

Sara: There was at least one chore we shared with the villagers: fetching water. A one kilometre walk up a steep hill. We had fun learning how to carry water buckets on our heads. I still feel rather incompetent when I see five-year old girls carrying much bigger buckets on their heads than I can. This was rather amusing.

J.H.: They must've laughed at you somewhat?

Sara: Primarily at our attempts to speak Tshiluba, the local language. Educated folks speak French, but most of the women and children speak only Tshiluba. In the villages especially. We had numerous contacts with the various schools in Kalenda: the primary, secondary and nursing schools. It was a lot easier to relate to the teachers, since they spoke French and shared some of our interests. Numerous children became very fond of the participants. There were even some Zaïrians who worked with us at rebuilding the hospital: as many as twelve of them.

J.H.: What about the Zaïrian nuns?

Sara: They were our most important contacts. They ran the hospital and decided what needed to be done. As well, they introduced us to the villagers, set us up in our house, and generally helped us adjust. The Catholic church plays an important role in the village. Everyone goes to church on Sunday, which provides an opportunity to socialize.

J.H.: But not all participants are Catholic.

Sara: No, but this didn't prevent us from attending the sermon. The influence of religion is still very strong in this country, much stronger than in Canada. The nuns were a very strong presence in the church, both here and in neighbouring villages. It's interesting to observe the influence that traditional African religions have had on Christianity, especially at the level of the music and rhythms accompanying church services. It was rather different from what we were used to.

J.H.: I observed this at the midnight mass, which I attended with all of you, including participants from Mwene Ditu. The men were on one side of the church and the women on the other. Only the women sang ...

Sara: That's simply their tradition.

J.H.: I noticed you were part of the choir ...

Sara: I like to take part in what's happening, though I didn't manage to learn all their songs.

J.H.: The women sang for two whole hours ... while dancing!

Sara: It was rather unusual to see women dancing in the church. A custom we might take back to Canada! Although it is practiced in some churches ...

J.H.: Did you discover any fundamental values in Zaïre which we may have lost in Canada?

Sara: People are very close to one another within families, including extended ones. For example, if you have a cousin in another town, you'd think nothing of going to live with him for three years while you attend school. This kind of solidarity is very strong here. And respect for the elderly is very pronounced, another important value we could heed.

J.H.: Your Zaïrian counterparts will be shocked when they realize Canadians shuffle the elderly off to retirement homes.

Sara: They certainly will, and that's understandable. After all, that isn't a proper way to treat seniors.

J.H.: That's not how we did things in Canada barely a few decades ago. How can we explain our sudden change of attitude towards the elderly?

Sara: Our society has moved away from the extended family, favouring a more materialist and selfish lifestyle. A great deal of importance has been placed on production. We must ceaselessly produce; once you're no longer productive, you're put on the sidelines. It's become a trend in numerous areas of our society. Since we don't acknowledge that people may have talents other than a simple capacity to produce things, we place seniors in retirement homes.

J.H.: You'll talk about this and many other things during your presentations in Canada.

Sara: There are so many things to relate! You have to ask yourself: "What do I focus on?" "How do I condense the essential into an hour-and-a-half presentation?" I'd like to get people to question their own culture and values by discovering another culture. I'd like to sensitize them to what's happening around the world, to problems and their causes, to the reasons they persist and to why they're connected. I'd like people to ask: "How is my life related to someone in Zaïre?" It's not easy to ask yourself that type of question when you've never wandered beyond your community ...

J.H.: What do you think are the best means to touch hearts and prompt attitude changes?

Sara: I see our role as a mere starting point. We obviously won't manage to change anyone's life or attitude. This can only happen through a very long process. We may touch those who've already started thinking about world problems. We're only a tiny part of the process. I don't think I can change anyone radically ...

J.H.: Who knows?

Sara: Who knows? At least I'll give it a try.

J.H.: Will you head to university after the Canadian tour?

Sara: I'll definitely start university in September. Nothing's going to stop me this time.

J.H.: Not even Canada World Youth!

Sara: No. One thing the program really gave me is a desire to learn, to acquire academic knowledge. Experience is obviously essential, but I want to understand what others think by reading what they've written, something I haven't yet had time to do. I'll probably choose a university in Montreal or Ottawa, because I'd like to continue improving my French.

J.H.: What will you be doing in ten years?

Sara: I'll probably be in Canada. Though I'd like to continue travelling and work overseas, I believe the most important thing we can do as Canadians is stay in Canada and help change the attitude of our compatriots and the structures which affect the Third World. The most important work to be done is in Canada. So, in ten years, I'll probably be returning from a three or four year work experience overseas, probably in the area of education.

J.H.: So you think we can change the attitude of Canadians towards the Third World with a determined effort? And take on other industrialized countries after that ...

Sara: Absolutely. The economic structures that hinder the development of poor countries must be changed within industrialized nations. Everything must begin with a change in attitude by Canadians, Americans and Europeans.

J.H.: An enormous undertaking for you and the other participants!

Sara: It's somewhat like the Zaïre program: we must see our role as a small part of a huge process, and not expect immediate answers and instant results.

Sara Whitehead's Comments on the Canadian Tour

When thinking about our tour, the following images and impressions come to mind: flashes of the Canadian Shield from the windows of our van as we sped through central Canada at a frantic pace ... The faces of hundreds of children from small towns, smiling as Lusamba, the girl who was our Zaïrian counterpart, inititated them to the rhythms and pulsations of Zaïre ... Browsing through and

Afro-Canadian beauty shop with Lusamba ... The openness and warmhearted hospitality of our host families.

Sara Whitehead Ten Years later

On returning from Zaïre, Sara studied at McGill University and the University of Guelph, earning a bachelor's degree in international development. She then studied medicine at McMaster University and, given her interest in rural communities, completed a family medicine residency in northern Ontario.

International issues continue to interest her, and she's travelled a great deal. She practiced pediatrics and family medicine for five months in Thailand, and then earned a master's degree in public health from Johns Hopkins University.

Sara now lives in Sioux Lookout, Ontario, where, as programs medical officer, she provides public health services to twenty-eight Oji-Cree communities. She's married to Philip White[1]*, and they have a son named Elijah.*

1 We'll catch up to Philip White in Thailand, on page 260.

7. Fergus Horsburgh

From Alberta to Mali

Fergus and his Zaïrian counterpart, Mauwa Kikungwé, amid the harshness of a Quebec winter, during the Canadian tour.

Fergus: I was born in Montreal and raised in Chateauguay and Montreal West. I lived there until I was fifteen years old when, after my parents' divorce, my mother and I moved to Edmonton. I went to high school for a year, but dropped out before finishing.

J.H.: So, you're one of those!

Fergus: One of those ... I worked as a truck driver for six or seven months before getting a job with the University Games in Edmonton. At the time, I was just planning to work and save money. For a rainy day! At one point I heard about Canada World Youth from my sister, who'd been through Katimavik. The two organizations are closely related.

J.H.: Let's say they're sister organizations.

Fergus: That's right. I went through the Canada World Youth interview and was accepted. Though I was getting ready to leave, I worked as a truck driver in the day and a janitor at night. I did this until the training camp for Mali began, in Saint-Liguori, Quebec.

J.H.: Saint-Liguori! You were far from knowing you'd return three years later with the Zaïre program! Had you chosen Africa?

Fergus: I'd have preferred Bolivia, since I was fostering a child from that country. The selection process, however, decreed that I go to Africa. It wasn't so bad, since the continent has always appealed to me. Following the orientation camp in Saint-Liguori, my group moved to a small farm community called Saint-Roch-de-l'Achigan, where pigs are raised and tobacco is grown.

J.H: Since you'd lived in Montreal, I assume you were bilingual ...

Fergus: Not really. I managed to speak French with some difficulty. One thing Canada World Youth and Katimavik have given me is a good command of French. When I arrived in Saint-Roch, I managed to make myself understood. My Montreal friends had even taught me some *québécois* slang. However, I became fluent after a few months of immersion with my host family, the Lafortunes. They were a young couple, and I used to look after their twins. I thought it very interesting, since this was my first experience working with children. Though I spent some time tending the pigs, most of the work I did was in the tobacco field. I'd once spent a two-week summer holiday on a farm, but never realized all the work farmers have to do. It was unbelievable.

J.H.: You haven't yet told me anything about your Malian counterpart.

Fergus: Ah! Baïsso! He was from Bandiagura, in Dogon region. Actually, he was the only Malian from the Dogon region. There were some difficulties at first, in Canada. His attitude towards girls in the group was awkward. Like many Africans, he had a wrong impression about Canadian women, of white women generally. Impressions conveyed by Hollywood "B" grade movies, where women are often portrayed as loose. All that lovely violence and romantic nonsense: what a mix! So, perhaps Baïsso took this for reality and got rather fresh with some of the girls at the Saint-Liguori training camp. This gave him a bad reputation. As a result, even I had misgivings about him. We talked about it somewhat, but this created some distance between us. One night, during our trip to Ottawa, Quebec City and Montreal, we went for a long walk: I wanted to talk to him about this situation before we left for

Mali, and I began to see his point of view. "Well," he said to me, "I really thought your women were like that ..." He felt his attitude was normal. The Malians would wonder: "Why are you making such a fuss. That's how your women are. Look at them walking around in those jeans. What do you expect?" Appearances may have justified them somewhat.

J.H.: Did you get a culture shock on landing in Mali?

Fergus: I think so. But I never really understood the meaning of "culture shock" ...

J.H.: Nor I.

Fergus: I probably did have a shock, though I don't like that word. Let's just say I was hit by a barrage of varying information. For instance, just by travelling through Bamako, the capital: all the new sounds, strange voices, the smells ... Twelve of us were crowded into a *Land Rover* as we headed to our village. People stared at us in astonishment as we drove by; they were probably wondering what the devil we were coming to do here. "Where are they from? What do they want from us?" Back in Canada, TV force feeds us images of an Africa where people starve to death and crowd into camps where misery prevails. That's not the whole story. People do suffer somewhat. Malian's often say: "*On souffre ici*!" But they may be talking about when they had to give the village chief a goat because a few lizards died when their house burned down. They refer to this kind of oddity as suffering, a word to which they ascribe a very special meaning. But they don't complain about life's hardships; they accept them as inevitable. "That's life!"

J.H.: Where did you go after Bamako?

Fergus: We moved to Sirakorola, a village in the Kalengoulou region.

J.H.: Names that remind me of something: I believe I'd visited your group ...

Fergus: The most difficult part was living in an agricultural camp run by the military, and located one kilometre from Sirakorola. Even a single kilometre made socializing with locals more difficult. That was the first time I lived in a large group. A tough experience, but not all that bad. Arguments often occurred; numerous problems had to be settled. Unavoidable things. We nevertheless managed to work well as a group. For instance, we built a washroom for the small clinic in the village, and helped some of the camp people with the harvest. They were young farmers from far-off villages who spoke only Bambara, and to whom the military were teaching new farming methods. "Good use of military money I'd say!" We became good friends with these young farmers. One of them was called Djeeba. I can still picture him clear as day. He spoke neither English nor French, only Bambara. We really got along, working, playing soccer and wrestling with him. He'd often invite us to share a meal with his family. We were very good friends. At the end of our stay, when he realized we'd be leaving soon, he dropped by to visit the participants. He had a very serious and concentrated look. He suddenly uttered a few words in French—probably the first time in his life he'd spoken the language! He said, in very rough but understandable French: "*En va toujours amis*." It took him awhile to get all this out, amid a stream of Bambara I didn't understand. The incredible effort he made to convey his friendship really touched me. It was super. I'll never forget Djeeba ...

J.H.: What else did you bring back from Mali?

Fergus: Mali helped me get rid of numerous prejudices. I always considered myself rather open-minded, but came here thinking everyone lived in small huts where people were dying; that they were pretty ignorant and unaware of what was happening in the world, while we North Americans were able to study geography, history and politics especially, since the media bombards us with it daily. Malians don't appear to know about all these things. I wonder if they need to. They know who their president is and that's it. However, they attach a great deal of importance to the family—something we seem to have forgotten in Canada. Over there, the family counts for nearly everything. An entire family will live under the same roof: parents, grandparents, sons, their wives and children. Everyone works together in a communal field, which really impressed me. And they show the greatest respect to their elders. Whereas in Canada, as soon as you reach sixty-five or seventy, and become a little more frail, you're packed off to a senior's home! Those who can't afford it know the government will house their elderly parents, sometimes in places that look a lot like prisons.

J.H.: This never struck you in Canada?

Fergus: A little. But I felt this had always been the case and would continue to be so.

J.H.: It hasn't always been that way.

Fergus: Within my lifetime at least. I'd sometimes think: "Oh, this is terrible." But never went so far as to criticize, since I'd never known anything different. In Mali, I got to see the respect shown to the elderly, how much they're considered an asset to the community, "*un trésor*." Unlike the Aztecs, Egyptians and other peoples, who have a written history, Malians transmit theirs orally from one generation to the next. Elders pass on information, telling stories while seated around a fire. It's terrific!

J.H.: What about Mali's development problems?

Fergus: I saw so much red tape it made me sick! Everywhere red tape slowed things down. It may be unavoidable, but getting the least thing from point A to point B created an incredible waste of time, due to transportation problems. It's fine to talk about development aid, but before helping people, you at least ought to know their names! You should avoid showing up and saying: "Here we are! We're now going to change this and help you do that, etc." They may not even want your help ... It's not a question of helping them, but of working "with" and "for" them. I resented the idea that we were there to "help" these people ... It's a bad attitude ...

J.H.: As you know, Canada World Youth is not an aid program ... You were sent to Africa to learn and share.

Fergus: Which is good.

J.H.: Following the Mali program, did you decide to return to school, dearest dropout?

Fergus: Needless to say my parents were urging me to. My father had done pretty well for himself, he had some money and wanted to help me with university. I'd hoped Canada World Youth would help me finally decide, but it didn't work.

J.H.: So we failed with Fergus!

Fergus: Heavens no! Perhaps the program didn't urge me to resume studying immediately, which may seem negative, but it's probably because I came out of it with more questions than answers. Returning to Canada gave me an even greater shock than landing in Mali.

J.H.: Such as?

Fergus: The media! I was staggered to realize how important the media is in Canada, how we accept whatever it says as gospel, which is ridiculous. If you say: "I went to Africa," people often answer: "Oh, wow! that's really neat. Did you go on a safari?" It surprised me how misinformed many people are about Africa. Perhaps it's understandable: their only information about the continent comes from media soundbites and glossy National Geographic photos. In any event, I feel safe in saying that the majority of Canadians are ignorant about Africa.

J.H.: Your father must have tried again and said: "Fergus, you have to finish high school."

Fergus: But I didn't. I got another job and moved into my own apartment. I went to see my mother in Edmonton. And put some money aside! As my father said: "You should go to school; if not, then at least put some money in the bank." That's when I started thinking about Katimavik, especially because I wanted to continue brushing up on my French—which isn't easy in Edmonton!

J.H.: What did your father say following your nine-month stint with Katimavik?

Fergus: The usual! But he may have been starting to wonder about me: "Well, maybe university isn't for this kid. Not everybody's cut out for sitting in a classroom for years on end." He suggested I get a trade. So I apprenticed with a cabinetmaker for two years. I had my own apartment and was working to support myself: paying for groceries, rent, power. I think this helped me mature. One day, I thought that maybe I didn't want to be a cabinetmaker or carpenter for the rest of my life. I then took some night courses ...

J.H.: At last!

Fergus: To my amazement, I got a good mark, B+. And one day, I got a call from Canada World Youth. Daniel asked whether I was interested in the special program with Zaïre. I said yes, but wanted a day to think about it, and talk it over with my girlfriend, parents and friends. Three weeks later, I arrived at the Saint-Liguori camp.

J.H.: ... for the second time!

Fergus: The same old camp, same cook and everything.

J.H.: And by going to Zaïre, you were returning to Africa.

Fergus: Moreover, when I got there, I told myself: "Oh, I'm so glad to be back!" And I'd spend hours at night simply marvelling at things as simple as a palm tree. The simple joy of saluting people and shaking hands with everybody. In Canada, they call in the police if you shake a stranger's hand!

J.H.: I suppose that group living in Kalenda caused you some problems, as it did to other participants. But when all was said and done, your group seemed pretty tightly knit.

Fergus: We became friends, especially towards the end. Though I didn't get to know everyone, I became rather close to three or four participants, including Zaïrians of course. In our communal house, absolutely no difference is made between Canadians and Zaïrians.

J.H.: What about problems related to the huge work project?

Fergus: We arrived here planning to renovate two hospital pavilions, fix the roof on the maternity ward and central pavilion. We didn't get to do everything since too many people had their own priorities. At one point, we had three or four bosses! Our co-ordinator, Philippe, had his objectives and insisted we reach them. Sister Justine had her priorities and Pelé, the Zaïrian carpenter, had his. When I worked with him, I had to adjust to his methods. We finally managed to co-operate and get things done. We renovated the residence, but could've done a lot more had we been better organized, and only had one "boss." We at least got to socialize with the villagers, village chief, and Zaïrian sisters, who are very happy with our work. The same applies to Mama Mpinga, the woman in charge of the project and president of the Mama Mobutu Foundation.

J.H.: And the governor of the province came to congratulate you in person ...

Fergus: Along with the Canadian ambassador in Zaïre. They were both pleased. The reason I'm not perfectly satisfied may be that I realize how much more we could've done ...

J.H.: Maybe you're a perfectionist.

Fergus: To a degree. I like to do things as well as possible.

J.H.: Did you mingle with the villagers?

Fergus: It was somewhat difficult at first, since our house was rather remote: we hesitated to venture into the village. People didn't understand our language; we didn't understand theirs. One night, I heard some music coming from the village. I told myself: "Oh, what the hell, everyone here's asleep and I'm not even drowsy." So off I go! I grabbed a flashlight, and dragged along Abata, a Zaïrian participant I worked with. All kinds of music was being played in the village. People everywhere. They spotted me, immediately brought a chair, and offered me some *cinq cents*, a kind of corn-based alcohol. People were dancing, and I thought: "This looks like a lot of fun. Let's go!"

J.H.: What time was it?

Fergus: The middle of the night. We got there at about 11:00 or 12:00 p.m., and stayed over two hours. The moon was shining. At one point, some guy started dancing around me. I didn't know how to react. He was one foot away, still dancing. So I asked Abata, who was seated next to me, what I should do. I didn't want to offend anyone. He replied: "You should give him money and encourage him to keep dancing." I had some on me. You place money on the dancer's forehead. When I'd done so, everyone broke into laughter. I then told myself: "What the heck! Here I go!" With some help from the alcohol, I started dancing with this guy, amid everyone's roaring laughter. We danced for a few minutes; it was really enjoyable. I finally sat down again and asked: "Well, what's going on? What's this revelry about?" The answer: this rejoicing and laughter were to celebrate ... a funeral! That's the night I met Eelunga, who's become my best friend in the village. He's got his own place, where I'd go over some nights to play cards. I met a few of his friends. Since we're the same age, we talk about nearly everything. People here are really interested in finding out about Canada and talk openly about everything. One night, we started off talking about marriage ... and ended up discussing politics! And how they felt about Mobutu, the founding president of the MPR, the only political party in Zaïre. Sometimes we'd talk, or just play cards in silence. Other times, we'd do nothing; just while away the time. After this, I no longer hesitated going to the village and meeting people. I met the secretary of ITM, the *Institut technique médical*. I'd frequently visit him and talk with his children, who are about my age, i.e., eighteen to twenty-three. I befriended a carpenter. In short, I spent whole evenings in the village, answering people's questions about Canada. I really enjoyed this. You can't just show up to say hello and leave after five minutes. You have to sit down, take your time. You'll be offered corn or peanuts and spend at least an hour with your hosts.

J.H.: You obviously integrated into Kalenda very well.

Fergus: Mali had been more difficult. I'd made a few friends, but they weren't nearly as close as those in Zaïre. I may very well cry when we leave tomorrow ... That wouldn't surprise me at all. But then we'll return, and there'll be the grand Canadian tour. I'll make French presentations in Quebec and English ones in Ontario, in the Toronto and Peterborough area.

J.H.: Sometime in March, you'll again face living on your own.

Fergus: But my father will be happy to hear this one: I'm heading to university!

J.H.: Way to go, Fergus!

Fergus Horsburgh's Comments on the Canadian Tour

We've just spent six weeks travelling around Canada, telling people about the realities of Africa. It was an enjoyable and extraordinary experience for me; however, finding out just how ignorant Canadians are about Africa gave me quite a shock. I can't blame them. The media pounds them daily with images of starving Africans. It annoys me to see how they exploit a few sensational items to sell their damned newspapers, or make a few extra dollars with their beer commercials.

Moreover, we got a very warm reception throughout Canada, and people were genuinely interested in hearing what we had to say. This speaks well for young people throughout the country who, I believe, sincerely want to find out what's happening beyond their own borders.

I got a lot of pleasure and satisfaction in sharing my experience with them. To such an extent, that I've decided to study eduction at university, beginning in September. Unless Africa's beauty and charms inspire me to return ... But, this time, I'll resist as best I can.

Fergus Horsburgh Ten Years Later

Following the Zaïre project, Fergus worked as a cabinetmaker and then headed to Trent University. Before getting his degree, however, he took a year off to travel through China, the

Philippines, Thailand and India. During that time, his parents got back together and remarried.

After graduating from university, he moved to Calgary where he worked with street people. He also worked at a young offenders centre before heading to the University of British Columbia, where he completed a teaching degree.

Fergus is now married and the father of an infant son. He runs a class for children with behavioural problems in Surrey, British Columbia.

8.
Annik Lafortune

From Quebec to Costa Rica

Annik and her Zaïrian counterpart.

Annik: I was born amid the wind, cold and sand of Chibougamou. My father worked for mining companies and I spent the first three years of my life there. Afterwards, my family settled in Montreal, then Saint-Lambert, where I've lived for fifteen years. That's where I went to high school. I especially remember an English teacher who often talked of the volunteer work she'd done in Black Africa. This first contact with an international worker awakened me to the possibility of cultural and professional experience abroad.

Following high school, I turned to visual arts, a discipline which allowed me to express myself, think about life and communicate with people around me. Following two years of CEGEP, I wanted to learn new things, see what was happening in other countries and discover other cultures. I love to discover countries through traditional art, music and languages. I felt that cultural contact with young people my age was essential. Besides, I envied my brother Éric, who'd been a Canada World Youth participant in Bolivia[1].

J.H.: In fact, that's where I met Éric.

Annik: Exactly, during an evening party in the Andes ... When he returned we both talked a lot about Bolivia and the extraordinary experience he'd had. That's when I decided to send an application to Canada World Youth. I finally managed to be accepted into the Costa Rican program. The first part of the exchange allowed me to discover the Outaouais, a beautiful region of Quebec. My Costa Rican counterpart, Oscar, and I worked for three months at an agricultural co-operative in Buckingham, where we touched on all aspects of farm work. I taught my counterpart how to count in French when we had to make an inventory of nuts and bolts.

J.H.: While you learned to count in Spanish!

Annik: Precisely. Numbers first, followed by days of the week and then basic vocabulary.

J.H.: So you knew a little Spanish when your reached Costa Rica. What were your first impressions of that wonderful little country?

Annik: At first, I was astounded to see the preponderance of North American influence. For example, young people in San José listened to the same music and wore the same jeans we did, and major fast-food chains were located in the capital. I'd imagined that all Latin America was profoundly rooted in local traditions. I quickly realized that Costa Rica was an exception; it had maintained the traditions of European colonizers instead of native ones.

J.H.: A strange kind of Third World! What about the villages and your host family?

Annik: Living in villages was very different from the capital. There are no restaurants, no hot water, and power only a few hours a day. My family gave me as warm a welcome as it would've given one of its children. As a girl, I easily integrated ... into cooking, washing and keeping house. It was out of the question I do work in

---

1 We'll meet up with Éric Lafortune in Bolivia, on page 217.

the field; this was the exclusive domain of men. It took three weeks of negotiations and heated arguments to convince my "adoptive father" I was perfectly able to put on boots and do farm work.

J.H.: Were his apprehensions based on your capacity to do physical work?

Annik: Absolutely not! My greatest cultural shock was discovering the extent to which the roles of men and women were predetermined. Men work in the fields and women at home. Questioning this division of labour was inconceivable to them.

J.H.: What kind of values did you discover?

Annik: Every day I was confronted by a pervasive religion, strict morality and a predominance of the family. A lifestyle no doubt similar to the one my parents experienced forty years ago. I was also delighted by the great hospitality and warmth of Costa Ricans. Every day we'd take the time to salute people we met and visit friends or neighbours. In short, we took the time to live!

J.H.: Although Costa Rica isn't the most tragically impoverished country in the world, did you discover a few Third World realities?

Annik: It really is a Third World country, although there aren't the enormous social discrepancies found elsewhere. It boasts a vigorous middle class, a well-developed co-operative system and numerous national companies. However, large multinationals control most plantations. They employ underpaid workers, many of whom are black or Nicaraguan refugees. Salaries and working conditions keep them at a rather pathetic standard of living.

J.H.: And when you returned from Costa Rica?

Annik: I continued studying art education at Concordia University, while getting involved in a YMCA international co-operation program, with Bangladesh more specifically. I was still hoping for another co-operation experience abroad. Following two years at university, I managed to get into another Canada World Youth program, in Zaïre this time. It included a three-month stay in Africa, preparing audio-visual material and doing presentations concerning African development in schools throughout Canada.

J.H.: And, one day, you landed in Zaïre ...

Annik: It was a hot and humid night actually. We'd just crossed Europe and Africa in less than twenty-four hours before reaching Kinshasa. It was 2:00 a.m., but the atmosphere was rather animated! Awaiting us were the national television network, our Zaïrian counterparts and representatives from the Mama Mobutu foundation. They were as tired and agitated as we were. All these wonderful people escorted us to the centre where the orientation camp and our immersion into African life would take place. The integration went smoothly since everyone spoke French.

J.H.: The great departure for Western Kasaï took place a few days following your arrival in Kinshasa. For the tiny village of Kalenda, more specifically, where we are now.

Annik: A party atmosphere surrounded us as we arrived; the whole village was dancing and singing to greet us. We live in the remains of a large hospital the Belgians built in the fifties, during the colonial period. The hospital has hardly been maintained since their departure, for lack of means. As well, the civil war that raged from 1960 to 1965 seriously damaged the building.

J.H.: So your job was to make this jungle hospital more functional.

Annik: In fact, we were to repair it as best we could with materials provided by the Canadian embassy. That's when the realities of an underdeveloped country struck me the most. Our task was complicated by faulty transportation systems, lost merchandise and scarce tools. We had to manage with the means at hand. The more repairs progressed, the more we discovered the building's appalling condition. We even had to replace the beams supporting the roof. Quite an adventure! We'd been told at the outset that all we had to do was repaint the inside walls.

J.H.: Were your problems limited to material resources?

Annik: Of course not! We had to set aside our North-American ideas about construction and take into account extreme climatic conditions (torrential rains and scorching heat), relatively unskilled labour and a lack of materials. Despite it all, the Zaïrians remained jovial and taught us to laugh at situations that were sometimes discouraging. Besides, this is the reason I've kept such unforgettable memories of our project.

J.H.: What about contact with villagers?

Annik: Smiling was the best means of communication, since the people spoke the local language more than French. Even if Tshiluba is the province's official language, people in my village speak three other dialects. But there were a hundred or so students at the medical school that spoke French rather well. It was the language of instruction.

J.H.: What stands out in your mind, now that your stay in Zaïre is drawing to a close?

Annik: First and foremost, the simplicity of the people who make do with little. Walking barefoot, wearing the same clothes every day, carrying a seat to school—these are just some of the things that are part of their daily lives. I had to get used to the idea that this was as typical of Africa as taking the bus is in North America.

Furthermore, Zaïrian reality differs greatly from that portrayed by the international media. Our views are limited to reports concerning droughts, famines and wars. Once here, we're surprised to see skyscrapers, supermarkets or even traffic lights. The land is cultivated, the subsoil is rich in minerals—diamonds especially—and numerous rivers criss-cross the country. This helped me understand that a developing country is not necessarily lacking in natural resources, but rather devoid of structures allowing a fair distribution of wealth.

J.H.: On your return, a grand Canadian tour will give you an opportunity to convey your ideas about international development. How do you feel about it?

Annik: I'm very excited. I came to Zaïre to learn and I'm returning to share my experience in Canada. I'm particularly eager to tell Canadians about reality in Zaïre. Initially, I'm sure they'll have the same prejudices I had about Africa.

J.H.: Perhaps you'll be able to sensitize Canadians to the responsibility we all share in the development process.

Annik: And make them realize that countries around the world are interdependent. Besides, Africans have a great deal to teach us about human relations. But we have to take the time to get to know them.

Annik Lafortune's Comments on the Canadian Tour

With slide shows and scripts in hand, we began the Canadian tour with a lot of nervousness. A ten-day stopover in Montreal seemed like very little time for preparing to explain the gist of our experience and relate our adventure. During the six-week tour, our task consisted of combing the territory between Vancouver and Winnipeg. Our goal was to weed out prejudices concerning Africa that are mainly propagated by the media. The success of our presentations rested mainly on anecdotes concerning African life that were still fresh in our minds.

There were nine of us altogether: six Canadians and three Zaïrians spread into rural communities, suburbs and major cities. Abata, Todd and I made a fabulous team, filled with humour and creativity. Our Zaïrian counterpart quickly became the favourite wherever we went. We visited schools, colleges, universities, community centres, international assistance organizations and even media outlets.

Finally, the six-week tour convinced me that education is the best way to change the perception we have of others and thereby stimulate understanding and co-operation between nations.

Annik Lafortune Ten Years Later

Following the Canadian tour, Annik studied at Concordia University and became a visual-arts teacher. Since then, she's worked as a facilitator at Montreal's Museum of Fine Arts, and as a teacher in numerous elementary and secondary schools in the Montreal area.

She's travelled abroad a few times and still hopes to work in the area of cultural co-operation. Culture, popular traditions and languages still fascinate her.

Anyone who's been a visible minority in a country and experienced the absence of cultural references, can appreciate the ability she's developed in understanding the integration challenges facing ethnic minorities, in Montreal schools as well as in our society generally.

9.
Benoît Beauchemin

From Quebec to Jamaica

Benoît Beauchemin in the Rockies in 1990.

Benoît: I'm from Laval, Quebec, and was the youngest member of our group. I turned nineteen right here, in Zaïre. When I finished high school, I dreamed of taking a year off to travel a little before locking myself away in a CEGEP. To smooth the transition between the two levels somewhat.

J.H.: I know what you mean! It's awful to think that many young people are confined to classrooms from kindergarten to the end of university, without having any contact with the real world. A ridiculous system! Did you have any idea about what you wanted to do with your life?

Benoît: I was hesitating between sociology and international development.

J.H.: Even before knowing what international development was ...

Benoît: Exactly. It was a hunch. But since I wasn't altogether sure, I wanted a year to think about it. I was also interested in Katimavik. But shortly after the Canada World Youth interview, I was informed I'd be leaving for Jamaica.

J.H.: Is that where you wanted to go?

Benoît: Actually, my first choice was Africa ...

J.H.: ... which is where you are now!

Benoît: ... but I felt any Third World country would be interesting. The point was to discover another culture and be confronted with different ideas.

J.H.: The Canadian part of the program took place before you headed to Jamaica ...

Benoît: My group ended up in a quiet rural community called Woodstock, one-hundred kilometres west of Fredericton, New-Brunswick.

J.H.: Did you speak English?

Benoît: I managed a little. Now, near the end of the Zaïre program, I feel I'm relatively bilingual.

J.H.: Tell me about Woodstock.

Benoît: A farming community of about eight-thousand people. My counterpart and I lived and worked on a farm operated by an elderly couple, the Robinsons. There was an orchard with three-hundred apple trees, one-hundred acres of corn, and vegetables to supply the small family store.

J.H.: What was your family like?

Benoît: Simple folks, very gentle and very amiable. They introduced us to the region. Their son had already left home, but often came to help us on the farm.

J.H.: Was this your first experience in an anglophone environment?

Benoît: I'd travelled a little to Ontario, but this was my first in-depth contact with an English-speaking family. Much to my surprise, I experienced a culture shock when I arrived. I was astonished that this could happen while living with a Canadian family, in my own country. I realized, for the first time perhaps, that there are cultural differences between anglophones and francophones, in terms of values and outlooks. Differences that are often minor, all things considered.

J.H.: Tell me about your counterpart.

Benoît: Rohan Murray was from Montego Bay, a beautiful tourist town in Jamaica. He was from a large rural family: eight brothers and two sisters. He had worked in a store. We had a few communication problems at first, due to our cultural differences and my inadequate English. It took at least two months for us to communicate properly. From then on, everything was alright. I remember him as sensitive and intelligent.

J.H.: How was this young black person welcomed by the family?

Benoît: Very well. As expected, he became the centre of attention because he was a foreigner. Naturally, he went through a culture shock, but our family did its best to help him get over it. He really had no problem.

J.H.: Since this was a farming project, you both had to work on the farm ...

Benoît: We learned how to drive a tractor, a new experience for both of us. We also learned to spray insecticides, plant trees, work in greenhouses. I really enjoyed this first farming experience, to the point that when I returned to Canada, after Jamaica, I found a job in a Laval nursery. So I went on planting trees and taking care of plants. Experience which helped me get a job afterwards.

J.H.: That's not Canada World Youth's main objective, but it often happens. Did you basically like New Brunswick?

Benoît: Oh yes! I'll go back when I return to Canada. I want to see my host family, the Robinsons, again.

J.H.: Did you keep in touch with them?

Benoît: Absolutely. I'm even thinking of going back to their farm next summer. Without a salary; just for the pleasure of working there. After New Brunswick, we headed to Jamaica ... where another host-family, an elderly couple, awaited us. The father was retired and the couple seemed rather well off.

J.H.: And your work project?

Benoît: We were to build a community garden for the YWCA. The students who lived there did their own cooking. We helped them save lots of money by getting them to grow their own vegetables. As well, we taught them the basics of market gardening and introduced them to co-operation.

J.H.: Would you say you properly integrated into your Jamaican community?

Benoît: Very much so. Our family introduced us to their friends and we visited the families of other participants. I also made a lot of friends, mainly because our project allowed us to work in the garden with the twenty-five girls. Thanks to the rotation system, we got to know all the students living at the YWCA.

J.H.: Leaving these friends and returning to Canada must surely have been difficult ...

Benoît: It was. On my return, I spent three or four days with my host family in New Brunswick. I told them about Jamaica and showed them slides. We organized a small Jamaican party with the other Woodstock host families and their friends. It was strange, rather sad even, since our Jamaican counterparts were absent. There was snow, it was cold. A strange mood. In any event, we managed to organize a wonderful Jamaican party, right there, in the back country of New Brunswick, with the temperature at −15°C!

J.H.: You returned to Laval, and CEGEP lurked around the corner ... How old were you?

Benoît: I was eighteen. I joined Canada World Youth at seventeen and, once again, was the youngest participant in the group. This was February and CEGEP began in September. I had no money and decided to get a job in a nursery, thereby using the knowledge I'd acquired in New Brunswick. I managed to earn enough to enter CEGEP in the fall, where I'd been accepted in social sciences. Everything was fine. I was returning to school. That's when I was offered the Zaïre program ... I didn't hesitate very long, since I knew at the time I'd one day study international development, a decision I'd taken as a result of the Jamaican experience. The Zaïre program would allow me to acquire more knowledge in that area and discover another culture, another Third World country. Postponing studies for another year was the least of my concerns. I knew school would always be there, but another opportunity to get practical experience in Zaïre might never arise. So I began reading up on Zaïre, preparing my baggage while working part-time at the Canada World Youth office in Montreal.

J.H.: When you landed here, in Kalenda, you were plunged into group living, which was a new experience for you.

Benoît: It's very demanding. Simply having to face the same fifteen people every day when you get up! Quiet moments are rare, as is personal time to think, write and read. Cooking, doing dishes, cleaning ... But I learned a lot. With time, group spirit and solidarity emerged. We spend every day and do everything together. I'm sure we wouldn't have known one another as well had each participant lived with a host family. Bonds between the members of this group seem much stronger than those I had with the Jamaican program participants. Naturally, conflicts arose and there was some friction; however, we'd immediately call meetings to solve problems. On the other hand, we missed something by not living with Zaïrian families.

J.H.: Your group seems to have fully integrated into Kalenda ...

Benoît: We have. For the past month and a half we've felt totally at home.

J.H.: And what about your enormous work project?

Benoît: It consisted of rebuilding, as best we could, a huge half-destroyed hospital, already overrun with vegetation. An especially arduous task since participants had hardly any construction or carpentry experience, save Fergus. He sort of became our leader.

J.H.: You're all experts now!

Benoît: We learned a lot about construction. It was a good experience. But we had our share of surprises. For example, the tools and construction materials we needed took three weeks to reach us from Kinshasa. I also remember that, one day, between 150 to 200 people suffering from the sleeping disease arrived at the hospital, which was in absolutely no condition to receive them. All the roofs leaked. So we had to fix them quickly to prevent the rain from falling on these poor patients. Problem was we couldn't work later than 12:30 p.m., due to the intolerable heat.

J.H.: All these people suffered from the sleeping disease?

Benoît: It's widespread in this region. It's caused by the bite of a tsetse fly and attacks the spinal cord, ultimately breaking down the nervous system. Patients experience general weakness and trembling; if nothing is done, death follows.

J.H.: Can it be cured?

Benoît: There is a rather effective treatment, but it must be administered at the beginning of the illness. After a certain stage, nothing can be done: death occurs in less than two months.

J.H.: Who treats your 150 to 200 patients?

Benoît: Belgian doctors who travel from one village to the next, visiting health clinics and administering treatments. Once in awhile they come to Kalenda.

J.H.: Do you have any contact with patients?

Benoît: That's not easy. We worked on the roof, desperately trying to shelter patients from the rain. We were in the midst of the rainy season and it would always pour at the end of the day. We had to move quickly. And patients remained inside, tired, exhausted or asleep. In short, contacts were difficult. We saw a lot more of their families.

J.H.: Though your hospital had no doctors and lay half in ruins, it did have Zaïrian nuns ...

Benoît: That's right and the hospital is their whole life. They run the maternity wing, which functions rather well. We also fixed its roof. It handles about thirty births a month.

J.H.: You seem to get along famously with the Zaïrian nuns ...

Benoît: Oh yes! They helped us a lot when we arrived in Kalenda, giving us furniture and all the material we needed. Their advice also helped facilitate our work and our integration into the community. They're very charming and have a wonderful sense of humour. We have a great time with them.

J.H.: I met Sister Justine, the superior. Some participants told me she's a saint.

Benoît: I'm sure! She's devoted many years to the hospital. She believes that if it isn't entirely renovated, it will at least be functional. Which would greatly benefit people in the region.

J.H.: She's a nurse, she delivers babies...

Benoît: I've even heard she performs some operations, given that she has a knack for surgery. Circumstances force her to dabble in everything, under extremely difficult conditions, with minimal equipment. Sister Justine, like all the nuns, plays a very active role in the Kalenda community. There's no doctor in the hospital, which is a tragedy. With all the patients already there, and others who'll come once the hospital is renovated, at least one doctor is absolutely needed. We found a house that might be suitable for a doctor, but the roof leaked, the ceilings had collapsed and the walls were damaged. So we decided to fix it up and make it liveable ...

J.H.: As bait for a prospective doctor, in short ... I visited the house: it's clean, enormous, almost resplendent. If I were a doctor, I'd feel like living there.

Benoît: At least we'll leave with this hope, this joy: maybe the house will attract a doctor to Kalenda, which would prompt Zaïrian authorities to make the hospital truly functional.

J.H.: You had another task besides construction: preparing presentations for the great Canadian tour that awaits you on your return ...

Benoît: We divided the group into four teams, two of which are responsible for preparing a typical presentation, in anticipation of the prospective discussions we'll have with the various audiences we'll meet. The two other teams are producing a slide show depicting life in Kalenda, which is considered a typical Zaïrian village. We discuss culture, family life, problems related to water. Another slide show will talk more generally about Zaïre and its development problems, about Africa and the views Canadians have of it, which are often distorted by the information we get. The Mwene Ditu group proceeded in the same fashion. So when we get back to Canada, we'll have to translate the narrations of our four slide shows into French and English and then record the soundtracks. We'll have a week and a half to do all this!

J.H.: Your first audiences will be Katimavik groups located throughout Canada.

Benoît: We're really eager to meet them. Though we don't get bored here in Zaïre, we look forward to embarking on the great tour, to do something different and meet people.

J.H.: What region of the country will you cover?

Benoît: We'll spend one week in Quebec and five weeks in Ontario.

J.H.: Will your Ontario presentations be mostly in English?

Benoît: Most of them. I'm happy about this because it will help me improve my English. Oh! preparing these presentations wasn't easy with all the work we had to do at the hospital. We worked on construction in the morning, when it wasn't so hot. After lunch, we'd take a short nap because we were really tired. And, in the afternoon, we'd throw ourselves into the presentations. Naturally, cooking and cleaning came on top of all this ...

J.H.: You did your own cooking?

Benoît: We hired an old woman, but she couldn't manage on her own: cooking for fifteen people is a lot of work. Especially in Africa, where everything is always complicated and takes time: we have no electricity, no running water ... we have nothing. And no microwave oven!

J.H.: What do you eat?

Benoît: Mostly *fufu*, the basic staple. It's a heavy dough made of corn flour and manioc. Very good for the stomach. *Fufu* is eaten with vegetables, fruits or rice. We'd have goat meat once in awhile.

J.H.: Did you buy a live goat?

Benoît: Yes and we'd have someone from the village slaughter it. Once every three weeks. Every day, two participants would help the cook prepare meals, scrub pots and do the cleaning.

J.H.: You'll be in Kinshasa in a few days ...

Benoît: ... and shortly thereafter in Saint-Liguori, Quebec, to put the final touch on our presentations. Then we'll head out in small teams of one Zaïrian and two Canadians.

J.H.: I've been told your groups can count on seven-hundred solid bookings. You won't run out of work! What do you plan to do after this?

Benoît: I haven't decided, but would like to visit my Jamaican family, to see if things have changed over there. I'll certainly get a job. As well, I'd like to make more presentations in Laval and Montreal.

J.H.: In addition to all those you'll have already made?

Benoît: That's right. And then, in September, I'll start studying social sciences.

J.H.: This time for sure!

Benoît: I've postponed school twice because of Canada World Youth ...

J.H.: And after social sciences?

Benoît: I'm nearly convinced I'll be going into international development.

J.H.: So, you don't have too many regrets about your experience with Canada World Youth?

Benoît: Absolutely not! Despite some frustrations and a few minor problems, how can I regret an experience with Canada World Youth! I haven't lost two years of school. On the contrary, I learned a lot, especially about myself and problems of the Third World. I think I've gained a greater openness of mind, which isn't the case for all my friends who stayed in Laval to study. Thanks to Canada World Youth, I got to understand my potential. I'm now aware I can do things that seemed impossible only yesterday. For example, I know I can travel anywhere in the world without a hitch. I've acquired a lot of self confidence, probably because Canada World Youth helped me overcome obstacles I'd have normally considered insurmountable.

Benoît Beauchemin's Comments on the Canadian Tour

Our stay in Zaire was unforgettable, and the Canadian tour that followed was certainly, for all of us Canada World Youth participants, a unique opportunity to relate what we'd been through in Africa and our new impressions about that part of the world. I hope we managed, in our own way and given the means at our disposal, to dispel stereotypes about Africa that often prevail in our society. Above all, I hope we succeeded in opening the minds of younger audiences, for whom I personally felt a special responsibility.

For me, the tour was a theatre of memorable encounters. Not only with Katimavik organizers and participants, with whom we lived in municipalities along our itinerary, but also with various groups that we shared our adventures and impressions with, while answering a flurry of questions. Of course, I remember that our hosts always gave us a warm welcome and that audiences were extremely diverse. A quality that compelled us to be extremely adaptable.

I remember one thing in particular: one day, we were to make a first presentation before a kindergarten class. The average age of our audience was five or six years. We'd brought back African masks from Zaïre, and this was likely the first time these children had touched any of this type. They observed and listened with fascination to Nkoyi Mabiku, the Zaïrian girl who was our counterpart. We took out a world map and showed them where Canada and Africa were located. Early in the afternoon, we met with a group of seniors in a home. They marvelled at our African adventures, while we were fascinated to hear their anecdotes from another era. In the evening, our last presentation took place before a group of international development students at the University of Scarborough.

I recall we were nervous at the prospect of discussing international development with these "experts."

After going through two Canada World Youth programs, I realized that huge misunderstandings and disparities exist between northern and southern countries. I understood we all have a responsibility to act and show solidarity.

Benoît Beauchemin Ten Years After

At the time of the Zaïre program, Benoit was eighteen years old and the group's youngest participant. With hindsight, he says his experience with Canada World Youth definitely had a major impact on his professional orientation and personal outlook. Following the program, he studied for six years, completing a college degree in social sciences (1988), a bachelor's degree in political science from McGill University (1991) and, finally, a graduate degree in international development from the University of Ottawa's Institute of International Development and Co-operation.

Over the past few years, his travels have taken him to a few troubled regions, namely the Republic of Haiti and the Middle East.

Benoit is now twenty-nine years old and the main associate with an international-development consulting firm in Montreal.

II. The Mwene Ditu Group

Let your foot venture down untrodden paths.
Let your mind wander into uncharted thoughts.

Lanzo del Vasto

1.
Yvonne Sabraw

From Alberta to Pakistan

Yvonne and Mangando at work int the Mwene Ditu hospital.

Yvonne: I was born in Saskatoon and lived there five years. I spent the rest of my life in Calgary. Before joining Canada World Youth, the most important thing to me was being involved in competitive gymnastics with a club in Calgary. This took most of my time, and was *the* most important thing in my life. My family came afterwards ... School was a distant third. Even in high school, I was still seriously involved in gymnastics, but started to ponder my future a little more. I thought I might like to become a doctor, perhaps to work in a developing country, or something of that nature. So I quit gymnastics and totally dedicated myself to studying; I wanted high marks to get into medical school. I then read something about Canada World Youth in a community newspaper, an article probably written by a former participant. After reading it, I thought to myself: "Oh! I'd love to participate in that program!" I submitted an application, but was turned down because I wasn't yet seventeen. I was crushed! I was sent another application form the following year. I filled it out and sent it, without getting my hopes up too much. I was absolutely thrilled when I learned I'd been accepted. Finally, something new to put my energy into!

J.H.: And your program was to start somewhere out West?

Yvonne: In Saskatchewan. This was Canada World Youth's first program with Pakistan. It wasn't my first choice. But I was so happy to be in Canada World Youth, that I'd have accepted to go anywhere. In fact, my first choice was Africa, which would've allowed me to be in Quebec for the first half of the program. I was a little worried because this was the first exchange with Pakistan, and I'd heard all kinds of stories about initial experiences. During a first year, no one really knows what's going to happen, everything will be poorly organized, etc. For example, if you go to Indonesia, which has been an exchange country for years, everything runs smoothly and you're certain the program will be well organized.

J.H.: There's some truth in that.

Yvonne: But, at the same time, I did learn a great deal, precisely because I belonged to a group that was to break the ice with Pakistan. We had fewer restrictions and didn't have to listen to comments such as, "last year, participants did this or that, or last year, host families were like this or that." Everything was open. And we took advantage of the situation.

J.H.: What about Saskatchewan?

Yvonne: I was already familiar with Saskatchewan. When I learned I'd be in Rosetown, Saskatchewan, I told myself: "Well, I'll sort of be home for three months."

J.H.: A small town?

Yvonne: Four thousand residents, I believe. We lived with a great host family: the mother and father were really wonderful. They had three young children, and I had the impression of being with my own family. It was a perfect situation for my counterpart, who wanted to live with a family. She missed hers terribly, and we were really lucky to find a family where love was very much in evidence. At first, I feared we might have religious problems, since the parents were Christian fundamentalists and my Pakistani counterpart obviously Muslim. We did, in fact, have some interesting discussions on religion. Our host family was excited about having someone from another culture and they gave their all to the program. For example, our parents would bake a cake whenever a participant's birthday occurred. Even when we started living in groups, near the end, my counterpart and I would go back to visit them ... and eat their cookies! Whenever group living depressed us a little, we'd go back to see "mom" and "dad," who quickly cheered us up.

J.H.: How did you get along with your counterpart?

Yvonne: We had ups and downs! Sometimes we compared our situation to a pre-arranged marriage, something my counterpart, Fatimah, fully understood since that's how people get married in Pakistan. When parents decide you'll marry a certain boy, there's nothing you can do: you have to get used to the idea. I often told myself that had Fatimah and I been in the same school, we'd never even have thought of being friends. We're so different! Differences of personality more than culture.

J.H.: But ...

Yvonne: But this taught us a great deal and we finally did a lot of growing together. It wasn't a matter of saying: "Oh! you're my best friend in the world and I really want to be with you all the time!" In any event, we *had* to be together and *had* to communicate and overcome the cultural barriers between Canada and Pakistan. Although we hadn't chosen each other, we were stuck: whether we liked it or not, we were to live side-by-side for six months. And we needed each other to survive. We'd gotten closer by the end of the program and were able to better appreciate what we'd learned. I believe many of our problems were caused by a lack of maturity. We'd argue over nothing: "You did something I didn't like, and I'm going to ignore you for the rest of the day." But this helped us mature: together we managed to get rid of our childishness. Although we never really became the closest of friends, we respected each other because we'd helped each other grow.

J.H.: What kind of work did you do *together* in Rosetown?

Yvonne: There were several work projects. Mondays, we'd volunteer with a senior citizens' home. Tuesdays and Wednesdays, we worked in a community sports shop, and Thursdays at a hospital clinic or a farm. I especially liked working with seniors; this was a new experience for me. I suddenly understood that these elderly people were human beings. I no longer said to myself: "Well, they're old people, and we have to be nice to them." I thought of them as friends whom I looked forward to seeing! And all of them were more than three times my age! I also learned a lot from my counterpart's reactions; to her, seniors are an integral part of family life. She was crushed when she saw them confined to an institution. After the first day, she went home and cried and didn't want to go back: "How can you get rid of your seniors in such a way? How can you be so heartless?" She missed her family; all she could think of was her grandmother in Pakistan. Over there, she'd visit her every day after school, and there'd always be someone to take care of her. I had to explain as best I could that some of our seniors like to live in this kind of institution, since they feel more independent. We mustn't imagine their situation is worse than it is. Perhaps they don't want to burden their relatives. In short, I attempted to provide my counterpart with a Canadian perspective. But I greatly respected her point of view since she was right: most of those seniors don't like being confined to an institution. They'd bide their time waiting for their children to visit ... Children who'd show up to chat for barely an hour before leaving again, which greatly saddened their elderly parents. That's why they fell in love with Fatimah, who sorely missed her grandparents back in Pakistan. She quite simply adopted fifteen grandfathers and fifteen grandmothers in Canada. It was wonderful. I also made some friends in that home, but Fatimah took them all to heart.

J.H.: You headed to Pakistan following a three-month stay in Saskatchewan. How did you feel when you got there?

Yvonne: I had a strong culture shock. Folks at Canada World Youth had prepared us as best they could, but ... But that culture differs greatly from ours. We certainly didn't feel as free as in Canada, since the state exists solely because of religion. Without it, there'd be no Pakistan.

J.H.: And India would be a little bigger ...

Yvonne.: Everything is determined by Islam: customs, traditions, even the laws. People dress and behave as they do because of religion. We'd prepared ourselves mentally for all this; however, it's an entirely different story when reality hits you in the face. What struck us first was the segregation between men and women. Right from the orientation camp, boys were billeted in Islamabad, the capital, while girls were lodged in a Girl Guide house, outside the city. We were no longer a Canada World Youth group, but rather a feminine Canada World Youth group and another masculine group.

J.H.: That's still how it is.

Yvonne: Things would have been easier had we remained together, but we really wouldn't have integrated into the Pakistani culture. We'd have been a tiny Canadian bubble in the midst of Pakistan. We'd just spent three-and-a-half months together in Canada, and were a group of good friends, both boys and girls. And, suddenly, you become insecure because of the culture shock ... and you can't even hug half your friends! During orientation sessions, girls would sit on one side of the hall and boys on the other. We sometimes felt the need for emotional support. "Hang on! You'll make it!" And we couldn't even touch our friends. It was like a barrier between us. Without this emotional support it was even more difficult getting used to the hard realities of Pakistan.

J.H.: And following the orientation camp?

Yvonne: One group of girls headed for Lahore, another for Rawalpindi, while the boys stayed in Islamabad. I was with the group that travelled the furthest; the one that went to Lahore. This was good. Lahore is a very beautiful and historic city.

J.H.: A wonderful city indeed.

Yvonne: Islamabad is more westernized. When we landed in Pakistan, all the Pakistani participants told us: "you'll see, Islamabad is a very Western city." But that's not how I felt when I saw it: "This isn't Western at all. It's nothing like Canada. This is so completely different." But when I returned after two months in Lahore, I realized just how westernized Islamabad was. Lahore is an old and traditional city surrounded by walls, filled with crazy little streets where camels plod along. People sometimes built houses in the middle of the street, so we'd have to go around them. My host family belonged to the upper class, which really bothered me at first. When I became a Canada World Youth participant, I told myself I'd end up living somewhere in an African hut or a grass shack. That's what I wanted to do. I'd talked a great deal about this to Lison, another Canadian participant. We were really upset with Canada World Youth. We wanted to run away and live somewhere in a straw hut. And if they wouldn't let us, we'd just quit the program! We really wanted to identify with the city's poor folk, and with poor people from a developing country in general. We wanted to live with them, feel things the way they do and curse the horrible rich people. But the attitude of rich Pakistanis towards the world's poor is much like that of Canadians. Things are easier in Canada. We know we're rich, but we don't have to deal with abject poverty. But when you're rich in Pakistan—as I was!—you can't ignore the misery around you. I had a lot of difficulty getting used to being surrounded by poverty, and facing this reality: "Hey! you're a rich person!" I couldn't just say: "I'm poor" and despise those horrible rich folks. Because I understood I was one of those horrible rich people I'd have preferred to curse! And I realized the members of my host family were good albeit rich people. When you live with them, you find out they're decent people. They care about their families. And yet, despite everything, you ask yourself: "How can they ignore all the poverty around them?"

J.H.: However, you did finally manage to get along with your rich family from Lahore.

Yvonne: Yes, but we only spent a month with them, and never got the feeling we really belonged, as had been the case in Saskatchewan. A rather loosely knit family whose members, however, I still refer to as "brothers" and "sisters."

J.H.: What kind of work did you do in Pakistan?

Yvonne: I worked for the Pakistan Society for the Rehabilitation of the Disabled. Primarily with the school for younger children, as well as in the hospital. It was difficult, since everything took place in Urdu, the country's language. And so I learned a little Urdu, especially from the children I worked with.

J.H.: Did you finally manage to get along in Urdu?

Yvonne: When necessary. For example, when I gave directions to rickshaw drivers or had to communicate with people from various organizations. But the language is so unique and its grammar so different from ours, that I couldn't hold a deep conversation. Though I couldn't sit with someone and speak effusively, I managed to ask questions and understand responses.

J.H.: But a lot of Pakistanis speak English, don't they?

Yvonne: They do. My family, for instance, spoke English as well as Urdu. And the same applied to my school's head mistress. English is the country's second language. When I taught English to the school's children, I had to use Urdu to help them understand. At the hospital, we only spoke Urdu with the nurses and patients, who spoke no other language. We had to explain to them, in Urdu, that I wasn't a doctor, even though I was white, and explain to the teachers and nurses that being white didn't mean I had things to show them. That's the impression they have of us: "If a white person visits us, it's because he or she is going to tell us things, tell us what to do, explain to us why our way of doing things is wrong and why their's is right." And I spent my time repeating: "No. I want to learn from you, I've come here to learn and observe. I've come to see how you do things; surely not to tell you what to do." And for them, **wow**! it was a kind of culture shock to see a white girl sit with them, pay attention to what they had to say and listen to their stories.

J.H.: What's the most important thing you learned in Pakistan?

Yvonne: Never to judge another culture. We're often tempted to judge, to say a country is good or bad. But we must finally understand that all is relative. Who are we to say that Pakistan is okay, but that arranged marriages and segregation are not? There are good things in Canada, as well as bad, like shuffling our seniors off to institutions. It's enough to say: "That's how it is!" so we can learn and understand. And if things can be improved, this should be done while taking their context into account. Nothing is better simply because it's from Canada, the West or Pakistan.

J.H.: So you became more tolerant?

Yvonne: Absolutely! It's a question of life or death! You go crazy if you don't learn tolerance—really—especially in a country as different as Pakistan. Let live and never judge.

J.H.: Are there any Pakistani values that you found particularly worthwhile?

Yvonne: People talked a great deal to me about the closeness of families, something I was able to appreciate in the families of the teachers I worked with. But this wasn't evident in my host family; however, there was a spirit of co-operation. For example, a cousin lived with the family while studying. For the entire month I thought she was one of the daughters: "Not at all. Her mother works abroad and she's staying here while studying."

J.H.: When you returned to Canada following such an experience, did you feel any different?

Yvonne: Returning home wasn't easy, especially since I had to finish high school. I'd left school to join this program—the equivalent of ten years of learning compressed into six-and-a-half months! And when I returned, I had to face a situation exactly like the one I'd left. Oh! those high school students! I no longer had the impression of being one of them, while I had to pretend I was. It's very difficult for any former Canada World Youth participant to return to school, since they have all these new ideas about peace, personal development, international development, cultural differences. I was wondering how I could change society, while my classmates talked about the last party, the drugs they took, movies they'd seen, etc. And I'd talk about world peace! We no longer had anything to talk about. While standing at the bus stop, I felt like telling someone: "Did you hear what happened yesterday in such a country? Or how about problems in Israel? And Nicaragua?" People look at you with amazement, and say: "God, you're strange! You're so weird! What's gotten into you?." You feel very different as a result. In a way, this is good, but you feel lonely. I no longer wanted to be like other students, I only wanted them to be a little more open. I'd never felt more open. I'd look at them and think: "Wow! That's how I used to be!" In fact I mustn't have been exactly like that, since I already had some notions about international development ... and had chosen to join Canada World Youth! In short, I tried to talk to other students, but it was pointless. This cloud, however, did have a silver lining, since it forced me to look for groups in Calgary that were interested in development. I had no choice. If I didn't want to go crazy, I had to find people that would understand what I talked about. My family was really helpful when I returned. In their eyes, I hadn't changed that much. I'd come back and was still a member of the family. I tended to criticize them a lot. But they pointed out that, although I purported to be tolerant of other cultures, I was being intolerant of them ...

J.H.: There's some truth to that!

Yvonne: They were right. That was a good slap in the face for me! Soon after I returned, I'd keep saying: "We waste way too much water and food! Why do we do this?" Until I realized that we have to be tolerant of our culture as well as others. And just because I'd been elsewhere and seen different things, didn't mean I'd changed my lifestyle all that much. I was still very Canadian. I finally went back to the bars, and started buying groceries from multinationals since I couldn't find them anywhere else. I had to live like a Canadian and had no right to criticize the Canadian lifestyle, but had to make small changes to my life first.

J.H.: So you finished high school?

Yvonne: Yes. Since my school was special, I was able to finish the two months I had remaining, instead of going back for a whole semester. And I found a job afterwards.

J.H.: What kind of work?

Yvonne: Housekeeping and maintenance in a historical village in Calgary. I did this until September and then did a year of university.

J.H.: What did you study?

Yvonne: I opted for Science. On returning from Pakistan, I was no longer sure I wanted to become a doctor. I'd seen too many doctors twiddling their thumbs in the hospital where I'd worked. I was frustrated by their claiming to be helpless for lack of high-tech equipment found just about nowhere in Pakistan. They could've done more than say: "Well, if I had this incubator or X-ray machine, I could perhaps help this child; otherwise, there's nothing I can do." And then I'd see nurses who really tried to help, though they had even fewer resources. When I returned to Canada, I told myself: "I no longer want to be a doctor. I absolutely want to be a nurse." But some of the people I spoke to reassured me: "Look, all doctors aren't like that. You can change things. You can be a good doctor." As a result, I continued to be interested in medicine. I studied math and sciences. Following the first year, I decided not to rush things; once you take that road, with chemistry, biology and all the disciplines related to medicine, you're forced to forget economics, politics, sociology: things that interested me a great deal. So I told myself: "I'll take the time to study economics and politics, and learn more about development and the world generally; maybe afterwards I'll go on to medicine." That's where I was when I got a phone call from Canada World Youth ...

J.H.: Albert Schweitzer began to study medicine at thirty-three.

Yvonne: Yes. I think that's the best way to go about it. Once you begin to study medicine, you have no other choice but to continue. I greatly admire doctors who manage to be involved in development. Wow! They're under constant pressure to keep up with all the new techniques, and keep abreast of everything that goes on in their field. They surely don't have time to devote a year to studying political science, international development, the new international economic order. So, I told myself that's what I wanted to do, have a good foundation, clear ideas before I pursued medicine.

J.H.: So the call from Canada World Youth came at the right time?

Yvonne: More or less. I filled out the form and went to the interview in any event, telling myself: "Well, why not give it a shot?" But I didn't expect to be selected. In fact, I'd gone back to studying. Even after having been accepted, there were still some problems with my medical exam. So I started the university semester. I bought books and attended classes to the very last minute because my medical file was still under review. I told myself: "I really want to be in the Zaïre program. But if it doesn't happen, I'll have had an excellent year at university." So, one way or another ...

J.H.: You couldn't lose!

Yvonne: Precisely.

J.H.: In any event, you suddenly found yourself with rather strange participants, given that they were **former** participants.

Yvonne: It was different. It was nice. In fact, each time I meet a former participant, for example when I run into someone at a meeting of people interested in development who says: "Oh yeah, I was in Canada World Youth," we hit it off right away, and have so much to talk about! Imagine, then, the Saint-Liguori orientation camp, where you meet seventeen former participants in one fell swoop. We exchanged ideas, talked about our programs, related everything we learned ... At that pace, we were emotionally exhausted after a few days. Especially in my case, since everything took place more or less in French; I felt I was banging my head against a wall. I didn't have a clue about what anyone was saying. At first, I knew very little French. I'd been allowed five days of immersion with Carole—a francophone participant—and her family.

J.H.: Five days! That's not much of an immersion.

Yvonne: I'd learned a few words here and there, during my other exchange, since my group leader was francophone and many of my really good friends were Quebeckers. But between Pakistan and Saskatchewan, you don't really have a chance to learn French! Surely not enough to hold a conversation. I could ask for a glass of water.

J.H.: When you reached Zaïre, did you have a culture shock similar to the one you had in Pakistan?

Yvonne: Not at all. I found it one hundred per cent easier to integrate. As soon as I reached Kinshasa, I realized how much easier it was. Life in the village is so much less constrained. I'd prepared mentally to have an experience similar to the one in Pakistan, but there are far fewer restrictions. Though I knew Africa differed from Asia, I was ready to make all kinds of concessions. Religion, the behaviour of people, their aloofness, etc. When I got here, I was astonished to see uncovered arms and legs; women walking with their heads up and not veiled. A breath of fresh air. I immediately felt at home here and haven't had any problems adapting. Even if there are many cultural differences, they're nothing compared to what I'd just experienced in Pakistan.

J.H.: Here, in Mwene Ditu, you were able to live with host families, unlike Kalenda participants who had to settle for group living.

Yvonne: My family! Oh! I use the word "fantastic" too much. Well, let's just say they're a wonderful and truly good family.

J.H.: Not as rich as your Pakistani family?

Yvonne.: No, they're not. Perhaps they're one of the wealthier families in the village, but that isn't saying much. They don't live in a straw hut, but have only five knives to serve seven people. It's that type of family. Their house is more "modern," but they don't have a lot of clothes. They own nothing that would lead us to believe they're well to do or belong to the middle class. A very traditional family. They cook in the open air and eat with their fingers ... *fufu* and manioc greens most of the time, and fish. In short, a lifestyle that differs greatly from that in the West.

J.H. Despite all this, you had no trouble adapting?

Yvonne: No, not really.

J.H.: Even to *fufu*?

Yvonne: Oh! *fufu* ... I didn't like it when I was in Kinshasa. I'd put a tiny bit on the side of my plate and say: "How will I ever handle this?" But now I rather like *fufu*, which is part of the basic diet here. It wouldn't even occur to me not to like *fufu*. I eat it, even if it's heavy in the stomach. Let's say I eat as much of it as I would potatoes in Canada. All the other family members eat huge portions and they really love it. I like it, but in moderation ...

J.H.: So, how did you get along with your family?

Yvonne: Very well. They really helped me learn French. I had to learn a little Tshiluba to understand my mother, who speaks only that language. However, I certainly learned less Tshiluba than I'd learned Urdu in Pakistan, since I first had to learn French. French is the language I use to communicate with most people ... I'm getting there, slowly but surely. I have no choice. Until I began living with my host family, I still had a choice. If I couldn't explain myself in French, I'd switch to English, and there was always someone in the group who could understand me. This was the case in Saint-Liguori and Kinshasa. When I began to live with my family, where Tshiluba was spoken most often, I'd use French, since I didn't understand a word of Tshiluba: "Oh! would you please allow me to speak French? I want to speak French!" As a result, I used French rather than English to help me along. My Zaïrian family helped me learn French more than anybody else.

J.H.: In a small isolated village in Western Kasaï! What about your counterpart?

Yvonne: Khoni. She's five years older than me, but I only realized it after a few weeks. She's the main reason I was able to adapt to the family so easily. She fits into the family very well.

J.H.: Although she's from another tribe?

Yvonne: Yes, she comes from another region and doesn't speak Tshiluba. However, she does speak Kicongo, Lingala, French as well as her mother tongue, a dialect. My counterpart speaks three or four languages, like everybody else in this country.

J.H.: Canadians must be amazed to realize these simple people manage to learn three or four languages ... while we have problems with only two?

Yvonne: With only two! I feel so stupid to be still grappling with French, while Khoni has the option of speaking her maternal dialect, Kicongo, Lingala or French!

And she's now learning English, because of the Canadian tour. There's no problem for these people: they switch from one language to the other. That's how it is in my family: they speak their maternal dialect, Tshiluba, then switch to French. They understand Lingala and speak Swahili. That's four languages in my family alone! They always speak French to me, even if they get somewhat frustrated. But Khoni is never frustrated when she speaks French to me, and I really appreciate that. She's very understanding and mature. This experience is very different from the one with my Pakistani counterpart, with whom I argued for no reason, save lack of maturity. I now feel I've matured and am better able to maintain a good relationship, no doubt because I learned so much in Pakistan. And Khoni is really very mature and in control of things. As a result, we've developed a really good relationship, despite some communication problems. This hasn't disconcerted us; on the contrary, it's helped us learn. She's also helped the family a great deal. They think of her as an older sister, although she didn't really take the place of the older sister, who's in Kinshasa. Khoni is like an older sister who always has something wise to say about a situation. They seek her advice. Oh! she's ...

J.H.: ... a marvellous girl!

Yvonne: Oh! Yes!

J.H.: So, what did you do over all these months?

Yvonne: I started out planting grass! Blade by blade. After two or three days, we decided there were a lot more important things to do in this village than planting grass. I ended up helping other participants paint a school.

J.H.: But didn't you have to rebuild a small hospital?

Yvonne: That's right. A small hospital for tubercular patients. We began with three ramshackle buildings: crumbling cement, broken windows, doors falling off hinges, no ceilings, no roofs. Repairing the entire hospital gave us a great deal of satisfaction. When I think about it, we arrived at this disastrous work site only seven weeks ago, in unlit buildings, with dust-covered floors, broken bricks, pieces of wood, old mats scattered about, and a partially collapsed roof ... Standing before this spectacle, we wondered: "Oh, God, do they really expect us to fix all this? Help! This is an absolutely impossible task!" We got to work in any event ... We burned all the garbage, took down parts of the ceiling that had collapsed, cleared the overgrown vegetation that cluttered the road linking the hospital to the main highway. Villagers who had some expertise gave us a hand in mixing cement while we rebuilt the roofs. We repaired and painted the walls. Lynn and I made mattress covers. Beds were repainted. In short, we rebuilt the entire hospital. In many ways, it's **our** hospital.

J.H.: From now on sick people will be treated there, and lives saved ...

Yvonne: I hope so. We all felt immense satisfaction yesterday at the official inauguration. From here on in, though, it all depends on the Zaïrians. It would be too bad if they failed to maintain the hospital properly; but there's nothing we can do about that.

J.H.: It was impressive to see the governor of the province inaugurate the hospital while villagers sang and danced ...

Yvonne: They were showing their gratitude to Canada World Youth participants.

It was an excellent cultural exchange; it was wonderful to see Zaïrian and Canadian participants working together to help the community. We got to know all the women and children from the surroundings who came to see us work. We'd chat with them during our "mango breaks."

J.H.: You gave something to Zaïre; what did you get in return?

Yvonne: So many things ... Music, for instance. I learned their dances ... My host family was gracious and warmhearted. The experience was very rewarding. They were always willing to help me, whatever the time of day or night. They'd explain the least thing to me and were delighted when I helped prepare meals. They couldn't have been any more hospitable or warmhearted!

J.H.: How will Zaïre affect the rest of your life?

Yvonne: One of the tangible things I learned was the importance of having a close family. I learned this in seeing mothers with babies on their backs, taking them everywhere, and in seeing older kids caring for younger ones. By observing kids playing with the simplest toys, I understood it was possible to live modestly. I'm rather proud to be Canadian, for all kinds of reasons, but I don't like the idea that we need all those Atari games, that we need something to keep us amused all the time, instead of simply enjoying what we're offered by the people surrounding us, our family, our friends. We're always looking for a new movie to enjoy, the latest record or video game, while overlooking the joy we could get from the person with whom we go to the movies or listen to a record. Everyone has a family. We should take advantage of it.

J.H.: Are your views on development clearer today?

Yvonne: The Zaïre and Pakistan programs helped me grow a great deal in that respect. Before, I was interested in the development of other countries. I'd always tell myself: "How can we help *them*?" Now, I realize that development also applies to *us*. I'd like to help Zaïre, but also know it can help itself. For example, there's no reason anyone in this village should go hungry; but Zaïrians, not Canadians, will have to solve these problems for themselves.

J.H.: When participants rebuilt community wells, weren't they helping the Zaïrians a little?

Yvonne: Yes, and that was a good work project. But the community really doesn't *need* us to build wells. We obviously gave them the impetus, but villagers did a lot of work themselves. For example, in areas of education and nutrition, Canadians can't provide a great deal of help by sending food and money to Zaïre. I'm starting to feel we're kidding ourselves if we believe we can solve the problems of developing countries by sending them things. Perhaps the greatest obstacle to development is a lack of awareness by rich countries. We try to divide the world into *us* and *them*. And we always talk about *those* countries having to change their attitude. But we forget that everything is interrelated through economics, politics ... For me, it's primarily a question of respect and sharing. If we show developing countries respect, then we'll be able to offer them significant assistance. We must also recognize that we have a lot to learn from them. Development will only occur when all of us work together to improve conditions both in Canada and the Third World.

Yvonne Sabraw's Comments on the Canadian Tour

The Zaïrian program was a wonderful experience, but I feel the Canadian tour was the most interesting part. Looking back, the Canadian tour gave me as much, if not more, than I'd expected. For two reasons: first, because of what I learned; second, because of the interest Canadians demonstrated towards our presentations.

I owe most of what I learned to the two participants who accompanied me: N'Sombolayi, my Zaïrian counterpart, and Michael Smith, my Canadian counterpart. It was exciting to prepare and improve our presentations together. They were very open and lively, which allowed us to exchange ideas and become very close friends. Of course, it was pretty tough going. We travelled through four provinces in six weeks, doing four or five presentations a day: it was exhausting! But we finally got used to the gruelling pace by trying to have a little fun while working.

One thing still amazes me: how much Canadians *need* and *want* to learn more about other countries, the lifestyle of others, particularly that of people in the Third World. They want to understand development. This is especially the case for rural Canadians. Students were fascinated to hear about the realities of Zaïre, and really pleased to be able to speak to N'Sombolayi. Their previous notions of Africa were rather vague: jungles, deserts, wars, starvation. I'm beginning to wonder how the world can improve when we don't even realize that human beings, not that different from us, live on the other side of the world. Human beings whose culture, traditions and outlook we must respect.

The people we met during the Canadian tour really wanted to know more, so we were able to share our experience and provide them with a better perspective on Africa. And help them feel that the world is *one*! Development becomes a lot more meaningful to them when they realize it's not about sending money here or there, but that it's a process that must take place within their community, as well as in the Third World.

In short, we felt we accomplished something over those six weeks. I only hope that more Canadians get to meet men and women from other countries and, especially, understand how important each individual is to world development.

Yvonne Sabraw Ten Years Later

Following the Zaïre program, Yvonne moved to Quebec to continue learning French. She studied sociology and political science at McGill University, and then switched to the physiotherapy program in 1988. She graduated with a bachelor's degree in physiotherapy and worked at Montreal's Constance Lethbridge Rehabilitation Centre for three years. During this time, she worked as a volunteer for the Yellow Door Coffee House. In 1994, Yvonne returned to her home town, Calgary. Following a two-month trip to Central America, she went back to practising physiotherapy at the Alberta Children's Hospital. She continues to play an active role with Amnesty International and the Arusha International Development Resource Centre.

2.
Éric Larouche

From Quebec to Jamaica

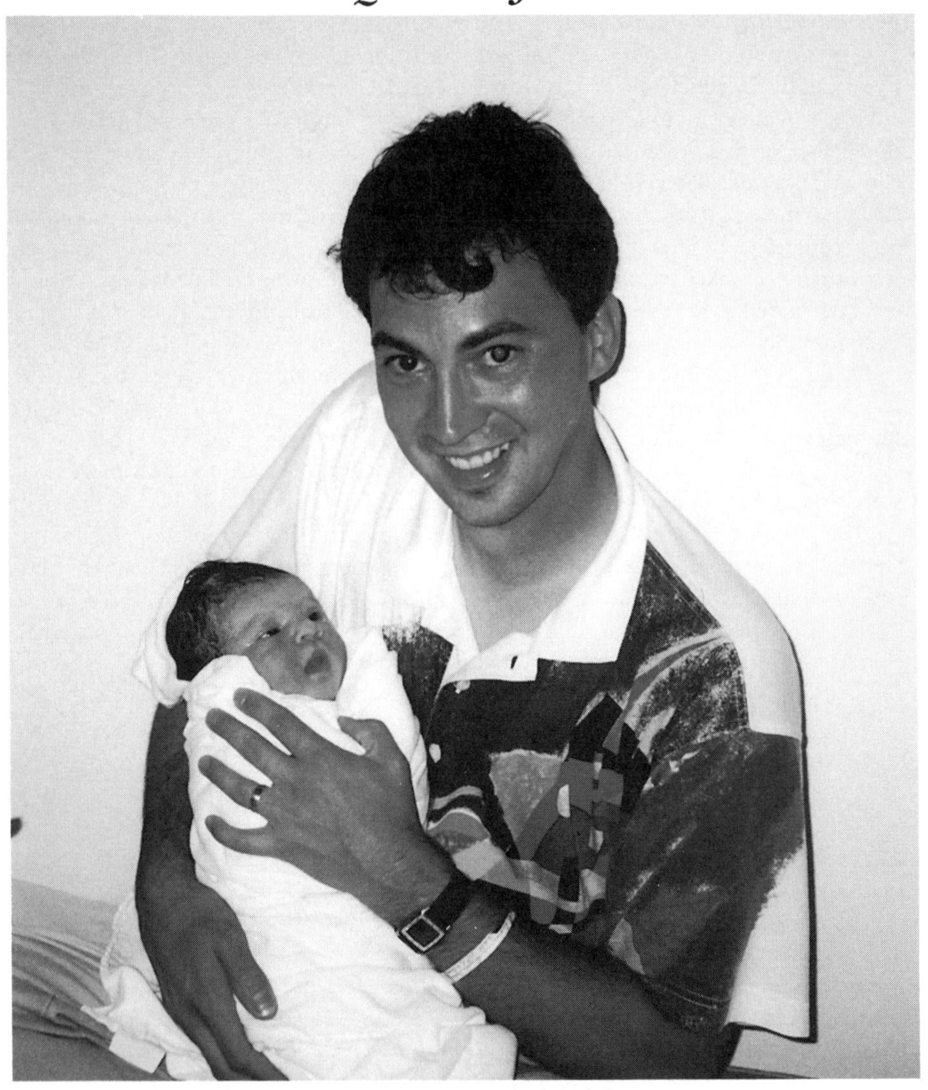

Éric Larouche with his daughter Léonie, ten years later.

Éric: I'm twenty-one years old and was born in Saint-David de Falardeau, a small village with two thousand people in the Saguenay-Lac-Saint-Jean region. I finished college two years ago, and had specialized in humanities with an option in law.

J.H.: You wanted to become a lawyer?

Éric: That's right. During the last year, I read a Canada World Youth ad in a student newspaper. It mentioned exchanges with the Third World ... Energetic youth ... Three months in Canada, three in a developing country ... Needless to say this immediately caught my attention. Especially since I'd been fascinated by the accounts of participants I'd met by chance: we'd talk for hours ... I needed to experience something different, before shutting myself away in a university with very serious people. I felt I was still too young, I wanted to attend the school of life before ending up in the other one.

J.H.: What do you mean by the school of life?

Éric: Forgetting about classes and theory, having a real adventure, somewhere, getting work experience, even in Canada.

J.H.: With a little luck, I imagine, and a good interview, you were accepted as a participant in Canada World Youth's program with Jamaica. Why that country instead of another?

Éric: It was luck. I felt like participating in Canada World Youth. It didn't matter whether it was Asia, South America or Africa. For me, the important thing was to live in a developing country. Jamaica was a stroke of good luck.

J.H.: You first had to go through the Canadian part of the program?

Éric: My group, consisting of seven Canadians and seven Jamaicans was sent to Gagetown, a tiny village with five hundred inhabitants in central New Brunswick. People were mostly farmers and descendants of English loyalists. A beautiful green village, located on the banks of the Saint John River, where everything grew in abundance.

J.H.: Since you were from the Saguenay-Lac-Saint-Jean region, I suspect your knowledge of English was limited. And yet, you were going to live in an English-speaking community for three months, with an anglophone counterpart from Jamaica.

Éric: Language! This was the greatest challenge I ever faced. I was nearly unilingual. The orientation camp had been rather difficult, but I could at least count on translations provided by other bilingual participants. The problem really cropped up when I found myself alone with my counterpart, Newton Robinson. On the farm, I managed to communicate as best I could thanks to family members who knew a little French. My counterpart and I finally managed to communicate with signs and mimes. No one else could guess what we were saying. But sometimes we'd need ten minutes just to say: "Could you get me a hammer?" It was certainly interesting!

J.H.: During which time you weren't learning English!

Éric: This was only a first step towards learning to communicate with my Jamaican friend: we shared the same room and worked together all day. But as time went by, English words came, sentences piled up. So the first English words I learned were about working on the farm. A very slow and rather painful apprenticeship. But following this three-month immersion, I was already managing to understand what people said and be understood by them. One hurdle had been cleared. I'd leave for Jamaica, where English is spoken, with greater confidence: I was at least able to speak their language.

J.H.: Besides this miracle, what do you remember most about New Brunswick, a province that's a neighbour to yours, in a village even smaller than yours?

Éric: The Canadian part of the program is absolutely crucial. You have to experience things in your country before tackling another one. Living with a Jamaican and observing his reactions to cultural differences gave me a hint of what awaited me in his country. As well, it was very rewarding to participate in the communal activities and celebrations of people in this small village. And our host family must've also found the experience rewarding, since it was relentlessly confronted to other cultures, particularly Newton's, whose reactions often amazed us.

J.H.: Do you think your group changed Gagetown in any way?

Éric: Without a doubt. All those conversations with young people in the village, all those intimate chats with host families, who were exposed to another culture for the first time. At least, this lays the groundwork for a greater understanding between the people of Canada and another country. For example, when we watched TV news together at the end of our stay, members of the family showed keen interest, not when an item dealt with Jamaica, but when it pertained to some country in Africa, the Carribbean or South America. Newton would sometimes tell them: "The situation just described really exists in my country." This was an introduction, a modest initiation to the world of development. And so, yes, I believe our group did change Gagetown, somewhat, if only in making its people a little more concerned.

J.H.: Listening to you, I can't help imagine what a remarkable country Canada could become, should a program like Canada World Youth one day be available to all young Canadians ...

Éric: That would be the beginning of a new era for Canada. It would be wonderful to see all Canadians in regular contact with all developing countries, wanting to understand them better and provide more efficient aid. The important thing isn't help, but knowing how to help.

J.H.: May heaven and the Treasury Board hear you! So, from Gagetown, you suddenly headed to Jamaica's enormous capital.

Éric: You can say that again! Half the country lives in Kingston. We were greeted at the airport by a swarm of radio and television journalists, government representatives, and people from the Canadian High Commission. Which shows how much Jamaicans are really interested in Canada World Youth and, perhaps, that we had a small mission to accomplish in this country. It was obviously important for them to acknowledge the arrival of young compatriots returning from a unique experience in Canada, accompanied by young Canadians wanting to live in Jamaica for over three months, simply to work with the people, co-operate, exchange ... It was easy to see the Jamaicans expected a lot from us. A few days following our arrival in Kingston, groups were spread into host communities. Mine was located at the very centre of Jamaica, a small farming village called Christiana.

J.H.: Was Newton still with you?

Éric: Naturally. We once again shared a room, and worked on a farm with the father, growing potatoes, cabbage, tomatoes and corn. A few cattle were raised as well.

J.H.: What kind of house did you live in?

Éric: A hundred year-old house dating back to the slavery period. It had been used by plantation owners to house their sugar-cane harvesters ... who'd travelled from Africa completely against their will. A very modest house which had been enlarged to meet our family's needs. We were comfortably lodged, and even had electricity, running water ... and television! On arrival, I had a few misgivings about the nutrition. Quite wrongly. To my great amazement, I was delighted with Jamaican cooking. And, since we lived on a farm, we were never short of fresh vegetables. What a novelty and pleasure to go outside and pick oranges or bananas from a tree, or cut a stalk of sugar cane. Everything was within easy reach.

J.H.: You didn't mention culture shock at all ...

Éric: Seeing so many new things created more amazement than culture shock.

J.H.: Amazement or wonderment?

Éric: Both amazement and wonderment at all these differences. For example, the great hospitality of villagers who ceaselessly invited us into their homes, and offered us beer. Simple and honest folk, who live at a different pace. If they don't feel like harvesting today, they'll do it tomorrow, next week or next month. It's rather unimportant to them.

J.H.: Perhaps this habit of procrastinating delays development in Jamaica and elsewhere?

Éric: It may be a factor. But the worst problem is transportation. Fertilizer and insecticides take forever to reach farmers who urgently need them to ensure the success of their crop. This is a serious cause of underdevelopment.

J.H.: It's unavoidable that a country as culturally and economically rich as the United States have so much influence on a nearby small country. Do you think this will affect Jamaican culture in the long run?

Éric: Yes; this can increasingly be seen. Fortunately, Jamaicans still have deep African roots, and maintain traditions and habits which are specific to them: funeral ceremonies, for example. Even the Jamaican language bears a profound African influence.

J.H.: Isn't English the official language?

Éric: Of course. But among themselves, Jamaicans speak a dialect which is a mixture of English, Spanish and Swahili.

J.H.: Do you understand this dialect a little?

Éric: I was eventually able to understand. But it's very difficult for anyone who only speaks English to manage.

J.H.: Are people encouraged to speak this language, which is specific to Jamaica?

Éric: Not at school, where Englishis mandatory. But it's more or less encouraged for cultural reasons. It's the preferred language of poets and singers.

J.H.: Leaving that beautiful country must've been difficult for you.

Éric: After seven months of group living, it wasn't easy to leave the Jamaican participants, say farewell to our friends or even the villagers with whom we'd had such good relations.

J.H.: What about your host family?

Éric: Leaving a family with whom you've lived intensely over numerous months isn't easy. I'm still in touch with them.

J.H.: You don't leave Jamaica, you tear yourself away!

Éric: That's the word: you tear yourself away! I've kept a faint hope of returning one day to see people I knew, and discover other aspects of a country I believe to be filled with mystery. As for the culture shock, it awaited me on returning to Canada! In mid-January 1985! The problem wasn't so much the cold, but reintegrating the North American environment, rediscovering North American habits, learning to live at home again. It took maybe three months. The worst thing is you've just lived an exciting experience ... which seems to interest no one! Folks who haven't experienced similar things can't understand them. Insignificant details are all they care about: what do people eat? How do they dress? Still, I managed to make friends and meet a few groups of young people from my region, with whom I was able to share profound experiences and have serious discussions. This perhaps allowed them to go further afterwards. I realized in the end that I couldn't dwell on this experience, and had to stop dreaming of returning to Jamaica. This would lead me nowhere.

J.H.: But you owed a lot to Jamaica, it had no doubt changed you somewhat.

Éric: It often happens that the effects of this program are only noticed many months afterwards. Only then do we realize we've changed. I still felt like continuing the adventure, and getting more involved with development, without really knowing how. I worked with youngsters at a summer camp: by getting involved in my midst, I realized I could further the cause of development, even in Canada. I stopped thinking it was absolutely necessary to travel abroad to change things.

J.H.: Did this discovery have an effect on your career choice? Did you still feel like becoming a lawyer?

Éric: Following the summer camp experience, I decided to enter university ... to study education!

J.H.: Is Canada World Youth responsible for such a radical change of direction?

Éric: Absolutely. Three days before classes began, I got a call from Canada World Youth informing me about the special program with Zaïre, which would take place during International Youth Year. I only had a few days to decide: "Zaïre or university?" When Canada World Youth finally accepted me into the new program, I felt that university could always wait, whereas such an opportunity might be unique. The really interesting part was that an extensive tour would take place to increase public awareness about international development, after the three months in Zaïre.

J.H.: So you told yourself: "Why not?"

Éric: Yes, why not continue attending the school of life before entering the conventional one. When I landed in Zaïre, I must say I was amazed at its similarities to Jamaica. The scenery was the same. Vegetation, people, types of buildings. So, no culture shock! I immediately felt at ease in these new surroundings that seemed so familiar. The major differences with Jamaica, at all levels, hit me when I arrived in our village, Mwene Ditu, in Western Kasaï.

J.H.: Did you have a counterpart?

Éric: Unfortunately not! We couldn't all have one since the group consisted of nineteen Canadian participants, and only nine Zaïrians.

J.H.: So you found yourself alone with a Zaïrian host family.

Éric: A large family, an extended family as it's known around here, with the father, mother, children and a bunch of cousins, nephews, uncles and aunts. No fewer than ten people lived in the house. An additional seven or eight family members lived in another hut on our property.

J.H.: Is the father responsible for all these good folks?

Éric: Right down to the least little cousin! The family plays a very important role in Zaïrian society. It helps each individual through the stages of life: education, work, marriage.

J.H.: A few customs likely to impress a young man from Saguenay-Lac-Saint-Jean.

Éric: And make you to think. You finally ask yourself: "Have modern societies lost touch with fundamental values, or have these old African societies stopped evolving?" The answer can be found in living with a Zaïrian family.

J.H.: Before this interview, you took me into your family, introduced me to your mother and father—that's what you call them—as well as your brothers and sisters. I noticed that the mother, a woman who's still young, had shaved her head, and that of all the children. I'd seen nothing like this elsewhere in Mwene Ditu. What did it mean?

Éric: A death occurred in the family barely ten days ago. My father's mother died. So, close relatives came to mourn for a week. They had their heads shaved, as is the custom, and slept on the floor inside the house. They neither washed nor changed clothes.

J.H.: This must have upset your life with the family.

Éric: I had to adapt to all kinds of situations. The house was always filled with people as villagers came to console the family. They'd come to cry, eat, dance even, since mourning doesn't exclude some festivities. We'd eat at all sorts of hours. In short, I didn't rest much during that week!

J.H.: But you had a unique experience ...

Éric: Which I'll probably never re-live!

J.H.: Besides living with this wonderful family—which I got to know thanks to you, and which seems love you a great deal—what did you do in Mwene Ditu?

Éric: We had a choice between three work projects. At first, I worked in a kindergarten school with Carole, another Canadian participant. This was a new school, and it completely lacked educational material. There was nothing: no scribblers, no books, no benches for the children. All instruction was oral. Children between three and five years of age did endless recitations in French, a language they didn't understand at all. They spoke only Tshiluba, one of the four national languages of Zaïre, the others being Lingala, Kicongo and Swahili. However, the official language, and that of instruction, is French.

J.H.: Since you'd already chosen a career in education, this work project was very appropriate.

Éric: A very fulfilling experience which enabled me to discover the aptitudes I had for education. I also enjoyed working on the wells with the other participants. There's no shortage of water in Mwene Ditu, but a serious problem with supply and purification. Building wells helped provide the people with filtered water. However, it has to be boiled, which requires the burning of coal—something people can't always afford. So they drink un-boiled water, which causes all kinds of illnesses. Another interesting work project was rebuilding of the Mwene Ditu hospital, which had been abandoned many years ago and was lying in ruins. We finished the work on schedule, and the sick will now be admitted into the new hospital.

J.H.: Your stay is coming to an end. You must now think about returning to Canada.

Éric: And especially the grand Canadian tour awaiting us, and for which we're well prepared. We'll be split into small groups of three participants: one Zaïrian and three Canadians. We'll be spread into three major regions: the West, the East, and the centre, i.e., Ontario and Quebec. We expect participants will give over seven hundred presentations in six weeks. In grade schools, high schools, as well as general and vocational schools, CEGEPs, universities, social clubs, etc. I feel well prepared, because of the Jamaican experience, which was a kind of introduction, and because of Zaïre, which makes up the body of the work. Only the conclusion needs to be written ... I'm in no hurry. Who knows what the future holds?

Éric Larouche's Comments on the Canadian Tour

During our tour of the Maritimes and Quebec, I was pleasantly surprised by the welcome that host families and Katimavik groups gave us. Besides putting us up in their homes, they helped us throughout the program. We got to know many people already interested and involved in development. For example, we met former host families in the Joliette area who'd taken part in a Canada World Youth program with Mali. People obviously develop a co-operative spirit as soon as they become aware of these problems. Now there's a means of improving the world!

One day, while we were with a Katimavik group, a participant told me our presentation had given her the itch to participate in Canada World Youth. She really wanted to get more involved and have an intercultural experience. Others told us we'd managed to sensitize them to the reality of Third World countries and motivate them to get involved in a concrete manner.

Éric Larouche Ten Years Later

After saying goodbye to all participants, who'd become a genuine family, Éric returned to live with his family in the village where he'd grown up. Finding his bearings was difficult following such an intense experience; however, he quickly managed to reintegrate his community with the help of friends. After working as a facilitator with the Centre du Lac Pouce *and an instructor at a summer camp, Éric became a facilitator with the* Jeunesse Étudiante Chrétienne du Saguenay-Lac-Saint-Jean *from 1988 to 1992.*

He afterwards worked as a sales representative for the La Source *book store in Chicoutimi. His work took him to the four corners of the Saguenay-Lac-Saint-Jean and North-Shore regions.*

Following this work experience, he returned to school in September 1993. He's very fond of nature, and has chosen a career in ornamental horticulture. He's now married and recently became the father of a beautiful daughter, Léonie. Though he works as a landscape consultant in Chicoutimi, he hasn't forgotten his Canada World Youth experience. He remains sensitive to international development issues and would like to re-live a co-operation experience with his family in the near future.

3.
Stephen Gwynne-Vaughan

From Ontario to Mali

Stephen, when he still had a beard and long hair, with Mwene Ditu friends.

Stephen: I'm twenty-three years old. Before joining Canada World Youth, I worked at a valve-making factory in Ottawa. I quickly realized I wasn't cut out for that kind of work. I'd dropped out of high school to travel around Western Canada. On my return, I decided to finish high school, after which I'd decide what to do with my life. My girlfriend is actually the one who introduced me to Canada World Youth. She brought home an application form one day. I made a copy by hand and filled it out ...

J.H.: You copied it? Did your girlfriend want to use the original herself?

Stephen: Exactly. She'd obtained the form at her school, and the deadline was rapidly approaching. I said to myself, on the spur of the moment: "Hey! I really feel like travelling!" I'd already travelled quite a bit since my father was in the armed forces. That's how I got to go just about everywhere in Canada and the United States. As well, I told myself that Canada World Youth would provide the perfect opportunity for me to determine what I want to do with the rest of my life. Like all new participants, I had pre-conceived notions about the program. And it was hard for me to imagine what life would be like in Africa.

J.H.: Had you chosen Africa to begin with?

Stephen: No. More than anything I'd wanted to participate in a French language program. When asked which part of the world I wanted to go to, I said: "Anywhere, as long as French is spoken." I live in Ottawa and many of my friends are bilingual. When I'd go places where everybody was French Canadian and speaking their language, people would notice I was anglophone and, poof! they'd all switch to English on my account. One day, a friend of mine said to me: "You know, I'm fed up always speaking English for you and repeating everything just because you're a unilingual anglophone. Why don't you try to learn French?" So I then decided to make an effort, but learning French in an anglophone setting isn't easy. Thanks to Canada World Youth, I can now manage in French, and I certainly intend to continue improving.

J.H.: Your prayers were answered; you joined a program, half of which would take place in Quebec, and the other in Mali. Did you know where that country was located?

Stephen: No. Before I went, the name Mali meant absolutely nothing to me. As is often the case, names from the colonial period are more evocative. I therefore remembered French Sudan and, of course, Timbuktu, an ancient and romantic city ...

J.H.: Perhaps not in reality ...

Stephen: Perhaps not ... In any event, I felt I was setting out on a grand adventure.

J.H.: But the trip to Timbuktu began somewhere in Quebec?

Stephen: That's right. In a small farming town near Montreal, Saint-Félix-de-Valois to be exact. People call it *Saint-Félix-de-Volaille* ... Chicken City. And so, I lived on a farm that had 125,000 chickens, sixty dairy cows and two hundred beef cattle. Some of the chickens laid eggs for market, while the others specialized in eggs intended for reproduction.

J.H.: You worked on this farm with your Malian counterpart?

Stephen: Yes, his name was Mohammed Side-Tourey. Oh! I won't forget our first encounter with the Malian participants! How distant I felt from this man who was to be my counterpart for the rest of the program! He was older than the others, in his thirties.

J.H.: That's unusual. But on occasion, some African countries have a broader definition of what we refer to as youth ...

Stephen: Indeed. Besides, Malian participants are chosen by their government, according to its criteria. Mohammed didn't look much older than me, but he was extremely conservative. A Muslim gentleman, with a very conservative mentality and a certain aversion to change. And I was the oldest Canadian participant ...

J.H.: How old were you?

Stephen: I was twenty, and the most radical member of our group. I wore an earring, had long hair and the whole bit ... And I'd lived alone in an apartment before I joined the program, which certainly wasn't the norm. This immediately created certain conflicts between Mohammed and me: he couldn't understand that I wasn't living with my parents, that I didn't send money to help them, etc. He couldn't understand this kind of behaviour, which created a few problems at first.

J.H.: Did some of your difficulties stem from your speaking French to each other?

Stephen: That did have something to do with it, since it was really difficult for me to express my feelings or the reasons underlying my attitudes. Our conversations were mostly very brief. In fact, we only had conflicts about our attitudes concerning family life and personal lifestyle. But we finally got along after a month. I learned to communicate with Mohammed, without using words even, with gestures, which can be rather subtle.

J.H.: You must have looked like a hippie to this devoted Muslim ... and maybe you were one, in a way.

Stephen: I was a hippie, no doubt about it, with long hair and everything. You might say I was rather radical. Where most children follow the wishes of their parents, I'd left home at sixteen. The reason: I wanted to find out what I wanted to do with my life, discover myself, set definite goals. I felt that everything had been too easy during childhood and then throughout high school. I was quite successful in high school, and in sports, without ever really trying. After breaking a leg, I had to forget about sports, find something else to do, which wasn't easy. Canada World Youth offered the opportunity of leaving my normal social environment and observing it from a completely different perspective. The program gave me lots of new ideas and convinced me to develop and improve myself.

J.H.: Your friend Mohammed and you were billeted with a host family in Saint-Félix-de-Valois. What kind of family? How did they react to this tall guy from English Canada and that tall Malian? People with black skin must be rare in Saint-Félix-de-Valois.

Stephen: Yes, but our host family was special, given that one of the girls was to marry a Muslim from Morocco ... who, moreover couldn't leave Morocco, which caused a great commotion. Two of the sons worked on the farm. An enormous farm, as I mentioned. The mother also worked on the farm, while one of the girls worked at a neighbouring farm. A kind of extended family if you will, since the grandchildren also lived there. Even a few cousins worked on the farm. What struck me most, is that the family had no problems with Mohammed, considered as someone completely different, whose strange behaviour had to be tolerated. In fact, they had more trouble with me! I was laid up with gastro-enteritis during the first week. Without wanting to be critical, I could only be amazed by their stoicism and hard work. For example, during the day, the father had another job at the neighbouring slaughterhouse. And yet there was tons of work to be done on the farm. We missed him quite a bit, which disconcerted him. Upon returning in the evening, he couldn't help saying: "Oh! this hasn't been done or that hasn't been done." I mentioned that these people lived a stoic life. For example, their television was in bad shape: the vertical hold didn't work and the pictures went up and down, which is hard on the eyes. And the house lacked a few of the comforts I was used to. They didn't have a stereo, only a tiny radio. They had no dining room table. And yet, they had a lot of money in the bank. Their lifestyle lead me to believe that Mohammed and I were perceived as cheap labour rather than participants in a cultural exchange ...

J.H.: It's rather strange for rich people to live that way ...

Stephen: Yes, but I think I finally managed to understand the father. He had very little formal education, whereas the mother was a teacher. She was the real brains of the family. The father had an immense capacity for work—twenty hours a day! Absolutely incredible! He was always worried, and very stubborn. I suppose he had a difficult part and couldn't imagine blowing money on things he considered useless.

J.H.: As you said earlier, what first attracted you to Canada World Youth was the dream of travelling to a far-off country. Perhaps, as often happens to participants, you felt that spending four months in a Quebec village was something you had to go through, the real objective being Africa.

Stephen: I was actually very pleased about going to Quebec. My first goal was to learn French. I wanted to get to know my neighbours, my fellow Canadians. That's why I wanted to learn French. I was completely immersed in French during my stay in Saint-Félix-de-Valois, which allowed me to think. Things were very different from home. I'm from the city, and moving to the country, to a small town, helped me learn something every day.

J.H.: Did your attitudes towards French Canadians change?

Stephen: They were reinforced. As I said, most of my friends in Ottawa are bilingual anglophones or francophones. So knowing French seemed to be another way of understanding my brothers, my Canadian friends, better. As well, I learned a lot about agriculture, about Canada's roots, because cities get food from the surrounding countryside and towns. One hundred and twenty-five thousand chickens on this farm alone! That's 250,000 barbecued chicken wings!

J.H.: At a certain point you had to bid farewell to this family ... and to the 125,000 chickens! Your group took off for Mali and, one day, landed in the strange city of Bamako. Was this a shock to you?

Stephen: Without a doubt, there's always a culture shock, but you don't notice it right away. It was ... I can't say Shangri-La ... It was new; everything, absolutely everything was different. What you notice first is the lack of comforts and luxuries we take for granted back home. We were put up in a rundown youth hostel and had to make due with the contents of our knapsacks. A simple trip to the market was quite an adventure: new sights, smells, sounds, new languages. Although French is spoken in Mali, numerous languages and local dialects are used more often.

J.H.: French is spoken by perhaps ten per cent of the population?

Stephen: Perhaps. Bamako is a huge city. Since we couldn't afford it, we didn't party around in posh hotels; instead, we focused on and thoroughly explored the downtown area.

J.H.: After a few days in Bamako, you were sent to your villages. Was yours very far from the capital?

Stephen: Ah! it seemed like the middle of nowhere! Light years from Bamako! In actual driving distance, I don't imagine it was more than two-and-a-half hours from the capital. But for the folks in my tiny village, Bamako was the place to go, it was paradise. Everyone dreamed of going there.

J.H.: What was the name of this village located so far from "paradise?"

Stephen: Narena. It's a tiny village on the road to Guinea, the major road, the *only* road. It was filled with potholes, which caused our vehicle to break down before we reached the village. This made us realize how important an adequate transportation infrastructure is to an economy ... As for the culture shock, it didn't really hit me until a week after I'd reached Narena. We were to live in a group, just outside the village, which was disappointing. It meant that integrating into the community, a small farming community, would be that much more difficult.

J.H.: What did they grow?

Stephen: I believe millet was the only thing grown there. Mali is in the Sahel region, and therefore very arid. The drought had lasted sixteen years. The fields looked pitiful and it was impossible to grow vegetables without irrigation. The country set up a rural-reintegration program to bring city people, especially from Bamako, back to the country. The objective was to settle these people in villages throughout the country and teach them more effective agricultural techniques, rational nutrition and sanitation practices. The program seems to have been successful. For instance, in Narena, we took care of a small garden where we grew lettuce and a tomato or two, which helped improve the people's nutrition.

J.H.: So you lived in a group ...

Stephen: Consisting of seven Malian and seven Canadian participants and two group leaders. We lived in a mud-brick, tin roofed house that had four rooms. Four or five to a room.

J.H.: Boys on one side and girls on the other ...

Stephen: Definitely. In Mali, people of opposite sexes hardly mingle. It's a Muslim country. I realized that houses with thatched roofs were much more comfortable. The sun beats down on a tin roof and the house becomes a pressure cooker. I couldn't help but think: "Ah! but with the right technology! Something must be done: we're cooking in this house!" And yet, we'd been given what was thought to be the best house in the village.

J.H.: In Africa, having a tin roof is a sign of prosperity ...

Stephen: I suffered a good deal because of that darned roof. But I'd visit with friends most of the day because their houses were cooler, and because one of our goals was to integrate into the community. We didn't have much in the way of work projects, except for the gardening and, of course, we did the *récolte*, I can't even remember the word in English.

J.H.: The harvest? My God, you're forgetting your English!

Stephen: Ever since I've been living in French ... I remember that we picked some peanuts at harvest time. And, especially, that we built improved ovens in the homes.

J.H.: Appropriate technology, finally, since these ovens help save a lot of wood for cooking.

Stephen: The scarcity of wood for cooking is a major development problem, especially in the Sahel region where desertification swallows countless kilometres of arable land every year.

J.H.: And every day the women must travel further to gather wood ...

Stephen: They're also the ones who must fetch water.

J.H.: I'm told that gathering wood for cooking takes up a good part of the day.

Stephen: Especially in this region where a tree is found only every kilometre! Moreover, women use extremely dull axes—very crude tools. The wood, baobab for example, is often very hard, as are some of the bushes. I tried on many occasions and wasted a great deal of time attemptng to cut that darned wood. And yet, women accomplish this thankless task every day! What energy they must exert! It's amazing that they can survive, given the few calories they ingest, and the constant effort required by other domestic tasks.

J.H.: So, tell me a little about those improved ovens, which you made with earth, I believe ...

Stephen: We use termite mud mixed with sand and water. The ovens are shaped by hand and affixed to the ground. Wood is inserted through a hole at the bottom, and a grill is placed on top for cauldrons. There's a little feed-off hole which serves as a pot warmer while something else cooks on the grill.

J.H.: How much wood can be saved using this system?

Stephen: Hard to say. I don't know how this can be measured precisely, but it does boil water three times as fast as a regular fire. And hot water can be kept on the pot warmer while the rest of the meal cooks on the grill. Without this system, a great deal of energy is wasted, since two or three fires must be used.

J.H.: You mentioned earlier that one of your goals was to integrate into that village located at the back of beyond. How did you manage?

Stephen: Since we worked and lived in a group outside the village, each of us had to leave the group and explore the village for himself. On the first day, I walked down the road and stopped at the first straw hut I encountered. Two small children came running out: we seemed very, very strange to them. They'd touch us and then look at their hands to see if they'd turned white! We had to be persistent; we remained somewhat apart even if we sparked a lot of curiosity. We asked ourselves what we were doing here. One day, since I didn't know anyone yet, I knocked on a door haphazardly. This happened to be the house of a tailor busily working away. I said hello, and introduced myself: "We live over there, down the road, and are going to be here for a few months." I continued on my way since I wanted to buy some cigarettes. Which provided an opening line: "Could you tell me if there's a store in ..." I was looking for excuses to stop here and there. By the second day, I was already a friend, since people remembered me from the previous day. The important social ritual, where men gather to drink tea, offers a good opportunity to make contact. In fact, my counterpart, Mohammed, one day told me: "Well, you're absolutely going to have to learn how to make this tea." I finally learned, which really amused the villagers, perhaps because I was the only one from the group who took interest in this. We all drank tea, but I was the only Canadian participant who knew how to make it. People really got a kick out of this: "Hey, look at that young white guy making our tea!" In fact, the tea ceremony was the major social event every afternoon. In the first part of the ceremony, you fill a small teapot with water and add tea leaves. You boil it until a third of the liquid is left. The result: a thick liquid, so strong it would knock your socks off. It can keep you awake for a week! It was incredible. Villagers call this *thé d'homme*, or man's tea. Canadian participants weren't really crazy about the stuff, save for those looking for a good shot of caffeine. It was very strong and very sweet. To make the second pot of tea, the same leaves are used, water is added, and the concoction is reduced to a third; but, the tea is weaker since much of the caffeine has gone. So more sugar's added! The men wouldn't have tea from the third pot, since it was very weak and very sweet. It was given to the women and children. I recall giving them a good laugh: I was very good at making the *thé d'homme*; it was so strong that the women even hesitated from drinking from my "third pot." The men thought this was very funny.

J.H.: This must have helped you integrate into the village.

Stephen: Without a doubt. Teatime is that part of the day when men sit around to chat, share stories, learn, especially from the older men who've acquired so much wisdom and experience. Well, they tried explaining things I had difficulty understanding ... But I remember trying to explain snow to them ... I had to give up! You mustn't forget I was just beginning to speak French, with people whose second language it is ... and who often only spoke Bambara, the local language. I needed a translator, which complicated things.

J.H.: Not always easy, but a lot of fun, right?

Stephen: Fun?

J.H.: Perhaps that isn't the right word ...

Stephen: Right! When people asked me afterwards: "Well, how was your trip?" I couldn't say I had a "lot of fun." We had group-dyanmic problems, serious ones, and our work projects could have been more successful—they didn't have the impact I'd hoped. On returning to Canada, I began seriously thinking about what the program had taught me. I often thought about people in Narena, especially the youths with whom I'd often spoken. They had so few opportunities for advancement, for leaving the village even, leading a more exciting and enriching life ... Whereas I had virtually unlimited opportunities, because I'm Canadian ...

J.H.: But you weren't without knowing that at least twenty per cent of our young people are presently unemployed. Despite this, you thought ...

Stephen: I'm speaking for myself, of course. All I had to do was get into something; all I needed was an idea, and nothing could stop me. I'd tell myself: "Find something you like and you can succeed." Perhaps this was overconfidence. Finding a job might not be that easy. That's why I decided to finish high school and then study journalism, which would provide an opportunity to travel and continue learning a little every day. I gave presentations on Mali as soon as I returned to Canada, at my high school for example, which wasn't easy, due to my "dubious" reputation ...

J.H.: You were still a hippie in the eyes of your classmates?

Stephen: More than ever! In appearance at least: I'd grown a beard and wore an African booboo brought back from Mali. So, in appearance, I was more than ever a hippie; but a lot less so down deep. I'd resolved to move ahead within Canadian society, where so many opportunities were offered. I especially wanted to continue learning. Before Canada World Youth, I hadn't managed to find a career that really interested me, and I had trouble focusing my energy. The program gave me time to think about my environment, my life, and the opportunities before me. I continually wrote down my thoughts. I wrote ceaselessly. So I told myself: "Well, you like to write. You want to learn? You want to travel? Journalism!" I therefore began to work during the day, to provide for myself, and to study in the evening. Afterwards, I registered at Ryerson's Journalism School in Toronto but, following the first semester, I was quite dismayed: journalism wasn't what I thought it was. Ryerson is a very practical and pragmatic school where you're taught to write ... in support of the status quo! You're trained to become a big city reporter, whereas I wanted to be a roving correspondent to see the world. I especially didn't want to live in downtown Toronto and write about violent deaths and other tragedies. Without denying that aspect of society, I felt a more positive attitude was required, to write more about the good things in life instead of sensationalizing things and seeking to uncover its seedier side. That's when I got a call from Canada World Youth. I'd found a job with American Express. It was summertime, school was out and I'd already decided to switch disciplines. Everything was going perfectly: I had a weekend job and had registered at the University of Toronto in International Development, since I already had some background in the field and was very interested in it. Having eliminated journalism, I still wanted to write, travel, live and learn, but in a more positive sense this time. I could have an impact. And I'd get more personal satisfaction by helping people while I learned. International development, like journalism, is a field that doesn't offer huge salaries. However, it offered everything I wanted.

J.H.: And the phone call ...

Stephen: So I received a call one afternoon: "Hi, this is Daniel Renaud from Canada World Youth. We're putting together a special program with Zaïre ..." I was staggered! I jumped out of my chair! I couldn't believe it—a second chance! I was especially surprised to be chosen for this second program, given the group dynamic problems we had in Mali. Daniel asked me: "Would you like to go?" And I said "yes!" right away. He replied: "No, no, you'll need some time to think about it." I answered: "I don't need time to think about; this fits in perfectly with my plans. That program will offer the best practical experience I can expect; moreover, it will help confirm the choice I made pertaining to international development. If this is the path I'm to follow, I'll return convinced more than ever. If it's not for me, well ..." I didn't even want to think about that. I'm very happy to have had the opportunity of coming to Zaïre, and I'm sure I chose the right path.

J.H.: So you joined the special program with Zaïre. Special in that groups are made up of former participants, and its primary goal is sharing the Zaïrian experience with many Canadians, through presentations to be made on your return to Canada. How did it go?

Stephen: Oh! To begin with, I arrived at the training camp late, due to some misunderstanding. I became the butt of numerous jokes. I was known as "Steve-a-day-late Gwynne-Vaughan" for the rest of the program! I was pleased with the idea of improving my French in Zaïre, a francophone country like Mali, but with a greater potential for development and a bright future. I was rather depressed after being in Mali, because problems in that country seemed insurmountable, for climatic reasons especially. Whereas Zaïre has so much potential. I was determined to get to know Zaïre as much as possible. And then, devote myself to preparing our presentations. And finally, to pull my load in the work project. I tried to come here without any pre-conceptions, but a few disappointments awaited me. Since we're all former participants, the presentations should have been easy to make. We were all rather familiar with development, a topic we feel strongly about. We nonetheless had problems. As in all groups, one problem followed another. Participants handed in work late, others had differing points of view, but we had to integrate them into the group. Canadian participants already knew one another, whereas we'd barely met the Zaïrians. So we had to take the time to learn about their perception of things, which differed from ours on just about every subject, be it male-female relationships, infrastructure, transportation systems, communication, politics. We couldn't just decide a question from a Canadian perspective. A lot of time was needed. Even we former participants lacked the experience of more elaborate presentations needed for the grand tour around Canada. A whole new world to discover. How would we convey this or that message? We naturally had the technology, the medium, but that wasn't enough. We used photos and texts. Fine. But what exactly would we talk about, how would we present this or that subject in complete objectivity? There was no shortage of problems! To my delight, however, I must admit that we solved most of them.

J.H.: Forget the problems for a moment, and tell me about your Zaïrian village, Mwene Ditu.

Stephen: On arriving, we were greeted by the *Missionnaires du Christ-Roi*, a group of really terrific nuns. They'd organized everything: work projects, host families, etc. Everything was in place. I was to be billeted with a doctor who was a bachelor. I was really pleased about this, since it provided greater freedom to leave the house and explore other parts of the community. I didn't have a counterpart and this prompted me to meet as many people as possible, to chat with a neighbour when I got the chance. My host, the doctor, wasn't much older than me, and had lived in a large modern city. So he understood me and we got along famously.

J.H.: He lived alone?

Stephen: No, he lived with a friend, what they call a little brother around here. I believe I somewhat took his place, since he had to sleep on the couch and I got the bed. At the beginning, I had to get used to the language, the food, the lifestyle, the mealtimes, etc. Nothing like travelling to make you appreciate the good home cooking back in Canada! In Zaïre, the diet is very repetitive. I had to get used to my doctor having a servant: master-servant relations are very rigid. For example, though I'd have liked the man to sit and eat with us, that was impossible. So, getting used to all these little things took some time. When I think about it today, it all seems rather unimportant. However, even if this is my second African experience, the culture shock still hit me three weeks into the program, when work projects were already well under way.

J.H.: Rebuilding the hospital?

Stephen: I'd chosen the work project designed to provide Mwene Ditu with drinking water, since I'd done research on water problems around the world. The project started on a very small scale. We were to clean and repair two or three wells, and perhaps build one. The first one we were to clean didn't work at all; it had been rather poorly built by a Peace Corps group about four years ago: they hadn't dug deep enough to reach the water table. Perhaps the water table is lower, I don't know; it nonetheless couldn't be reached, especially during the dry season. Repairing this seemed ridiculous. So we decided to rebuild it completely. A difficult task given our inexperience in this field, the language barrier between us and the population, not to mention the cultural barrier: for example, we had a hard time getting along with the village chief. We were really depressed at the beginning. We all thought: "Gosh, this is an impossible task!" This was an enormous undertaking for three participants. The convent's sister superior gave us a sort of really good kick in the butt and said: "Quit moaning and groaning; start digging! Do something!" And, she then told us: "In any case, the experience will benefit you. You'll learn something, even if you don't manage to build a good well." So day after day we dug and dug, made all kinds of plans, and then finally cried out for help: "Send us someone who's already built one of these contraptions!" We'd completely demolished the old well and dug a great deal. It was time to rebuild; for that, we needed help. The good sisters finally dug up two specialists from the region who'd previously built wells. Precisely what we needed: an idea or two and a little practical experience. We immediately got to work; four days later, construction was complete. Though the specialists provided a few good ideas, we also chipped in with a few of our own. Together, we managed to build a good well that ought to last many years, provided it's properly maintained. We then checked out the village to determine where the population was densest and where the need for drinking water was greatest, and decided to build two or three more wells.

J.H.: In listening to you, I can't picture these wells. Do they provide houses with water, or what?

Stephen: Mwene Ditu is built on an escarpment, i.e., the city is located above the surrounding area. Wells are located in the lower areas, at the foot of the escarpment, where water naturally accumulates. The water either comes from the ground through an artesian well, or flows to the bottom of the hill. To collect water, an enormous hole must be dug, deep enough to reach the impermeable layer of clay. The reservoir is then filled with gravel that acts as a filter. The hole and canal are afterwards filled with larger pebbles and charcoal to filter the water some more. The whole thing is then covered with plastic and dirt, so that nothing can be seen from the exterior. Water from the old wells contained worms and I can't imagine what. The reservoir was an old rusty barrel containing contaminated water. Today, the well provides twenty four litres of filtered water per minute through two pipes. The area has good drainage, no stagnant water and the water quality can easily be tested by the doctor.

J.H.: Your efforts helped provide drinking water to roughly how many families?

Stephen: Including our seven wells, I believe they'll serve thousands of people. Every day, hundreds of women come to fetch water. We've managed to interest customary and district chiefs, and the local population. As well, the teachers—I met school directors and prefects—have promised to inform the people, youth especially, about the importance of boiling water and properly maintaining the wells. We emphasized that these wells weren't a gift from heaven, that they belonged to the people, especially since they helped build them, and that they had to keep them in working order, or else the project was doomed to failure. I believe it will work, because we reached an agreement with those responsible for the *Salongo* (community work day): they've promised to send three volunteers every week to clean the canal and areas surrounding the wells.

J.H.: You'll obviously leave something behind in Mwene Ditu ...

Stephen: Yes.

J.H.: You must be proud of yourself.

Stephen: I'm glad we got support from local and regional authorities, from schools and churches, and the population in general. Only this can provide long-term results. Mwene Ditu now has a local team of well builders and even an inspector. We realized that if we really wanted to leave something in our wake, we had to train a few people to do exactly what we'd done. We administered tests to a few unemployed youths, and selected those who seemed most capable of doing this type of work, thereby creating a few jobs. I believe all this should be helpful.

J.H.: Do you still consider yourself a hippie, after carrying out such an important project?

Stephen: Am I still a hippie?

J.H.: Whatever that is!

Stephen: Exactly, whatever that is! No, I think not. This project helped me realize that development must be based on co-operation. I won't leave here saying: "I've done my work. Now let's forget about it!" Since people here shared their values with me, just as I did with them, I can only go home and continue working. This has motivated me enough to get started on all that needs to be done in the years to come. Basically, there is no such thing as development: it's an ongoing process which must get the attention of all those concerned with improving life and living standards the world over. Hippies tend to live at the fringes of society. But I feel more involved than ever, I've realized I can't leave decision-making to others and that I have an important role to play in the building of a more just society. We too often place personal pleasure ahead of social needs. We only have to observe the decline of the family's role in our society to realize this. After living in Africa, where the family is the focus of life and a source of wealth, not necessarily material, I question whether our society is as "developed" as we think. And I wonder if we shouldn't place more emphasis on improving society by emphasizing the family, rather than economic change, which is so dependent on state intervention.

J.H.: You learned a great deal, Stephen ...

Stephen: It would be hard to determine everything I learned during such a program. Learning while working benefits participants in ways that can't really be measured. This has nothing in common with traditional forms of learning that are geared towards finding a job. Canada World Youth helps us learn more about the human condition and brings us into contact with life's most fundamental aspects. My constant and daily contact with people from the most varied backgrounds opened my eyes and gave me new ideas. This unique experience helped me understand the wisdom behind the statement: "Development demands that we think globally and act locally." That's exactly what I plan to do. Starting today!

Stephen Gwynne-Vaughan's Comments on the Canadian Tour

In my opinion, the Canadian tour was the most important part of the special program with Zaïre. It was certainly the most intense. Something new for Canada World Youth and *very* new for all participants. In the beginning, we were running more on energy than organization, but we learned as we went along. At the end, after working out numerous details, we were giving quality presentations. Following the tour, we agreed that the experience had been positive, and the impact important. We realized that this was a first experience and perhaps a precedent for Canada World Youth.

As well, the tour reaffirmed several ideas I'd had for some time. First: the greatest obstacle to real international development is that people don't understand the global system and the part they play in it. Second: People, youth especially, are willing to learn more about the global system. Third: If people did have a better understanding of the global system, and the inequalities it perpetuates—especially as far as the Third World is concerned—they'd want to change things. Fourth: If enough people demand changes, changes will be made.

Stephen Gwynne-Vaugh Ten Years Later

After the Canadian tour, Stephen went back to the job he'd given up to participate in the Zaïre program. However, he wanted to learn more about "development" and Canada's willingness to improve its foreign aid, rather than simply criticizing the work of others. He therefore registered in the University of Toronto's International Development Studies Program.

Steve finally got a haircut and, to support himself while doing graduate studies in geography and international development, worked as a counsellor with young offenders at prisons and half-way houses in Ottawa.

In 1991, Steve returned to Africa to work with emergency relief programs in Angola, Mozambique and Liberia. He's been director of Action internationale contre la faim *in Mozambique, where he co-ordinated development programs related to health, drinking water, nutrition and security.*

He recently returned to Ottawa to pursue graduate studies in international development at Carleton University.

4.
Lynn Lalonde

From Ontario to Bangladesh

Lynn Lolonde practising *Tshiluba.*

Lynn: I'm from l'Orignal, a village between Montreal and Ottawa along Highway 17, in the Ottawa Valley. The region is both agricultural and industrial. We're three children at home. My father is a farmer who also works across the river in Quebec as a laboratory technician. So I was raised on a farm and lived in a small village. I attended a Catholic primary school and then went to a bilingual school in Vankleek Hill. Most francophones took some courses in English, while anglophones took some in French. Right from my first year in high school, my father encouraged me to take some English courses. After a few years, I took half of them in English, including physics and math.

J.H.: You were already straddling both cultures ...

Lynn: Exactly.

J.H.: And you quickly became bilingual ...

Lynn: Yes. I'd participated in the Department of Natural Resources Junior Ranger program, which helped me a great deal. My family also helped me become bilingual, since my mother is English and my father French.

J.H.: At what stage of your studies were you when you heard about Canada World Youth?

Lynn: I'd completed grade thirteen, at the halfway point of which you start thinking about university, and what you'll do with the rest of your life.

J.H.: Did you have any ideas?

Lynn: I'd thought about university and was particularly interested in forestry. I wanted to become a forester.

J.H.: You like the forest?

Lynn: Yes. I've always loved nature, no doubt because I was raised on a farm and because of my Junior Ranger experience. One day, I went to see my guidance counsellor, who was also a friend, and asked her if she knew any programs allowing youths to travel and work abroad. She'd just received a Canada World Youth brochure and application form. I filled out the form just for fun at home, and then talked about the idea with my parents. Though my mother basically agreed, my father wouldn't hear of it. I love him dearly and we're very close; yet this was the first time he categorically objected to one of my plans. He even said that if I got involved with Canada World Youth, he'd no longer help me through university. I mailed the form anyway and, a few weeks later, Canada World Youth invited me to an interview. The program is basically unknown in the region where we live, but my father managed to obtain information from a priest and one of his friends. They completely reassured him about the value of Canada World Youth. Soon thereafter, the Toronto regional office phoned to say I'd been accepted. However, I'd been selected for the Bangladesh program ... whereas my first choice had been Africa. One of my aunts had taught in Zaïre, so I'd heard about the country in early childhood. And I relished stories about people who'd travelled to Africa or elsewhere. I could sit for hours, enraptured, before someone relating his adventures and giving slide shows. I devoured *Géos* and *National Geographic* magazines. When on the phone with the Toronto office, I again insisted on going to Africa, but finally settled on Bangladesh ... without the slightest idea of its whereabouts! Furthermore, the Canadian half of the program with Bangladesh would take place in British Columbia, giving me the opportunity to discover Western

Canada, something I'd always dreamed about. I was really excited and literally jumping for joy.

J.H.: So in September of that year you found yourself somewhere on the Pacific coast, along with other participants.

Lynn: Following the orientation camp on Vancouver Island, we headed for the three communities assigned to the three groups. I ended up in Powell River, where I'd be able to polish my English. Our group leader was called Bob. An extremely interesting chap: he was a vegetarian, the first I'd ever met. I don't even know what a vegetarian eats in winter!

J.H.: No meat in winter!

Lynn: Nor in summer, I gather! I had another shock on meeting my Bengali counterpart, Rajchahi, with whom I was to live the next seven months: she was twenty-four and I'd just turned nineteen!

J.H.: You must've learned a little Bengali?

Lynn: Yes, a few words during the orientation camp. And I was proud of my counterpart, with her long black braids, her pierced nose and elegant sari.

J.H.: That must have impressed your host family?

Lynn: Our family was special: the father was twenty-five and the mother twenty-three ... which is to say my counterpart was older than the family's mother! A family plagued by illness. The mother had been operated for cancer, and her twins, barely two-years old, had also been through surgery.

J.H.: Did you all get along?

Lynn: Rather well, considering the age proximity. Our group was very energetic, and we always felt like doing lots of things together; my counterpart, however, was very conservative. This created a difficult situation. For instance, when we'd go swimming at the pool, she wanted to jump in the water wearing her sari! I like to walk briskly ... but Rajchahi straggles behind, since people in her country walk slowly, etc.

J.H.: What about the work experience?

Lynn: We worked with the mentally handicapped, which taught me a lot, though I found this emotionally difficult. I worked at the carpentry workshop with a seventy-year old woman who led a team of handicapped people. My counterpart gave sewing lessons while practising her English, which was rather rough. I afterwards worked in forestry, and then with a veterinarian, something forbidden to my counterpart.

J.H.: Why?

Lynn: In Bangladesh, animals are apparently taboo. They can't be touched. As soon as a dog brushes against a sari, it can no longer be worn, unless it's repeatedly washed. It was therefore out of the question for a Bengali to work with animals at a Canadian vet's.

J.H.: You learned different things ...

Lynn: I learned a great deal from the handicapped. I realized how much they need love and attention. Bengalis were amazed that we put them in institutions. As well, they couldn't believe that seniors, even when healthy, are placed in retirement homes. One day, my counterpart exclaimed: "I can't believe you treat seniors that way; our society reveres them enormously!"

J.H.: That reaction is nearly unanimous among our Third World participants, who are scandalized by the way we treat seniors in Canada.

Lynn: After the British Columbia experience, I was a little nervous about going to Bangladesh. I wondered how I could adapt to such a different culture. Spending three months living with Rajchahi gave me an inkling of what awaited me, though she was a very good counterpart.

J.H.: What was your first impression on landing in Bangladesh, at the Dhaka airport, no doubt?

Lynn: Lots of people had come to greet my counterpart. She was surrounded by friends and relatives, while I was alone, exhausted, overwhelmed by the heat, carrying my luggage. I sat on my bag, bordering on tears. Canadian participants asked me to join them, but I didn't want to leave my counterpart. I ended up in a bus with her and all her family, with everyone speaking at once in Bengali. I didn't understand a word. I had my nose stuck to the window and was fascinated to see a crowd scurrying about in all directions, to glimpse my first coconut trees ...

J.H.: A first shock, right?

Lynn: I suddenly realized I was an empty jar. But beginning to be filled ... I found myself somewhere in Dacca, at Rajchahi's parents, in a modest living room: four walls and a few sofas. I felt that this was how the poor live in Canada. I was observing, not judging. And being observed. People made comments on my hair, my skirt, comments gradually translated by my counterpart. I finally admitted I was exhausted and would like to turn in. I then experienced genuine panic. I felt completely alone, at the ends of the earth, with no drinking water and lost. Although I did have a counterpart I'd known for three months, I often had trouble getting along with her. At about 8:00 p.m., I hear the wailings of a rooster having his throat slit. At 11:00 p.m., I find myself on the floor seated on a mat for the evening meal. I was somewhat familiar with Bengali cuisine, but suddenly realized I was eating the rooster whose death cries I'd heard three hours earlier. Little things of that sort profoundly shook me. I'm given a bowl of rice, a coconut is split. I'm thirsty, but I don't dare ask for boiled water, knowing this is a rarity in Bengali homes. In any event, with the Bengali I spoke then ... I finally lay down on a mattress, beside my counterpart. It was very warm. I ceaselessly told myself: "Calm down, Lynn! Don't get excited! Takes things as they come, one day at a time ..." The next morning we all boarded a bus that would cross Bangladesh, in search of more of my counterpart's relatives. I found the landscape rather similar to Canada's ...

J.H.: Really? What about the palms, the banana trees?

Lynn: There were green fields as far as the eye could see. Everything in Bangladesh is cultivated. Fields and more fields. Hardly any trees or hills. Everything in the delta lowlands is flat, right up to the border with Burma (now called Myanmar). We finally ended up in Chittagong, where we were to spend a few days with my counterpart's relatives. I'd never drunk tea, and they served it very often. I gradually got used to it, especially when considering it replaced boiled water. I'd brush my teeth with tea! For someone from l'Orignal, it was quite an experience to sleep on a wood plank, surrounded by six or seven people. We quickly began to laugh together, the others especially, given my laborious Bengali. My new friends gave me the grand tour, lent me a sari and taught me some native dances. In short, I had a good time and slowly began to integrate. A few days later we arrived in our host community, Phultola, which means "flower plant."

J.H.: And your host family?

Lynn: It was located ten or fifteen minutes from the village, in the heart of the country. A rich family for country folk, but poor when compared to their village counterparts. People had to fetch water from a pond, where they also bathed. My parents were very old and not very talkative. However, I chatted a great deal with the children, the youngest of which was fourteen. My sisters read English, but couldn't speak it. This forced me to learn a little Bengali, enough to get along. And furthermore, we communicated a lot with gestures. It's astonishing.

J.H.: And the work experience?

Lynn: We were supposed to build a small community centre, but were short of materials. There weren't any bricks, nor anything else! A mason finally arrived and, while he built the walls, we made the floor by carrying clumps of mud. All morning. In the afternoon, along with Annie, a participant from Baie-Comeau, I tried to integrate into village life, for example, by helping a cook in a small restaurant.

J.H.: I realize the program with Bangladesh wasn't easy. In fact, there were so many organizational and logistical problems that Canada World Youth had to give up on that country. I hope we'll return some day. In any event, would you say you still learned something over there?

Lynn: A difficult program indeed, but terrific as well. I really got to like Bangladesh. On arrival I was, as mentioned earlier, an empty jar that was beginning to be filled. I learned about the importance of religion to daily life ... I learned patience ... Luckily, my Canadian parents taught me the value of an open mind. I learned that people, be they from Bangladesh or Canada, are essentially the same.

J.H.: How right you are!

Lynn: They may dress differently, have distinct customs and skin colour, but I realized Bengalis have the same aspirations we do. Listening to them, I discovered they spoke about the same things as Canadians: relatives, friends, food, clothing. People are basically the same.

J.H.: What did you do on your return to Canada?

Lynn: I admit that during the first year I had difficulty reintegrating our society, getting back on my feet, dreaming again, setting goals for myself. I then went to university for a year.

J.H.: In which discipline?

Lynn: International development, with the Scarborough Co-op program.

J.H.: You mustn't have been the only former Canada World Youth participant ...

Lynn: Among the twenty-five students who attended classes during the first year, only three or four weren't former participants.

J.H.: Things must have been pretty lively!

Lynn: We were perceived as a rather strange group on campus ... with our evenings dedicated to this or that country, our exotic dinners and slides ... I finished the year very successfully, but the idea dawned on me to study nutrition, a science that could really help the Third World. In fact, I've always been interested in nutrition, especially since my parents were concerned about it. One day, in mid-August, I was told I'd got a call from Canada World Youth. I was ecstatic to learn that the organization hadn't forgotten about me. I got another call from Daniel Renaud, who related the story about Operation Zaïre. But first, I had to talk it over with my parents.

J.H.: They must have been somewhat disconcerted?

Lynn: On the contrary. My father told me: "I'd hoped something like this would happen. I'm happy for you." Following the Toronto interview, the orientation camp and everything else, here I am in the heart of Zaïre.

J.H.: One more shock!

Lynn: Not really. What changed things considerably was that many Zaïrians speak French. I began to learn Tshiluba, the language spoken in our village, Mwene Ditu. I was told not to bother, that after three months I'd never again use Tshiluba. I promised myself never to say this about any language. Learning a new language is always a rewarding experience.

J.H.: What about your host family?

Lynn: My counterpart, Riba-Riba, and I share a wonderful mother. A widow with twelve children, half of whom still live at home ... as well as countless grandchildren! I get along really well with everybody in the village. Things are more laid back than in Bangladesh! We don't have to wear long sleeves, people like to dance, sit in small groups and chat over a beer. Even in Canada, people still find it strange for women to drink beer. Women here are astonished that I hardly consume any beer. Although Zaïre is a beautiful sun-drenched country, it does have numerous problems. For example, people are badly nourished. Food isn't scarce, but people don't know how to use it, nor how to transport it from one place to another. In Bangladesh, however, there weren't any transportation problems, there were plenty of buses to carry people and goods. And there are many diseases in Zaïre ...

J.H.: Despite everything, you adapted more easily to Zaïre than Bangladesh?

Lynn: Without a hitch. I never miss Canada. I love living over here, I adore Zaïre, a country I've been hearing about since I was very young.

J.H.: Over here, at least, you had a wonderful work experience: rebuilding the Mwene Ditu hospital, which had been abandoned for I don't know how many years.

Lynn: First, I spent a week whitewashing an old home for widows—the most extraordinary week in my life. Our widows had been more or less abandoned by society. They no longer had any family. Many suffered from goitre, others were crippled, and one was blind. They had to beg for food, though beggars are rare in this country. Their house, which I was whitewashing, looked like a Canadian barn—one we'd hesitate to put animals in. I wish I could've done much more for these women, but understood their society must take care of them. One day, our group dipped into its kitty to buy them food. They were very happy and thanked us every day with their smiles and *"mayos!"*

J.H.: Which means?

Lynn: "Hello! How are you!" They stretch out their hands to us, i.e., with both hands opened. Poor women who own absolutely nothing. They collected tiny pieces of paper ... which could make up a novel. I then worked in a kindergarten, with Ian, before joining the others at the hospital where we worked as "unskilled" labour, under the direction of tradesmen, such as carpenters and masons. Another way of integrating, another opportunity to think.

J.H.: This was important work, since the hospital will soon admit hundreds, even thousands of sick people ...

Lynn: That's right, numerous tuberculars and people with the sleeping disease, etc., will be treated in this hospital. The need is huge. One day I managed to go on a tour of the bush with a local doctor. We went to Kambaye, eighty kilometres away.

J.H.: In Africa, distance is calculated in time spent on the road instead of kilometres ...

Lynn: We left at 6:00 a.m. and reached Kambaye at around 10:00 a.m. The road wasn't very good and I got seriously rattled in the back of the vehicle. But I considered myself lucky to be going into the bush with a doctor, midwife and nurse. We screened and vaccinated people at a cattle farm, gave enemas and a crash course on nutrition. We came back at day's end, in the midst of a tropical storm. My heart was in my boots when we had to cross a river on a tiny ferry ...

J.H.: Throughout this commotion, you also had to work on presentations you were to make on returning to Canada?

Lynn: Of course.

J.H.: Do you know what territory you'll cover?

Lynn: Quebec and Ontario. This will be the most interesting and important part of the program for me. I'd done a few presentations here and there, in schools and social clubs, when I returned from Bangladesh. But this time things will be really well organized, with people awaiting us everywhere, with Katimavik groups among others. It'll be terrific. I'm really looking forward to it.

J.H.: You dream about it ...

Lynn: Oh! yes, I'm really excited. All participants are dreaming about it. But it'll only last six weeks, all good things come to an end.

J.H.: And you'll have to think about your future once again?

Lynn: I now have two years of Canada World Youth and one year of university under my belt. I started with an empty jar which is now overflowing! It's given me some ideas ... I mentioned earlier my interest in nutrition. I now have an even keener interest in this discipline, especially as it applies to the Third World.

J.H.: The jar is overflowing with plans and dreams ...

Lynn: I think that's what makes up a human being: the ability to dream, to make plans for the future, have ideas to improve the living conditions of others. I don't imagine all those people in the Third World should have a car, television and fridge, but I believe we must help them fulfil their basic needs, and improve their quality of life. Moreover, they've preserved values we've lost—in the area of human interaction, for example. Since they don't have telephones and TVs, they're still able to sit under the moonlight and chat. Whereas people in Canada suffer from a shortage of human contact.

J.H.: So, you want to change the world?

Lynn: There was a time I wanted to change everything. But now I'd be happy to change a tiny corner of the planet, to influence the lives of a few people. That's all I want. Even in Canada, there's room for a lot of development: there are still too many poor and undernourished people. And we have enough people able to improve the lot of the needy. For my part, I want to be involved with the Third World, that's where I'll be able to help improve things, even if only a tiny bit.

J.H.: I get the feeling you love our Third World brothers and sisters a great deal ...

Lynn: Yes, absolutely. People in this county are without masks: we can see their heart!

Lynn Lalonde's Comments on the Canadian Tour

What struck me most during this tour, is the amazing number of teachers who completely dedicate themselves to educating the next generation. They have a heartfelt desire to sensitize their students to international-development problems, to make them understand how this concerns them individually, and how they can play a part. Many of the teachers I met in Quebec and Ontario were terrific people, as are many of those we met in each of the communities visited.

I didn't realize so many people of that quality existed: profoundly dedicated folks. This really touched me.

Lynn Lalonde Ten Years Later

Following the Canadian tour, Lynn attended McGill University where she obtained a bachelor of sciences degree in nutrition. She worked in the community health field in Terrace, British Columbia, then travelled to Eastern Europe, Turkey and Greece in 1991. After returning to Canada, she worked for three years as a nutritional advisor with the Eastern Ontario Health Office. She went back to school in 1994, and obtained a bachelor of education degree from the University of Ottawa.

Lynn has been married since 1992. She lives in the Thousand Islands and teaches in an immersion program in Kingston, Ontario ... and still dreams of travelling!

5.
Ian Bell

From Newfoundland to Sri Lanka

Ian Bell, a great environmental advocate, ten years later.

Ian: I'm from Corner Brook, Newfoundland, but was born in Halifax, where my father was attending university. I returned to Newfoundland when I was six-months old.

J.H.: Halifax didn't have time to spoil you ...

Ian: I consider myself a real Newfoundlander! I went to grade school and high school there, and studied two years at Memorial University's regional college in Corner Brook. I was still quite young ...

J.H.: What did you study at university?

Ian: A little of everything. I was very confused during the first two years. I didn't really know what I wanted to do. I was only sixteen when I entered university. It's hard to know what you want at that age.

J.H.: You had no idea?

Ian: Not really. I knew I wanted to do something worthwhile with my life. But what exactly was the big question mark.

J.H.: When did you first hear about Canada World Youth?

Ian: I heard about it way back, from my cousin, Dave Bell, who'd done the program with Honduras about ten years ago. I remember this very clearly because his Honduran counterpart spent a few months with his family. And then, years later, when I was at university, a former participant with the Bolivian program, Adrian Kehoe, came to talk about his experience to our geography class. I was completely enthralled by what he said, and sent in an application immediately. I ended up on the waiting list! So I went off to study at the University of Waterloo, in Ontario. When I returned home for the Christmas holidays, a large brown envelope awaited me with an application and a letter urging me to fill it out. I got the much-awaited reply before year's end: I'd been accepted! I was jumping for joy!

J.H.: Had you indicated which continent you preferred?

Ian: I'd mentioned Asia.

J.H.: Why? Were you already dreaming of Asia in Corner Brook?

Ian: I don't know ... It seemed like the ends of the earth, an interesting place, surely ... I picked Asia, though I could've chosen any other continent. I ended up with the Sri Lankan program.

J.H.: And where did the Canadian part of the program take place?

Ian: In Nova Scotia's Annapolis Valley.

J.H.: A stone's throw from your home.

Ian: That's right. I was a little disappointed at being so close.

J.H.: You'd have preferred British Columbia ...

Ian: Naturally!

J.H.: ... or Quebec even?

Ian: Quebec, of course! Anyway, I ended up in a village barely twenty miles from my uncle's farm! So I knew the Annapolis valley quite well. The Canadian part of the program was nonetheless very rewarding.

J.H.: It must have been even more so for your Sri Lankan counterpart.

Ian: His name was Gerald D.K.C. Premanath, a brilliant fellow from a rural Sri Lanka. He'd done excellent organizational work for his local youth organization, the National Youth Service Council, which explains why he'd been chosen for the program.

He was extremely thrilled about it. A very good person, with whom I got along very well. He really got along with the host family.

J.H.: A farm family, no doubt?

Ian: Our parents weren't typical farmers. They'd bought the farm four years earlier; the father was a teacher. He taught in the winter and ran the farm in the summer.

J.H.: What kind of family?

Ian: Oh, a wonderful and very interesting family. The father was called Doug Joyce. He'd come from Britain as a child with his family. They'd lived in Halifax at first. A really good guy with whom I got along really well. Very bright. On top of being a teacher, he was a hard worker and a good carpenter. He could do anything on the farm. And he had a good sense of humour. My counterpart and I worked very hard, but it was worthwhile with a man of that calibre ...

J.H.: A large family?

Ian: Not really: the father, mother and two children. When we arrived, there was also a young Quebec girl participating in an exchange program with Doug's daughter. And a girl from Sudan who was studying at Acadia University, and spending her vacation with the family. This was all quite interesting.

J.H.: Indeed. So after three months you had to leave that wonderful family and head to Sri Lanka ...

Ian: At other end of the world! Very exciting ...

J.H.: So tell me about the other end of the world ...

Ian: Sri Lanka's incredible! After Corner Brook ... My group settled in the northern part of the country, near Anuradapura, the former capital. An area where agriculture and tourism are economic mainstays. My counterpart and I lived with a host family in the centre of a small village called Katakalliyawa. Once again, I was fortunate to be with an exceptional family. Both parents were university graduates. The father spoke perfect English, besides the other two Sri Lankan languages. He had a profound knowledge of his country, which allowed us to learn a lot. Life in the village was really enjoyable; it didn't take me long to feel very comfortable there.

J.H.: And what a beautiful country!

Ian: Unbelievably beautiful.

J.H.: What did you think of Sri Lankans?

Ian: The people are very close to one another. They're very close to the environment, their community, their work and life in general. They know how to share. They're very cordial, always ready to talk to you or invite you for dinner. Very open people thrilled about welcoming Canadian youths, those young white people who'd come to live and work with them in their village. Sri Lanka had long been a British colony; let's just say the villagers were used to whites that were a little different from us. I'm sure we managed to change their impression of the Western world. It was a very valuable human experience.

J.H.: What kind of work did you do in the village?

Ian: We worked really hard on building a road. It was strenuous physical labour: digging, carrying dirt, working with local tools, the *manatoo* and *udela*. But adaptation problems and the sweltering heat prevented us from working more than four days a week, and six or seven hours a day. An extremely intense experience: a new way of living and eating, a new environment.

J.H.: Did you make numerous friends?

Ian: In Nova Scotia at first. Elizabeth, the girl from Sudan, became a very good friend. We write quite often. I also stayed in touch with my family in the Annapolis Valley. I stayed with them for a few days at the end of the program.

J.H.: And in Sri Lanka?

Ian: I made plenty of friends in the village. Naturally, the father of the host family was my best friend. There was a family in the village I was particularly close to. They were well-off rice farmers. They lived a kilometre from my house, but I'd often visit. This was at the beginning of the rice season and I became particularly interested in the irrigation of ricefields. I followed the entire process, from the day the rain began, to when farmers started plowing, spreading chemical fertilizer, right through to the planting of young rice clusters. Unfortunately, we left before harvest, but only just.

J.H.: Are you still in touch with friends you made during the program?

Ian: Absolutely. I actually got a letter barely two weeks ago.

J.H.: In Zaïre?

Ian: Exactly. From Ann Lynagh, a participant with my former group who lives in Alberta. I regularly correspond with three or four others. Do you remember when our group called on you at the Senate in Ottawa? I spent the evening with one of the girls that had been in the Sri Lankan program. At the end of this program, I plan to travel through Canada and visit all my friends along the way.

J.H.: Following your two Canada World Youth programs, I take it you have friends everywhere.

Ian: All over the country, from the west coast to the east. I'm really looking forward to seeing all of them again.

J.H.: So you returned to Corner Brook following the Sri Lankan program ...

Ian: It was very strange ... Suddenly coming back, changing environments from one day to the next. What struck me most wasn't so much the cold as the radically different atmosphere of Western society.

J.H.: What were your plans for the future at that point?

Ian: Nothing specific, save returning to the University of Waterloo. I wasn't exactly thrilled, but it offered something interesting and positive.

J.H.: In what discipline?

Ian: Environmental studies, with a major in geography. But I wasn't really sure where all this would lead. I finished my second year; after that, you have to decide on a particular option.

J.H.: Canada World Youth would again delay your decision ...

Ian: Norma Scott, from the Atlantic regional office, called me and I realized I had a good chance of going to Zaïre. I was accepted shortly thereafter. Since I was one of three unilingual anglophone participants, I had to be in Montreal before the others to undergo a five-day French immersion. Quite an immersion! I didn't speak a single word of French at the time, though I'd long felt I should learn the language. There's no reason for me not to speak French. I live in a bilingual country. Many people speak the two languages, so it's obviously possible. You have to make the effort. I was really intimidated at first ...

J.H.: Where did this five-day immersion take place?

Ian: With Annik Lafortune's family; she's one of the francophone participants in our group. I studied a great deal. Both Annik and the francophone environment helped me a lot.

J.H.: But five days, even with Annik, hardly seems enough.

Ian: Even with Annik ...

J.H.: And you'd be living numerous months in French, since Zaïre is a francophone country.

Ian: So I realized I'd absolutely have to learn French, failing which I wouldn't get much from the program.

J.H.: I can see you succeeded.

Ian: I've come a long way. I understand quite a bit, and can hold a conversation. Zaïre is a great place to learn French. It's fun just to go out and talk with people. And it's not intimidating; everyone comes up to you to talk. I wasn't afraid of answering them, even if my French was still shaky.

J.H.: So here we are in Zaïre.

Ian: I got a shock on arriving, like everyone else. A shock to the senses because of the heat, vegetation, the new environment. But I quickly became very comfortable, especially when I reached our village.

J.H.: Mwene Ditu.

Ian: A word meaning "people of the forest," or "village in the forest."

J.H.: Or what's left of it.

Ian: It's nearly disappeared over the last twenty years. It's a serious problem. Several other things have also disappeared: elephants, many other types of animals ... and the Belgians!

J.H.: Do you remember the first day with your host family?

Ian: I remember the first night. We arrived late; the entire family had been awaiting me for hours. My mother showed me my room and the rest of the house before serving me a large plate of rice and beans, a choice dish in these parts. Zaïrian cooking is very simple and based on flour. One vegetable per day. Food isn't that important to me. I have a good appetite and eat my fill. I'm always touched to see my mother devote so much time and effort to preparing meals. And I know that it's excellent food by Zaïrian standards. Our family eats three meals a day, which isn't the case for everyone around here, to say the least. Many people are lucky to eat once a day.

J.H.: Tell me a little about your host family.

Ian: I consider myself fortunate to have such an agreeable family. A traditional and extremely Catholic family. Their not wealthy by village standards, but neither are they poor. They manage to maintain a relatively high standard of living by working very hard and using all the tricks imaginable to earn a little money. The father died five or six years ago. Only the mother and one of her daughters remain, along with some grandchildren.

J.H.: How do they earn a living if the father's dead?

Ian: They own the small house. The kitchen is located in a house beside the first one; they rent a small apartment in it. The family owns another house which it rents, as well as a field it cultivates somewhere. And the mother runs a few "small businesses."

J.H.: What kind of "small businesses?"

Ian: For example, she brews a traditional alcohol drink, a sort of corn-based beer. It's rather amusing that such a profoundly religious woman sells alcohol, but she knows it's profitable ... and the family has to live! She allows the corn to ferment until it sprouts, and then brews the beer.

J.H.: Is it good?

Ian: Not really. It's doesn't hold a candle to Canadian beer, but it's palatable. Not in large quantities! So my mother sells beer and produce from her field. As well, many of her children attended university and help her out somewhat financially.

J.H.: It's unusual for a widow to be able to send children to university.

Ian: No doubt, but our mother knows all the tricks. She's learned to survive.

J.H.: Did you have many friends in the village?

Ian: Scads. The people are friendly and love talking to you. And since I have to practice French ...

J.H.: But the villagers don't all speak French ...

Ian: More than you might think. Those who reached high school speak French. Anyway, all my Zaïrian friends speak it. I'm always amazed to see these simple people, who have few means, speak French, as well as their own language—Tshiluba, in this case—and often a third, even a fourth language. What amazes me even more is that they want to learn English. Many people come up to me in the street to try their English: "Hello, mister. How are you?" They'd really like to learn.

J.H.: Why?

Ian: That's the question I've often asked them: "You speak French—your national language—and Tshiluba, your mother tongue. Why the devil do you want to learn English?" They study English in school as third language. Besides, people in Mwene Ditu have plenty of spare time and always want to learn something new. They're extremely anxious to learn ...

J.H.: What about your work project?

Ian: I spent the first six or eight weeks building wells, an excellent project. It was hard work but we learned a lot about building wells and a lot about the villagers who were very involved in the project. We'd show up at the site, and the local chief was already there, with a schedule for the day and ten or so men ready to help us. Not to mention the women who helped as well. There were many curious bystanders who'd watch and ask questions. Near the end, the group leader, Sylvie, asked us to help rebuild the hospital: it was to be inaugurated in three weeks and a lot still had to be done. I was happy to pitch in.

J.H.: What kind of work did you do at the hospital?

Ian: Masonry, painting, carpentry. We built the roof, covered it with sheet metal and panelled the ceiling with plywood. I even cut glass, which was quite an interesting experience. Unfortunately, I broke about thirty large panes while learning ...

J.H.: Scott Elliott told me the same story. Quite a disaster!

Ian: But everything was ready for the official inauguration ceremony, that took place this morning!

J.H.: Terrific! So you'll be able to leave with a clear conscience on Sunday.

Ian: Thinking about leaving saddens me profoundly. There would've been a lot more to learn, so many things to do. I could spend months here, even a year. But I'm also thrilled about the grand tour awaiting us back in Canada.

J.H.: Which region will you cover?

Ian: I'll first do presentations in the Atlantic provinces: one week in Nova Scotia, one week in New Brunswick, a few days in Prince Edward Island, and then three weeks in Quebec, where I'll be working in French. This really excites me.

J.H.: Who'd have thought this possible barely three months ago? What will you tell all those Canadians?

Ian: We'll try to expose them to a new culture and give them a new perspective on Africa. We'll talk about all those preconceived ideas making the rounds. We'll introduce them to the reality of Africa. We'll have done a lot if we manage to get people thinking and interest them in issues related to development in Africa and elsewhere.

J.H.: And following those painstaking six weeks?

Ian: I'll go back to Newfoundland where I've got a summer job lined up at Memorial University. In the fall, I'll resume studying geography at the University of Waterloo, with a major in resource development. And, if possible, I'd like to study for a semester in another country, perhaps even Sri Lanka, since I know the University of Waterloo has programs with many foreign universities.

J.H.: The two programs you did with Canada World Youth will no doubt help you ...

Ian: No other educational experience compares! And I'll try to obtain some credits.

J.H.: Other former participants have obtained some from their university.

Ian: Perhaps a credit in Third World geography, one in sociology and another in French ...

J.H.: What about a final word?

Ian: I'd only like to say that Canada World Youth programs provide absolutely fabulous experience! It certainly was for me, and I'm sure it will be for anyone wondering about life and seeking to discover himself. To really understand who you are, it's very important to get away from everything you know: your community, family, habits ... Immerse yourself into group living, and travel to a new country where you have to rediscover everything and fend for yourself. The best way to understand yourself is by trying to understand others.

Ian Bell's Comments on the Canadian Tour

We left the tropical bliss of Zaïre in early 1986 and returned to the ice and snow of Canada. The temperature in Montreal was -20°C ... something Zaïrian participants had to get used to, along with Western culture. We got warmed up at Montreal's YMCA, then headed to our countryside retreat to plan our six-week tour of Canada.

The tour would allow us to share our Zaïrian experience with Canadians. We worked in teams of three (two Canadians and one Zaïrian), using Zaïre as an example of a typical developing country. We'd produced a slide show and presentation directed at whoever would listen. My group travelled for six weeks throughout Nova Scotia, Prince Edward Island, New Brunswick and eastern Quebec.

I remember an endless stream of classrooms, community centres and church basements. We made as many as six or seven presentations a day, travelled in a cramped minibus and slept in a different place each night. I remember struggling in my very poor French, trying to share my experience and give people an idea about the life of the average Zaïrian.

I don't know if our audiences learned anything, but I sure did!

Looking back, I recall the experience was intense and rewarding. It prompted me to continually challenge myself—something I still do. And if asked to do it again, I'd hop the next plane to Montreal at the drop of a hat!

Ian Bell Ten Years Later

Following his experience in Zaïre, Ian worked for a year in Alberta and then returned to the University of Waterloo to complete a bachelor's degree in environmental studies. He spent four months in northern Pakistan doing work on his thesis with the Snow and Ice Hydrology project. He returned to Newfoundland in 1988, and now works with the Water Resources Management Division at the Department of the Environment.

Ian and his wife have two children and live in beautiful Corner Brook on the west coast of Newfoundland. While Ian remains interested in international development, he devotes most of his volunteer time to promoting local development. He was involved in organizing a very successful symposium on the environment and is currently vice-chair of the Corner Brook Stream Development Corporation. This corporation seeks to develop green space along Corner Brook Stream for recreational and educational use. In short, Ian is fully involved in a wide variety of projects related to development and the environment.

6.
Carole Godin

From Quebec to Ecuador

Carole and her little Zaïrian sister, Suzanne.

Carole: I'm from a small village near Quebec City called Les Écureuils. I grew up in a large family of seven children, which I left when I was seventeen-years old. My father is a former member of Parliament and civil servant who became a farmer; this allowed me to get acquainted with the running of the farm, where I worked as a teenager. Following high school, I headed to a CEGEP in Quebec City to study dental hygiene, a discipline which really didn't correspond to my aspirations. In fact, I really didn't have a clue about what I wanted to do with my future. That's when I should've joined Katimavik, or at least taken a break to really determine what I wanted to do. But I felt pressure from my family to continue with CEGEP. They went on about my having to "find a steady job ... " Following a year of confusion and inner searching, I decided on a complete change of direction. I headed to a small CEGEP in La Pocatière to study humanities, i.e., psychology, geography and sociology. I enjoyed it. I met people interested in nature and joined an outdoor club whose members were very concerned with the environment. I'd swim and practice ballet-jazz at the club. Since I was rather far from home, I didn't return to see my parents on weekends; so I explored the La Pocatière region, which is beautiful. There were plenty of lovely villages to discover with my friends from the outdoor club: Saint-Pascal, Saint-Roch-des-Aulnaies, Kamouraska ...

J.H.: Something to make you forget about dental hygiene?

Carole: Oh, yes! But after a year in La Pocatière, I got the urge to return to Quebec City, to be closer to my parents. So I ended up at the CEGEP in Limoilou, which I'd been told had excellent geography courses. Classes were indeed very stimulating! I also worked a little at the CEGEP library and daycare centre during the school year, and continued with the ballet-jazz I'd started to learn in La Pocatière. So I finished CEGEP without really knowing what I'd be doing in university. That's when Canada World Youth accepted me: at last! time to take a break and travel, something I'd been dreaming about. I was told in June that I'd take part in the program with Ecuador, which was to begin in August. So I had a few months of free time. Since I'd taken clown lessons on weekends, I was able to organize a small clown troop with a bunch of friends.

J.H.: I don't really see you as a clown ...

Carole: There are two sides to my personality: the very serious part ... and the other one!

J.H.: You had to show your serious side for Canada World Youth to accept you. A clown may not have been so well received!

Carole: I'm not sure; there are quite a few clowns in our group!

J.H.: Really? But you were a real clown for a number of months ...

Carole: A very fulfilling experience. We produced a show in Quebec City, taking care of everything: publicity, negotiating contracts, etc. Performing before various audiences gave me greater self confidence. And then the Canada World Youth program began in August in Ontario.

J.H.: Where exactly?

Carole: In North Bay, a city of fifty thousand people where a variety of work projects awaited us in a women's centre, a museum, a YMCA, schools, etc. I worked in an art gallery with Roman, my Ecuadoran counterpart. He was the source of most of our problems during the program. In fact, I'm the one who'd chosen him, more for the challenge than for any affinity I may have had with him. I felt very self confident during the orientation camp, and observed this boy with whom the others had trouble working. He was truculent and rather selfish.

J.H.: So you chose him anyway. For the challenge.

Carole: That's right.

J.H.: You told yourself: "I'll take him if no one else will!"

Carole: No, not really. Roman was bright and had interesting ideas, despite his difficult character. So I told myself: "He seems open and I think we can build something interesting together." I had many letdowns. Perhaps because I started out with the idea of changing him.

J.H.: Unfortunately, we always want to change those we love!

Carole: Those we love? I don't really think I loved him! We finally managed to get along, later in Ecuador. But the beginning was extremely difficult.

J.H.: Naturally, you both lived with the same family in North Bay ...

Carole: It wasn't easy for him, since it was a single-parent family: the mother, who wasn't often at home, and her fourteen-year-old daughter. Roman and I worked in an art gallery with Sharon, the mother. We'd often return home in the evenings without her, since she was very busy. Roman had never been away from his family before, and thought it sad to return to a house where nobody awaited us. The intense family spirit found in Ecuador was lacking. Moreover, it was a new experience for him to be in a family consisting only of girls ... who didn't speak the same language as he! Sharon had been to Mexico and knew a little Spanish, which really pleased Roman. We had a lot of trouble getting along because we were so different! I must admit I was rather individualistic back then, whereas Roman enjoyed group living and sports. I realized, following the program, that I hadn't really tried to help him. For example, I'd write letters as he loitered and say: "Come on, Roman, listen to music, read a book, write!" That was a little rough. I'd have had to play some sports with him more often, things like that. At one point, he became more independent and would venture out alone to visit his friends. I thought this was fine since it would help him discover his independence. Truth is, however, we weren't very good counterparts.

J.H.: Did you speak English back then?

Carole: I was completely hopeless during the first week, but learned rather quickly. I had a good base, having done a six-week immersion in Halifax.

J.H.: What about Roman?

Carole: He spoke only Spanish, which added to our problems. He didn't seem motivated to learn English. I could've learned Spanish from him; but we were in Ontario and I decided to concentrate on English.

J.H.: Following those difficult months, the whole team left for Ecuador ...

Carole: Total joy! The first time I'd ever left Canada, and I was heading to a country in the south! Roman and I lived with a good host family on a plantation where coffee, cocoa beans and oranges were grown. The father had been dead for two years. The mother and her son were the only ones left, the remainder of her eleven children having moved out. The son ran the plantation. His style rather resembled Roman's, but I really got along with him. His name was ... Victor Hugo!

J.H.: Victor Hugo?

Carole: Isn't that a great name? Though he shared some of Roman's values, he was much more open. For example: Roman would often tell me: "Why talk about it? That's how I am, that's how things are in Ecuador, and you can't change this." Whereas Victor Hugo would say: What are things like in Canada? How does this or that work? Oh, how different! How strange!" In short, we had good conversations. We didn't always agree, but he was never negative and discussions always ended on a positive note. When Roman realized I got along with Victor Hugo, he mellowed out and became more obliging. We really had nothing in common: I was somewhat feminist and he was rather macho. Nonetheless, we finally managed to get along fairly well.

J.H.: You finally changed him ...

Carole: A little I think. I regret not having kept in touch with him. I'd really like to know what became of him. He kept telling me during the program that he wanted to go into the army, which really disappointed me. We'd had a study day in Ontario concerning militarism and all the problems it causes. I was especially angered that he'd chosen that course and told him so. He'd answer: "Things in Ecuador aren't like they are here. Finding a job isn't easy." So security is what he was seeking. I was really hard on Roman at the beginning of the program. I became more tolerant in the long run, since I'd been exposed to other values. I finally accepted differences. Though I'd previously given little importance to the family, I discovered the values attached to it in Ecuador, and how much I needed them. In Ecuador, the large house was always filled with people. Plantation workers replaced absent children. A large extended family ... And all these people continually asked me about Canada.

J.H.: In Spanish, of course. How did you manage?

Carole: I'd begun to learn Spanish with Roman, who didn't speak English. However, since people in this part of Ecuador speak very quickly, I didn't understand a thing at first.

J.H.: In which part of the country were you?

Carole: In Caluma, a coastal village in the province of Bolivar. Three hours from Guayaquil, the city where we sold coffee and cocoa beans. Travelling to it allowed me to see some of the country. I went to stay with Roman's family over the Christmas holidays, in Gualaceo, near the city of Cuenca. An exquisite region, and very different from the coast, with an almost European look. Its people are more relaxed and speak slowly, which allowed me to understand them better than people in Caluma. Folks in Gualaceo were even amazed I managed so well in Spanish, after barely one month.

J.H.: You worked on a plantation in Caluma?

Carole: That's right, two days a week, in the cocoa-bean dryers. We also worked two days a week at the school, where I taught English. I also did a little activity leading with groups ...

J.H.: The clown surfaces again ...

Carole: Precisely! I did a few tricks, played the flute, taught French songs to the children. It was great!

J.H.: I don't doubt it. I imagine you must have had some group projects as well ...

Carole: We participated in group work days, the *mingas*, as they were called. One day, a special task awaited us in San Pablo de Pita, a village also hosting Canada World Youth participants. A bridge was under construction, and the road leading to it had to be built. The elevated road had to be protected from heavy rains, so we reinforced its edges with stones encased in wire netting.

J.H.: We haven't talked about the shock you may have had when you reached Ecuador.

Carole: I didn't really get a shock when I landed in Quito, the capital, which is really beautiful. Of course, we were struck by the tropical vegetation, the intense heat and all the people walking along the roads. The shock was greater, especially for Ecuadoran participants, when we reached the small village of Caluma. Most were from relatively well-off families and had rarely ventured beyond large cities: Quito, Cuenca or Guayaquil. They were completely oblivious to their own country's rural reality.

J.H.: Canada World Youth often helps young people from the Third World discover development problems in their own back yard.

Carole: Even in Canada, we realized that Ecuadoran participants disagreed when, during a study day, we talked about illiteracy and other development problems in their country. They got angry: "That's not true! It's not how you say it is!" They even argued with the group leader, although he knew the situation in Ecuador very well. They got a shock on reaching Caluma, being exposed to poverty for the first time in their lives. Some of them, for example, refused to live with a humble family in San Pablo de Pita. This prompted serious arguments between Canadians and Ecuadorans. We called them spoiled children! During a meeting, one Ecuadoran participant tossed out: "It's easy for you Canadians. It's as though you were camping here for a few months!"

J.H.: Yet they finally managed to adapt ...

Carole: Yes, and they were happy in the end. We'd had an orientation camp in Quito, with former Ecuadoran participants, before settling in our villages. They related the experiences they'd had during previous programs. We asked: "What part of the program did you prefer? Which was most rewarding: the Canadian or Ecuadoran phase?" Without fail, Ecuadorans answered: "The Ecuadoran phase," since they'd discovered a previously unknown aspect of their country. Most of the Ecuadorans were from relatively well-off families and easily adapted to life in Canada. It's when they arrived in the small villages of their country that they had to give up comfort and make compromises.

J.H.: I once visited your villages: they're very poor.

Carole: Caluma was more or less okay; but San Pablo de Pita was really poor. That's where the strongest participants were sent, those having no problems with their counterparts. The others settled in Caluma.

J.H.: How did the departure go?

Carole: It was heartrending. I would've liked to stay longer, but this was impossible. Basically, I'm glad we left, because I'd probably never have come back!

I'd adapted very well to Caluma and my host family. I felt we could've achieved more, and done more concrete things; however, we had to live at the pace of the local people, and three months is rather short to complete any project.

J.H.: What did you do after returning to Canada?

Carole: I had the intention of registering at Montreal's circus school ...

J.H.: Dearest clown!

Carole: ... but I wasn't sure I'd be able to afford it. So I decided to work in a summer camp for the handicapped throughout June and July. As for September, I'd have to wait and see. What a discovery the handicapped were! I learned a great deal and had a lot of fun with them. A very rewarding experience in human terms. We did skits, swam and camped together. In July, Terry Preston phoned me from Canada World Youth's regional office in Toronto. She was looking for former participants to help with the orientation camp for new recruits in Maple Lake. I accepted and became the language co-ordinator with a group of Canadian—and Ecuadoran!—participants.

J.H.: You certainly had a few things to tell them ...

Carole: Strangely enough, I felt closer to the Ecuadorans than to the Canadians ... It's easy to see I've come a long way! Three weeks later, Terry Preston asked me: "Did you hear about the special program with Zaïre that Canada World Youth is organizing this year?" I was interested, of course. A few days later, Philippe Mougeot, the co-ordinator for the new program phoned and suggested I head to Toronto for an interview. I was accepted! Afterwards, one of the group leaders, Daniel Renaud, asked if I could take in Yvonne and Sue—two anglophone participants with the special program who needed a quick French immersion before heading to Zaïre. They spent a few days with my family in Les Écureuils, which allowed me to get to know them. I gave them a tour of Quebec City and we then headed to Canada World Youth's Montreal office. You were there, apparently, looking forward to our arrival. We joined the other participants at the Saint-Liguori orientation camp that night. Group living once again. We expend a lot of energy building relationships, friendships even, only to have distance take them away from us afterwards.

J.H.: Some of those friendships are lasting; former participants still see one another often, even after many years ...

Carole: Oh! yes, I know I'll see some participants again, even if they live far away. Thanks to the program, we have friends to visit throughout the country.

J.H.: In the meantime, you'd head to Kinshasa to make new friends.

Carole: We stayed there only a few days before heading to Mwene Ditu, where we are now. The day following our arrival, we were spread out into the various host families. Mine is terrific and we get along famously. A family with eleven children, though only seven still live at home.

J.H.: That makes eight, with you ...

Carole: That's it. Young children: the oldest girls are fifteen and seventeen years old. Both of them are like counterparts to me: I share my room with them, we go to the market together, prepare meals ... and have a lot of fun! I have very few communication problems with the family, since the father and three oldest children speak French. The mother doesn't speak the language, but understands it. We sing together. I've brought a book of songs and we sing in the evenings as we prepare meals. They now know numerous Quebec songs. And they've taught me traditional dances from the region. A wonderful swap which gave me a lot of pleasure. When I dance their dances, they tell me: "Look, you're a real Zaïrian!" The father is rather learned and we talk a great deal. He relates Zaïre's history, the problems that followed independence, etc. He asks me to tell him about what I observed during the day and whether anything seemed strange to me. He then explains these things to me, by putting them in their context. He takes a lot of interest in my adaptation to the food, the lifestyle, the habits.

J.H.: Did you get used to *fufu*?

Carole: Adapting to the lack of variety wasn't easy. We eat *fufu* once or twice a day! It's made with corn flour and manioc and resembles uncooked pie pastry. Absolutely without flavour. I don't like it very much, but have no choice since it's the basic food.

J.H.: Still, you don't eat *fufu* exclusively ...

Carole: It's generally served with two other dishes. We often eat cooked manioc leaves flavoured with tomatoes. It looks like spinach. The other dish is goat meat, or fish that's either dried or fresh. It hardly varies from one day to the next. On special occasions, rice, potatoes or beans are served.

J..H.: Is *fufu* nourishing?

Carole: Not really. It's poor in vitamins, but quickly gives you the impression of being sated. Zaïrians roll it into tiny balls and swallow it whole. Everyone laughs at me, since I chew my *fufu*.

J.H.: What other family custom impressed you?

Carole: People spend all their time in groups. I found this difficult at first: I'm still somewhat of a loner, though much less than last year. So I need time to write or read. At first, I felt a little guilty whenever I'd retire to my room. People would worry: "What's going on? Is Carole sick?" And I'd tell myself that staying in a group was rather futile if we didn't do anything together. But I've changed. I now take pleasure sitting with the family and understand the comfort they get from being together. Children are very important to Zaïrian families and are the centre of attention. They sing songs, do recitations or sit on our knees and babble. Even if they don't speak French, it's always easy to communicate with them. I was particularly close to my sister Suzanne. I'd accompany her to the pre-school where I worked three days a week with Éric, another Canadian participant. We prepared educational material for the children, gave lessons and sang songs with them. This brought me closer to Suzanne.

J.H.: Did you visit other families from the neighbourhood?

Carole: My next-door neighbours host another participant, Yvonne, and her counterpart Khoni. So we inevitably see a lot of each other. They come over to my place to chat, I go over to theirs to dance. Their whole family came over to visit mine at Christmas. I really like Éric's family and often call on them. In fact, it's really easy to integrate into this village, because the people spontaneously come over to talk to us. It's even easier than with a Canadian family. Villagers I don't know drop by the house and ask if they can visit with me: "We'd like to talk about Canada ..." It's okay, when I'm up to it ... They're especially interested in Canada's social life: family, marriage, education.

J.H.: Your work project surely wasn't limited to the pre-school.

Carole: I spent my time between working there, building wells and rebuilding the hospital. At first, participants were spread over the three projects. We finally concluded it would be more interesting for participants to rotate from one project to the next, thereby multiplying their experiences. So I went from the school to the hospital, then to the wells, until we all had to concentrate on the hospital, to complete the work before inauguration day.

J.H.: You did terrific work on the hospital.

Carole: I'm really happy about this ... A real development project. As were, indeed, the wells. Perhaps work at the school wasn't as useful ... I found it rather frustrating at first. Discipline is very strict and certain things seemed unjust to me. For example, one slogan said: "Who speaks Tshiluba?" And the children would answer: "An ignoramus!" I thought it unjust to treat the local language in this way, even if it was to prompt children to learn French. In difficult cases, children are still caned.

J.H.: I can't imagine you hitting a child ...

Carole: In fact, I protested when others did. They absolutely couldn't understand my reaction. People thought this was rather funny ... There was this little girl rejected by all the others. I believe she had psychological problems of some kind. The children called her a witch, they rejected her all the more considering she had a great need for attention. The children would shout: "Get out of here, witch! Go on, leave!" The little girl refused to leave and got pushed around. One day, I took her hand and told her to follow me into my classroom. She immediately began to show progress: she raised her hand, came to the blackboard and answered questions. I was really happy, until she began to regress once again. She took her liberties with me: I'd spoiled her too much. I then understood that education wasn't my vocation! Especially in a school devoid of resources like that one. For example, children between three and four years of age are squeezed together, five to a bench. They'd inevitably squabble, hit one another and cry. So how can they pay attention to what's going on at the front?

J.H.: On top of spending your time between three work projects, you also had to concentrate on your presentation for the Canadian tour ...

Carole: We began with nothing. We had information but were basically at a loss on how to present it. After working really hard, we got results I'm rather pleased with. It's rather theatrical, but we at least managed to explain development in Africa, based on our experience in Zaïre. What I wanted to accomplish in Ecuador, I achieved here.

J.H.: You now have a basic idea of what development means ...

Carole: It's a beginning, but I still have lots to learn. I'm very eager to undertake the Canadian tour, and share my experience with others.

J.H.: You'll be doing this for at least six weeks.

Carole: Exactly. And if I really enjoy it, I'd like to continue in that direction. Study development and group animation in Montreal. I'll mention this to Luc, who'll be my group leader during the Canadian tour. He's also done development education.

J.H.: You'll tour Ontario?

Carole: And Quebec. Two weeks in French and the rest in English. That's another challenge. I'm able to communicate with people, even in groups, but in front of a class, it's another story.

J.H.: It must be exciting to think you'll communicate with hundreds, even thousands, of Canadians ...

Carole: It's really great! Like a dream ... And everything will be perfectly organized: transportation, accommodations, everything. There'll be people everywhere to welcome and listen to us.

J.H.: Like the Katimavik groups with whom you'll share accommodations in some communities.

Carole: That's also great! I met a few Katimavik participants last year, but have known about the program for many years, since my parents have often been a host family. When I saw participants in the streets of Les Écureuils, I told my mother: "Mom, it would be great to have Katimavik participants at home!" My parents are very open and have been hosting participants since then, even anglophones. At first, my mother would say: "Since Carole isn't here and I don't speak English, it would be difficult to host anglophones." She's now used to it and welcomes participants from everywhere.

J.H.: Do you know who'll be on your team during the tour?

Carole: Lynn and Mangando. Lynn is a Franco-Ontarian and Mangando is Zaïrian. I really get along with him; he has a good sense of humour, asks the right questions and has an excellent analytical mind. A Zaïrian with whom I believe our Canadian audiences will have no difficulty communicating. I'm really proud of the Zaïrian participants. They're very aware of the happenings in their country, and don't only focus on the good side of things. They understand the purpose of the tour, and realize they'll be the centre of attention and asked more questions than Canadian participants. And all this interests them to the highest degree.

J.H.: What do you think you'll do following the six-week tour?

Carole: I'll quietly return home to rest for a few weeks. Make maple syrup with my parents, go horseback riding, visit a few friends. And then find a job in the Quebec City area, or in Montreal, and work until September. Perhaps return to the summer camp for the handicapped ... A year over here, another over there ... I want to improve my English and might live in an anglophone province ... I might study group animation at the University of Quebec in Montreal, with development education, naturally, topping the list ... Or perhaps spend a year in Quito to improve my Spanish ... What's certain, for the moment at least, is that I don't want to spend three years in a university, and then the rest of my life pursuing a "career!"

J.H.: You're not the type ...

Carole: No, that still doesn't interest me. Perhaps I'll get there ... later!

J.H.: Would you say the Zaïrian experience changed you in any way?

Carole: Whereas Ecuador helped me become a lot more tolerant, Zaïre changed me intellectually. I see things differently. I previously had a tendency to impose my North American point of view and judge the customs of others. No longer. Finally, the main thing the program taught me ... was that I had a lot more to learn!

Carole Godin's Comments on the Canadian Tour

I realize how lucky I've been to be part of such a program: a superb group, a wonderful exchange country, Zaïre, where we learned a great deal, and finally the Canadian tour which took me from Vaudreuil, Quebec, to London, Ontario, and through New Liskeard, North Bay and Toronto.

The groups, schools, host families that welcomed us were fantastic, and showed keen interest in our presentations. Despite all this interest, however, we were astounded to see how little people know about the Third World, given that we live in a country where information and means of communication are at everyone's reach.

In Canada, we hardly suspect the existence of Zaïre, whereas, over there, in the midst of the African savannah, children know a lot about Canada, even if they must carry benches on their heads because there aren't any in the schools, even if they have no books.

I found the tour rewarding: it provided me with more insight concerning development, taught me group-animation techniques and helped me understand that Canada has a long way to go to really understand problems concerning international development.

Moreover, so do I ...

Carole Godin Ten Years Later

Following the Zaïre program, Carole worked in Quebec City as a facilitator with an association that organized intercultural exchanges. Her main occupation was hosting groups of teenagers from Ontario and the United States who were spending a few days in Quebec city to learn about the province's culture.

The following year, she registered in the nursing program at Quebec City's François-Xavier Garneau CEGEP, while keeping her part-time job as a facilitator. She participated in the intercultural training program given by Garneau-International at the college. Carole completed this program by doing a three-week apprenticeship in Haiti, in May 1988.

In the spring of 1990, she earned her college diploma and worked in two Quebec hospitals. She afterwards settled in Rivière-du-Loup, where she works mostly in the emergency ward of the Grand-Portage regional hospital, while studying nursing at university. She occasionally co-operates with Canada World Youth, giving information seminars on health and sexuality to participants.

Between studying and working, she's managed to make a few trips to the United States, Mexico, Venezuela and France. She also returned to Ecuador, a country she remembers fondly. She wanted to expose her nearest and dearest, who travelled with her, to the pleasures of being in that beautiful country where the people are warmhearted and friendly. All of them really appreciated the experience, particularly an evening spent in a village with the people she'd lived with.

Carole is now married and is getting ready for another rewarding cultural experience, since she'll be heading to China in a few months to adopt a little girl.

7.
Scott Elliott

From British Columbia to the Dominican Republic

Scott in his Indonesian village in 1992.

Scott: I was born in Port Moody, British Columbia, and lived there until I was eighteen-years old.

J.H.: What did you think of school?

Scott: It was boring and not very challenging. Most of my time went into social activities and sports rather than studying. I nonetheless graduated in 1982, and was even chosen class valedictorian. I'd sent an application to Canada World Youth just before graduating, really hoping to leave my home town and experience something new. Otherwise, I felt I wouldn't have much of a future. Unfortunately, Canada World Youth wasn't in the cards.

J.H.: You weren't accepted?

Scott: No, but I'd also sent an application to Katimavik.

J.H.: You wanted to cover all the bases!

Scott: That's right. Though my friends were heading to university, I really didn't want to begin studying in the fall, nor stay in my hometown to find a job.

J.H.: You didn't know what to do with your life?

Scott: Not really. I had a clear idea of what I didn't want; more school or a meaningless job. I knew I wanted to travel, to see something new and do something with my life.

J.H.: Did Katimavik accept you?

Scott: A week after being turned down by Canada World Youth. Wonderful news! Next thing I knew, I was on a plane headed to London, Ontario. In fact, this was my favourite part of the program, the best of my three rotations. Ten of us lived together and worked at the Museum of Indian Archeology. A crash course in learning to co-operate with others!

J.H.: What about the second part of the program?

Scott: It took place in Quebec's Lac Saint-Jean region, in the village of Chambord.

J.H.: Chambord? My wife was born there!

Scott: Ah oui! An extremely beautiful region! In retrospect, I realize I didn't integrate into the community as well as I could have. The best part of this rotation was my three-week stay with a local family. I learned a lot of French and, especially, a great deal about Quebec culture. The family ran a dairy farm, a new experience for me: we'd rise at 5:00 a.m to milk the cows, do countless things all day, play with the kids ... then retire at 7:00 p.m. Coming from the city, I'd never experienced life on a farm. I've gained a great deal of respect for farmers.

J.H.: Where did your group live during the third rotation?

Scott: In Fort Saint John. I worked in the theatre department at a community college, and then at a school for "problem" youth, the Fort Saint John Alternate School.

J.H.: Where is Fort Saint John?

Scott: Northeastern British Columbia, at the mile fifty-four mark along the Alaska Highway.

J.H.: So you were back in your province.

Scott: But in a region I'd rarely visited. I'd only been to southern British Columbia.

J.H.: What did you do after Katimavik?

Scott: I returned to Port Moody, got a summer job and registered at a college in

September. I really didn't want to, but there were no interesting jobs and I had nothing else to do. On the night I registered, I got a phone call from the alternate school where I'd worked as a Katimavik volunteer. They offered me a job as a child-care counsellor. I was only nineteen and this was a unique opportunity. So I withdrew from college and headed to Fort Saint John. Before I knew it, I was working full-time, counselling, teaching physical education, tutoring, and helping students on work-experience placements.

J.H.: So what happened afterwards?

Scott: I sent Canada World Youth another application in the spring ...

J.H.: Never give up!

Scott: ... and was accepted. As luck would have it, the Canadian part of the program took place in Alma, in the Lac Saint-Jean region ...

J.H.: You were predestined for Lac Saint-Jean!

Scott: Apparently. That's where I really learned to speak French. So I speak it with an English accent ... and one from Lac Saint-Jean.

J.H.: I believe you were with a group from the Dominican Republic ...

Scott: That's right.

J.H.: And you had a counterpart ...

Scott: His name was Luis Demetrio Baez Rodriguez ... or Luigi for short. We had fun learning to communicate: Luigi is Spanish, I'm English.

J.H.: So which language did you speak?

Scott: Very broken French. With a lot of signs! However, my French is now much better.

J.H.: Tell me about your host family.

Scott: My God! It was quite an experience. We lived with the Trudel family for three months. They had five children, which might not be a big deal to some people; however, I'm from a family with only two children: my brother and I. I suddenly ended up with five very active young brothers and sisters, whose language I was only beginning to learn—that was something! But I really enjoyed the experience.

J.H.: What did you think of Lac Saint-Jean?

Scott: A wonderful region. It was very different from what I'd known growing up. I thought people would be biased against me because I was English, but everyone was really nice. Since I was the only anglophone working at the CEGEP, students came to see me to practice their English. I'd muddle along in broken French and we managed to understand each other very well. I also had the opportunity of organizing activities with Solidarity International for World Food Day. This was my first experience related to development education. It helped make development and disarmament issues less abstract to me.

J.H.: And from there, you headed directly to the Dominican Republic ...

Scott: The first time I'd travelled outside Canada or the United States. I didn't know what to expect. We landed in the middle of a hot and humid night. Exhausted ... and very excited!

J.H.: What were your first impressions?

Scott: I was rather overwhelmed! I didn't know any Spanish, since I'd been mostly grappling with French in Quebec. We were given two Spanish lessons, a brief four-day orientation, then shipped off to our counterparts' villages to spend a few days until the community projects were ready. We were given quite a welcome when we reached Luigi's village. It's really small and Luigi had become a celebrity, having been to Canada and all. I think the entire village population (two or three hundred) was there to meet him. I felt really lost, since everyone spoke Spanish. I'll never forget the day. Seated with some of Luigi's cousins, I was trying to follow the conversation. After a couple of hours, I was rather dazed and remember thinking: "What am I doing here?" It was quite the shock!

J.H.: Tell me about the Dominican Republic.

Scott: Definitely one of the best experiences of my life. We lived in a small town; everybody knew us, or wanted to, which really facilitated our integration and our understanding of their lives and reality. My work project helped me get to know people. Luigi and I taught English at local schools. A good challenge, since I still couldn't translate anything into Spanish. I'd explain a concept or English word to Luigi *in French*, and he'd translate it into Spanish. Quite a complicated system, but it worked because students were eager to learn. I also worked on building houses for very poor families—an OXFAM project—and dug ditches with the villagers for over a week. I really enjoyed the experience, since I was able to do something concrete for the community and got to know many villagers.

J.H.: You haven't mentioned your host family ...

Scott: La Familia Mendez. We lived on a small farm on the outskirts of town, beside a river. The family lived very simply, but all its basic needs were met. It was almost self-sufficient, since the farm provided casaba, beans, pigs, oranges, bananas, not to mention the peanuts and coffee we sold in the market. Our house was the last one on the power grid ... By the time electricity reached our house, it could barely energize the light bulbs.

J.H.: What was the village called?

Scott: Loma De Cabrera.

J.H.: Give me your impressions about the country, in the area of development, for example.

Scott: This was my first experience in a developing country, and I was rather unaware of what was going on. However, many things really impressed me. One of my first shocks was learning about the use of arable land. Sugar cane was grown at the expense of basic staples. We visited numerous sugar-cane plantations and saw how workers were exploited. I couldn't understand the logic of this system, until I learned sugar was one of their only cash crops. It allows the government to repay loans to the International Monetary Fund. It seemed a waste of valuable land and resources. I was also very impressed that babies and children seemed so happy. During the three months I spent in the village, I rarely heard a baby cry. It certainly wasn't due to a lack of babies, though infant mortality was very high, but parents took extremely good care of the children. They were happy, even if they had next to nothing, materially speaking, unlike their Canadian counterparts who are often too spoiled. People here love to celebrate. Families often go out together, to dance merengues and salsas. It was very important for them to look good on nights they went out. Even if their clothes are old, they're always clean and well pressed. This wasn't my style! I'd always considered faded jeans and T-shirts acceptable for any occasion. I've since acquired a little pride; I'm more conscious of the way I dress. I was always a little rebellious and felt my way of dressing should've suited everyone.

J.H.: That's typical of young Canadians!

Scott: It is, but my Dominican experience helped me change my attitude in that regard.

J.H.: Did you manage to learn any Spanish?

Scott: My Spanish wasn't bad at all after three months. I managed to get along. I spent a month in the Dominican Republic after the program, and my Spanish improved drastically. I lived with Luigi and his family, with no Canadians around. A total immersion.

J.H.: You then returned to Canada. Somewhat changed, perhaps?

Scott: Absolutely. The Dominican Republic taught me a new way of living. I'd lead a sheltered suburban life, without the least idea about what was happening in the rest of the world. I began to question some of my values. I realized Canadians live at a frantic pace and don't take the time to enjoy life's simple pleasures. Though Canadians are very sociable, their use of time is too rigidly structured and makes no allowance for the unexpected. I realize this is a generalization, but it's often the case. However, I must admit I proved this generalization wrong during the trip I made from Montreal to Vancouver, following my return.

J.H.: So what happened?

Scott: A friend and I left Montreal for Ottawa. I stayed there with André, a participant who'd been with me in Loma De Cabrera. I worked a few days for a furnace salesman, going door to door trying to get interviews for him. I soon took off for Toronto to see Brian, another past participant. I worked long enough to buy a bus ticket back to Vancouver—stopping all along the way to visit former participants.

J.H.: You now had friends throughout Canada ...

Scott: True friends! Most of them I'd met while in Katimavik or Canada World Youth. This allowed me to stop in every province. And these friends could understand my experience, and all I'd learned. Since none of my Canada World Youth friends lived in the region, I felt completely lost when I reached Vancouver. As for high school friends, they were completely unable to understand all the changes in my attitudes. I'd discovered so many things which I thought were impossible to talk about to anybody who hadn't had a similar experience. It was very difficult for me to renew acquaintances with people I hadn't seen in three years, and try to summarize all I'd been through. You can't explain this in ten minutes. I soon moved back to Fort Saint John, to continue working with children, either in groups or individually. After Canada World Youth, I couldn't resign myself to a "regular" nine-to-five job. I needed work I thought was worthwhile and could make a real difference. At the end of the summer I was beginning to ask: "What will I do next?" That's when I heard about the special program with Zaïre. I applied, was accepted ... and here I am!

J.H.: So tell me about Zaïre ...

Scott: Reaching Zaïre was very different from landing in the Dominican Republic. It was a lot easier, and I was much more comfortable, probably because I expected a culture shock. Following a brief stay in Kinshasa, we headed to Mwene Ditu, the village we're in now.

J.H.: Tell me about Mwene Ditu.

Scott: On arriving, I learned that Miango, my Zaïrian counterpart, and I would be living with Papa Raphaël's family. The initial experience was rather surreal. I remember being quite nervous when we said hello to each family member ... before we were left alone for what seemed a long time. It was so dark that, the next day, I was unable to recognize people that had been there the night before ...

J.H.: Was there no electricity?

Scott: Neither electricity nor running water. But this wasn't really a problem. By town standards, the family was relatively well-off: they had lanterns, water jugs, wood for cooking, a broken gas refrigerator and a rudimentary outhouse. What else could you could ask for!

J.H.: How did you get along with the family?

Scott: Numerous minor reasons prevented my rapid integration. For example, I referred to my "father" as Papa Raphaël for over a month, but no one knew who I was talking about. The villagers knew him as Tszambila, since they'd stopped using Christian names. I wasn't very comfortable at first, since we were treated so differently. Miango and I would eat with two of our "sisters." The conversation was rather stiff and formal. We barely had any contact with other family members. All that's changed now, and we're much more part of the family. I take the time to talk to my "mother." She doesn't speak French and I still don't know more than ten words of Tshiluba, the local language. I speak French to her, though she doesn't understand it too well; but she laughs. We don't understand each other much, but we have fun.

J.H.: How many children are there in the family?

Scott: Four girls live at home. Now and again, *Fiston* shows up. I think he was a grandson who lived next door; he was perhaps two years old. Other children are scattered along the road between Mwene Ditu and Kinshasa. It's sometimes hard to tell who's family and who isn't. It's totally different from the way I grew up.

J.H.: There's no limit to a family's size! What do you think about the amazing and boundless solidarity between family members, including nephews and cousins?

Scott: It was a revelation. I love their concept of the extended family. Yet Zaïrian families aren't necessarily very close. Some children don't see their parents for many years. This seems strange to me, since I see my family many times a year. But these families have a lot of solidarity. Each member depends on the others, each has a role and responsibility. Anyone can become a family member: a cousin, a distant relative you've never met ... or someone like me! They become part of the family as soon as they set foot in the house. Instantly. Things are different in Canada!

J.H.: Perhaps we've lost a few traditional values over the years ...

Scott: Definitely. The values I found here resemble those my mother told me she'd known while growing up on a Saskatchewan farm. I believe it's something related to interdependence. People here are used to sharing and aren't afraid to depend on others. They need one another to survive.

J.H.: What did you work on while in Mwene Ditu?

Scott: Numerous projects. I started with the Lycée Mobutu, a school run by the nuns, repairing and painting the building. I afterwards switched to the wells which were designed to provide drinking water to the population. I got there at the right time. Steven, Ian and Miango had done the groundwork and got the community involved. Taking part in the water project gave me a real taste for hands-on development work. I was excited to work on a real development project. As a result, development was no longer an abstract concept, or something that happens "over there." I worked manually, digging dirt, but was contributing directly to building a fresh-water spring that would benefit many people. That's a good feeling. One day, forty or fifty men, women and children helped us extract white clay from the well. Children aren't usually encouraged to take an active part in the work, but on that day we invited them to join in. We then started smearing their faces with clay ... They had a great time, were really playful, and much more helpful afterwards.

J.H.: Steven, the project's driving force, seems convinced it's off to a good start.

Scott: He was the project's main catalyst. He wanted it to succeed and ensured it got done. Impressive work.

J.H.: How many wells did you build altogether?

Scott: I was involved in building only one well, though our group built seven. We drafted proposals for the village chiefs concerning all Mwene Ditu's wells.

J.H.: Hundreds of people will benefit ...

Scott: Thousands, more likely! As long as they maintain them, of course. The ideas, materials and technology are local, so outside help won't really be necessary. But enthusiasm often dwindles, and people fall back into old habits.

J.H.: What did you do besides building wells?

Scott: I spent two days a week on that project and three teaching English. Schools are worse off than in the Dominican Republic. Many people readily admit the education system is going downhill, which is really sad.

J.H.: What's the main problem with Zaïrian schools?

Scott: Money, resources and priorities. Buildings are made with mud bricks and have thatched roofs: the walls often collapse. The only materials on hand in schools where I taught were extremely worn-out blackboards ... and the chalk I had! Students brought their own chairs, often a *Lido* powdered milk can. Only half of them had pens and paper. Teachers are considered qualified as soon as they've done six years of high school. They're paid between seven hundred to one thousand zaïres a month—about twenty-five dollars Canadian. Though the cost of living is much cheaper than in Canada, it's extremely difficult to live on that kind of salary. Teachers manage by having "small businesses" on the side, which eat into the time they should devote to the classroom. It's discouraging for them. Teachers and students often come to school without energy in the morning, since they haven't had a decent breakfast. Many kids don't even attend school, often for economic reasons: they're needed to work on the farm, family business or in diamond mines.

J.H.: Let's forget about the school for a moment; tell me about the hospital you worked on ...

Scott: This was one of the group's major projects. We rebuilt a hospital that hadn't been used since independence. I'm very proud of what we accomplished. Difficulties kept arising, and made things discouraging at times. For example, I was asked to cut glass one day. Having never done this, I broke quite a few panes. We had few resources and it was very frustrating to waste them.

J.H.: Especially when considering the price of glass in this country!

Scott: Prices are crazy! The disappearance of material was another frustration. I think eighty per cent of our tools vanished, which really hampered us when, for example, we had to make do with two hammers instead of twelve.

J.H.: People must really need hammers!

Scott: They do. And I understand the situation; we all do. Around here, if you own a cement trowel, you become a mason; if you own a hammer, you become a carpenter. Ownership of tools identifies your profession. I'd have understood if people had taken our tools at the end of the project. I have no qualms about this. In fact, I thought it was rather neat to create jobs by providing a few tools. But they could at least have let us finish the work.

J.H.: You nevertheless completed your project. The hospital was rebuilt ...

Scott: Enfin, c'est prêt! *Oui*!

J.H.: I've heard patients will arrive soon ...

Scott: That's right, today.

J.H.: What did you think of the inauguration we attended today?

Scott: I was really impressed. A very interesting ceremony which attracted many people. I'd expected a good turnout: the governor's presence, and that of a Canadian delegation, made it an event not to be missed. We were so happy to have completed the project!

J.H.: Did you get to know many villagers?

Scott: It took months to really integrate. The kids are a lot of fun. I understand barely half of what they say, since most speak only Tshiluba. So conversations are extremely basic but we still have a good time. I know many people now, and get along with everyone. With some, conversations are limited; with others, I can talk about anything. You start to build strong bonds. I gave a few souvenirs to a friend this morning; he gave me the tusk from a wild boar he killed when he was twelve years old, i.e., twenty-three years ago. It's not beautiful, but has character, due to the story behind it. A very special gift.

J.H.: So, do you feel as comfortable in Mwene Ditu as you do in Vancouver?

Scott: Probably more so. I'm comfortable with the community and lifestyle. More at peace with myself than when I was in Vancouver. It's not easy to explain.

J.H.: By the way, your French is very good.

Scott: I've improved a great deal since I got to Zaïre, but still make a lot of mistakes. I understand and speak it well. However, I'm sort of lost when the conversation gets more complicated. I still lack vocabulary and grammar. I'd have to take courses and read some books.

J.H.: Time has come to return to Canada ...

Scott: So soon! But I'm really looking forward to the Canadian tour. I'm very excited!

J.H.: You'll get to put your communication skills to good use. In which region, exactly?

Scott: Western Canada. I'm sure it won't be easy to travel from Vancouver to Winnipeg, and do presentations every day for six weeks. Lot's of moving around, thousands of miles on the road. Our Zaïrian counterparts are in for a minor shock, mostly because of the cold. But I'm sure they'll be fine.

J.H.: You expect a lot from the tour?

Scott: It's one of the main reasons I joined the program. I naturally wanted to discover Africa, but I'm thrilled to get a chance to tell people about our experience and about life outside Canada. We'll talk to thousands of people, stay with Katimavik groups and travel across the country! There's a genuine lack of communication between young people from Canada and the rest of the world. If everyone knew how people live elsewhere, and why they live that way, they might think about remedying certain injustices. As well, development education is absolutely necessary in Canada, though our school systems hardly bother with it. Our tour will somewhat compensate for this shortcoming.

J.H.: You had plenty of time to think about your future during the program ...

Scott: I'm still very interested by Katimavik and Canada World Youth, organizations that correspond to my desire to work with young people. I'm not sure yet, but I may very well become a group leader with both programs! I'll see what happens. I'd like to attend university, since I often feel under-qualified. I'm proud of what I'm doing, but am sure I could do more.

J.H.: Good luck, Scott!

Scott Elliott's Comments on the Canadian Tour

The Canadian half of our exchange was very intense and exciting. Our goal was to reach out and share what we'd learned and experienced through Canada World Youth. I'm sure I learned as much as the people we talked to.

Our groups started the tours on Vancouver Island, in British Columbia, and continued as far as Thunder Bay, Ontario. During our six-week trip in a van, we polished our presentations, learned to live out of a knapsack and feel at home anywhere. We were warmly received by host families and Katimavik groups, with whom we shared stories ... and ideas on how to improve the world.

Pauline, Mauwa and I, did presentations before diverse groups, ranging from grade-school students to seniors in intensive care. We learned to adapt our presentations to audiences varying between six and three hundred people. Responses were fantastic. We'd always run out of time—we had to answer one more question, give additional information, or relate another story. We shared our experience with over

3,800 people during 93 presentations.

The tour convinced me our education system has shortcomings. The lack of knowledge and sensitivity to the world around us was all too obvious. Little emphasis is placed on life skills, personal growth and development education. The Zaïre program opened my eyes to what surrounds me. A kind of education not available in a classroom, unless it's open to the world. An experience I'll never forget, which encouraged me to continue studying.

The value of living in another part of Canada, or another country, cannot be sufficiently emphasized. I believe such an opportunity should be given to many more young people from Canada and around the world.

Scott Elliott Ten Years Later

Following the Zaïre program, Scott headed to university to continue his education. His studies took him to Ontario, Spain and his native British Columbia, where he obtained a bachelor's degree in business administration from Simon Fraser University.

He's maintained a profound interest in issues related to youth and international development. Among other things, Scott has worked for Canada World Youth as a project leader. He's now the organization's development and communications director, as well as a member of Katimavik's board of directors.

8.
Pauline Mckenna

From Ontario to Togo

Pauline returning from the market, somewhere in Togo.

Pauline: Following high school, I headed to the University of Ottawa to study business administration.

J.H.: So you wanted to be a business woman and make lots of money?

Pauline: I was planning on a business career. Without too much enthusiasm, I must admit. In the middle of the school year, I heard that Canada World Youth applications had been received. I'd always toyed with the idea of travelling to the Third World some day. I'm from a strict Catholic background; when I was young priests told us in church about Third World missionaries. I was very interested but really didn't know what I could do about it, or perhaps didn't have the courage to ...

J.H.: ... become a missionary nun?

Pauline: Absolutely not. So Canada World Youth accepted me and I made up my mind very quickly: it was yes! School could always wait.

J.H.: You'd chosen Africa?

Pauline: It was my first choice; the continent has always fascinated me. Asia and Latin America didn't interest me as much. So I was thrilled, especially since this was to be a francophone program, which would give me the opportunity to learn French. The first part of the program would take place in Quebec, the other in Togo.

J.H.: And you learned French?

Pauline: I did.

J.H.: What was the name of your Quebec host community?

Pauline: Sainte-Hélène, a village near Saint-Hyacinthe, about two hours from Montreal. I was from a large family and had been raised on a farm in Ontario. So I ended up on a Quebec farm, living with a large family! I didn't expect things to be very different; I nonetheless learned a lot from my Quebec experience.

J.H.: Did you have any problems being accepted by your host family?

Pauline: Oh! no, they accepted me right away, and I adapted without a hitch, since I was from a large family.

J.H.: Along with your Togolese counterpart?

Pauline: Yes. His name was Kokou and he was wonderful. It was difficult at first, due to cultural differences and all. Our conversations were rather trivial ... Besides, there were so many people in the house that we barely had time to talk. We had to adapt to each other and build a climate of trust before being able to communicate properly. When problems arose, we tried to discuss them quietly, submit our opinions, as different as they may have been, and finally managed to find a solution. In fact, this is how participants dealt with group problems. Kokou and I had a lot of respect for each other, which allowed us to solve our communication problems effectively.

J.H.: What was his social background?

Pauline: He'd just left a small village that was very poor. Later on, in Togo, we spent a few days with his family and I met his relatives and friends. They radiated incredible warmth and hospitality. I was from the other end of the world, but they immediately made me feel at home. That's hard to beat!

J.H.: Let's come back to your Quebec family ...

Pauline: I think Kokou and I really helped them understand that there's another world beyond theirs. It's always rewarding for an ordinary family to be confronted by the reality of another part of Canada and another part of the world. People have a great need for seeing something beyond their own existence and taking an interest in that of others.

J.H.: Did you and Kokou work on the farm?

Pauline: We shovelled fertilizer and brought in hay, things like that. Which really suited me.

J.H.: And one day, the great departure took place, Africa, Togo ...

Pauline: Oh! the people were so wonderful, friendly and warmhearted! That's what I'll remember most about their culture: the incredible warmth. You feel welcomed right away. When people enter the house, you must shake the hand of each one. It's a spontaneous gesture, a personal contact with each individual encountered. They'll bend over backwards to ensure your comfort and happiness. This helped me a great deal. When you're from a large Canadian family, like me, you're used to sharing everything, but since there isn't always enough to go around, everyone must ensure he gets his share. I personally hesitated to share what I owned. So I ended up in Togo with extremely poor folks who didn't hesitate to share the little they had. You enter a house and are immediately given food, even if a child was about to eat it. Sharing is very much a part of Togo. It's a cultural characteristic we've lost in Canada. Canada World Youth's greatest merit is to provide an opportunity to leave everything behind, live elsewhere and discover new values. The organization allowed me to leave my small Ontario town, and take a break from university, where I was getting mired in routine, like everyone else. I wanted to leave this. The program allowed me to stop everything and take the time to think, to realize things were happening beyond my tiny community, to look elsewhere, to acquire my own moral values and put some order in my ideas ... without being submitted to the influence of my family or friends!

J.H.: How did you look at your future before Canada World Youth?

Pauline: Well, I thought I'd spend three or four years at university, as my brothers and sisters had done, then get a job and probably get married. The prospect didn't excite me very much. I'm pleased to have broken out of that mould, since numerous possibilities are now open to me; there are many things I want to do because I now have the strength and courage to do them.

J.H.: So your three months in Togo were worth it?

Pauline: An excellent experience from any point of view. In fact, I didn't want to leave ... I'd liked to have stayed in Togo, if only it had been possible.

J.H.: Participants must return home after the program. They sometimes go back to their host countries on their own, as hundreds of former participants have done.

Pauline: I know ...

J.H.: What was the work project in your Togolese village?

Pauline: We built energy efficient ovens in the houses, because the shortage of wood for cooking had become a serious problem in our region, located in the southern part of the country. We built seventy ovens in the three surrounding villages. And taught people how to build and maintain them.

J.H.: Besides saving energy, i.e., wood, I believe these ovens were also safer for the children ...

Pauline: Children risk being scalded when a cooking-pot is perched on three stones. At first, the reaction of people frustrated us somewhat: "Well, those whites are going to teach us new techniques!" And, in fact, we did give them lessons. But the villagers didn't build the ovens: they left that task to participants. We tried to remind them we'd leave some day and that they *had* to learn to build and maintain the ovens. For example, they had to be sprayed with water once a week to prevent the clay surfaces from cracking. We built an oven for the woman who prepared our meals. By the time we left, she was no longer using it and chickens were starting to lay eggs on it. Getting the people to accept such a radical change was difficult. Yet, isn't this so in our own society? Is it any easier to get Canadians to change their ideas and ways of doing things? Our frustrations were part of the learning process!

J.H.: Did any Togolese values touch you particularly?

Pauline: The Togolese have a lot to teach us. For example, their family structures are much stronger than in Canada. Togolese families value sharing, mutual respect and support. In Canada, we're becoming more individualistic and materialistic.

J.H.: And you wanted to become a business woman and make lots of money barely a few months ago ...

Pauline: Indeed! Money is no longer very important to me. I'll settle for the basics and having healthy children.

J.H.: How did you handle returning to Canada?

Pauline: Oh! I found it difficult to renew contact with my friends, who only cared about fashion and the dresses they wanted to purchase! These things no longer matter to me, but I'll respect the opinion of my friends if they really value them. They noticed I'd changed, but I didn't want to impose my new values to them. I was ready to tell them about my experience, what I saw, how I felt in Togo, if they wanted to listen, but ... the first months weren't easy. Just because I felt nobody understood me. It's normal, I'm sure ...

J.H.: Former participants have often told me the same thing ...

Pauline: So you feel like finding someone who understands you. That's why I wanted to spend the summer with Kate, a former participant with Costa Rica. This helped me in a way. Yet, it may have hindered me as well: we spent too much time talking about all the things we had in common. I afterwards threw myself into working with seniors: I'd visit them and help with housework. I didn't earn much money, and think some people must have been astonished that a twenty-two year old girl spent her time visiting a ninety-three year old man, cleaning his place, then sitting and chatting with him. But I thought this was wonderful. I didn't earn much but was happy. The seniors were happy. That's another thing I learned in Togo: never neglect seniors.

J.H.: Hadn't this dawned on you before you went to Togo?

Pauline: Perhaps, but I hesitated because of what people might have said; they would've surely thought me unusual: "Why the devil are you doing this? Why are you wasting your time with the elderly?" But I had the courage to answer when I returned from Togo: "If that's your opinion, too bad!" I'd acquired the courage to shoulder my decisions.

J.H.: Was this full-time work?

Pauline: No, part-time. I also did other minor jobs. Then I had to return to university. There was no other alternative. I went back without really knowing what I wanted to do; but I was sure I no longer wanted to go into business! Perhaps social sciences, since I wanted to work with people. Following the first semester, I turned to recreology, no doubt because I'd had a happy work experience at a camp for young offenders. I now believe I'll pursue a career in recreology.

J.H.: And work with young people?

Pauline: Not necessarily. I think I want to start with young people and then switch. What's most important is working with people who need help and who'll benefit and grow from your involvement. There's no way I'll sit in an office before a pile of paper! I prefer a gym filled with children. I feel it's more useful.

J.H.: So you took recreology for a year at university?

Pauline: Yes, while working at a community centre. During the summer I got involved with a camp for children suffering from cancer, which had recently opened in Ontario. I was thrilled.

J.H.: And then fall came along ...

Pauline: Fall, indeed! My return to university was all set. I'd rented an apartment and was thinking of continuing to work at the community centre, while raising funds for the camp for young cancer patients, and a few other minor things. That's when Canada World Youth contacted me about the Zaïre program ...

J.H.: It must have been exciting to be with eighteen former participants who'd been through the same program, though in different countries. Everyone must have immediately felt at ease ...

Pauline: No. At first, I didn't feel comfortable at all. Certainly less than I'd been during the first orientation camp with the Togo program. Things improved following a week or two, but I still didn't fully understand what this "special" program was about. I finally caught on at the very end of the orientation camp. Once I'd accepted the goals, I finally felt at peace with myself, and at ease with the group. I was still somewhat worried about the Canadian tour that was to follow our three-month stay in Zaïre. How could we change the mentalities, ideas and values of our Canadian audiences? But I told myself it would be a start if our presentations managed to change the attitude or prompt the interest of a single person. Of course, I didn't think we'd have to limit ourselves to one individual, though Canadians are far from ready to accept the development concept. No doubt they'll be less inclined to welcome the cultural side of our presentations, and realize there are people in Africa who have a different culture, but who are human beings like us, with similar values, needs and aspirations. I felt it would be meaningful if Canadians thought about these things, and that those who are in a position to, should become more fully involved in development.

J.H.: You're three months ahead of yourself! You've already returned to Canada and are wondering about the prospective reaction of your Canadian audiences. Let's begin with your arrival in Zaïre ...

Pauline: I didn't feel the least culture shock this time. Zaïre resembles Togo in many ways: the people, markets, traffic, bars, the way women dress. All this reminded me of Togo.

J.H.: Like Togo, Zaïre is a francophone country. Did your fluency in French facilitate things when you arrived in Mwene Ditu?

Pauline: After a few weeks, I no longer had any problems communicating with people.

J.H.: With your host family, among others?

Pauline: Oh! yes. A wonderful large family with nine children, many of whom had already left home. I live there with Lusamba, my friend and counterpart. She really helped me integrate into the family by explaining things to them. For example, during the first days, the family insisted we eat separately on a table inside the house. I didn't say anything at first, thinking this was due to a form of respect. Finally, I got them to understand I wanted to live with them and like them. They relented after awhile and I now do as I please: I shower, wash my clothes, take care of the house. Problems have vanished. I owe all this to my counterpart, Lusamba, who's from Kinshasa. I think it's so much better to have a counterpart and live with a family. Group living is fine, but I think you learn more with a family.

J.H.: Was the food a problem for you?

Pauline: I had trouble getting used to it, both in Togo and Zaïre, because of its drabness. We Canadians are used to small portions because of the variety of our food. Here, portions are huge since only one or two dishes are served at each meal. It's not easy.

J.H.: Do you consider *fufu* to be drab?

Pauline: Unless you add *pilipuli* ... At first, I had trouble telling my parents why I wasn't eating: "You don't like our food?" they'd ask. I answered that I did, but that it took getting used to. After a few days, they asked whether I wanted to eat something besides *fufu*. I admitted I'd have liked rice or something else. So they began preparing rice and small dishes, like sardines, especially for me. A few weeks later, I asked them to stop doing this, since I'd finally got used to Zaïrian food. From then on they treated me like any other family member.

J.H.: Did you have any health problems?

Pauline: None at all. I'm very glad to be in excellent health.

J.H.: What about your work project in Mwene Ditu?

Pauline: The main project was rebuilding the hospital. We repainted a school during the first week, which didn't really thrill me since I didn't feel I was doing something useful or helping the people. Naturally, the school looked really good afterwards, but I wanted to do something more concrete. However, rebuilding the hospital contributed something significant to the village.

J.H.: And after three months of unrelenting work, you assisted to its inauguration this morning ...

Pauline: After working on various projects, including the wells, all participants turned their attention to the hospital over the last month and a half. A wonderful group effort where each gave his all. I'm really proud of the results. At least we'll leave something concrete in our wake. As I was coming over to do this interview only moments ago, people stopped me in the street to say: "Thanks for rebuilding our hospital!" This means more to me than hearing the governor's speech at the inaugural ceremony. All day, children have followed and surrounded me, repeating: "Thank you! Thank you! Thank you!" I was very touched.

J.H.: Did you have a lot of contact with the villagers?

Pauline: Less than I wanted. I should've put more effort into it; however, we didn't have much spare time. Every morning we'd work on wells or something else from 7:30 a.m. to 12:00 p.m. and then go home to shower and eat with the family. We'd go back to work at about 2:00 p.m. We gave English lessons three days a week to the Zaïrians who'd accompany us on the Canadian tour. We then had work sessions pertaining to our presentations that lasted until 5:00 or 6:00 p.m., five days a week. We'd head home afterwards to have dinner, served at 7:00 or 8:00 p.m., depending on families. I'd turn in after dinner, or sometimes talk with Scott and Miango, the participants who lived across the street. We were short of time, but I admit I should've tried to meet more people.

J.H.: At least you weren't idle. You briefly mentioned your presentations ...

Pauline: I worked mainly on the visual part of our slide show with Steve, Khoni and Mangando. We wanted to use slides to illustrate some of the development problems found in Mwene Ditu and elsewhere in the Third World: a lack of drinking water, malnutrition and inadequate education. Since we couldn't deal with all the problems at once, we concentrated on those three. We'll show how Zaïrians are trying to solve them and how this concerns Canadians. Our presentations will try to introduce Canadians to development by reminding them that millions of people like us face these problems. Zaïre is only one example. We'll ask three questions at the end of our presentation: "What is development? Why must everyone get involved? How can it be done effectively?" To urge people to look beyond their community and start thinking ...

J.H.: What territory will you cover?

Pauline: My team will travel through Canada's four western provinces. I consider those six weeks as the most important part of the program. Without that prospect, leaving Mwene Ditu would sadden me even more.

J.H.: Zaïre seems to have affected you more profoundly than Togo ...

Pauline: An effect that's different rather than more profound. The Togo experience was more cultural, whereas Zaïre exposed me to development problems. What's certain is that Zaïre opened my eyes to the realities of development, something I plan to get more involved with following this program.

J.H.: And you'll return to university ...

Pauline: I have two more years of university; I plan to complete them and probably travel again afterwards. I don't want to settle into a job for the moment. Perhaps I'll work in a Third World country for a year or two ...

J.H.: Do your plans completely exclude a business career?

Pauline: As I said earlier, I want to devote my life to people, particularly children and teenagers. I now realize that what's most important, what makes me happy, is helping others.

Pauline McKenna's Comments on the Canadian Tour

There's no doubt: the second part of the special program with Zaïre was the most important. The research and hard work done in Mwene Ditu allowed us to reach our Canadian audiences.

Throughout the tour, I was ceaselessly amazed by the concern of people who, for example, wanted the school system to include a development-education program.

Many students admitted they never even studied Africa ... it was no longer part of the curriculum! And they were completely unaware of the word development. Our presentations therefore allowed those students to at least discover one aspect of Africa and, more importantly, piqued their interest in the continent. Things will change around the world when people are better informed about what's happening in developing countries. There's no other way.

Pauline McKenna Ten Years Later

After completing the Zaïre program, Pauline joined her sister in Europe for a two-month backpacking trip. On returning to Ontario, she worked at Camp Trillium, a centre for children with cancer. During the fall, her urge to travel took her on a two-month discovery tour of Ecuador and Peru. In January 1989, Pauline accepted a position as assistant director of programs with the Trillium Childhood Cancer Support Centre. Soon thereafter, she was appointed executive director of the centre. This program, designed to help children with cancer and their families, is one of the largest in North America.

Pauline recently left the Trillium Childhood Cancer Support Centre, and will be heading to Queen's University to study in the Outdoor Experiential Education Program. On December 23, 1995, Pauline married Darryl Upshaw in a small church in Jaco, Costa Rica. The witnesses to the marriage: two former participants with the Quebec-Costa Rica program, Kate MacDonald and Reiner Estrada.

Pauline and Darryl hope to return to the Third World one day, to work in the field of education.

9.
Paul-André Pétrin

From Quebec to Costa Rica

Paul-André doing his laundry.

Paul-André: I'm from Grenville, Quebec, a village near the Ontario border. Following high school, I headed to the CEGEP in Saint-Jérome, to study humanities.

J.H.: There's no great commitment to studying humanities; you're not bound to anything.

Paul-André: Perhaps! I then headed to the University of Sherbrooke, to study preschool and elementary education.

J.H.: That's rather more serious! Were you really thinking about becoming a teacher?

Paul-André: I honestly didn't know. I'd thought about psychology at first, but hadn't been accepted. Education was my second choice. So I told myself: "Well, why not? At least I'll be dealing with something concrete." It wasn't easy, since I lacked motivation. So, I decided to send an application to Canada World Youth during the Christmas holidays. If I didn't feel like returning to university the following year, I'd at least have another option. I went through all the steps, without getting my hopes up too much, and was finally accepted. Putting off my education was a serious decision, so I hesitated for awhile.

J.H.: But, since you really didn't know what you wanted to do with your life ...

Paul-André: That's right. I still had important questions about my future. Rather too many! But you don't get an offer from Canada World Youth every day. So I jumped at the opportunity and told myself: "Come on, go for it! Take a chance! You're young and university can always wait."

J.H.: You therefore joined the program with Costa Rica.

Paul-André: Exactly. And the Canadian half was to take place in Granby, Quebec, where my counterpart and I ended up with a wonderful and typical Quebec family. The father was a tailor, while the mother stayed at home to take care of the two children: a six-year old boy and nine-year old girl. Our relations with the family were quite simply marvellous.

J.H.: Tell me a little about your Costa Rican counterpart.

Paul-André: His name was Jorge Barrentes.

J.H.: I know him, he's a friend of mine. Tell me about him anyway.

Paul-André: A great guy! I couldn't believe my luck: first, to end up in Granby, where I wanted to be; then to live with a decent family I really got along with, since the parents were young and open; finally, to have a counterpart like Jorge. It was super. We naturally had some minor conflicts, but were really close to each other.

J.H.: Tell me about his background.

Paul-André: He was from the middle class, like me, and had also been to university. All of this greatly facilitated communication between us. We could talk about anything.

J.H.: In French?

Paul-André: At first, Jorge had only a basic knowledge of French, but he learned quickly. He had no trouble after barely three weeks.

J.H.: What was the nature of your work project in Granby?

Paul-André: Jorge and I worked in the extended-care ward at the hospital. We helped two recreation specialists entertain patients. We played some music and dabbled in visual arts. We organized the Christmas and Halloween celebrations ... and even another wonderful party!

J.H.: Often with patients who were at the brink of death!

Paul-André: Being with these people was a new experience for us. We were intimidated at first ...

J.H.: Because they were at death's door?

Paul-André: That's right, or because they were handicapped, could no longer speak ... or had been abandoned! I noticed that our so-called developed society still has serious problems to solve. The experience also helped me discover non-verbal communication. For example, there was an old man who could neither move nor talk. So I'd play guitar for him, and his eyes would immediately begin to shine. It was beautiful!

J.H.: Was this your only work project?

Paul-André: Well, it kept us busy seven hours a day!

J.H.: And how did Jorge manage?

Paul-André: We both found it very difficult to face so much misery every day; however, we finally got used to it and established good relations with patients. The two supervisors trusted us and gave us a lot of leeway. We worked very hard, often to the point of exhaustion. But it was worth it.

J.H.: You had to make sure you deserved going to Costa Rica ...

Paul-André: Indeed! When I reached that beautiful country, I spent two weeks with my counterpart's family, some thirty miles from the capital, San José. A relatively well-off family, very authentic. Warmhearted people. In short, genuine Costa Ricans! I was part of the family after two weeks, and they didn't want me to leave ... The host community that awaited us hardly resembled what I'd expected. I'd imagined it as a small village deep in the mountains, surrounded by coffee plantations. We ended up in a small city in the northeast, near the Atlantic coast, in a banana-growing region. Our host family lived right in the city and had all the Western comforts: TV, electric stove, *Jeep*. I was somewhat disappointed, since I'd expected a more radical change of scenery and a little exoticism. But, with time, and despite my host family's relatively Americanized lifestyle, I discovered the special nature of Costa Rican culture.

J.H.: What about the work project?

Paul-André: We helped a professor of agriculture at the city's agricultural college. Every morning, Jorge and I would check the beehives. Very interesting work, despite the painful stings ...

J.H.: And the rest of the day?

Paul-André: Besides spending time with the family or other participants, I tried to integrate into the community. It wasn't easy at first. My Spanish was very rough and I was often likened to the *gringos*. I made headway slowly but surely. For instance, I'd often drop in at the seniors' activity centre, and listen to their wonderful stories, while improving my Spanish. Once in awhile, I'd play guitar with the church choir. I'll never forget the surprise I got when I arrived. I told myself: "So, this is Third World? Where's the misery?" The development problems didn't stare me in the face, since they were less sensational than what I'd seen on TV. I gradually began to understand why this country, where people seem so happy, is nevertheless a developing country. I realized this following our inquiry into the pollution caused by banana plantations.

J.H.: Banana trees pollute?

Paul-André: The streams which flow through these plantations provide people with water that's often contaminated with pesticides used on farms, as well as with other kinds of garbage. At the beginning of our brief inquiry we interviewed many of the people in charge of *Standard Fruit*, an American multinational banana company. We then spoke to the peasants, labourers, community health workers, etc. That's when I realized how much the people were being exploited, and the extent to which these countries are economically dependant on large companies. This isn't immediately obvious, since multinationals like to pretend they're great benefactors which create employment. We also helped young Red Cross volunteers organize a blood-donor clinic. I was amazed at the important role played by young people in Costa Rican society. For example, the president of the Red Cross's youth branch was twenty years old. I wonder if this could be possible in Canada. Young Canadians hesitate to get involved and take their place in society, due to the gulf that lies between generations. As well, the program taught me not to judge people: whatever a person's age or lifestyle, each has something to teach us and it's always possible to establish a good relationship on some level.

J.H.: My! You've learned a lot of things! Even Spanish ...

Paul-André: I never would've thought it possible to learn another language in only three months.

J.H.: And yet ... you also learned that the program would end one day ...

Paul-André: Oh! It was really difficult to tear myself away from my group! But the worst thing, after having been through such an intense experience, is returning home alone, resuming your daily routine, reintegrating yourself, looking for a job, making new decisions.

J.H.: Speaking of decisions ...

Paul-André: My first decision was to return to the University of Sherbrooke to complete my bachelor's degree in education. I needed money to do this, so I got a job in a Montreal daycare centre. I had to get used to the big city: the subway, the noise, the crowds. This exhausted me!

J.H.: Poor little country boy!

Paul-André: Indeed! But Montreal is where I'd hear about the special program with Zaïre. I got some information at the Canada World Youth office, but without too much enthusiasm, since my return to university was already in the works. Was I ready to leave again? I'd only been back five months, and was still somewhat disoriented. To my great surprise, however, Canada World Youth selected me.

J.H.: Hurrah for Zaïre!

Paul-André: There you have it! The trip to Africa naturally attracted me, but what especially convinced me to go was the prospect of the grand Canadian tour that would follow. This was the perfect opportunity to get relevant experience, since I was interested in education.

J.H.: Unlike Costa Rica, Zaïre must have seemed a genuine developing country to you. Especially when you arrived here, in Mwene Ditu, your village.

Paul-André: I've been told it's a city ... It has a population of about 125,000 people.

J.H.: That many? Yet it looks like a large village. I haven't seen a single house with multiple storeys.

Paul-André: There's one over there: the police station.

J.H.: All right, there is one. The others are plain huts made of mud or concrete, which give Mwene Ditu the look of a village, And your host family lives somewhere over there ...

Paul-André: A wonderful family! I don't have a counterpart, since there isn't one for everybody in this special program. However, I share a room with a guy who's my age. He's twenty-two. In fact, he was like a counterpart: he helped me a great deal to integrate, especially in youth circles.

J.H.: What does he do for a living?

Paul-André: He's a teacher. He finished high school two years ago and now teaches at the *lycée*.

J.H.: How much does he earn a month?

Paul-André: About $20.00 Canadian.

J.H.: Is that enough to live on, over here?

Paul-André: He manages to, since he still lives with his parents. But the other teachers who have families quite simply can't manage. In the market, a bag of flower costs 800 zaïres. So, when you earn 750 zaïres a month ...

J.H.: Do you essentially get along with the rest of the family?

Paul-André: They always stay close and want to keep me entertained. They fear I may get bored. I didn't say anything, but this bothered me somewhat, since I sometimes like to be alone. After awhile, they realized I was comfortable with them and happy. So they began treating me without ceremony, like a regular family member, but always with a lot of respect and affection. Earlier, I mentioned my brother, the teacher, who earned $20.00 Canadian a month. Seeing this, I told myself that living in Mwene Ditu wasn't expensive, that such a salary could provide for most needs. I hadn't known genuine poverty in Costa Rica. In Zaïre, however ... We're in a diamond-mining region and lots of money changes hands. As a result, the cost of living is higher than elsewhere. Diamonds or no diamonds, the peasants don't earn any more. For example, a pagne that costs 200 zaïres in Kinshasa, sells for 500 zaïres in the Mwene Ditu market.

J.H.: And if you converted zaïres into Canadian dollars?

Paul-André: A Canadian dollar is worth about 40 zaïres.

J.H.: So a pagne, such as those worn by women, costs about $13.00. Is that expensive?

Paul-André: Very expensive, when considering the average earnings.

J.H.: How can a married teacher who earns $20.00 a month afford a $13.00 pagne for his wife?

Paul-André: He can't without extra income. If he owns a small plot of land, his wife will sell fruits or vegetables in the market.

J.H.: Does your brother have extra income?

Paul-André: No, because he lives with his parents. He's still young and relies on his father. He doesn't even pay for his share of the food. His fondest dream is to study in Kinshasa one day; so he's saving up. Speaking of my brother ... He gave me a lot of help with my slide show, which I wanted to focus on Zaïrian youth. I wasn't sure I'd be able to work my way into youth circles. I thought they might consider me as a friend ... or an overly curious tourist. Luckily, my brother is the activity leader for a group of young people. He has two brothers who are roughly his age, and tons of friends. I hit a bull's eye. I fell on the ideal family.

J.H.: You seem to have a knack for always falling on the ideal family.

Paul-André: Isn't life wonderful!

J.H.: You seem to get along with your brothers; what about other family members?

Paul-André: It's more difficult because of the language.

J.H.: They only speak the local dialect?

Paul-André: The father gets along in French, but the mother speaks only Tshiluba. There's no problem with young people my age, since French is taught in school from grade five. Naturally, I'd have liked to talk more with my parents. The absence of a common language, however, didn't prevent us from establishing a wonderful friendship. One day, my mother fell sick. I'd told my brother: "Tell her I'd be happy to take her to the dispensary if her ailment persists." People always hesitate to go to the dispensary because they may have to pay for medication. In any event, the mother gave in and asked me to take her to the dispensary, which I did. That night, the father came into my room to thank me, striving to speak French: "Thank you ever so much, my son, for taking your mother to the dispensary. You really are my son." I was profoundly touched that he considered me his son. An unforgettable moment.

J.H.: What a marvellous experience!

Paul-André: Absolutely! At first, I felt I was a burden on the family, but finally realized I was like an open window on the world to them. My parents, brothers and sisters had such a thirst for knowledge. Their openness of mind, their curiosity about the outside world made me think about the attitude of Canadians, who are far from having the same desire to discover other cultures. They often look at the world with only an ethnocentric bias.

J.H.: But do you realize how few Canadians have had, like you, the exceptional luck of living numerous months with a Zaïrian family? Though I've travelled somewhat, I've never had that luck.

Paul-André: You're right. It's a great privilege ...

J.H.: As for rebuilding the hospital, I assume you worked with the others?

Paul-André: It was a huge undertaking. Watching us work, the villagers finally began thinking their hospital might be built. They began to take interest in the project. That's why the work gave us a great deal of satisfaction: we felt we were contributing something to the community. The participants who built the wells—seven wells altogether—also provided something very significant. They especially took the trouble to train four young villagers to continue our work and maintain the wells after we leave. I also did a lot of work with the slide-show team, every day for two months. I was so eager to attend meetings, that I couldn't sleep the night before! Unlike the slide show on Costa Rica last year, this one would be used to the hilt. So we put all our heart in it.

J.H.: You must have been rather proud, this morning, at the hospital's inauguration ceremony, with the governor, the singing, dancing, speeches and all.

Paul-André: This project gave me a better perspective, one from Africa. I not only understand things better, but *feel* them with my whole being. I lived with a family where the mother has to fetch water two kilometres away. One litre of water weighs a kilogram; she carries up to twenty-five of them in a jug balanced on her head. I lived with people, shared their tasks for a few months, and sincerely believe that living conditions can be improved with some organization and a little help.

J.H.: Are you eager to return to Canada?

Paul-André: Fear of the "readjustment shock", as it were, has completely disappeared. Being exposed to Zaïrian culture has shown me the extent to which I'm North American. And I accept it. I look forward to the beginning of the grand Canadian tour!

J.H.: Do you know what territory you'll cover?

Paul-André: Part of Quebec and the Maritimes.

J.H.: That's where we'll see if you have the makings of a teacher ... In what language will you do presentations?

Paul-André: Three weeks in English and three in French.

J.H.: Any plans for the future?

Paul-André: I'm wary of them ... You remember, last year, two days before returning to the University of Sherbrooke, Zaïre fell in my lap. It's not that I don't know where I'm heading: I want to go everywhere! Decisions will naturally have to be made and that stimulates me.

J.H.: What will the Paul-André seated in front of me be like in ten years?

Paul-André: Still young I trust! Perhaps not physically ... But I hope I don't fall into the trap, the routine, the comfortable lifestyle ... and end up no longer able to change anything! To remain young, I'll continue taking risks and keeping my eyes wide open ...

J.H.: And never lose your ability to be amazed.

Paul-André: That's right. But it's easy to lose; you have to work at it constantly.

J.H.: Do you think your future will somehow relate to development?

Paul-André: I met many deeply committed people during this program. They inspired me and I want to work with them later on. We have a basis, a few ideas and some contacts. One way or another, what I'll do with the rest of my life will relate to development, be it local or international.

Paul-André Pétrin's Comments on the Canadian Tour

The tour was designed to offer Canadians a new perspective on Africa, introduce them to the concept of development and encourage them to get involved. I sincerely believe our success in meeting these objectives went beyond our expectations.

During the tour, I learned to continually outdo myself, overcome fatigue, control my emotions, nervousness and shyness. With Sue and Miango, I got to make seventy presentations before the most diverse audiences, from grade-school students to seniors, not to mention radio and TV interviews.

The experience I acquired during six weeks of intense work with both my teammates was priceless. What I've retained most is the desire of people to learn more about the outside world. As well, I was struck by the lack of resources in this area, and people justifiably complained about this.

What particularly troubled me was how little Canadians know about foreign cultures, especially when you consider that the communications sector is extremely developed in our country. Even teachers who were very interested in development admitted they lacked resources, guidance counsellors, or simply a time slot to talk about development with their students. In that respect, Canada World Youth's grand tour was dead on.

Paul-André Pétrin Ten Years Later

Following the Zaïre program, Paul-André returned to Montreal to complete a bachelor's degree in the teaching of French as a second language ... and immediately returned to Canada World Youth in 1988-1989 to work as a project leader with the Ontario-Uruguay program.

Since 1989, he's been working as a trainer with an adult education centre in Verdun, in southwestern Montreal. Music is also becoming increasingly important in his life, though surely not as much as his four-year old son. Finally, he admits without hesitation that Canada World Youth provided him with some of the most meaningful experiences in his life, and that the three important years he spent with the organization, at the beginning of his adulthood, will continue to inspire him and confirm his desire to work at improving the world.

PART THREE

Hello, World!

I have memories of cities that are like memories of love.

Valery Larbaud

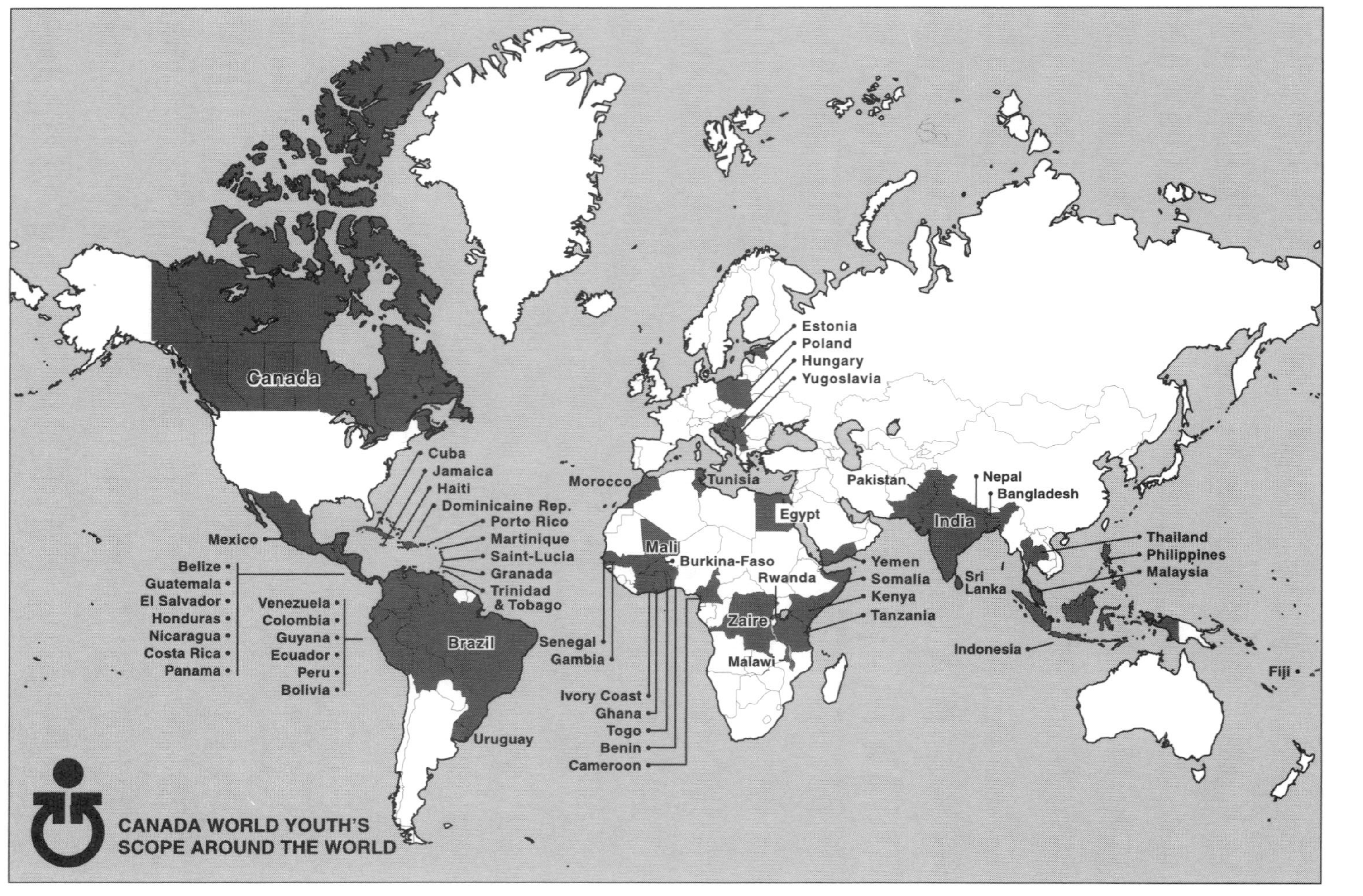

In its first twenty-five years, Canada World Youth has had programs in sixty or so countries spread over five continents.

Note to readers

I'm fully aware no one reads introductions, forewords and preambles. But if you really want to know about the origin of the texts that follow, you'll have to resign yourself to consulting page 12, where this is clearly explained.

Since you'll do no such thing, I might as well repeat that *Part III* assembles a few excerpts from the travel log I write during missions abroad for Canada World Youth, or on private trips.

A way to once again say hello to a dozen or so countries of the world.

1.
Bolivia

1981

Two Bolivian *campesinos*, friends of Erik Lafortune.

January 27

Within two hours, I've travelled from the humid heat of Asuncion, capital of Paraguay, to the cold and rain of La Paz. Perched in the Andes at 3,650 metres above sea level, the city has one of the highest altitudes in the world.

I'm greeted at the airport by Canada World Youth's co-ordinator in Bolivia, Yvan Labranche, and our friend, Francisco Pereira, director general of the *Instituto Boliviano de Tecnologia Agropecuraria* (IBTA), Canada World Youth's counterpart in Bolivia. A happy reunion. I'm driven to the hotel, where I'd expected to keep chatting with Yvan, but it's past 10:00 p.m. and curfew begins at 11:00 p.m.

January 29

We were scheduled to leave at 7:00 a.m., then 10:00 a.m., to visit participants in Coroico and Caranavi. We finally leave La Paz at 12:00 p.m.—five hours late, which seems normal in Latin America ... The IBTA provided us with a *Jeep*, the only type of vehicle able to travel on side roads during the rainy season. We even have a driver, *El Gordo*. Reynaldo, the Bolivian co-ordinator, accompanies us. Since our vehicle has an extra space, Yvan invites a young Canadian woman from Edmonton to join us. She's passing through La Paz and wants to visit Yungas, i.e., the beautiful tropical region where Canada World Youth projects are located.

La Paz is nestled in a large valley surrounded by mountains. Heading towards the Yungas, we scale a mountain named La Cumbre that's 4,869 metres high, before descending—and climbing repeatedly! The scenery is imposing, staggering, phantasmagorical. But the circuitous road is enough to fill the bravest traveller with dread. I won't even try to describe its horror, certain as I am I couldn't accurately depict it to Canadian readers. Let's just say a small dirt road winds through the Andes, clinging to a nearly vertical cliff, hugging ravines often over four or five hundred metres deep. With no guardrail. Curves follow one another; they vary between 100° and 160°. The only road signs are small white or black crosses marking spots where trucks have fallen, often carrying dozens of people to their deaths. The most recent ones are still decorated with lilies and gladiolas ...

The road is so narrow that two vehicles can only pass each other in the rarest of places. When they meet, the one climbing—always painfully—has right of way. The other backs up carefully until the road widens enough to allow passing.

On reaching a small village, we learn that a major rock slide hasn't yet been cleared. An endless line-up of heavily loaded trucks, with ten to twenty travellers clinging to each of them. In some cases, they've been waiting for four days. Yvan and Reynaldo walk away in the hope of being able to go over the scree: perhaps they'll find some vehicle beyond it that would allow us to go on our way. In a tiny corrugated sheet-metal cafe, the size of a handkerchief, I eat an egg and bread with Cathy, the young Canadian. After an hour, we decide to look for our friends: a nearly two-hour stroll under a sun that's fortunately filtered by a layer of clouds. To kill time, we count trucks stopped on the roadside. When we reach the ninetieth, we meet Yvan and Reynaldo who'd also counted trucks all the way back to the slide: seventy-four.

Therefore, 164 trucks, on *this side*. Since each carries an average of twenty passengers, 3,280 men, women and children have been forced to camp out, many over the last four days ... Water and supplies are beginning to run out.

Yvan and Reynaldo inform us that, despite the determined efforts of bulldozers, the road won't be cleared for a few days, perhaps more if heavy rain resumes. So, what do we do? A road is under construction higher up the mountain. Trucks are forbidden to use it; in any case, they couldn't climb the particularly steep slope leading to it. A *Jeep* might manage. Still, we'd need permission from the military personnel watching over the area. Yvan gets it without much difficulty, thanks to a safe-conduct signed by the minister himself. "But it's at your own risk!" says the sergeant. What about the rest of the road?

One small inconvenience: we'll have to wait for the work to stop and road crew to leave, at about 6:00 p.m. ... We finally make it through, with quite a commotion, when we hurl the *Jeep* up a particularly steep slope, half pebbles, half clay. Afterwards, we spend another two hours over bad corkscrew roads, always at the edge of a cliff. A thick fog blankets the Andes, we can only see a few metres ahead, but at least the ravines have "disappeared" ...

After expending huge amounts of adrenaline, we finally reach Coroico, where a Canada World Youth group wasn't expecting us: we were supposed to head for Caranavi today, which is three or four hours from here, and stop on our way back, after tomorrow. We're too exhausted to travel one more kilometre. Fortunately, a few participants are still in the village, while the others are living with the *campesinos* with whom they work.

When in Coroico, participants live in the village school, which is vacant since school is out. They have evening meals in a tiny eatery where we meet up with some of them. A happy bunch under the benevolent authority of Gilbert Côté, the group leader: Jacqueline Larson from Edmonton, Jean-Jacques Desgranges from Sudbury, Duane Thomas from Ottawa, and Tannis Loescher from Neepawa, Manitoba, and their Bolivian counterparts. We share *arroz con pollo* and a lot of news. After listening to a brief concert of Andes music under the stars (two panpipes, a Spanish guitar and a *charango*—a Bolivian string instrument), we make our farewells ... But only until after tomorrow, when, as planned, we'll return to Coroico. Moreover, curfew begins at 11:00 p.m.

January 30

To make up for lost time, we leave at 5:00 a.m., i.e., one hour before curfew ends. Well ... ! We assume soldiers at the checkpoint will be sound asleep. If any problems arise, we can ask to see the mayor, a close friend of participants ...

During the first hour, we drive in the pitch black, placing our fate in the hands of our driver, *El Gordo*, i.e., the fat one. Fat yet small: his legs seem to have a hard time reaching the brakes. He settles for placing his fate in the hands of all the saints in heaven, by making three signs of the cross before each stage. The least distraction on his part, the least brake failure, and we plunge into a ravine to our certain deaths.

Daybreak revealed marvellous scenery, which we'd have appreciated more had *El Gordo* driven more slowly and sounded his horn before rushing into the most unbelievable turns. We were in God's hands! And since the slide probably still hasn't been cleared, we won't likely meet other vehicles. In theory. But in practice, after negotiating a hairpin curve, a huge truck looms out of nowhere. Shouts. Drivers slam the brakes. The two vehicles stop in the nick of time: fifty centimetres separate the bumpers. A frontal collision would've likely hurled us into the abyss.

After three startling hours, we arrive in the tiny village of Santa Ana. This is where participants who work in the Caranavi region live. Caranavi is a village of colonists located a few ravines away, according to Guy Bordeleau, the unflappable group leader.

We have breakfast with them: bread, margarine and black coffee. What pleasure to meet these boys and girls once again; we'd barely had time to meet over four months ago, during their training camp in Saint-Gédéon du Lac Saint-Jean, Quebec. And what surprise to observe they've all become *trilingual*. Brian Gorlick from Winnipeg tells me about his discovery of Quebec, and his love for the Lac Saint-Jean region, where he'll return next summer to polish his French, by taking an immersion course in Jonquière. Yet he says this in remarkably proficient French. And he speaks Spanish just as well. He's astonished about what's happening to him: "In less than five months, I've learned *two* new languages. Unbelievable! No school could've given me as much." Stephen MacDuff from North Augusta, Ontario, adds: "In addition to two languages, I now understand my country a lot more! Not to mention Bolivia, development, etc."

We join participants at their worksite in the afternoon, somewhere on the mountain. With the help of *campesinos*, they've cleared some land to make a tree nursery. With heavy blows of their machetes. Each shows me the blisters on his hands. Ah! our participants are proud of themselves! And the *campesinos*, all of them members of a co-operative supported by the IBTA, seem delighted about this unexpected and symbolic collaboration. The *campesino* leader improvises a brief speech to thank *Juventud Canada-Mundo* and "*nos hermanos Canadienses*," "our Canadian brothers." Hearing such things in this remote corner of Bolivia is enough to move you profoundly ...

Someone requests a group photo. Since we're fifteen or so, we'll have to line up in two rows. An elderly *campesino* says, laughing: "Canadians can stand behind and we Bolivians, who are much smaller, will stand in front." They're small, of course, due to the malnutrition that's plagued them for generations ...

January 31

Departure for Coroico around 1:00 p.m. *El Gordo* makes three signs of the cross. Let's hope this doesn't prevent him from keeping a sharp eye on the two thousand turns ahead of us!

The rainy season takes a short break; today the sun shines brightly. The Andes seem more beautiful than ever, especially since they're luxuriant, contrary to their arid Altiplano sisters. Those spared from vertigo (unlike me!) can admire the bottom of the valley, some three or four hundred metres down, where a sparkling river undulates like a long silver snake.

We reach Coroico and call on participants met the day before yesterday, and those who were absent. A wonderful trilingual group, as well: Louis Chiasson, a New Brunswick Acadian, Jackie Larson from Edmonton ...

We visit one of the co-operative's experimental coffee plantations with IBTA agronomists. A delightful one-hour stroll along the mountainside, thankfully in the shade of tall trees needed by coffee plants. *Campesinos* explain the problems with this type of farming, particularly the leaf "rust" that has afflicted Bolivia, and which can reduce the crop by half. Éric Lafortune from Montreal talks about the terrible disease with heartfelt concern.

A brief speech by the *campesino* leader. He praises the work of participants, and thanks *Juventud Canada-Mundo* from the bottom of his heart for sending them to his remote village.

In the evening, IBTA agronomists offer a dinner in my honour, but more in recognition of Canadian and Bolivian participants. Dishes typical of the region and a small Andean music ensemble. A table set in the open air, in an interior court. We chat, laugh and, inevitably, dance Bolivian dances. I still need a lot of practice ...

February 1

It's with great regret that I leave Coroico, a marvellous old village whose streets are paved with time-worn cobblestones dating back to the colonial era. All the houses seem to be of different colours, very bright and dazzling in the midday sun. The *plaza* is filled with Indian women decked in native costumes, and strange tiny round hats. Located halfway between the Altiplano highlands and the tropical region, Coroico enjoys an ideal climate throughout the year.

But the real reason this enchanting village has a hold on me, is my apprehension about the nightmarish road to La Paz. It's impossible to determine if the rock scree has been cleared, since reports are either vague or contradictory.

Today, *El Gordo* is nervous on the brakes and brazen with the clutch. But he's especially too sparing with his horn for my taste. Following two narrowly avoided frontal collisions, I beseech him to use his horn in turns of 120° or more. He laughs, says "*¡Si! ¡Si!*" but does as he pleases.

Bolivian drivers are usually excellent, which explains why the population hasn't been decimated more seriously. But accidents happen. A short distance from La Paz, we notice an overturned and half-destroyed truck; it tumbled thirty or so metres after poorly negotiating a turn. Perhaps its passengers managed to escape, but a few kilometres further, the fall would've been five-hundred metres ...

We finally approach the scree: the road is still closed and will likely remain so for a few days. Since we have a four-wheel drive vehicle, we might still take the road that's under construction, a little higher up the mountain. Soldiers guarding its entrance inform us a recent dynamite blast has blocked a stretch of the road with large stones. It's Sunday, and the road won't be cleared until tomorrow. Faced with the prospect of sleeping in a *Jeep*, we decide to have a look. The soldiers shrug their shoulders and let us through. A heap of stones blocks the road in the place mentioned. A *Jeep* had preceded us, and its six passengers are removing the rocks. We lend them a hand; in a short while, we've opened a passage large enough for a *Jeep*.

The moral of the story: never believe what the military says!

2.
Senegal

1982

The mysterious and wonderful Larry Huddart.

December 18

Larry Huddart will remain one of the most wonderful men I've known during my lengthy life. He spoke little, and never about himself. (I couldn't say as much!) Only by chance did I learn a little about his extraordinary life. Among other things, he'd been vice-president in charge of the Quaker Oats company's Latin American activities for a very long time. But this unusual businessman was also a poet—which changes everything!

When I met him, likely in Vancouver, where his wife Carol was a judge, he'd already given up a brilliant and lucrative career, long before the age of retirement, to the great surprise of his friends. None of us were aware he only had a few years to live due to a serious illness; he wanted to devote them to the young people of Canada. He dedicated much of his time and incredible energy to the Lester B. Pearson International College in Victoria, but Katimavik got the best part of this. For two years, he and I were its co-presidents.

To learn about the movement, he'd rented a camper and spent numerous months travelling throughout our enormous country to visit Katimavik groups, often located in the remotest areas.

Larry Huddart was also very fond of Canada World Youth. One day, as I was getting ready to leave for Mali, where we had a program, I invited him to join me. At his own expense, it goes without saying. He was thrilled, especially since this great traveller had never set foot in Africa.

We'd planned to meet in Dakar, the inevitable stopover on the road to Mali.

Dakar, 12:00 p.m. Both of them finally arrive: Carol, bubbly and happy to feel at ease in French Africa—her knowledge of the language makes the place seem familiar—and Larry, the mysterious Larry, whose infinite discretion is quite an impressive weapon. We hug and exchange compliments ... Over the past years, I've spent untold hours with Larry, talking about Katimavik, its ground-breaking mission, its constant need for expansion, which is regularly thwarted by callous bureaucrats and fickle politicians. But this trip was a snare: I'd finally have the time to get to know him and perhaps fathom his mystery.

Without hesitating, I suggest we make a short pilgrimage to Gorée Island. The island is a focal point of Black Africa: the ignominious slave trade began here on a large scale, and any trip to the continent should begin there. Countless Africans came to this island and were herded onto slave ships that took those who survived to their white masters in America.

The Huddarts would therefore get to know West Africa by visiting Gorée Island. Together we explore the sandy streets—humble Whites among smiling Blacks who seem to have forgiven "us" ... I'm the mentor, the guide, white as I am. I have credentials: I spent a week on the island three years ago, since I'd been invited to be a guest speaker by the tiny University of Mutants for Intercultural Dialogue, founded by Senghor. "Look, up there, that was my room, facing the ocean ..." The Huddarts are *rather* unimpressed, but listen politely.

We walk on the soft sand found on the beach, squares and streets ... There are neither cars, motorcycles, nor even bicycles on Gorée. This former marshalling yard for slaves is now a peaceful haven where anyone, black or white, can sense more freedom than anywhere else, and be momentarily liberated from the tyranny of machines, gadgets, computers, and what have you.

We do the grand tour, walking in the opposite direction from tourists. We reach the House of Slaves whose back door gives directly onto the ocean: once through this door, the Senegalese, Guineans and Malians would head to America without any hope of seeing Africa again.

The sun has set and the chilliness of December makes us shiver. Unfortunately, all the emotions aroused by visiting Gorée Island don't prevent us from being hungry. We're somewhat embarrassed by our hunger, since countless men, women and children literally starve to death on this continent. "The only sorrow is that we aren't all saints," as Leon Bloy said. Carol, Larry and I admit we're not saints and that we're hungry ... and I know a little restaurant at the end of the island, cheerfully called *L'Hôtellerie du Chevalier de Boufflard*. We sup on a skewer of mutton, white rice that's a little grey and sticky, and a bottle of rosé that's almost too chilled, almost too good ... Happy to be together.

Feeling like a seasoned Goréeite, I say to the Huddarts with the confidence of a colonial from the "golden era": "Let's go in the bar (cool sea breezes wafted over the terrace and we were beginning to shiver). I know the owner. And the owner's wife who minds important things, like the cash register. They once travelled to Canada. No, not to Vancouver. It's too far, rains too much, and they speak English there. They've been to Quebec, to Île d'Orléans, to Saint-Joseph-de-la-Rive, to Saint-Anne-de-Beaupré ..."

The boss recognizes me. He's elated. I gain esteem in the Huddarts' eyes. They realize I'm *well known* in Gorée, and will be able to count on me for the rest of the trip! The boss is so happy to see me—to see Canadians, actually—that he offers us a liqueur. "Not just anything, but a bottle for special occasions." When I tell Marcel (now, come on, we got acquainted three years ago, and then there was Saint-Jean-de-la-Rive ...), when I tell Marcel the Huddarts are *anglophones* from Vancouver, he's momentarily put off; but everything changes when Carol starts speaking French to him.

Another small liqueur. He furtively changes the record that's been spinning aimlessly since we arrived. I glimpse the cover: Line Renaud and, of course, she's singing *Ma cabane au Canada*, a tune extolling the ridiculous image the French had, and still have, of Canada, including Quebec. He cranks up the volume: *Ma cabane au Canada* sweeps over half Gorée Island. We feel as though an RCMP officer will burst into the bar any minute ... and ask Marcel for his licence!

All this was very enjoyable, but we had to return to Dakar on the 8:00 p.m. boat. And get ready for the big trip to Mali, during which I may get better acquainted with the secretive and gentle Larry ...

I did manage to learn a few things. At sixteen, he set out to discover the world on a tanker, rubbed shoulders with Jack Kerouac, Henry Miller, Aldous Huxley, Allen Ginsberg, and others. He even had a brief writing career: future biographies will highlight short stories published in the *Saturday Evening Post*, even poems featured in a distinguished American literary magazine. He later walked a thousand kilometres across Australian wilderness, marking a trail for the country's government, etc. Good old Larry. The Quiet Canadian ...

3.
Colombia

1986

Columbian *campesinos.*

December 20

I'm greeted at the Bogota airport by the two Canada World Youth co-ordinators: Naseem Jammohamed, the Canadian, and Jairo Viafara, the Colombian. They see me to my hotel, where we exchange gossip, news, documents and letters. I hadn't known either of them, but over the next days, would observe them in action and appreciate their work.

December 21

Up at 6:00 a.m. Breakfast with Naseem and back to the airport to take the plane to Medellin, capital of the province of Antioquia, where a group of Canada World Youth participants is located. Less than an hour's flight, the first leg of a long and arduous journey.

We're met at the airport by *Doctora* Magola, regional director of ICETEX (*Instituto Colombiano de Credito Educativo y Estudios Tecnicos en el Exterior*—whew!), the para-governmental organization that's been Canada World Youth's counterpart in this country over the last thirteen years. Also awaiting us, an old friend, *Señora* Betty Rodriguez, head of ICETEX services in Bogota and directly responsible for the program. I'm very sorry to learn she'll retire at the end of the month: "I'm making my last official visit with you today. I'm pleased about this, since Canada World Youth will be the fondest memory of my career with ICETEX."

Señora Rodriguez has been our staunch ally for some years. Despite her precarious health, she didn't hesitate to accompany me on this trip over roads that are sometimes in very bad repair, always rather treacherous, and typical of the Andean region.

Speaking of health, I have to mention mine, since it was to complicate my trip somewhat. I've always vaunted my iron constitution and uncommon resistance to fatigue, with justification. I was even convinced that my twenty-one day hunger strike last March hadn't harmed me. Three days before leaving, I saw a doctor about some general pain in my bones and joints. Diagnosis: serious decalcification caused by the fast, provoking joint, hip and, alas, coccyx irritations! I left Montreal with appropriate medication, and apprehension about the hours of travelling by plane, car and certainly by *Jeep*, all of which should be sparingly undertaken by someone with a tender coccyx.

The trip from the airport to Medellin is severe strain enough: nearly an hour on a road hugging the mountain, often broken up, eroded on the cliff side, or besieged by debris on the other. A road that would be condemned for safety reasons in Canada. Moreover, Colombian drivers are so brazen when negotiating curves, that we felt we escaped a good dozen head-on collisions by the skin of our teeth. This is normal for *Señora* Rodriguez. Although each jolt prompts me to cry out, since my poor bones are being rattled, I've enough discretion to avoid the slightest remark. As for the unbelievable road dangers and unruly traffic, I'm just amazed that I forgot the anxiety of my last trip to the Andes, and that, after a certain interval—all adrenalin having been drained—I adopted a fatalistic attitude. I no longer noticed the picturesque little shrines niched into rock walls, or the small white crosses planted every several hundred metres along ravines, or simply painted on a rock: each represents a terrible accident claiming the lives of many people, or a few dozen in the case of buses or trucks crammed with passengers. Suddenly, I can't help smiling, thinking of my fainthearted grandmother who nearly had a nervous breakdown and called on all the saints in heaven whenever we ventured up Quebec City's Côte-de-la-Montagne, in my grandfather's old but powerful *Packard* ...

An infernal road with sublime scenery. We wind our way down to the valley floors, and then climb to new summits with peaks sharply silhouetted against the blue sky, then down once more, up again, down ...

Arrival at Medellin. Another two hours on similar roads to a remote village called Los Micos, where seven Colombian participants and an equal number of Canadians await us. Plus two group leaders.

We arrive late, which seems inevitable and normal in this country where a thousand unforeseens lie in wait for the traveller. Already well-integrated into the country, participants show no surprise and quickly serve us a lavish traditional Antioquian meal, such as you'd never find on a weight-loss diet: *arroz* (rice), *frijoles* (large black beans), *patacones* (fritters stuffed with cheese and guava paté), *chicharran* (slices of fried fat, reminiscent of *oreilles de christ*, Quebec's grilled bacon strips), etc.

Since there wasn't much time for chatting with each participant, we organized a meeting in the small school at Los Micos, a hamlet of some three or four hundred inhabitants. They related their impressions of the program, readily convincing us they're a perfectly happy group. Their only regret: having to leave the village and, especially, their host families in a few weeks. *They unanimously agree the program should be extended by a month*.

Since Christmas is just around the corner, I give each participant a paperback in English, French or Spanish with a brief comment. But Naseem, the co-ordinator, is the most successful: she gives everyone a beautiful colour photo with each participant in the spotlight, and, on the back, a sentence or two referring to the event ...

Participants tell us enthusiastically about life in Los Micos, about community project, and activity programs for children, who are very numerous among the *campesinos*. But mostly about life with their respective host families, the coffee harvest, gardening work, etc.

I've rarely met a group so representative of Canada's cultural mosaic: Sylvie Joly, the group leader, is a Quebecker and former participant in Senegal; Grant Thistle from Newfoundland; Kirby Smith, a native from Pincher Creek, Alberta; Pedro Orrego from Toronto, whose parents fled Pinochet's Chile; Rachel Bégin, a unilingual French-speaking Montrealer who, in six months, learned English *and* Spanish; Roanne Racine, a Franco-Ontarian; Traci Jang from Vancouver, whose father is Chinese; and finally, Yukio Ouellet, from Quebec City, whose first name and perhaps slightly narrowed eyes are the sole indicators his mother is Japanese. In short, a range of young Canadians about which our selection service has good reason to be proud.

In the little time I had, I nevertheless managed to establish a more personal contact with Yukio, who tells me just how much the program has changed his "perception of others and myself"; with Rachel, whose excitement is visible when speaking of Canada World Youth, "the greatest thing that's ever happened to me" and, finally, with Kirby, the native Indian from Alberta who's over six feet tall. He invites me to visit "his" family, whose house is near the school: it's actually a cottage with a red-tiled roof, surrounded by flower beds, banana trees, chickens, dogs and, most of all, a throng of children. Kirby introduces his "mother," "father" and numerous "brothers" and "sisters." He obviously has no qualms about referring to them as such, and shows obvious affection for these *campesinos* who may have traits in common with Canadian natives.

One of Kirby's "sisters" is a slim teenager whose father immediately explains is deaf-mute. In fact, before participants arrived, she'd more or less been considered the village idiot. Taking an interest in her, participants realized she's very intelligent. They taught her to read. One thing is certain: she's no longer considered the village idiot ...

Kirby, who understands the kind of trip I had to make to spend a few hours with his group, as well as my program over the coming days, asks me point-blank: "At this pace, how many more years do you think you'll be able to continue?"

Without too much thought, I answer: "Bah! At least another twenty!" I'll then be eighty-three ...

Host families came to share a meal with participants, and I exchanged a few words with everyone; but Jairo insisted I meet them more formally, around a table. It's nearly 4:00 p.m.: we should be hitting the road to Medellin, where we're scheduled to hop the plane to Bogota. And tomorrow, our schedule begins at 7:00 a.m. ... Since my itinerary is set by ICETEX and our co-ordinators, it would be inconsiderate of me to disrupt logistics ... The two co-ordinators try to reassure me: they'll head for the airport right away and get boarding passes for the whole group, thereby giving *Señora* Rodriguez and me a few more minutes with the host families. Questions, answers, Señora Rodriguez is in fine fettle, the minutes go by, I start to get seriously anxious and, at the end of a comment, suddenly interject a resounding "*¡Feliz Navidad*!" And then get up.

"Don't worry," says Señora Rodriguez, "we've got all the time we need!" Which allowed us to chat another ten minutes before leaving. It was 4:30 p.m., and we were a three-hour drive from Medellin airport, where we were to take the 7:30 plane, the last one to Bogota.

We exchange impressions about participants, the *Señora* having spoken mostly with Colombians, and I with Canadians. "Do you know, she said, "that we already have three hundred former Colombian participants throughout the country? It's about time they form an association. This would be a wonderful network of young people particularly active in their milieu."

Once we hit the road, neither the *Señora* nor myself make the slightest reference to the possibility we'll miss our plane. With infinite discretion, I glance at my watch: 7:25 p.m. And the airport isn't even in sight! Our only hope is that the plane has been delayed, a rather common occurrence. 7:30 p.m. The driver, who hadn't spoken the entire trip, exchanges a few fleeting words in Spanish with *Señora* Rodriguez, possibly hoping I wouldn't understand:

"We're five minutes from the airport ..." the driver says.

"Good. There's still hope," answers *Señora* Rodriguez.

"But ..."

"But what?"

"The gas tank's empty!"

In fact, the needle was on E; in any minute, our car was to join all the other broken-down vehicles along Colombian roads.

But fate was on our side: the car finally reaches the airport. It's 7:35 p.m. Our two frantic co-ordinators are on the ramp brandishing boarding passes: "Hurry, the plane hasn't yet taken off." We scurry, but still have to wait for *Señora* Rodriguez, who's no longer of age to jog. Too late: they've just closed the plane doors! My Colombian hosts parley with anyone who has an air of authority or wears a uniform. No go. Engines rev up. Technically, the plane has left, even if it doesn't take off till 8:00 p.m. Morale plummets. Since there isn't another plane before tomorrow morning, the program for the next two days will be jeopardized. Naseem is discomfited, the *Señora* has lost her unflappable composure, Jairo continues to try everything. Suddenly, he arrives triumphant: "A small company plane leaves for Bogota at 8:30 p.m. It's 8:25 p.m. There's a chance." Another sprint to the other end of the airport. We curse the Avianca company for not whispering a word about this competitor's flight. We arrive as the plane's doors are closing. We once again miss the flight by a hair's breadth, and there are no other planes on the tarmac. In short, a catastrophe. Floor cleaners get to work, shopkeepers close their shutters, long rows of ceiling lights go out simultaneously, as though to push us out with heavy whip lashes. We no longer have a car and the thought of a nightmarish two-hour taxi trip to bed down in Medellin doesn't cheer anyone ... especially the one whose coccyx is already acting up. I learn there's a small town called Rionegro fifteen minutes away. It has the only hotel in the area, *El Oasis*, and I suggest we head there. We'll catch the first plane for Bogota tomorrow. Embarrassed at the error we've made, and just as exhausted as I am, my companions offer no resistance. I evoke a few thoughts about this hotel for them; perhaps it's a relic from the colonial era where we can sip warmed wine before a grand fireplace, while the owner makes us a nice and juicy omelette *à la criolla*. Morale is clearly on the upswing.

In fact, Rionegro is a totally charming, small colonial town, not yet ruined by modern reinforced-concrete monstrosities. Streets with one-storey houses, tiled roofs and black wood railings juxtaposed with milk-white walls in the moonlight and modest little street lamps. The sole exception to this lovely architectural harmony: the *El Oasis Hotel*, a three-storey, totally hideous concrete block. At least, rooms are available, even a restaurant, where we have fine-sounding Spanish dishes that are absolutely inedible.

A short night on tiny, very hard beds, in other words, excellent for the spine of anyone without aching bones.

December 22

Not having foreseen this Rionegro stopover, I have neither razor nor toothbrush, which simplifies morning ablutions. Up at 5:30 a.m. The hotel management, which spares no effort to please its distinguished clientele, offers us a *tinto*, i.e., a black coffee (from Colombia!) with two sugars. It's still night, but in the pale dawn, the jittery blinking of simple Christmas decorations and the antics of several inebriated *campesinos* remind us the *Navidad* is three days away.

This time, we reach the Medellin airport an hour and a half prior to our flight's departure, *as should be the case*, and land in Bogota at 9:00 a.m.: the plane we were to take to continue our journey has already left. However, we devised a solution, no doubt painful for my coccyx, which allows us to more or less respect the next two days' schedule. Instead of flying from Bogota to Butaramanga, and, from there, driving to Pitiguao, a village where a group of participants live, we'll rent a car in Bogota, and drive to San Gil in the district of Santander. From there, we'll head to Pitiguao in an all-terrain vehicle provided by ICETEX. In all, nearly *nine hours* on the road.

San Gil is a beautiful town whose colonial architecture is mostly intact. We have a quick look at the *plaza central*, the time needed to switch from an ordinary car to an all-terrain vehicle, which is essential over the very poor, bumpy road to Pitiguao. This village of three to four hundred inhabitants survives as best it can by growing sisal, whose market was seriously affected by competition from synthetic fibre. As well, they grow some sugar cane and yucca, a tuberous plant vaguely resembling the potato, which is a staple of their diet.

Pitiguao participants were to serve it proudly, along with the region's traditional dish, a thick soup, certainly rich in calories, made with beans, peas, corn and meat.

Another terrific group. A few strong personalities, as different as humanly possible from one another. Gina, a lively, pretty and enthusiastic Colombian wears a funny little straw hat that looks great on her. I tell her so. A few minutes later, she comes and offers it to me with a note saying, "*Especialmente para ti. De Gina. Recuerdo de Colombia*." Another Colombian participant, Audanago, wears a beautiful woollen bag across his shoulder, in the style of the region's *campesino*'s. This time, I make no reference to the bag. Audango prods me: "Say, do you like my bag? Then I'll give it to you." Before I can even protest, he empties the contents and puts it over my neck: "After what Canada World Youth has given me, it's the least I can do for the initiator of such a good idea." I'm not used to such spontaneous remarks and never quite know what to say. For example, when Paul Cormak of Westhill, Ontario, tells me about his life in a nutshell: "First, I had the extraordinary opportunity of being a Katimavik participant. That completely transformed me. I then decided to go into agriculture, in the area of international development more specifically. That's why I craved the Canada World Youth experience, particularly with Colombia where I can learn about problems faced by small farmers.

"And what will you do back in Canada?"

"First, I have to earn some money to keep studying. Next summer, I'll take an immersion course to improve my French. In Rimouski, probably. Thanks to Katimavik, I already manage farely well in French. Our group spent three months in Baie Saint-Paul, an absolutely wonderful village. After that, I'll head to the University of

Guelph to study tropical agriculture. And later on, I'll work on agricultural development in the Third World."

When I hear a twenty year-old boy relate such things, in a small remote Andean village, I realize the efforts of all those who've worked for Canada World Youth (and Katimavik) have been worthwhile.

I talk some more with Caroline Thibault, of Sherbrooke, who's also learned English and Spanish, "besides everything else" during the program. "When I got here and found myself with this *campesino* family in their poor house, I had a moment's anxiety. 'I have nothing in common with these people,' I told myself. 'Absolutely nothing!' I've got to know them since, and realize they aren't so different. They have the same basic concerns, often the same reactions: they're like you and me."

And there was Kathie, of Castelgar, British Couombia, who discovered the program when her home town hosted a Canada World Youth group. (India, 1985-86). She can't get over it when I tell her I know Castelgar: I travelled there last year with General Malothra to visit the group from India. Canada World Youth's world is very small, dear Kathie ...

And Laily Kent, from Gloucester, Ontario; Willa Baker, from Athabaska, Alberta; Neil Burns, a Vancouver artist who designed the team's T-shirt and was very proud of it; and Louis-Martin Pepperhall, an authentic *Québécois*, sharp, composed, with an excellent sense of humour, which doesn't prevent him from being more serious when talking about Third World issues or world peace.

Naseem gives everyone a "personalized" photo, which elicits laughs and comments. I hand out paperbacks and Canada World Youth pins; what causes genuine enthusiasm, however, are two-day old copies of the *Globe & Mail* and *La Presse*. Participants have been practically without news from Canada for nearly two months.

Canada World Youth and ICETEX visitors receive the same gift: a jute sack decorated with the signature of every participant, and filled with samples of products typical of the region: a half-kilo of green coffee, a platano, a lemon, a yucca, a half-kilo of raw sugar cane, sandals with soles made from an old rubber tire, and a half-litre of *aguardiente*, the national liquor.

A more formal meeting with host families comes next. I don't manage to elicit any critical remarks.

One woman exclaims: "Oh, we're already quite sad that participants will leave in three weeks ..."

Another: "We should have more participants, for a longer time."

A bronze-complexioned *campesino* says: "Thanks to your program, our community will never be the same again!"

Finally, an elderly lady gets unanimous applause when she says: "We want you to send another group next year!"

A few musicians, guitarists and singers, join the group crowded into a room in the house of Caroline's family, festively decorated by participants: Christmas balls, streamers, *bienvenidos* written in jute rope, etc.

Since there's obviously no hotel in this small village, we're put up in two rooms, one for women, one for men, in a tiny convent in the *plaza*. We each get a thin mattress, unrolled on the cement floor, and a woollen blanket. Neither sheets nor pillows, no luxury to create a scandal in the *Ottawa Citizen* about my travel expenses!

The only drawback: I don't sleep a wink all night!

December 23

For once, I'm excited about rising at 4:00 a.m. Twenty minutes later, we're on the road, even more terrifying at night, travelling through darkness constantly slashed by truck lights bursting out of nowhere: since ours is the smaller vehicle, we always have to back up somehow or other, when meeting another vehicle, until the road is wide enough for two of them to pass.

Adding to the surreal character of this road, where disaster looms around every curve, are sinister creatures that surge out of the night: the *Años Viejos*, a sort of life-sized scarecrow decked in tattered raiments filled with straw and stuffed with firecrackers, that represent and already mock the Old Year 1986. On December 31, at midnight, these effigies to the span of time over which we have no control—the year just passed—will be burned in public places. *El Año nuevo* has the benefit of the doubt: it might bring good fortune, peace, prosperity, who knows? And if it doesn't keep its promises, it'll also be burned in effigy next year!

I won't describe the road between Pitiguao and San Gil: no portrait could convey the reality. Save for this shred perhaps: Naseem bought a box of fancy biscuits in San Gil. She eagerly opened it when we reached Pitiguao: all that remained was a fine yellow powder. See what I mean?

An overturned truck blocks the road, just before we reach San Gil. No victims, but the vehicle could easily have plunged into the ravine, only a metre away: in that case, there'd have been no survivors; only another little white cross to mark the spot.

Not knowing how long the delay would last, we decided to walk as far as the town. An hour's walk under a clear blue sky and an ideal temperature: about 21°C.

We leave San Gil at 8:00 p.m. in a sturdy *Jeep* with the regional ICETEX director, Fabio Paez: he loves Canada World Youth and, because of this, succeeded in getting ICETEX to assign groups to his division (Boyaca) three years in a row.

The road from San Gil to El Ermitano is the worst we've seen in Colombia. In short, it took an hour to travel eight kilometres.

Once again, the effort was worth it: it's sheer joy to get to know the Colombian and Canadian participants, including Ariane Zurbuchen, a Quebecker who lives in a village I've never even heard of: Saint-Georges-de-Clarenceville; Arnold Blackstar, a native from North Battleford, Saskatchewan; Karen Durling of Dartmouth, Nova Scotia; Stéphane Gagnon from Mont-Joli, Quebec; Teri Clark of Edmonton; Christine Graves and Brent Homan, both from Gloucester, Ontario.

Participants tell us about life in the community with their families, their involvement in organizing children's recreation. They're now laying the groundwork for Christmas festivities, and participating in daily *novenas*, which are semi-religious and semi-folkloric ceremonies.

All host families and friends had been invited to partake in a meal that, of course, highlighted the region's specialty, a type of huge, very spicy pork sausage—the *longahiza*—eaten with tiny potatoes fried in their peels. A delicacy ... that those with delicate stomachs or vegetarians should beware of!

They prepared a genuine celebration for us, with dancers, popular poetry recitations and musicians brought in from San Gil. It's only 4:00 p.m. and already time to leave this idyllic village nestled in the Andes, the *campesinos*—so real, simple and hospitable—and, of course, our participants.

But there's the El Ermitano-San Gil ordeal by *Jeep*, the three-hour drive between San Gil and Tunja, and as a finale, the three-and-a-half hour bus ride from Tunja to Bogota.

After these three memorable days, I was happy to fall into a real bed around 10:30 p.m. ...

December 24

Breakfast with Naseem, whose great compassion and intelligence I discover more each day. This petite young woman, of infinite discretion, almost self-effacing, possesses considerable character and sensitivity.

We head over to meet Dr. Oscar Ibarra, director of the *Fundacion Cultivar*, a non-governmental organization.

Last year, the eruption of the Nevado del Ruiz volcano disrupted at least one Canada World Youth group, located in the midst of the disaster zone. Participants were evacuated to Bogota, where they helped the Red Cross with disaster victims, particularly children.

Canada World Youth's national office received a $30,000 donation from Oxfam-Quebec, a sum entrusted to two Canadian group leaders: Jan Gelfano and Douglas Reiner, who decided to help victims for four months, *following* the return of participants to Canada.

One project Jan and Douglas helped set up: a carpentry workshop primarily designed to build furniture for Cambao residents, who lost everything following the volcanic eruption. In recognition of our two group leaders' contribution, the workshop bears the name *Taller de Carpinteria JAN-DOUGLAS*.

December 28

A lengthy stroll in Bogota's old colonial quarter with Augusto, a former Colombian group leader, who has a marvellous knowledge of the city's history. Jody, Naseem and I discover a most pleasant facet of this harsh city. A jaunt that helps reveal Bogota's human face.

Is it possible that these friendly Sunday strollers, out with their lovely children, belong to one of the world's most violent societies? Besides army and guerilla skirmishes, or the drug-trafficking Mafia's settling of accounts, the city boasts the country's highest murder rate. Colombia is certainly a "democracy," but one always more or less subject to martial law, with police barricades on all roads and omnipresent constables armed to the hilt.

In some provinces, *guerilleros* (left- or right-wing, it's never quite clear which) oppose the central government; but the country's real evil remains the production and marketing of cocaine and other narcotics. Drug moguls defy the government, corrupt the politicians, the military and the police, and assassinate those who resist them. Moreover, there's a complicity between the two states within the state: the drug traffickers and the *guerilleros*.

Every president and government promises to deal decisively with both, yet never goes far enough due to lack of courage, be it plain or political: nothing changes! Colombia's dual problem seems nearly insoluble ...

A country with roughly Canada's population, rich in resources (petroleum, iron, precious stones, coffee, cotton, rice, sugar cane, etc.); but poor as well (slums, Bogota street urchins, ever-widening gap between the rich and *campesinos*).

The three hundred Canada World Youth Colombian alumni have a huge task cut out for them!

4.
French Guiana

1987

Henri Charrière, also known as *Papillon*.

December 30

I had no reason to be in Cayenne, save to find the road to Paramaribo, the capital of neighbouring Suriname. I didn't want to reach Brazil too soon, since participants had barely settled in their community. So it was agreed I'd stop in Suriname, where I'd scheduled a meeting with Mr. K. Texel, deputy minister of foreign affairs, to discuss Canada World Youth: the way things are going, we'll soon run out of South American countries!

On reaching Cayenne, capital of French Guiana, I learn that the political situation has abruptly deteriorated in Suriname, a former Dutch colony: airlines no longer stop in Paramaribo, and the border with French Guiana is closed. A catastrophe! I consider heading to Brazil early; but the next flight is the one I'm scheduled to take on January 5. In short, I'm a prisoner in Cayenne!

January 1

I celebrate New Year's Day alone, in a nondescript, practically deserted hotel. Although the establishment is good by Guyanese standards, this *Novotel* would be considered quite ordinary in Canada. Still, prices are relatively high. There's no beach: French Guiana's coast is covered with a grey mud you sink into like quicksand. And the sea is unappealing where there is sand: it's dirty, brownish, and heavy with alluvion from the numerous rivers that flow into it, including the Amazon. Tourism doesn't have much of a future in French Guiana.

This former colony is a Department of France ... as Algeria once was! A tiny department—seventy thousand people—where separatism is becoming fashionable.

To reduce the costs of my stay and for a change of scenery, I decide to move on ... to a modest inn (of the Spanish style, i.e., where travellers find nothing, save what they brought), magnificently situated at the centre of Royal Island, one of the three Salut Islands. The others being Saint Joseph Island and Devil's Island.

In the last century, a French officer of Jewish origin, Alfred Dreyfus, had been unjustly accused of treason, and was imprisoned here for over four years. He was the island's sole inhabitant, save for a few well-armed guards who watched him day and night, and were forbidden to talk to him. The Dreyfus affair began October 15, 1884, when the officer in question was arrested. It literally split France in two camps: the *anti-dreyfusards*, and the *dreyfusards*, the most famous being Emile Zola, whose *J'accuse* shook France like an earthquake.

The Royal and Saint Joseph islands once served as French Guiana's prisons, and many penitentiaries are located along the coast between Suriname and Brazil. Convicts were incarcerated in wretched conditions for breaking some stupid rule or committing a crime. Attempted escape was obviously one of the more serious offences; it earned perpetrators several *years* of seclusion, often in a type of cage, where they were barely fed and condemned to absolute silence.

Royal Island, where I'll spend three days, is the largest of the three, but seems smaller than Île Saint-Hélène, near Montreal. It bears many traces from the penal colony era, which lasted nearly a century, i.e., from 1852 to 1946. It's difficult to conceive that France, a country of revolutions, freedoms and civil rights, created such a barbaric institution and maintained it for so long. And hard to believe that more than fifty thousand people were condemned to rot in this unhealthy country, often until they died from exhaustion, mistreatment, malnourishment, poorly treated tropical diseases, etc. These prisons were called the "dry guillotine." Though the French were right to be appalled by Nazi concentration camps, they didn't close these prisons until after the war. A stain on their honour. A crime this poor colony—now called a Department of France—still suffers from. Its development has always stagnated and continues to languish, although France built a launching base for *Ariane* missiles. The century of penal colonies forever withered this corner of French Guiana, the only South American country still under the thumb of a European power.

To such a point that, since 1946, French authorities have taken steps to erase this blight from their history: numerous structures built by the penal administration—i.e., the prisoners—have been torn down. The rest has been abandoned, as in the Salut Islands, to tropical vegetation, the most effective and least expensive demolition method: the roots of some trees can crack the thickest stone walls, rip iron doors off hinges, and bend the bars of cells.

By the end of this century, little will remain of these prison relics, and the rare former prisoners still alive in Cayenne, Saint Laurent du Maroni and elsewhere, will be dead and buried. Prisons will finally be forgotten and French Guiana can begin to live as if nothing had happened.

Minute, papillon! In 1970, a prisoner who escaped from French Guiana in 1944, wrote a book published by Robert Laffont, which became an overnight best seller. It's been translated into numerous languages. Hollywood even made a film; the author became famous and was in great demand.

His name was Henri Charrière, and the book is entitled *Papillon*—the nickname petty thieves gave the author in Paris before the war, which he obviously kept at the penal colony. Thanks to Papillon, the whole world rediscovered French Guiana's penal colony, which sorely wanted to be forgotten. His book kindled our outrage at the appalling living conditions imposed on prisoners. It allowed us to applaud the author's successful escape in 1944—preceded by a failed attempt that earned him two years in solitary confinement.

Will this country be cursed forever? What's certain is that the Guyanese ardently decry Papillon, likely because they're somewhat jealous, since his book made him a millionaire and an international celebrity. Officially, he's criticized for exaggerating, even inventing, many of the adventures. He's an excellent story teller who, let's just say, got a little carried away ... I got to know Papillon very well during his 1972 stay in Canada—when I ran the Éditions du Jour, through which Robert Laffont had published a Canadian edition of his book—so I tend to forgive him this shortcoming. Perhaps because I grew rather fond of this warmhearted, cheeky, profoundly humane man; and mostly because, when all's said and done, you can't deny that Papillon spent thirteen years in a horrible prison, including two locked in a cell on Saint Joseph Island. And he did escape twice, making sacrifices and feeling pain that exceed the limits of human resistance.

Papillon died of throat cancer in 1972. He was seventy years old and living in Spain. A few weeks earlier, he'd written to express heartfelt thanks for the concern and kindness I'd extended to him during his stay in Canada.

So, fifteen years later, I end up in the place he cursed with unforgettable intensity ...

January 3

Life drifts by smoothly and exquisitely in this little paradise known as Royal Island. I'm staying in the room of a former prison guard: four thick stone walls, hardwood shutters, corrugated sheet-metal roof, a recently installed shower on the verandah. It's almost monastic, but surrounded by incredible beauty! A footpath allows a tour of the island to be made in an hour, with green light filtering through coconut trees. Extraordinary vegetation: mango, lemon and banana trees, and others covered with flowers that cascade in huge clusters, pink or red hibiscus groves that burst like fireworks in the shaded undergrowth.

The ruins of a building suddenly emerge; rusty bars on its windows recall the men incarcerated here, for days, months, years. Many died or went crazy. In fact, a house for lunatics was built a little further on. Bars are in evidence there too.

I often feel alone on the island. With a few ghosts for company, including those of the children of prison guards; they died like flies and had a cemetery specifically reserved for them. Even torturers had plenty of opportunities to suffer. The children's cemetery still testifies to this. I approach a cracked stone and read an epitaph:

JEAN GIRAULT
DIED AT NINE MONTHS
JANUARY 18, 1925
WITH MUCH SORROW

In the afternoon, I visit Saint Joseph Island. Though more mysterious and beautiful than Royal Island, it harbours as many morbid souvenirs, odious buildings, cells and cages where some men were demeaned by others.

5.
Bhutan

1988

A Bhutanese woman heading to the market.

January 12

We fly over beautiful Bengali ricefields at very low altitude, and observe their varying shapes and assorted hues of yellow, brown and green. Here and there, water-filled paddies glimmer like mirrors randomly laid out on a huge quilt ... An extremely turbulent flight; without a seat belt, I'd be banging my head on the ceiling of the small, eleven-seat Twin Otter.

Suddenly, extremely high mountains loom up, indicating we're nearing Bhutan. We don't fly over them, but weave along valleys or gorges at the bottom of which streams sparkle like rivers of diamonds. A strange sight then appears. We fly very close to a mountain and see a *Dinky* truck driving along a small winding road. The strange part: the truck is *higher up* than our plane.

Breathtaking scenery, deep valleys, peaks occasionally streaked with snow: not the ideal place to make a forced landing. After an hour-and-a-half of turbulence, we make a smooth landing at the Paro airport. The village population is between two or three thousand. A representative from the Ministry of Foreign Affairs has been awaiting me since yesterday with car and driver. He's a young man wearing the national costume, as do most Bhutanese. A kind of striped kimono that reaches just above the knee, made from fine, hand-woven wool. It seems rather flimsy, given the harshness of Bhutanese winters. A wool cardigan, jacket, and raincoat buttoned to the neck don't prevent me from shivering. "We're used to it!" says Ugyen Namgchuck, my new guardian angel.

A one-and-a-half hour drive to Thimpu, the capital. So much the better! My stay will be brief and I want to take in all the scenery. The very narrow road is carved into of the mountainside and runs along valleys. The scarcity of traffic is reassuring, since each encounter elicits strong emotions.

High mountains, etched here and there with narrow terraces, where vegetables, wheat or barley are grown, resemble those of nearby Nepal; however, the unique architecture of even the most humble dwelling attests to a completely different culture. Houses are very attractive and made of bricks and wood ("without a single nail!" says Ugyen). Ground floors are mundane, but second storeys are trimmed with painted wainscotting. Their large-paned windows are often unglazed, and can be closed from inside with tiny white shutters. A pointed roof resting on four wooden pillars caps the building. Forage, provisions and firewood are stored in this manner of open-air granary. Roofs are covered with long wooden shingles secured by symmetrically placed rocks ("without a single nail!").

All we saw along the way were hamlets with a dozen or so houses. A large village finally appears ... But it's Thimpu, the capital! About fifteen thousand people. Low-roofed houses, whose woodwork is decorated with traditional motifs, create a wonderful harmony along main street. "The king," Ugyen explains, "personally examines the plans for every new building, whose exterior, at the very least, must respect Bhutan's architectural traditions." Long live the king!

The ministry put me up in a hotel called the *Molithang*. It's likely the best in the area and perched on a mountainside a few kilometres from the centre of

Thimpu. The only drawback: we're in off-season and the hotel isn't heated. It's as cold as a freezer.

I'm given a suite that's huge and "heated," i.e., equipped with a tiny heater that struggles to keep the temperature above 10°C. I get the strange feeling I'm the hotel's only guest ...

A senior official from the Ministry of Foreign Affairs drops by around 9:00 p.m. to go over tomorrow's schedule. He assures me I'll meet with at least two ministers to discuss Canada World Youth.

I suddenly realize that, due to my hasty departure, I haven't had time to eat since 7:00 a.m. I inform one of the hotel's rare employees. He speaks little English. Since either opening or heating the restaurant is out of the question, dinner will be served in my room, which suits me perfectly. Chinese noodles strongly flavoured with ginger and vegetables in a sweet-and-sour sauce.

I think I'll turn in early ... Crushed beneath a pile of wool blankets, I sleep wearing a bathrobe, socks ... and cap! Still freezing.

January 12

Ugyen and I reach the government building around 10:00 a.m. It was built by the king's predecessor, in the superb Bhutanese style. Guards present arms to me in front of the door. *Wow*! A tall, whitewashed building—obviously much older—rises in the midst of a huge courtyard. "It's a Buddhist monastery," Ugyen explains. Its presence at the core of the king's ministries and offices highlights the extent of religious influence on this society.

I have an appointment with His Excellency Dawa Tsering, minister of foreign affairs. In practical terms, he's the country's prime minister, though the position has been abolished. Bhutan is an absolute monarchy, and all powers reside in the king.

Mr. Tsering knows Canada well, and we have a common friend: Maurice Strong. The latter had promised to tell the minister about my visit, which he obviously did. "The letter was mailed a month ago and reached me yesterday," says Mr. Tsering, smiling.

He talks enthusiastically about another Canadian, Father Mackey, a Jesuit from Montreal, who's spent most of his life developing an educational system sorely needed by Bhutan. He's become a sort of legend in the country, and has received the highest decorations from the king, who, in a rare gesture, made him an honorary citizen of Bhutan. The minister asks why Father Mackey doesn't have the Order of Canada. Why not, indeed? I feel like telling him that Canadians took a lot longer to discover Dr. Bethune, also a Montrealer, and a great hero to a billion Chinese ...

And we talk about Canada World Youth. The idea seems to please him, but I'll have to discuss it further with his colleague, Lyondo Tashi Tolgyel, the minister responsible for education.

His Majesty, King Jigme Singye Wangchuk is a young (thirty-two years) and vigorous man who wants to modernize and develop his kingdom. He even allowed a few tourists in a few years ago. Despite transportation problems and a lack of adequate hotel facilities, about two thousand tourists visited Bhutan in 1987. But the king feels this was too many. "It was a mistake," he said to *Time* magazine (December 21, 1987). "It has corrupted our people."

Although tourism does provide these remote countries with valuable currency, it's contributed to the destruction of certain cultural or religious values. Unfortunately, I've seen it happen so often in my forty years of travelling that, if I were King of Bhutan, I might have the same reaction. As a practical step, he recently forbade all foreigners from visiting his country's twelve hundred monasteries and temples—the main tourist attractions. Tourism experts say this royal decision should lower to two hundred the number of tourists who'll visit Bhutan in 1988. This should reduce the damage!

Will this new isolationist trend affect the activities of the scarce NGOs that are just beginning to work in this country? Not necessarily.

I spend several hours doing the usual: cashing travellers' cheques, re-confirming my still uncertain *Druk-Air* flight, going to the post office, getting a new visa for Bangladesh, since I'm scheduled to return to Dacca on Thursday. Fortunately, there's a Bengali embassy in Thimpu. The town boasts only *one* other embassy: that of India, which has had considerable influence over Bhutan since the signing of a treaty in 1949, obliging Bhutan to "consult" India on foreign policy questions.

A few hours of sunlight remain before the cold sweeps over the land. I therefore venture out for a solitary stroll through the mountains surrounding the hotel. They're covered by a lush pine forest; every step reveals dazzling and indescribably beautiful scenery.

I get an unexpected visit from a young volunteer who works for the World University Service of Canada. She teaches at a school located a *three or four days'* journey from here, and is passing through Thimpu to meet her brother, who's come from Canada specifically to see her. Lisa and Nick Mayer are Bahaïs from Welland, Ontario. They remind me we met briefly following a speech I made before the International Convention of Bahaï Youth four years ago in London, Ontario. A meeting that brought together over two thousand young people. It definitely is a small world! And Thimpu is so small that they immediately learned the "senator" was in town. The Bahaï faith has always seemed a rather difficult concept to me, and out of touch with young Canadians. But the sincerity and personal discipline of the few Bahaïs I've met has greatly impressed me. For instance, how could I not admire this young Lisa, the only white person in her isolated village, who's been teaching Bhutanese peasants for nearly two years in extremely difficult conditions, for a purely symbolic salary?

January 13

Punctual as always, my young protocol officer picks me up at 10:00 a.m. The minister of foreign affairs has ordered him to show me Thimpu's surroundings and a few of the more famous Buddhist monasteries, royal palaces and temples.

Ugyen is almost too tactful and polite. He addresses me formally and throws in a "Your Excellency" every few words: "May I ask Your Excellency if Your Excellency would care for a cup of tea?" I have enough cultural awareness not to make him lose face by explaining I have no right to this title—reserved in my country for the governor general, ambassadors and bishops! In any event, I finally got used to it!

The monasteries often look like fortresses. Built atop high mountains and covered in whitewash, they resemble those of nearby Tibet.

We stop in front of a tiny pagoda open on all four sides. It shelters a huge prayer wheel—a metal cylinder decorated with Buddhist patterns. It must be around a metre across. The most devout passers-by stop and whirl the cylinder vigorously in a clockwise direction. A bronze bell rings at every turn. "Seven years and seven lents ..."

We admire the queen mother's palace—from the outside, naturally. She's said to have considerable influence on the running of the kingdom.

I never tire of Bhutan's scenery, of its lovely houses trimmed with frills, sometimes frescos, always in good taste, perched on a hilltop or anchored to a mountainside. White stupas with gilded spires glisten here and there, like upside-down tops. But what earmarks Bhutan's landscape are innumerable *dhars* that flutter in front of houses, in fields or in the midst of nature. *Dhars* are narrow streamers of white cotton, up to twelve metres long, on which prayers have been written for the dead, or sometimes the living. They're fastened along a pole made from a young fir tree. "A prayer is sent out whenever wind runs through the *dhars*," explains Ugyen. Usually, a single *dhar* is placed in front of a peasant's home when a death occurs in the family. But suddenly, out of nowhere, we see ten, twenty or more. I count several dozens lined up like soldiers along a mountain crest. They resemble a spirited little army of Gengis Khans ready to storm villages on the valley floor ...

I eat with the social services minister at 7:00 p.m., at a state dinner taking place in my hotel, which belongs to the government. The central heating has been turned on for the occasion. All of the fifteen or so guests are men wearing the national costume. We first meet in a lounge having couches on three sides. "Sit in the middle," the minister tells me, "so everybody can see you." He introduces me to each of the guests, all deputy-ministers or directors of this or that. Mr. Tsering, the foreign affairs minister and "first" minister, joins us soon thereafter.

I feel as though I'm at the other end of the world, a little out of place ...

But we start cracking jokes after two drinks. I relate a few travel anecdotes and emphasize how much I'm impressed with Bhutan, while the Bhutanese talk about Canada, a country they love more than it deserves. I hear about the wonderful Father Mackey, about John Hadwen, our former ambassador, Maurice Strong, and WUSC aid workers, "the best we have! (the other scarce ones are British, Australian or UN volunteers).

At one point, the foreign affairs minister says: "Oh! I read a good little book by Maurice Strong concerning the Third World. It was filled with ideas that were noble and generous, yet practical."

"Really?

"Yes. If I remember correctly it was called *The Great ... The Great ... something*!

"*The Great Building Bee?*

"That's it. *The Great Building Bee.*

"I've heard about it."

I hesitate for a moment. Modest as I am!

"Did you notice it had ... two authors?

"Yes, perhaps ...

"Well, the other author was, er..."

This called for a minimum of courage ... and vanity! But the result was worth it. I stopped being an ordinary Canadian VIP—and became a friend—as soon as my hosts found out I'd co-authored a book with Maurice Strong. An aura of friendship surrounded us for the rest of the evening. Friends of friends became our friends, including Senator Jack Austin, who'd accompanied Maurice Strong on his recent trip to Bhutan.

The conversation calmed down somewhat when three performers showed up to play traditional music. One strums a kind of guitar, with a magnificent dragon-shaped head. Another bows the two strings of a very long violin, "that comes from Tibet," says a minister. The third instrument has a dozen strings attached to a plank of sculpted wood. The musician hits the strings with two little hammers.

Six dancers suddenly appear; three of them are very attractive Bhutanese girls, the only ones I'll see all evening.

At dinnertime we move to another heated room where an impressive buffet has been layed out: a dozen very tasty and spicy Bhutanese dishes. The music has ended: scratchy loudspeakers blare out Strauss waltzes! But this doesn't dampen the conversation; it becomes increasingly warmhearted. There are no speeches, thank God, but everyone goes on at length about the friendship between Bhutan and Canada, with the names of Father Mackey and Maurice Strong frequently cropping up. In the end, "Senator Jack Herbert" becomes one of the family. Mr. Tsering, the minister of foreign affairs, goes as far as circumstances allow: "Sir, you have a real sensitivity to Bhutan's culture. This is very important to us. Canada World Youth is the type of organization we would be glad to welcome. When will we greet your young people? I don't know. But I hope it will be in the near future."

Given Bhutan's attitude towards all foreign influence, this statement seems to be a minor victory. Canada World Youth will some day come to Bhutan. In one year, perhaps two? I don't know. But the door is certainly open.

January 14

Up at 4:00 a.m. I get quite a surprise when I try to pay the hotel bill: I'm told I'm a guest of the Bhutanese government.

Ugyen awaits me at the hotel entrance. It's a blessing that I'll get to travel from Thimpu to Paro in the dark: I won't see the cliffs on either side of the road. The sun rises timidly as we reach the airport. Ugyen immediately takes me to the "VIP" lounge, which is as cold as a refrigerating warehouse.

"Your Excellency ...

"But we'll freeze to death in this room!

"Your Excellency, look ..."

Ugyen points to a miniature electric heater in a corner of the room. It should remedy the situation.

There's a hitch: a power failure has hit the airport!

"Sorry, sorry, Your Excellency ..."

The *Druk-Air* plane is scheduled to take off at 7:45 a.m. There it is, pretty as a picture, motionless, surrounded by attentive mechanics. Another hour before takeoff. It'll feel longer in this Siberian cold. Lord knows I'm no fan of jogging—far from it. But I start jogging. Frantically! For sheer survival.

The space around me is three metres by four, which means I circle like a caged animal. Fortunately, there are no witnesses, save Ugyen, who drops by to comfort me every half-hour. Suddenly, a flurry of activity surrounds the small *Druk-Air* plane. The pilot is revving the props and someone places my suitcase in the hold. Triumphantly, Ugyen hands me a boarding pass.

I keep jogging in any event, glancing at the aircraft at every turn. Horrors! Everyone scatters from the plane as though a bomb had been found on board. Ugyen comes up to me, crestfallen. "Your Excellency ..." Departure is delayed due to a storm, somewhere in India.

Hours crawl by. It's still dreadfully cold. I jog with the energy of a desperate man.

The pilot reappears around 12:00 p.m.

"Well?"

He smiles.

"The weather's still bad ... but we'll give it a shot."

Not something I like to hear from a pilot. But I really want to leave, and realize that five hours of jogging is just about my limit!

The *Druk-Air* plane finally leaves Paro and takes us to Dacca without a hitch.

6.
Indonesia

1989

Crossing the Kota Gadang Pasilihan River.

March 31

Up at 5:00 a.m. Bangkok airport, a three-hour flight. I land in Jakarta, greeted by a thousand memories that date back to my first trip here in 1973, when I'd negotiated Canada World Youth's initial agreement with Indonesia. The Canadian embassy seemed convinced I'd get nowhere, that it was almost impossible to reach a quick agreement with the Indonesians and yackety-yak. Yet I'll be joining in today's celebrations marking the fifteenth anniversary of Canada World Youth's program here, which has allowed 1,100 young people from our two countries to take part. We've had programs with forty or so Third World countries since Year I; none has lasted as long, nor been as successful.

April 1

I join the Canada World Youth delegation for breakfast: the chairman of the board, Harold Dietrich, his wife Joyce, our beloved vice-chairwoman, Norma Walmsley, Jean-Denis Vincent, Robert (Bob) MacRae, of Victoria, our archdeacon, whom we sometimes call the cardinal, Johanne Bourgeois, whom I met in Fiji when she was a young participant in 1973, and saw again a few years later as a group leader in a small Indonesian village. She's now a pillar of the Quebec office. And, of course, Gary Henkleman, an old hand, who was our co-ordinator in Indonesia before becoming our office manager in British Columbia. He's responsible for logistics during our stay here; we call him our "group leader."

I have an hour or two to spare, and suspect that the program devised by the Department of Education's tireless Dr. Washington Napitupulu will likely be very heavy; I therefore do a little shopping with the Dietrichs at a nearby store, where I know I can find splendid batik shirts. I might also allow myself to be tempted by a beautiful Balinese mask ...

So begins an adventure I'd have never related to a soul had there been no witnesses. Unfortunately, the Dietrichs were there; what should've remained secret by definition, given the personal or even intimate character of the matter, became widespread. Worse still, this event earned me the taunts of Canadian and Indonesian friends for the remainder of the trip.

I therefore must pull myself up by the bootstraps and get it off my chest. I was simply strolling around the sculptures, mostly Balinese, and suddenly stumbled on a *banana tree*. A wood carving by an anonymous Balinese artist. Life-size. With two banana clusters. That's right, two. Love at first sight! No use walking away, trying to lose myself in departments displaying wonderful shadow-theatre puppets, or change my mind by looking at splendid teak or rosewood *garoudas*, or fans as lovely as birds of paradise, I couldn't help it: the banana tree had me by the heartstrings. It seemed to beckon me with its broad, green leaves. I tried to talk myself out of it: "Oh, this is just a passing crush, a trivial flirt, I'll have forgotten it by tomorrow! And anyway, how could I ship that enormous wooden plant to Montreal? *KLM* will never allow this as one of my two items of luggage." I approach the banana tree and, making sure no one is looking, discreetly caress one of the leaves. It moved! Naturally. The leaves move because they're attached to the trunk with cotter pins. So they can be removed! That changes everything! Perhaps. I take a few leaves off and realize the trunk, carved from a single piece of wood, is still rather large. I hesitate. I consult my friends the Dietrichs, who've just come out of the batik department. To my great surprise, they encourage me, especially since I've managed to dig up a perfectly rational excuse: "You know the bay window in my dining room, on Prud'homme Street? It has a large tropical plant which gets lonely, probably because I'm seldom home. It wilted and died, quite simply to avenge itself for my lack of attention. I have to replace it every six months. Which costs a fortune! Let's face it, a wooden banana tree would last a lifetime and, when I die, one of my children will likely ... etc."

Harold is a sharp businessman and agrees totally. Joyce thinks a banana tree is perfect for my dining room's tropical decor. I hesitate no longer and head to the cash register! *American Express*. Everything is settled in five minutes. The packer is summoned. A lengthy discussion. We'll need two boxes, one of which may be oddly shaped, since the trunk has two branches. I briefly panic: "The box with the banana leaves and two clusters is rather large. But I could always saddle Jean-Denis Vincent with it, since he only has one bag and is flying back with me. But what if *KLM* refused to allow the tree-trunk on board?" The packer, who speaks no English, displays a beaming smile which doesn't manage to reassure me. I ask for the manager. His English is shaky. He fetches an assistant, then another, and a third. We have a long conversation in English and *Bahasa indosesia* "Well!" the manager says finally, "if *KLM* won't take your banana tree, you can always ship it by air cargo."

"Is that expensive?"

"I have no idea, but let's take a look."

Accompanied by three assistant managers, I follow him to his office through a maze located at the back of his shop, where there's no air-conditioning. I sweat profusely as the manager makes numerous calls and pounds his calculator:

"Air cargo will be exactly $1,050 US"

I nearly fainted. That's crazy! At that price I could buy a whole banana plantation, somewhere in Java, by the seashore ...

"May I use your phone? *KLM* will tell me if I can travel with a banana tree that's nearly 1.75 metres tall on their large plane."

It's 4:30 p.m. and offices are closed. We leave for Sumatra very early tomorrow morning, and won't return for three days.

"That's it! You keep my banana tree until Thursday—after all, I've already paid for it. And if *KLM* refuses, you'll reimburse me."

It's not that easy. I paid with a credit card; reimbursement is unbelievably complicated. If it's not too late we'll cancel the transaction and the banana tree will be set aside for me. I resign myself ... "See you Thursday! And don't go selling it to some rich tourist from Texas: the banana tree would be very unhappy there ..."

April 2

Up at 6:00 a.m. Departure for the airport at 8:00 a.m.—architecturally, one of the most beautiful in the world. We're heading to Pedang (a one-and-a-half hour flight), accompanied by our dear Dr. Napitupulu, director of non-formal education, culture and sports for Indonesia. He's the equivalent of a deputy minister of education in this country of 175 million inhabitants—the fifth largest population in the world. He's always been a friend to Canada World Youth; of all our Third World counterparts, he's among those best able to quickly and thoroughly grasp the program's objectives. He has a wonderful sense of humour and his company certainly won't be boring.

We're met in Pedang by a delegation from the Department of Education and a few former Indonesian participants from the region.

Lunch in a strange little restaurant, beside a pond astir with hundreds of beautiful black or red fish. They're caught with a landing net, skinned, cleaned and fried before our eyes. A delight.

April 3

This day ought to be the most memorable of our trip and begins at 6:00 a.m. An hour's drive to Solok, the district capital. We're greeted by the *bupati*, the Sumatra Barat governor's representative, likely the equivalent of a sub-prefect in France. Numerous former Indonesian participants accompany us. One of them, pretty as only Indonesian girls can be, has just completed the program in a district village. On her group's behalf, she gives the *bupati* a T-shirt bearing Vancouver's coat of arms, since they spent the Canadian part of the program in British Columbia. A card comes with the gift. Each participant has written something for the *bupati*: "Your sons and daughters will never forget you!" Or, "We'll keep the *bupati* in our hearts." A spontaneous testimony highlighting the extent to which the top district's official was intimately involved with the groups during the months they spent in the villages.

He was scheduled to be in Jakarta today, to attend the wedding of a friend's daughter—the friend being an important political figure. "I sent my wife in my place," he tells us. "I prefer going to the villages with you."

He knows better than we do the considerable physical effort needed to visit four remote villages, linked to the highway by incredible dirt roads, accessible only to all-terrain vehicles. Four such vehicles are parked in front of the *bupati*'s office. He climbs into the first one, equipped with a siren and a flashing red light.

We drive through an absolutely spectacular mountain region, likely one of the most beautiful in Indonesia: tall mountains covered in luxuriant vegetation right to the summit, gentle valleys carved into rice paddies that are sometimes light green, or ochre when the rice is ripe, or as dazzling as mirrors if still covered in water. Ricefields carve terraces into the hillsides; they resemble giant stairways.

After an hour on increasingly bad roads, we reach the first village, Tambak Paninggahan, where participants spent three months *two years ago*. Do the villagers still remember? We soon found out. A crowd awaited us at the village entrance to observe the poignant welcoming ceremony that's typical of this region. Several girls, wearing red velvet costumes trimmed in embroidery and gilded sequins, slowly approach us. One of them carries a plate filled with tree leaves, which she offers us.

We nibble on a small piece, while a second girl places flower garlands around our necks. A group with tambourines and other percussion instruments makes the moist air reverberate. A boy welcomes us on the village's behalf. We walk to the centre of Tambak Paninggahan, accompanied by a hundred or so villagers, and gather in the school yard. The best chairs from nearby houses have been placed in rows for guests of honour. The village chief makes a long speech in *Bahasa indonesia*, translated word for word by a former participant, a girl who learned English somewhere in Canada. The speaker carefully describes everything the village owes participants: construction of restrooms and a public bath, an office for the mosque, a stone wall in front of the school, etc. Participants learned martial arts, as well as local dances and crafts. The chief also underlines that friendship now unites our two countries, that former participants still write to their Indonesian "parents," etc.

Then come speeches by the *bupati*, by Dr. Napitupulu, Canada World Youth's founding president, etc. We're also served peanuts, corn, rice titbits and coconut milk.

Following the speeches, we're treated to a traditional dance performance and a martial arts demonstration by the two village champions. During one of the dances, the *bupati* drags Norma Walmsley onto the floor. Norma plays along and, thanks to her spontaneity and sense of humour, is a big success with the crowd. She's now recognized as our little group's premier dancer.

I'm relating what took place, but can't begin to describe what we felt on hearing moving testimonies from these humble villagers who were intensely involved with Canada World Youth, and now express their gratitude though this extraordinary celebration.

We get the feeling we're in another world, where friendship, hospitality and kindness are the fundamental values. We're all deeply moved and have trouble leaving these wonderful people who talk about their sons and daughters in Canada, smiling at us continually as though we were the real parents of those far-away children.

Atop a high mountain, a few kilometres from the next village, stands a promontory with a breathtaking view of a large lake that stretches out in the valley. With the help of villagers, our participants built a handsome concrete kiosk to shelter visitors. The building is now the pride of the village and, last February 13, the *bupati* changed the name of the mountain to *Tanjung Canada*, or "Cape Canada."

We reach the village of Balai-Balai Kagang, after a dreadful hour-long *Jeep* ride in 35°C temperature. Another welcoming ceremony, tambourines, yellow-orchid garlands, speeches, dances, etc. Guests of honour sit comfortably under a canopy, and villagers form a circle while standing in the blazing sun. The enormous trees that surround us create the impression we're in a huge open-air theatre.

The village chief says: "We're really sad to be separated from our sons and daughters in Canada, a country we now have close relations with. We're grateful for what they built in the village and in our hearts. Before participants arrived, we were really isolated, and no one came to see us. And now, strangers come to admire our scenery from *Tanjung Canada*. The world now seems closer to us."

To prove our participants were good English teachers, a group of children sings "You are my sunshine ..." Dancing, music, martial arts. The celebration continues!

Following the ceremony, they lead us to the village centre to see the clock tower participants recently built, along with restrooms and other useful constructions. Names of the fourteen Canada World Youth participants and two group leaders have been engraved on the tower.

Though the small dirt streets all have names, the village chief tells us he's changed some of them. Main street is now called British Columbia Street, after the province where the Canadian part of the program took place. There's also a Vancouver Street, and a Quebec Street.

The village chief invites us for lunch at 12:00 p.m. His house is surely the only one able to accommodate the forty-two guests—all men, save for three Canadian women who receive special treatment. Guests' wives are to eat *after* the men. We leave our shoes outside, and sit on carpets, around a long tablecloth covered with dishes: chicken, beef, fish, vegetables, fruits and a lot of rice. A local ceremony takes place before we eat: two villagers, one at each end of the room, hold a long dialogue which even Dr. Napitupulu doesn't understand. He only knows the speeches are polite formulas, hoping we enjoy our meal.

We're off to the third village, Kota Gadang Pasilihan, likely the most inaccessible. Recent rain has rutted the narrow dirt road. We drive fifteen kilometres an hour. Finally, the *Jeeps* can go no further and we must walk the rest. But a large river flows between two mountains and separates us from the village. "There's a bridge!" Dr. Napitupulu says, mockingly, as though to play a trick on us. The bridge is actually a narrow suspended catwalk where we must walk single-file on a bamboo trellis, hanging onto the wire that serves as a skimpy guardrail. Norma leads the way, as we courageously venture onto the footbridge which rocks like a swing. Jean-Denis Vincent and I, chivalrous as we are, allow the others to go first. We finally admit we both suffer from vertigo.

The river's grey waters are only ten metres below, but the current is swift.

"Any crocodiles down there?" asks Jean-Denis, laughing. We laugh mostly to save face, but advance with the greatest caution, watching each footstep on the narrow trellis, avoiding to look down. Dr. Napitupulu awaits us on the opposite bank, shouting "bravo!" as though we'd just scaled Everest. He isn't alone: a hundred or so young scouts in yellow and brown uniforms give us a wild round of applause.

We walk to a large concrete cistern built by participants. Villagers explain that mountain water now flows to their homes and gardens, whereas women previously had to walk for miles with water-skins on their heads to get it.

A similar poignant welcoming ceremony, with a few variations. A triumphal arch made of bamboo, Canadian and Indonesian flags wafting among palm trees, a village chief who endlessly describes the work done by participants. Besides building the cistern, they repaired village streets, built a volley-ball court, refurbished the tiny municipal office, etc.

Unfortunately, we can't linger in this lovely village, where houses are often built on piles, and whose pointed roofs resemble buffalo horns: we're already two hours behind schedule and must consider people in the fourth and last village who've put as much effort into preparing their celebration. We get rattled for over an hour before reaching Pasar Paninjauan, where ceremonies take place in pitch darkness that's occasionally punctuated by the flame of a storm lamp. We're brought to a stone platform covered by a red-cotton canopy, facing a small square where the crowd has gathered. The village chief mentions all the tears that flowed when participants left a few weeks ago, the splendid clock tower they built, which will remind villagers of them twenty-four hours a day, not to mention the fishpond they dug, etc.

It's nearly 8:00 p.m. when we return to Solok. Dirty, dog-tired and overwhelmed by the emotions of the day, another page in the story of Canada World Youth and a small step towards peace.

We'd have gladly hit the sack to recover from all this, but how could we turn down the *bupati*'s invitation to join him for dinner?

April 4

Up at 6:00 a.m. Since there are neither showers nor bathtubs, we wash local-style, splashing ourselves with cold water.

We reach Padang just in time to meet the province of Sumatra Barat's governor, the equivalent of one of our provincial premiers. He has tea served in his huge office decorated with carved panelling. He's fully aware of Canada World Youth's activities in his province, and insists Dr. Napitupulu send more groups here next year. "That won't be easy," says Dr. Napitupulu. "Several provinces await their turn ..." In other words, they're fighting over Canada World Youth!

Padang airport. A one-and-a-half hour flight, and we're back in Jakarta ... and my banana tree problem! I head straight for the *KLM* office. I'm allowed two items of luggage.

"Regardless of size?"

"Just a second, I'll check ... Maximum length: 150 centimetres."

"What if my parcel is 151 centimetres long ... or a little more?"

"It's against the rules. You'll have to talk to our manager at the airport."

What the heck! I like living dangerously! Accompanied by Norma Walmsley, I rush to the store. My tree's still there. I once again pay for it. Out come the wrapper, manager and assistant managers, all old friends by now. They easily found a large box for the leaves and banana clusters, but the trunk is a problem. There isn't a box big enough in the whole store. They finally dig up a fairly large one. But half the trunk sticks out, not to mention the two branches! They find another box for the upper trunk, but the branches still protrude. The manager has an idea and rushes off. He returns with two small boxes to protect the branches. The package is wrapped with tape and tied with lots of green nylon string. We congratulate one another as we admire our work: a box with exactly sixteen sides!

I can easily go down the three flights of stairs with the smaller box, but I'll need help for the monster. The manager gets a diminutive sales clerk to help me: he's much smaller than the package. He hoists it onto his back and, accompanied by Norma who's overcome with laughter, we make our way to the street, clearing a path through the astonished crowd of customers. The clerk flags down a taxi, which stops but races off when the driver sees the intimidating package. A second taxi. Norma climbs into the front seat with resolve, and shuts the door. When the driver realizes I also want to get in with my two boxes, he waves his arms in despair and politely asks Norma to get out. I suggest she return to the hotel without me, but she won't hear of it; she's having too much fun to miss a single episode of this adventure. Three more taxis pass by without even stopping. Night has fallen. Morale begins to tumble ... The little clerk has never faced such a situation but refuses to abandon us. He disappears for a moment and returns with a tiny policeman on a tiny motorcycle. He assesses the situation, stops a taxi with an authoritative gesture, ensures the "normal" box is put in the trunk which, naturally, can't be shut. I explain the problem with gestures: the strange two-armed box is nearly 175 centimetres long, and can't fit inside any taxi. He smiles and says he'll follow us to the hotel and carry the thing on his bike. I laugh at this odd suggestion. But with the help of onlookers that had gathered around us, the officer places the box upright on the seat of his motorcycle, just behind him. The little clerk sits behind the box, balancing it with his arms. Norma is laughing so hard that she's convinced she ruined the photos she took of this incredible event. And off we go, taxi, motorcycle, clerk, boxes, Norma and me, towards the hotel amid Jakarta's crazy traffic. After awhile, I lose sight of the bike and am nearly convinced the policeman and clerk dropped my banana tree and that a bus has smashed it to splinters. But no, they beat us to the hotel, safe and sound ... all three of them! I was certainly delighted to give them a large handful of rupees ...

Needless to say what the conversation topic was during the Chinese meal Canadians shared that evening. After coffee had been served, they insisted on going up to my room to see this strange box with their own eyes and, of course, be photographed beside it, to prove the authenticity of my banana-tree story to their friends.

April 6

Around 10:00 a.m., we visit participants from the Ontario and British Columbia teams: they've just returned from the province of Sulawesi Selatan, located some six-hundred miles from Jakarta, i.e., a two-day boat trip. They're getting ready for their brief performance this evening and resting before the long trip back, scheduled for Saturday. There are about a hundred of them and it's rather difficult to chat with each and remember names. But we'll all remember the profound happiness they display at having had a unique experience "that's changed us forever," a Toronto boy tells me. A young Vancouver musician has learned to play the traditional instruments of his village and even formed a group: "I have it all planned," he tells us. "I'll return in three years to study Indonesian music seriously." The usual wonderful mixture is in attendance: the Acadian from northeastern New Brunswick, the cheerful girl from Saint John's, Newfoundland, the guy from Edmonton who's never eaten so much rice, etc.

We share a traditional meal with participants: lots of rice, fine chicken brochettes with peanut sauce, small meat pies and bananas. Indonesian participants relate their stories about Port Hope, Ontario, or Summerland, British Columbia; Canadians tell us about life in Sulawesi villages. A curly haired Ontario girl shows us her photo album: "This is my mother grinding coffee ... There I am, harvesting rice in the paddy. Oh! my counterpart in her provincial costume! She's a terrific dancer. She was getting ready for the show we put on for villagers that night ... This hut is a restroom my host family built especially for my counterpart and me. There previously hadn't been a single one in the village, but our group built a large one for the community ... This is the party people organized on the eve of our departure ... etc." In the excitement, we even forget to tell our two Canadian co-ordinators, Wayne Lundeberg and Bill Doogan, and their Indonesian counterparts, that they're largely responsible for the obvious elation that prevails at the conclusion of this program, and which testifies to its success.

We leave participants until the super-farewell party this evening in Jakarta. It takes place in a huge hall where more than three hundred people sit at round tables decorated with orchids. Besides this year's hundred participants, and a few distinguished guests including the Canadian ambassador, nearly two hundred former Indonesian participants are here *at their own expense* from almost every province in the country. The effect is particularly stunning, since they're wearing traditional costumes from their region, as do Canadian participants, who were given the provincial outfit by the Sulawesi governor on their arrival. The girls are especially striking with their large necklaces and gilded diadems.

The ceremony unfolds according to Indonesian tradition: it begins with speeches by representatives from the Department of Education and Canada World Youth. The master of ceremonies is a young television announcer. She invites the following people to speak: Mr. Nasrun Azaar, Mr. Sunario, deputy minister of education, Dr. Napitupulu, Harold Dietrich and the founding president. We talk about the brotherhood of man, love, peace ...

A small-gift exchange among Indonesian and Canadian dignitaries follows, with a sumptuous buffet and a show including traditional dancing, singing and music—absolutely dazzling—performed by a professional group. But the evening's highlight was the number put on by participants. We were more than proud to see Canadians performing dances from Sumatra or Java with as much skill as their Indonesian counterparts. Sam, a young Torontonian, delighted everyone with his mastery of the tambourine and *angklung*, an unusual percussion instrument made from a hundred-odd pieces of bamboo. Another Canadian, a blond giant, led a group of participants in a demonstration of the martial arts typical of Salawesi.

And to conclude this memorable evening, the lovely television announcer asks everyone to form a ring around the hall. One of the trip's wonderful moments: three hundred young people from nearly all provinces of Indonesia and Canada, singing a *Québécois* song that's been extremely popular over the last fifteen years in the Indonesian program ... and which, to participants, certainly has no political undertones: *Gens du pays* by Gilles Vigneault. They've written a couplet in English and another in *Bahasa indonesia*, which alternate with the original French words, and expresses their ideal of love and peace:

"Youth of the world, now is your turn ...

Walk hand in hand and speak of love."
"Saudaraku giliran mu...
Untuk menyatakan cinta."

The emotion is so intense that Jean-Denis Vincent isn't alone in wiping a tear. It's getting late, we have to leave: farewells last over an hour! We'd like to talk to all participants and hear their wonderful stories. An Indonesian in his thirties gives me a hug. "Remember me? I was a participant in Year I, 1974. You came to visit our village ..." A tiny *Québécoise* hands me a slip of paper: "It's a poem I just wrote for you ... It's not Victor Hugo!" She disappears into the crowd before I can ask her name.

"*My* counterpart, *my* family, *my* village ...
Forever in my heart ...
Indonesia is a dream come true,
It's changed my outlook completely ..." etc.

April 8

Our group disperses, since we're not all returning to Canada along the same itinerary. I'm to go through Amsterdam with Jean-Denis Vincent. As we fly over Greenland he suddenly says: "I just realized what's happened to me, and why this trip stands out: *it filled my soul*!"

Yes, *KLM* did accept my banana tree. And though I'd expected the worst at Mirabel, the customs officer quickly reassured me: "It's a sculpture, of course, a work of art, and comes under clause 378: you have nothing to pay."

It's so wonderful when customs officers love art!

7.
Togo

1989

A Canadian participant and her Togolese counterpart preparing the family meal.

December 30, 1989

A first meeting with Togo's new Minister of Youth, Sports and Culture, His Excellency Messan Agbeyome Kodjo. He's thirty-five years old and was appointed in the cabinet shuffle that took place barely a week ago. The minister says to whoever will listen that "we've been friends, ever since we met in Canada." In fact, we met in Nanaimo, on Vancouver Island, "of all places," during my first trip there, when I'd been invited to speak at an international conference of two thousand young people from nearly every country in the world. That was in the summer of 1986, and I had indeed met Messan Kodjo ... who was far from suspecting he'd be Togo's youth minister two years later, and that we'd be discussing the resumption of exchanges between his ministry and Canada World Youth. Togo is fifteen thousand kilometres from Canada, and Nanaimo is five thousand kilometres from Montreal ... and the world is so small!

At 2:00 p.m. we leave for the northern city of Sokodé, where we'll spend the night. Tomorrow, we'll call on the host families in the two last villages where Canadian participants lived in 1985 and 1986.

The sky is grey, as it often is in winter, a season plagued by the harmattan: a dry, parching wind from the distant Sahara which carries a fine dust that darkens the sun, pollutes the air, and makes the Togolese cough. The strange light gives the landscape a surreal quality: palms, baobabs, teaks, and mangos are silhouetted against the hazy sky. We drive through fields of corn, yams, and sugar cane. As on all African roads, we see a cavalcade of women and a few men, walking in very upright positions, though they bear heavy loads on their heads. The region's shortage of water forces the women to walk up to twelve kilometres every day with a terra cotta jar or metal pail filled with water. Others carry wood, baskets of pineapples or bananas, or bags of charcoal.

We cross a vast plateau speckled with enormous termite hills that resemble Bavarian castles or gothic cathedrals. We see beautiful, serene Togolese villages and thatched mud huts: wealthier folks can afford corrugated-metal roofs; they're less attractive but more resistant. Life unfolds as it did a hundred, perhaps a thousand, years ago. Women crush manioc or yams to make *fufu*, a staple of the local diet. Men repair a wall eaten away by recent rains, young women sit on the roadside with small piles of peppers, oranges, manioc roots or tomatoes. Children play on well-graded dirt roads pushing along an old bicycle rim or small wooden truck made by a father or older brother. There's a degree of happiness in these villages where people have nearly enough to eat; however, improvements could be made in health-related areas, i.e., hygiene.

At nightfall, we nearly run over an enormous wild boar that bolted across the road. According to Mr. Batascome, the youth director, our *Peugeot* would've been a shadow of its former self following a head-on collision with the beast.

We check into Sokodé's charming *Central Hotel*, and are shown to our thatched, hut-shaped cabins.

Drinks in the open air, under palm trees, with notables from the prefecture, including the prefect, police commissioner, and youth inspector, i.e., the ministry's representative in this prefecture, N'Bebi Kome: he was the Togolese co-ordinator for the Canada World Youth program in 1984. A few other notables sit around a table, including a former participant who speaks fondly of the Canadian host family he lived with in 1984, in a Quebec village called Saint-Hugues. His "father," a Mr. Fontaine, regularly sends him letters, "and sometimes even a money order for Christmas."

December 31

Up at 6:00 a.m. I leave the hotel with the sub-prefect's assistant, since the prefect had to leave Sokodé at 4:00 a.m., and head to Kora, the president of the republic's native village, to wish the latter a happy New Year. Preceded by a police car and followed by another vehicle carrying the rest of the delegation, we head to Kparatao, a village that hosted a Canada World Youth group in 1985 and 1986. We stop in Sokodé to fill up with gas, and take the opportunity to stroll through the market. "Surprise me!" Diaghilev had shouted to Jean Cocteau. But there's no need to shout in Sokodé: the least gesture or object astounds us. A young girl sells branch stubs: they're actually local toothbrushes which are very effective and have built-in toothpaste. We spot a small booth: ten cigarette packs, some already opened since they're also sold by the unit, small soap bars, and a few pill bottles that I examine.

"Aspirin?

"Yes," says the young lady vendor, smiling.

"Chloroquine, for malaria?

"Of course!

"What about this one?

"For sore stomachs.

"And these red ones?

"The same.

"How about these yellow ones?

"Stomach aches."

As any polling expert would, I immediately conclude that Sokodé's population suffers more from stomach aches than from migraines or malaria. Finally, a booth that should please natural-product enthusiasts: completely natural remedies capable of curing every illness. My guide, Kantoni, doesn't have the time to identify all these excellent products, displayed by species if not by illness: the heads of toads, fish, snakes, urchins, crayfish legs ...

"Are they eaten just like that?

"No, they're crushed and mixed with other compounds. Each animal carcass cures a particular illness. Except AIDS, unfortunately!"

We reach Kparatao, located a few kilometres from the Benin border. Wherever we happen to be in this incredible, elongated country created by the whims of former colonial powers, a border is always nearby: Ghana to the west, Benin to the east, Burkina-Faso to the north ...

Kparatao's entire population is jubilant and awaits us at the village entrance. The chief welcomes us amid incredible pandemonium: tom-toms, rattles, and the strident *yu-yus* of women. We shake hands with at least fifty notables, magnificent in their finest Muslim outfits—the village is completely dominated by the Islamic faith.

A row of armchairs has been set up in the village square, under the shade of an enormous baobab and a few mangos.

A group of tom-tom players hammer the dry air, charged with harmattan dust. The crowd must include the village's entire population and forms a square closed on one side by the notables' chairs. There are hundreds of people, perhaps over a thousand, men and women in splendid, brilliantly coloured costumes, each one unique.

The program is a cheerful mix of folklore and yackety-yak. With rare exceptions, speeches made on such occasions are rather insipid. Nonetheless, I'm touched by the assistant prefect's speech—handwritten and likely prepared the previous evening, since my visit was organized at the last minute. I thank him for the exceptional welcome I was given. His reply: "It's nothing compared to what Canada World Youth has done for the people of Togo. A hundred of our young people have gone through the program. That's amazing. Your presence here, and that of young Canadians, is a victory over the distance that separates people. Thanks to Canada World Youth, we got to know and like each other, live together, and think of the world as a family."

A sort of master of ceremonies begins to ply his trade in the middle of the square. With numerous gestures, he prompts the crowd to respond to his slogans. One or two stand out: "Friendship between Canada and Togo, forever ..." The crowd replies: "Onwards!"

"General Gnassingbé Eyadèma[1], forever ...

"More power to him!

"Senator Jacques Hébert, founding president of Canada World Youth, forever!

"Onwards!" shouts the crowd.

Next up is a group of absolutely amazing men and women dancers. It's hard to understand the meaning of each gesture or body movement, but there's a shade of eroticism that fools no one.

Two flagpoles stand close together in the village square: one with Togo's flag, the other with the maple leaf. During my short speech, I couldn't resist making a Togolese-style flight of oratory: "With help from the wind, our flags are shaking hands, and even taking each other by the neck!" It's rather coarse, but draws a great burst of laughter and roaring applause ...

On behalf of his village, the chief offers me a national costume made from cotton that was grown, spun and woven here. This *agbara* makes me a "village son." I put on the large blouse, to the crowd's delight. An old woman then asks me to join her in a local folk dance, which must be the highlight of this improvised party. But no, fifty more dancers in white tunics and red tarbooshes clear a path through the crowd and treat us to an amazing performance, while kicking up a fine reddish dust by stamping the ground with bare feet. They're accompanied by seven musicians who

---

1 The president of Togo.

pound various-sized tom-toms. Between dances, the village chief's spokesman gives another speech: "It was a pleasure and honour for the village of Kparatao to host seven young Canadians who came to work with us in a spirit of peace and brotherhood. We admired the courage and determination of your young people, girls and boys, who worked in the fields and built improved ovens. Devices that remind us of their presence in our village. Long live the friendship between Canada and Togo!"

One more dance by young people from the Koranic school, another speech, and it's time to get under way, but not before speaking to each family that hosted participants in 1984 and 1985. On behalf of the others, one "father" says: "We've never stopped thinking of our children since they left for Canada; we ask the senator to do his utmost so they return to see us one day. At first, we were surprised to see Canadian girls insist on going into the fields and doing work traditionally done by men. Our girls followed their example. And now," he concludes, laughing, "my wife cultivates her own plot of land!"

It's 11:00 a.m. We're invited to a meal washed down with plenty of wine at the home of a local notable: rice, *fufu*, very spicy meat, etc. We had no idea we were expected at the Tchaoudjo prefect's official residence in an hour, for a reception and grand Togolese feast.

We leave Sokodé at 2:30 p.m. and head to Lama-Tessi, another village that hosted a Canada World Youth group. As was the case in Kparatao, my visit occasions a great public celebration with dances, songs, speeches and slogans chanted by the entire crowd. Three squatting flutists hop towards me and, for a few minutes, seem to play only for me. A wonderful speech by the village chief, who wears a white gandoura and a black fez covered in golden sequins that shimmer in the sunlight. On the village's behalf, he gives me a pick, mattock and large wicker basket: "Tools your participants used when they planted, weeded or harvested the manioc." A meeting with host families. Mothers speak very emotively of their Canadian "children." They remember their names: "Dominique, John, Lise, Mike ..." Some tell me they gave their participant's name to the first child born after his or her departure...

January 2, 1989

Before leaving Lomé, I sign a new protocol of agreement with the youth minister ... my buddy from Nanaimo! Canada World Youth will return to Togo this year, following a four-year hiatus.

"Canada World Youth, forever ...

"Onwards!"

8.
Thailand

1992

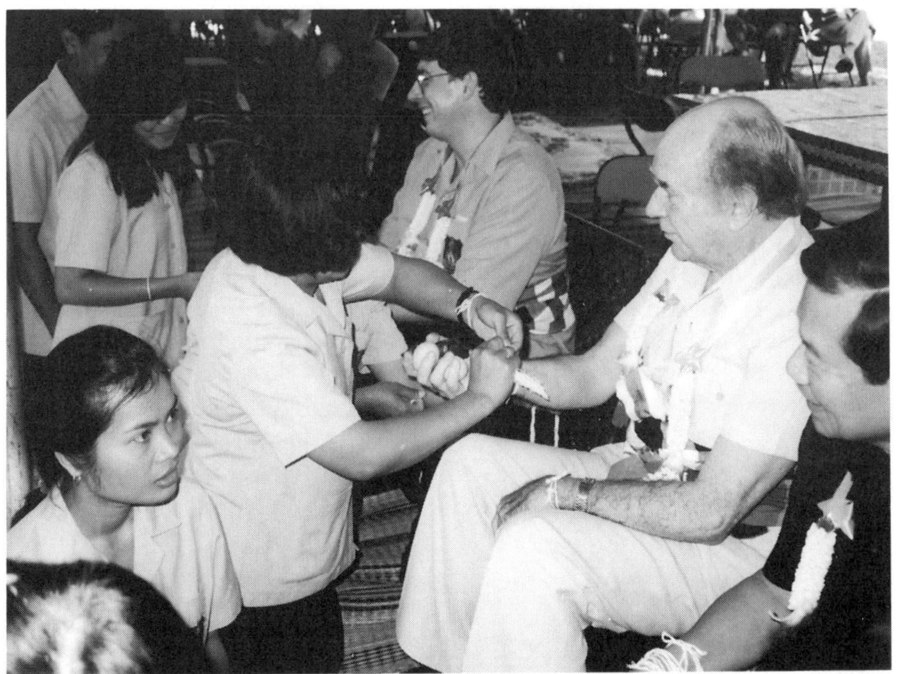

The welcoming ceremony in the village of Tambon Banlao, in northern Thailand.

January 3

My love story with Thailand began forty years ago, when I crossed that gentle land by *Jeep* during a trip around the world. I had no time to linger then, but swore I'd return on the first occasion.

The opportunity evaded me: I didn't see Thailand again until 1985, when I travelled there, not for leisure, but to submit Canada World Youth to the Thai government. They were so receptive that the program was set up the following year. It's been remarkably successful in the seven years since. Nearly three hundred youths have taken part, half of them young farmers from every corner of Thailand. Most of them, as I'd hear repeatedly in the coming days, have become leaders in their communities and particularly vigorous advocates of change.

I'm greeted at the airport by the two co-ordinators: Philip White and Jain, his Thai counterpart.

Jain is a terrific young man—the first adjective that springs to mind when I think of him with his disarming smile, a common feature among Thais. Before becoming a program co-ordinator, he's twice been a group leader over the last seven years.

As for Philip, he's what's known as a real old-timer. A participant ten years ago, then a group leader in Uruguay and Yemen, and now a co-ordinator in Thailand. He informs me he married Sarah Whitehead last year. She's a former participant I met in Zaïre in 1986[1]. What a close-knit family Canada World Youth is!

A few hours of lively conversation with Philip before the official dinner given by the director general of the Community Development Department (CDD), the Interior Ministry division responsible for Canada World Youth. Though the director general is relatively new to his position, he's obviously most interested in the program. To prove it, he'll accompany me to the three villages where participants are working.

January 6

Up at 4:30 a.m. We must leave for the airport early, before the Bangkok traffic becomes horrendous. It's dark, but activity is already intense. Noodle vendors serve their first customers along sidewalks, as other petty merchants set up flimsy displays.

An hour's flight brings us to Ubonratchatani, a large city in northeastern Thailand. We're met at the hotel door by a delegation from the ministry. An immense yellow streamer with an inscription in beautiful Thai lettering is attached to the canopy. Jain, Philip's counterpart, translates for me: "Welcome to Senator Jacques Hébert." I'd insisted my visit be as informal as possible, but the Thais wouldn't hear of it, especially since I was accompanied by the CDD director general, a person of considerable importance in the country's administrative hierarchy.

A three-hour drive towards the Laotian border. A region of rice paddies and

---

1 See interview with Sarah Whitehead, p. 93.

wading buffaloes. Lovely villages, airy houses built on piles due to occasional rainy season floods.

Two police cars, with red lights flashing, precede us, closely followed by a single motorcycle escort. Needless to say that regular traffic quickly divides to let us by. Only a few ponderous buffaloes, hides shining with mud, aren't so easily impressed. Our escort misses the turn at the crossroad, speeding straight ahead where they should've veered left. Laughter bursts out inside our minibus. A few minutes later, our crestfallen cops catch up with us.

A multitude greets us in the village of Tambon Banlao: the provincial governor, notables, CDD officials, Canada World Youth participants, host families, and numerous onlookers who wouldn't for the world miss activities that have taken so long to prepare. Several garlands are placed around my neck: jasmine blossoms with their heavy perfumes, and blue orchids.

They've built an immense dais capable of sheltering several hundred people in front of the Buddhist temple. It was hardly necessary, since we're beneath a green vault of mango and tamarind trees. The director general and I take place in the front row, before a monumental flower arrangement designed for the welcoming ceremony. Further back, nearly out of sight, a kind of secular officiant dressed in white sits on the ground and recites a long, chanted prayer, "to purify my soul"—just what I needed most!

The old man approaches on his knees, placing two eggs in my hand, as well as rice wrapped in a leaf. He rubs my forearm with a white cotton string, then ties it around my wrist. This is to ensure I'll have enough to eat for the rest of my life. A dozen old women (and the participants) follow him, each with a string to tie around my wrist.

The speeches and small-gift exchange that follow this quasi-religious ceremony are punctuated by spontaneous but brief bursts of applause. Participants in regulation sky blue shirts are seated, good as gold, in the front row of a crowd numbering a few hundred (regulation shirts are a Thai idea!). After over two months in Thailand, they've grown accustomed to the lengthy official ceremonies loved by people in this country, especially in the villages. I look at them from a distance (they're about a hundred metres away) and hazard the odd smile, as I catch the eye of one or another, never sure it's the proper thing to do.

In the midst of a wonderful flight of oratory from a powerful loudspeaker, a large, skinny and mangy dog quietly crosses the scene, casting a disgusted gaze at the distinguished guests.

A leading citizen stands up to tell us about the village, founded 175 years ago by refugees from neighbouring Laos. He describes its efforts at development and the contribution of participants. They've named a spokesman to explain the group's activity in recent months: Craig Candler from Edmonton, an excellent participant who's managed to learn the Thai language in two months. I catch a few English phrases in passing: "Interaction with the group and communities has taught us leadership and self-confidence. Dealing with numerous challenges has helped us acquire patience and tolerance of others ...

"We've all been given the chance to develop acceptance and open-mindedness ... so we might learn from the differences of others and improve ourselves and our knowledge as a result ... On returning to Canada, we'll try to share our knowledge, encourage others to improve themselves, be aware of others, and broaden their understanding of world issues."

Aa series of traditional dances follows, with the accompaniment of about ten local musicians. I wasn't familiar with any of the instruments. We were served copious amounts of tea and cookies throughout the long ceremony. From my perch, I manage to wink at Catriona Campbell, to at least inform her I was anxious for the ceremony to end so I might finally meet participants.

However, we still had to inaugurate the playground for village children, built by participants with makeshift materials. A commemorative plaque above the enclosure's entrance will likely remind future generations that eight young Canadians and eight young Thais from different parts of their respective countries came through this remote village. A throng of small children, unable to await inauguration, rushes to the swings.

We then visit a few host families, each billeting one Canadian and one Thai participant. Sherron Soo, from Vancouver, is of Chinese extraction. "They often mistake me for a Thai girl," she told me, laughing. "It creates odd situations." Her "family" lives in a handsome traditional wooden house built on piles. Access is by means of a long ladder. A closed room is reserved for participants. The rest of the family (five members) sleeps on mats in a single spacious room. The family has made a little shelter with braided-straw matting, so Sherron and her counterpart may wash discreetly ... with cold water stored in a large terra cotta urn. Sherron shows me the kitchen corner: a small hibachi with a few smouldering embers: "Rice, three times a day, vegetables, a little fish, meat occasionally." She appears perfectly happy and, like other participants, in a panic at the prospect of leaving her family, her village and Thailand in a few weeks.

A private meeting with participants, finally, under an immense tamarind tree filtering the sun's rays agreeably. A special moment that dispels all the hardships of travel. After an hour and a half of meandering conversation, when I've just stopped confusing Craig with Gordon and Elinor with Caroline, Philip tells me we have to leave. A three-hour drive back to Pratumrat, where the director general and I host a dinner for over two hundred guests.

January 7

Up at 5:30 a.m. We reach the village of Tambon Puay on schedule at 9:30 a.m. Everything is organized down to the last detail.

A billboard message greets me at the village entrance, and main street is decked out in flags along a stretch of at least one kilometre: the Canadian flag on one side, that of Thailand on the other.

A crowd of over four hundred awaits us in the large community hall. Guests of honour on one side and, on the other, our participants, with whom I won't be able to talk for several hours yet ...

The hall is decorated with numerous Canadian flags of all sizes made by the village women. Maple leaves take on the most astonishing forms. Some have stems as thick as tree trunks.

The ceremony is as long as it is stirring; it resembles yesterday's, save for a few details. For example, traditional dances aren't performed by professionals, but by participants. Canadians display as much skill as Thais in these dances, where arms, hands and fingers are busier than legs. Particularly remarkable performances were given by Dave Bronsard, a tall Quebecker from Aylmer, and Jos Lauzon of Windsor, Ontario.

It's obvious that villagers think highly of participants. A notable explains that local news is broadcast every morning through a loud-speaker located in the heart of the village. Every morning an item features participant activities.

We lunch outside under a mango tree, and I casually meet participants (at last!) in the shade of giant kapok trees that give the little park the look of a cathedral. As usual, we have lots to tell each other ...

I visit the families of several participants, including that of Jos Lauzon, who raises silkworms. Jos fully understands the lengthy process for obtaining silk, the endless thread that wraps cocoons. "To loosen the thread, you first have to boil cocoons. The worm can be eaten either boiled or fried. Not bad, and very nourishing," he says, placing a plateful of freshly boiled worms before me.

"Try them, you'll see ..."

"Er ... I like them better fried!"

Jos shows me a newly born calf, still tottering on frail legs: "He was born the day before yesterday. I helped the cow give birth. My counterpart and I learned the technique from our first host family, in Ontario."

Jos' "mother," surmising what her tall, fair-haired son is saying, laughs approvingly.

There's an Ontario farmer who doesn't realize that, thanks to him, a Windsor boy helped deliver a calf in Tambon Puay, a small village in northeastern Thailand.

January 8

Up at 5:00 a.m. Today, we're to visit a former Thai participant in Tambon Banrai, a small village in a western province, near Burma (or Myanmar, as the present regime prefers to call the country).

Along the way, we make a detour to a village of pile dwellers famous for its floating market. Since today's program isn't too heavy, my Thai hosts want to give me a few hours to relax. They couldn't have chosen a better place. Seated in a boat, we softly glide along the brown water of a wide channel among the hundreds of boats laden with fruits, vegetables and flowers. Long, narrow boats whose bows and sterns curl upwards like green beans, and steered by women, sometimes old, wielding paddles, and wearing wide-brimmed straw hats.

Neither the sound of a motor, nor the blast of a horn, only the lapping of water and voices of women hawking their goods from one boat to the next. Long, slender fruit baskets cross in passing, barely touching each other: bananas, pineapples, watermelons, oranges, limes, papayas, coconuts. Less pretentious, the vegetables pass in single-file: lettuce, cabbages, carrots, ginger, fresh herbs ... Another boat brushes past ours, filled to the gunwales with multicolored, strange and exotic fruit I don't recognize. Their heavy perfumes, however, summon a vague memory from my wayfaring youth. Traffic jams are frequent, yet seem to bother no one. This simply gives time to order a plate of noodles from a floating canteen, in the midst of which a small, charcoal-burning hibachi smoulders.

As a break from all this movement and colour, our boat slips into a nearby channel, narrower and quieter, lined with lovely wooden houses perched on piles. Then another channel, still narrower and barely wide enough for a single boat, opens onto a paradise of tropical trees and plants, where silence is broken only by the singing of birds.

Following these few hours of peace and delight, we take the road to Tambon Barai, where former participant Winit Limman awaits us. He's around twenty-years old and displays a beaming smile.

He offers us well-chilled coconut milk, then relates a story.

He was chosen as a participant in 1987, and spent three months on a dairy farm in Salmon Arm, British Columbia.

"I previously knew nothing about milk cows, since they're very rare in this part of my country. But my Salmon Arm host family helped me learn all about dairy farming. And thanks to Canada World Youth, I now have a little farm of my own. Come and see my cows ..."

He has fifteen fine cows and seven calves, and a kind of open-air stall: "An adaptation of my cowshed in Salmon Arm!"

All this was made possible through a loan obtained from a small fund set up by the CDD with the help of Canada World Youth. Winit has already paid back his loan, and the success of his venture provides a very stimulating example for the whole village.

"What I learned from Canada World Youth did more than help me build my own farm:

"1. I founded and preside over the Cow Breeders' Club, which has thirty members.

"2. I taught three hundred villagers the rearing methods I learned in Salmon Arm.

"3. I vaccinated sixty cows for neighbours.

"4. I prepared a plan for creating a small artificial insemination centre, another technique learned in Canada."

Winit has definitely become a leader in his community and describes his achievements and plans simply but with self-assurance.

He shows us photos just received from his Salmon Arms host family: "This is the farm where I learned so much. But it wasn't covered in snow, as shown in the photo, when I was there. Luckily!"

He talks about his Canadian counterpart, Patrick, with whom he still corresponds: "He just wrote to our host family which lives in Khon Kaen, a village in northeast Thailand.

"But they don't read English!"

"Patrick wrote his letter in Thai script," he answers, proud to have such a smart counterpart.

Here's a wonderful story to tell those who believe that Canada World Youth, while very useful to young Canadians, is less so for exchange-country participants.

January 9

Another early rise, another long trip in a minibus to the province of Singburi, where the third group of participants is located.

A traditional welcome. Garlands, flags, tea and small gifts. And several speeches. One of the notables, who manages quite well in English, introduces me as follows: "It's a great honour to welcome Canada World Youth's founding president, an honourable Canadian senator. In fact, you're the first honourable person to visit our village."

Both the CDD director general and I pretend not to have heard!

A long meeting with participants in an old wooden house built on piles (home of Mélanie Doyon's host family, a Franco-Ontarian from Sudbury). A very steep ladder leads to a spacious room covered with straw matting. Seated on the floor in Thai fashion, we chat for nearly two hours. Everyone relates experiences, adventures, dreams for the future. We laugh profusely; but a wave of nostalgia suddenly floods the room when a participant mentions that the program will end in just two weeks. "Tears will stream the day we leave," admits Heather McLean from Kamloops, British Columbia. She grabs her Thai counterpart's hand as she speaks ... both burst into tears.

Jake Buhler, from the Canadian embassy, who was accompanying us and being exposed to Canada World Youth for the first time, was more touched and bowled over than me ... I've witnessed countless moving scenes over the last twenty years!

Mr. Buhler is in charge of funds the embassy provides to assist small development projects. On the way back, I naturally told him about Winit Limmin, his fifteen cows, seven calves and, above all, his plans for setting up a small artificial insemination centre. Mr. Buhler promises to call on him in a few weeks ...

9.
Jordan

1993

In Lawrence of Arabia's fabulous country.

January 3

Following three days of efforts and intense negotiations concerning the possibility of establishing a Canada World Youth program in Jordan, I'm informed that my last meeting with the youth minister is scheduled for Thursday. I'll therefore have a few days of freedom and time enough for a vacation. At my expense, needless to say.

I hop a minibus to Petra at about 7:00 a.m. A four hour trip through a semiarid region, with a flat landscape gradually changing into pleasant rolling hills. Mountain ridges are blanketed with snow—how dreadful! Nevertheless, young shepherds graze their small black goats here. With disgust in their eyes, lanky dromedaries munch on scarce, dried plants; their dusty foliage seems hardly appetizing. We leave the Aqaba highway about halfway from our destination, and take a narrow road that meanders through increasingly imposing mountains. Strange limestone formations suddenly appear; they characterize Petra and its surroundings. Like a raging red sea, its fantastic breakers suddenly stilled.

Petra is unique in the world. A high point of man's history. The most spectacular vestiges are those of the Nabataean capital. Two thousand years ago, these ancient Arab people managed to build a city in the billows of this frozen sea, brimming with crevasses, jagged peaks and narrow gorges. In fact, temples, mausoleums and structures capable of housing hundreds, were chiselled out of the limestone instead of erected.

Since Petra covers a wide area, we hire the services of a small horse and its master, who may be no older than twelve. To reach the first relatively important monument, the Treasure Door, we must cover five kilometres through a gorge so narrow that two horses sometimes have difficulty passing, and so deep the sun never enters. Looking up, we at last manage to observe a strip of blue sky. These five kilometres will remain forever etched in my memory. One of the most spectacular natural beauties I've witnessed in my life—which has not been bereft of them.

I leave my small white horse and proceed on foot. A two hour stroll, but I'd need a thousand to see all the splendid facades of Nabataean tombs carved into the rock, and other more ancient monuments, including nine thousand year old ruins from the stone-age, vestiges of the Roman and Byzantine empires, as well as the more recent fortresses of the Crusades.

At 4:00 p.m., tourists, most of them Italian, hop the bus to Amman. As for me, I feel it would be an insult to Petra if I failed to stay the night.

January 4

An endless, exhausting and marvellous excursion through scenery well known to T.E. Lawrence. A Bedouin, the son of a late sheikh, discusses Lawrence as though he'd known him. He finally explains that Lawrence had been a friend of his grandfather's: "One of the Arab princes he mentions in the *Seven Pillars of Wisdom* ..." I'm obviously thrilled to meet an educated Bedouin who's read and enjoyed the marvellous book that had captivated me when I was twenty ...

Some scenes from the movie *Lawrence of Arabia*, starring Peter O'Toole and Omar Sharif, were filmed nearby ... and, of course, my Bedouin knew Peter very well!

I had the choice of hopping a bus to Aqaba at 5:30 this morning, or enjoying Petra until 1:00 p.m., and then taking a taxi costing me $37.50 (150 kilometres, a two-hour trip). Bah! To the devil with the expense! (Since Canada World Youth won't foot the bill ...)

Arrival in Aqaba around 3:00 p.m. I can't recall how many weeks or months Lawrence, with his proud Arabian warriors astride dromedaries, had needed to reach the city, back in 1917. However, his elation must have been more intense than mine; the taking of Aqaba was the ultimate victory against the Turks, who were allied to the Germans, and the beginning of the end for the Ottoman empire.

I check in to a modest hotel, which brings to mind motels typical of Abitibi during the 1950's; my room, however, gives onto a beach at the edge of the Red Sea. Today, the water isn't even blue, but rather a sinister grey. I'd expected the Aqaba temperature to soothe my old bones, and hoped to enjoy a bit of a warm spell before reaching Islamabad, which is glacial this time of year, not to mention New Delhi's merciless humidity in January. The temperature in Aqaba barely reaches 10°C. At least, I won't have to relate the same stories about Canada World Youth twenty times in the same day.

January 5

The sky is still grey and the wind is very brisk. I dress as I would in Montreal during November, and set out to discover Aqaba, a tiny city wedged between Saudi Arabia on one side, and Israel and Egypt on the other. A first stroll brings me near the Israeli border, where the port of Eilat—Aqaba's sister city—begins. When the wind blows in my direction, I hear voices ... which aren't Arab! Israelis who, no doubt, are also cursing the lousy weather ...

I walk nearly six hours, enough time to visit the entire town, its port, the only access to the Sea of Jordan, its beautiful beach, pleasant shops and sparse ruins, including those of an Arab fortress dating from the Middle Ages. All around, the presence of arid mountains, with pointy ridges and beautiful amber colour, in the midst of which Aqaba is embedded.

Comfortably muffled-up, sitting at the sea's edge, where a few rusty cargo ships await their turn to dock, in weather no swimmer would brave, I pore over *The Memoirs of Chateaubriand*. That I hadn't yet read this book at age sixty-nine, says a great deal about the type of education I received.

January 6

My vacation is temporarily interrupted: a car picks me up and drives me to the *Queen Alia Jordan Social Welfare Fund*, an NGO that wishes to receive participants from our Work Partner Program. I'm spared nothing: day-care centre, computer courses for children, drawing classes, sewing and machine-knitting workshops. A cup of coffee, curiously followed by a cup of tea, and a lengthy exchange with the director, an exiled Palestinian woman. In fact, legions of Palestinians inhabit this small country of 3,200,000 citizens.

In the afternoon, the sun suddenly breaks through the clouds. The sea, previously a depressing steel grey, begins to sparkle wildly. It couldn't last, but the temperature reaches 17°C, which isn't too shabby.

I again set upon Aqaba, whose market district is teeming with small shops, crammed with merchandise that overflows onto the sidewalk. The simple purchase of a pencil or two mandarins often sets the stage for interesting encounters.

For example, I enter into a tiny shop seeking *sibha* (Muslim prayer beads). Many Arabs recite them constantly. Not always for the sake of praying: "An effective way of relaxing," according to a Muslim friend in Ottawa, for whom I wish to purchase a modest souvenir. The shopkeeper is a handsome man in his fifties, sporting a solid black moustache, like the ones worn by most Jordanians. Even before talking "business," Rafik Alewah introduces himself, welcomes me to Aqaba, and offers a small glass of very sweet and steaming tea. The glass, fortunately, has a handle. A good way to hook a customer, but also a traditional gesture of hospitality.

I finally tell him what I wish to purchase. He displays two dozen *sibha* on the counter, of all prices and colours. From semi-precious stones, to the most gaudy glass baubles.

"Oh! this is for a Muslim friend? In that case, I have what you need," Rafik says, pulling another *sibha* out of a drawer.

"It's mother of pearl. Imported from Jerusalem, the holy city. Your friend will appreciate it..."

That very moment, the muezzin from a nearby mosque howls his harrowing calls to prayer...with the help of powerful loudspeakers.

"Since you have a Muslim friend, you understand that I must pray. Have another glass of tea. I'll only be five minutes."

Rafik unrolls his prayer carpet in the middle of the shop, kneels facing Mecca and immerses himself into prayers as though the rest of the world had ceased to exist.

Meanwhile, I scan various photos from the filming of *Lawrence of Arabia*, which cover a small wall. One photo features two Arabs in traditional garb, who look like brothers. I learn that the man on the left is Omar Sharif, the famous actor of Egyptian origin, and to the right, his understudy ... Rafek Alewah himself!

Once his prayer finished, he hastens to confirm he was the actor's understudy, especially during the dangerous cavalcades on camel back, with sabres drawn. Most of the shooting took place nearby, in 1962, in the spectacular Wadi Rum Desert. Some scenes were filmed in Saudi Arabia, and some even in Seville, Spain.

Rafik has a thousand anecdotes to relate about those eight exceptional months of his life, during which he rubbed elbows with international stars, including Gina Lollobrigida. "Eight months and seven days," he specifies with a touch of nostalgia.

"And now, I'm only a humble Aqaba shopkeeper, but a happy man. And, occasionally, I look at this!" he says to me waving a video-cassette of the new version of *Lawrence of Arabia*, which the producer sent him.

10.
Gabon

1993

A smile from Libreville, Gabon.

June 24

I wasn't scheduled to join the delegation of Canadian parliamentarians attending a conference of the *Assemblée internationale des parlementaires de langue française* (AIPLF) in Libreville, Gabon, from June 26 to July 3, 1993. A senator withdrew at the last minute, and I failed to convince any of my colleagues about the charms of Libreville in July. I was, therefore, the designated "martyr" ...

Besides, it may as well be said, I've always felt a quasi-physiological need to take in the hot, heavy and humid air of tropical Africa, at least every three years. That's how I am. Moreover, this trip provided an opportunity, outside the Senate, in complete freedom as it were, to be with two colleagues and friends: Senator Gildas Molgat, a very sympathetic Franco-Manitoban, and Senator Peter Stollery, an unusual Torontonian ... he speaks French and Spanish!

June 28

Convinced as I am that several senators and members from the House of Commons will write solemn reports, highlighting all the tiresome details of each long day of the assembly, I'll say nothing about it. Or almost ...

Anyhow, I've only kept a rather muddled recollection of the event. I vaguely recall an endless opening ceremony where important parliamentarians from various francophone countries played at who could give the longest speech, the one most crammed with commonplaces and hollow phrases about *la francophonie's* endless merits, in short, the dullest.

Fortunately, the Gabonese people invited children from Libreville schools to sing a song written specifically for the occasion. The following is a verse:

"Elected representatives from around the World
Have come to work
Elected representatives will work for unity
And they will ensure continuity."

What about senators? They, as well, have come from around the world, to work ...

We did, in fact, work in various committees, hoping that *la francophonie* would be the better for it ... and that "continuity" would be ensured!

Since Senator Molgat is a bureau member, his schedule was considerably heavier than that of ordinary delegates, such as Senator Stollery and myself. We did, however, meet him and his marvellous wife, Allison, every morning for breakfast at the *Pamplemousse*, a small and inexpensive cafe a stone's throw from the five-star hotel that housed delegates.

Libreville has the reputation of having the highest cost of living of any city in the world, save Yokohama, Japan. Gabon is a small country of one million inhabitants. Its economy boomed until 1985, mainly due to the export of petroleum, manganese, uranium, and exotic woods; however, here as elsewhere, falling oil prices have had disastrous effects on the economy. Nevertheless, Canada World Youth might eventually establish an exchange program with Gabon. I'd therefore asked the Canadian ambassador, between two AIPLF work sessions, to set up a meeting with the youth minister, Mrs. Bike who, unfortunately, was out of the country.

Instead, I'll meet the Minister of Housing, Land Registry and Town Planning, Mr. Adrien Nkoghe Essingone. The minister has invited senior youth department advisers to the meeting.

Following a one-hour discussion, I get the impression that Gabon would gladly welcome a formal offer from Canada World Youth which, moreover, could count on the enthusiastic support of our ambassador, Mr. Maurice Dionne.

July 1

To celebrate Canada Day, the ambassador holds a delightful reception in the gardens of his residence. The guest list includes delegates "from around the world." Conspicuously absent: the PQ MNA from the Quebec delegation, who refused the invitation from a "foreign country." The other day, of course, he'd attended a reception at the French ambassador's ...

Before leaving Ottawa, I'd convinced my colleague, Senator Stollery, to accompany me on an expedition to Equatorial Guinea, a country that borders on Gabon. He accepted without hesitation, since he loves to travel ... Almost as much as I do! "Jacques," he would tell me, "we're old Africa hands!" Senate pages were rather intrigued by the messages that Africa Hand I (me, of course!) sent to Africa Hand II, informing him about the progress of the "Equatorial Guinea" project.

Since there's no way of organizing a trip between Gabon and Guinea from Canada, I sought the advice of Mr. Maurice Dionne, our ambassador in Libreville. Through an exchange of fax messages, the ambassador informed me that travelling by road from Libreville to Bata, Guinea's principal city, was impossible, that he absolutely didn't recommend the only Guinean plane, a tiny, ramshackle and unsafe craft that ostensibly ensures a weekly link, etc.

I was about to give up on this small, inaccessible country, when the ambassador informed me that his colleague responsible for small development projects financed by the embassy, which is accredited in Guinea, will travel to the small city of Cogo, on the opposite side of the Rio Muni river, which can be crossed by pirogue. Should we deem this arrangement suitable, there'd be space for Africa Hands I & II.

Stollery and I are obviously pleased and, once the AIPLF convention is over, we join the expedition lead by an energetic and charming young woman, Mrs. Gaby Velghe, of Belgian origin.

11.
Equatorial Guinea

1993

The author raising a toast with Lord Peter in a pirogue on Rio Muni.

July 3

Departure from Libreville at 6:30 a.m. Expedition members hop in either of the embassy's two four-wheel-drive vehicles. In the first one: Gaby Velghe, her husband Olivier Sherpereel, an economist from the *Société française de conseil en développement*, Alain Richard, a French historian, and a Gabonese driver. In the other vehicle: Nicholas Dionne, the ambassador's young son, his Canadian girlfriend, Christine, and, of course, Africa Hands I & II.

A two hour trip on a fairly good road to Cocobeach, located on the Atlantic at the mouth of the Rio Muni. Despite its frivolous name, Cocobeach is the furthest thing from a Club Med resort: a small, rather austere fishing port. Fishermen moor their dugouts on a beach strewn with rubbish. With slow and noble gestures, they repair nets in the shadow of palm trees.

We wait over an hour for "our" dugout, which is longer than the others and equipped with a powerful outboard motor. At this point we're joined by Maria-José, a Spanish nurse who's to be our host in Cogo, where she oversees a small clinic funded by Spain. In fact, Equatorial Guinea is a former Spanish colony.

We leave Cocoabeach and Gabon around 9:30 a.m.: we'll spend the better part of the next two days in the dugout, on the placid waters of the Rio Muni, in a setting reminiscent of Tarzan films. For lunch, we eat sandwiches and, since there are French passengers, pâté, sausages and red wine.

Comrade Stollery—also known as Africa Hand II or Lord Peter—happens to be a remarkable amateur ornithologist. He put on quite a show as soon as a tropical bird skirted by our dugout. "There goes a great black-helmeted calao!" he exclaimed triumphantly. I wouldn't have taken him too seriously if Olivier Scherpereel, also familiar with birds of the region, hadn't corroborated Africa Hand II's observations.

Were it not for the knowledge of our two friends, I would've hardly noticed the beautiful and spellbinding birds which adorn this area. I could've never boasted seeing so many ospreys, whistling hornbills, Gabonese red-tailed grey parrots, herons, egrets, kingfishers, anhingas, red-throated bee-eaters, etc.

At about 3:30 p.m. we stop in Elon and are greeted by the village chief. The purpose of our visit: to check out a new kind of fish smokehouse built thanks to a grant from the Canadian embassy. We hand notebooks and crayons to the children. Their school is a modest shanty with a corrugated metal roof. The teacher gives a speech in Spanish, the official language of this tiny country of 300,000 people, where many local dialects are also spoken. We ask Africa Hand II to respond, since he pretends to speak Spanish—which turns out to be true. At first, we must plead with him, but once started, nothing seems to stop him ... which reminds me of his endless speeches against the GST in the Senate!

The village chief takes us into his home, the only concrete structure in Elon. He insists on offering us beer served at room temperature, i.e., very warm.

Later, Africa Hand II and I try to imagine the story of our host since the still-recent period when Spaniards were lords and masters of the country—independence was achieved in 1968.

I hesitate somewhat to relate the kinds of stories we told in the dugout to our expedition companions, who were a rather captive audience. To this day, they must wonder about the mental health of those two zany senators.

Bah! So what! Given the bum rap senators have received, I don't see how I could tarnish their reputation any further by relating, *verbatim*, Africa Hand II's hilarious monologue sprinkled with Africa Hand I's comments. Keep your chin up! Here goes!

Africa Hand II: Do you know how the good village chief, who served us warm beer, reached his lofty station in Guinean society?

Africa Hand I: Of course we know. But, since you're itching to tell us, go ahead!

Africa Hand II: Thank you, Africa Hand I. I'm in your debt. This good man, with beer as warm as horse piss, is called Antonio Bobolasso. *We must admit he has class*: two wives, eight children, five chickens and two ducks.

Africa Hand I: Enough already! We know how to count.

Africa Hand II: But did you know that the good Antonio, who's now village chief, had murdered his Spanish master the day of independence? *How about that?*

Africa Hand I: Of course, but you forgot to mention that Don Carlos, the master in question, was a filthy, racist and exploitive colonial ...

Africa Hand II: Yes, a disgusting character. A goddamn boss who booted his Guinean workers in the ass for forty years.

Africa Hand I: Forty-one years!

Africa Hand II: Okay. Forty-one years. That's right. Thanks, Africa Hand I. This doesn't change anything to the story, but might as well be precise. Being kicked in the ass for one more year is significant. Forty-one years. Yes. That's right. Thank you, Africa Hand I. *Gracias*. What was I saying before I was brutally interrupted?

Africa Hand I: Antonio...

Africa Hand II: Ah! yes, Antonio. He was Don Carlos's foreman, though that title didn't shield him from kicks in the ass.

Africa Hand I: Quite the opposite!

Africa Hand II: Quite the opposite, indeed. When one of Don Carlos's workers committed a colossal blunder, like stealing a bottle of rum or wringing the neck of one of the master's chickens, for example, he had no other choice but to hide in the forest for a few days. The unfortunate Antonio would get the kicks in the ass that his colleague had earned. By the end of the day, he could hardly sit down, and his wife Esperanza would rub his posterior with eucalyptus-scented palm oil. Antonio squealed like a pig at the slaughter. Bloody hell! You should've heard him! Meanwhile, Esperanza tried to calm him by talking about Equatorial Guinea's independence, which would happen someday, as it had in Nigeria, a former British colony ...

Africa Hand I: Long live Queen Elizabeth II!

Africa Hand II: The English understood before everyone else that they had no more bloody business in their colonies ...

Africa Hand I: ... and that it was better to exploit "independent" countries!

Africa Hand II: Exactly! The French took more time to understand. As for the Spanish ... they hung on miserably. In short, Antonio, with our regards for his aching posterior, was champing at the bit.

Africa Hand I: Like the Golden Dog...

Africa Hand II: What? What does a dog have to do with this? If I weren't constantly interrupted, I could finish my story which is, moreover, truthful and supported by indisputable historical documents. So, Mister Herbert ... We can manage without your Golden Dog!

Africa Hand I: If Lord Peter had any classical education, he'd consider my remark totally appropriate, since it evokes another historical fact...

Africa Hand II: Bah!

Africa Hand I: Besides, there's a tavern in Quebec City called *The Golden Dog*, on whose carved sign is a message that aptly summarizes Antonio's feelings:

"I'm the dog chewing the bone.
I chew it while at rest.
A day will come that hasn't yet come
When I'll bite whatever bit me."

Africa Hand II: Fine! Fine! What the hell! May I continue?

Africa Hand I: I don't see how anybody could stop such a chatterbox!

Africa Hand II: Anyhow, Antonio continued chewing his bone for forty years.

Africa Hand I: Forty-one!

Africa Hand II: Okay! Finally, the blessed day of Independence arrived. The whole town was ecstatic; people danced in streets, stinking with the heavy rum of freedom. Don Carlos and the other important landowners didn't celebrate; they had to wonder whether they should've written off their beautiful plantations and returned to Spain ... "What do those lousy Negroes plan to do to me?" Don Carlos moaned to himself, sipping a *Black Label*. They owe me everything ..."

Africa Hand I: Including numerous kicks in the ass!

Africa Hand II: "They owe me everything, but they'll quickly forget now that they're citizens of the Republic of Equatorial Guinea, a country those idiots believe is free." Don Carlos didn't know how right he was. Meanwhile, Antonio had nearly emptied a first bottle of rum with three or four of his workers.

Africa Hand I: There were four of them ...

Africa Hand II: That's right. There were four. Thanks Africa Hand I: you've finally provided a useful clarification. And then, Antonio said: "A day will come that hasn't yet come ..." Fat Pancho, who was drunk as a doornail ...

Africa Hand I: As a skunk!

Africa Hand II: Drunk any way you want, Pancho interrupted Antonio—as you do continually!—and said: "The country has been independent since the church bells rang at noon precisely. The day has therefore, hic! come ..." Antonio opened another bottle of lousy rum, which was emptied almost solemnly, yet very quickly. And, without further explanation, the four men quietly headed towards the master's house, where Don Carlos had just polished off his *Black Label*.

Africa Hand I: The five men.

Africa Hand II: What? But you said earlier that they were four. What kind of credibility can you have, Señor Herbert, when you keep fiddling with historical facts?

Africa Hand I: Calm down! Quick, a Valium! Yes, I did say *four* men, but with Antonio they were five.

Africa Hand II: That was obvious! The audience would've adjusted accordingly! But you insist on splitting hairs in five ... Where was I? Bloody hell! ¡*Madre de Dios*! Oh! yes, Antonio and his men approached the veranda where Don Carlos had just lit a fat cigar, something extremely dangerous since he was saturated with alcohol. Antonio solemnly broke the terrible news to him: "Don Carlos, your black rooster is dead." Though red at first, the master suddenly turned white as a linen shrub.

Africa Hand I: A shroud!

Africa Hand II: "That's impossible!" howled Don Carlos. "¡*Hombre de Dios*! Such a proud bird, one that all my chickens respected ... I don't believe you. He was still in such high spirits just this morning..."

Africa Hand I: "Well then, go into the henhouse and see for yourself," Antonio said.

Africa Hand II: Exactly! But do you want to tell the story yourself, or what? Go ahead! My lips are sealed.

Africa Hand I: That I'd like to see: Lord Peter keeping his lips sealed!

Africa Hand II: I'd be more than able, but the tale of this wonderful page in the history of Rio Muni, which has become the Republic of Equatorial Guinea, is coming to a close. Drunk as a doornail—or drunk as a skunk—Don Carlos staggered to the henhouse along with four, sorry, five men as drunk as he was. When everyone were inside...

Africa Hand I: Everyone is singular. Very singular...

Africa Hand II: When everyone *was* inside—Ah! you're a pain in the neck!—Antonio briskly shut the door of the odoriferous squall.

Africa Hand I: Stall!

Africa Hand II: "But my rooster's alive!" bellowed Don Carlos. "Maybe," whispered Antonio. "But you won't be for long. The time has come for you to pay for the thousands of kicks in the ass you've given us over the last forty years ..."

Africa Hand I: He should have said forty-one years...

Africa Hand II: Bloody hell! you're getting on my nerves! Do you want me to finish the story? As soon as Antonio had stammered the word *years*, the four men (the other four) grabbed Don Carlos and hanged him by the feet from a hook screwed into the ceiling. Taking a razor with a finely chiselled horn handle from his pocket, Antonio slit his master's throat—Slash!—in one fell swoop. Slash!—and he died shrieking "*Wawa*! *Wawa*! *Wawa*!" a strange word, unknown to the members of the small, yet attentive, audience. The men emptied one last bottle of rum before burying the unfortunate Don Carlos behind the henhouse, under an enormous pile of chicken manure.

Africa Hand I: The only unfortunate thing was that no one bothered to plant a cross, even a modest one, in the said pile, to honour the memory of a man who had, after all, been a great colonial.

Africa Hand II: For forty-one years!

We'll never know who more or less believed the amazing, yet true, story related that evening ...

We leave the village of Elon at about 4:30 p.m., and travel through a narrow tributary of the Rio Muni. It resembles a small canal streaming through a lush jungle, whose enormous trees form a green archway. Half uprooted by erosion, they eventually crash into the water, occasionally knocking out a brazen hippopotamus. Amazing ferns and pale-green bamboo groves gush like a water fountain in the setting sun. And the numerous birds that Peter and Olivier identify—sometimes in Latin!

We experience engine failure, but who'd complain in the midst of this earthly paradise! Night suddenly falls, like a theatre curtain, but the machinist provides a full moon, which makes the Rio Muni sparkle. Thin dugouts paddle by, their passengers silhouetted against the sky like puppets in a Chinese shadow theatre.

We reach Cogo in the pitch dark around 8:00 p.m. In the days of Don Carlos, the village had electricity, and even a dozen stylish street lights. A few years following the good colonial's horrible death in the sinister henhouse, the generator was switched off, seemingly forever: lack of fuel and spare parts.

Walking single-file in the dark, we climb a steep trail to the top of a hill, where Maria-José's small clinic is located; it has an electric generator that still works thanks to the consideration of Spain, the erstwhile and distant mother country. The Spanish doctor is vacationing, and Maria-José is the only white person for miles. Our visit pleases her, especially since Olivier, who is multi-talented, will prepare the evening meal while we sip an aperitif ... and while Lord Peter leaps into one of his improbable stories that finds him battling dangerous Colombian *narcotraficos*, or with rogues from the Foreign Legion, members of which he taught in Sidi-bel-Abes.

You take some, you leave some. I amuse myself by interrupting and contradicting him, by laying it on thick when he stretches truth beyond what even the most credulous Sister of Charity would swallow. In short, we thoroughly enjoy ourselves in Cogo. After feasting on the fare prepared by Olivier, his wife, the wonderful Gaby, takes us to Cogo's "discotheque," a wooden cabin where a dozen young "Cogolese" jig about, all of them boys since girls aren't allowed to wander into this den of perdition—a remnant of the education provided by the good Spanish sisters ... Gaby, who loves to dance, becomes queen of the evening. Africa Hands I & II don't wait until she tires herself out before returning to the clinic.

July 4

Sunday. One hundred or so Cogo residents, in their Sunday best, congregate in the imposing church. Though in ruins, the church is transfigured by the beautiful chants—more African than Catholic—that flood a vaguely gothic nave.

Following the sermon, I visit Cogo, a small town which must've been a charming administrative centre in its heyday. Little remains, save the shreds of a town hall, a small abandoned factory, electrical wires dangling here and there, and four old rusty gas pumps which stand as pathetic monuments to bygone days. Cogo's only link to the outside world: pirogues and the Rio Muni.

The people, however, are exquisitely kind. I get to know the tax collector: a small man who looks nothing like a tax collector. He shows me his two-room cottage, introduces me to his wife and three children, and insists on offering me a live goose. Although I love roast goose, I explain that the bird might cause certain problems with customs, at Mirabel...

I peel potatoes with Maria-José, who's somewhat enigmatic. What is this young nurse from Spain doing in Cogo? She could have an easier time of it in Madrid or, better yet, Seville ... Does she take herself for mother Teresa? I don't learn much, but feel a little closer to Maria-José ... because of the potatoes!

Back in our pirogue, we bid farewell to Cogo. A mandatory stop in Acalayon, a border post, where our passports are visaed, to enter and leave Equatorial Guinea *simultaneously*, something that should reassure the potentate who calls himself president of the republic, a dictator like those everywhere in Africa. Or almost ...

Cocobeach, Gabon. We reach Libreville around 8:00 p.m., where our ambassador, Maurice Dionne, awaits us at the residence with the pizzas of friendship. An extraordinary man, huge, sympathetic and jovial, who obviously wanted to hear all about our excursion. Lord Peter gladly obliged ...

12.
Albania

1993

Skanderberg, Albania's great national hero. "His statue will *never* be toppled!"

July 21

"What do you mean you're vacationing in Albania? Are you crazy?"

That's the kind of reaction I got for simply admitting I intended to take a brief vacation in Albania, Europe's poor cousin. In fact, Albania might even be said to be on the bottom rung of Eastern Europe, which isn't saying much.

When pressed to explain their astonishment, my people—who, of course, had never been to Albania—were effusive: "First of all, tourists don't go to Albania. That's that! The capital, Tirana, boasts only two barely adequate hotels. Besides, it's in the middle of nowhere. Neither credit cards nor travellers cheques are accepted. Only American dollars or other strong currencies. It's impossible to get out of Tirana. There are no rental cars, and you can't find a seat on the decrepit buses since they're always crowded. First come, first served! The food's horrible, and stores are empty. Why the devil are you going there?"

Our ambassador responsible for Albania, Mr. Rodney Irwin—forced to move from Belgrade to Vienna when hell broke loose in Yugoslavia—kindly warned me about the risks of travelling to Albania. He didn't, however, discourage me. A happy coincidence: his second secretary, Ms. Shelley Whiting, was to be in Albania at the same time as me. She'd be pleased to accompany me if I were willing to adjust my schedule to hers. And how!

I arrive in Bari at 7:18 p.m.—in Italy, trains are more punctual than people. Fifteen minutes later, I reach the harbour station, where I vainly seek the beautiful ship described in the colour brochure my travel agent gave me. I finally learn, uttering *prego* and *grazie* left and right—the extent of my Italian vocabulary—that the *Palladio* has been assigned a more prestigious itinerary (Bari-Greece), and that I'll have to make due with the *Expresso Venizia*, a much older and less comfortable ship. Too bad!

A procedure as simple as registering and having my passport stamped takes only two hours, inside a sweltering harbour station subject to power shortages every ten minutes.

I drag my suitcases to the boat, and then to my cabin, which is the size of a phone booth. No porthole. Since the cafeteria food leaves me totally indifferent, I dine on a piece of cheese and a quarter-litre of wine.

We leave the dock an hour and a half late, time enough to allow a hundred or so cars and trucks to board.

I soon realize I'm the only tourist among the two hundred or so passengers, the others being mostly Albanian workers needing a vacation in their country, after earning valuable currencies in Italy, Germany, Switzerland or elsewhere. A few Italians who do business in Albania, two Swiss missionaries ...

July 22

At 7:00 a.m. sharp, powerful loudspeakers urge us to rise, in Italian. We spot the port of Durres, but have to wait an hour before an Albanian pilot comes alongside to help the ship dock. Albanian immigration officers board the ship to stamp passports. The queue is endless. I see a taciturn Italian, slumped in a chair, sipping a cappuccino, and ignoring the crowd.

"You're not getting your passport stamped?

"No," he answers, looking disgusted. "I travel to Albania for a week every month—I run a small factory—and I've learned it's useless to stand in line for three hours ...

"Three hours?

"If not four. So I relax, have a coffee and wait for the crowd to disperse."

He's right. I order a cappuccino and sit beside him. But this strange Italian, who speaks little French, isn't very talkative. With great difficulty, I manage to get a few, mostly disparaging, comments from him concerning Albania: "A hopeless country ... Most factories are closed ... Running water only three hours a day ... A shambles ..."

I'm distressed that Ms. Whiting, from the Canadian embassy, is waiting for me on the landing dock. She'll wait four hours in the blazing sun with the driver from our Belgrade embassy, Milos Nedié, a Serb.

Seeing Ms. Whiting on the dock, waving a tiny Canadian flag, I realize I'm infinitely indebted to Ambassador Irwin. And, of course, to Ms. Whiting! Since neither taxis nor buses are in sight, I can well imagine the trouble an isolated traveller would have trying to reach Tirana by whatever means, not knowing a word of Albanian, a language like no other.

Comfortably seated in the embassy's *VW Passat*, I relax and admire my first glimpses of Albania, all undulating and luxuriant. An inconsistency scars this pastoral landscape: numerous reinforced-concrete pillboxes, built throughout Albania by communist dictator, Enver Hodja, after the country had fallen out with its Soviet brothers and renounced its Chinese brothers ... felt to be too revisionist! This tiny and proud country decided it had a monopoly on truth, and that the rest of the world was the enemy. Albania therefore had to protect itself against all possible invaders by building numerous bunkers, and pillboxes especially.

There are about 700,000 of them in this small country, only half the size of Nova Scotia. It's hardly believable: 700,000 monuments to human stupidity. Like enormous greyish warts, ugly, useless and unusable.

Like any self-respecting foreigner, we stop at Tirana's *Dajti Hotel*. Seventy dollars US per day, breakfast included. The other hotel, the *Tirana*, is bigger but far less suitable. During lunch, I realize that some of the criticism was well founded: the food is rather bad, even in the city's best hotel.

At my request, one of Ms. Whiting's Albanian friends gets hold of a guide who'll accompany me during the long stroll I'm planning through the small capital (200,000 souls). My guide is a twenty-year old medical student named Brunilda Basha. She's tiny, dainty and her English is just about understandable.

On casual strolls I often set myself silly objectives, which sometimes alter the course of events. For example, I look for a small duck to add to my niece Marie's collection ... In *Albanie*, published by the Seuil as part of the *La petite planète* series, I learn that Tirana still has cobblers who make custom shoes for a reasonable price. Brunilda is sceptical. I insist. And so, we're off through Tirana in search of cobblers, ending up in incredible alleys—places my guide never even thought of taking me. We finally locate a cobbler who'd be delighted to make me shoes. I want black ones;

unfortunately, he only has brown leather. "You won't find anyone better! I'm the last Tirana cobbler able to make custom shoes for you."

But he's lying. In a nearby lane, I meet Bilal Toska, a white-haired man with the proud bearing of a poet—of which there are many in Albania. He welcomes us in his home, showing us into a parlour adjoining a tiny shop. "Coffee?" He takes out an electric fan to make us comfortable as we chat.

I explain that my right foot is slightly larger than the right one (we can't be perfect!), and that custom-made shoes would please me immensely.

"*Po, po, po, po*!" he repeats energetically—which means: "Yes, yes, I understand, all right."

One small problem: Mr. Toska leaves tomorrow to attend his nephew's wedding, in the south, near the Macedonian border. A grand celebration in the works. And he plans to do some shopping on the other side of the border, in Macedonia, which was part of Yugoslavia until recently. I must leave Tirana Tuesday at noon, the day he returns from the wedding.

"Bah! I'll try to finish your shoes by then! *Po, po, po ...*"

He draws the contour of my feet on a white sheet of paper, and takes various measurements ...

Pointing to the pathetic shoes I'm wearing, he says: "As a bonus, I'd be happy to fix them, free ..." No way. I'll throw them out when I return to Montreal. We agree on the price: $18.00 US. I'm almost embarrassed ... In Canada, a pair of hand-made orthopaedic shoes would cost nearly $500.00 ...

Brunilda admits she's discovered a part of Tirana, thanks to my shoes.

She's Muslim. "But I don't practice. I don't go to the mosque. Having been raised under a communist regime, I've missed the religious education that might've motivated me. Don't forget that Albania was officially an atheistic state.

"Is this attitude also common among Catholics and the Orthodox (ten per cent and twenty per cent of the population respectively)?

"Yes, absolutely, among young people.

"And your parents?

"They don't practice either.

"Your grandparents?

"Oh! yes. They go to the mosque every week. Frankly, I have more of an affinity to the Catholic and Orthodox religions.

"Why?

"Because Western values interest me more than those of the East.

"Christianity also comes from the East.

"Perhaps. But it's a Western religion ..."

When I ask her to show me one of Tirana's important monuments, either a church or a mosque, Brunilda takes me to a very ordinary Catholic church, while, only a few streets away, stands the beautiful Hadji Ethem Bey mosque, built in the year 1211 of the Hegira ...

We pass by a pedestal scribbled with graffiti on the grand avenue: "A statue of Lenin once stood here. It's *kaput*, like that of Stalin, its counterpart across the avenue."

Numerous inscriptions are scrawled on the grey-stone pedestal, two of them in English: "Pink Floyd Wall Brake Down," and a more intelligible one: "Let the Sun Shine—10-12-92."

But an equestrian statue of Skanderberg still dominates this setting.

"How about that one?

"Skanderberg is our greatest national hero. His statue will *never* be toppled!"

July 22

At my request, our ambassador had scheduled a meeting with the Minister of Culture, Youth and Sports, Mr. Dhimiter Anagnosti.

I obviously have no mandate from Canada World Youth to negotiate anything. Though Albania isn't a Third World country, it's less developed and infinitely poorer than some Latin American, Asian and even African countries where we have programs.

However, there certainly exists in Canada, and other Western countries, an inclination, perhaps even the political will, to help former communist countries out of their present slump. Our Department of Foreign Affairs has even created a special fund towards that end. I'm therefore certain a program inspired by Canada World Youth could do wonders for Albania. But this mustn't be done at the expense of Third World countries.

The minister is in his forties and speaks rather good English. He's glad to finally meet a Canadian parliamentarian and talk about problems facing youth in Albania, a country whose average age is twenty-seven. Given the present economic chaos, we can well imagine the overwhelming number of unemployed youth. "They loiter in the streets," the minister says, "they get into drugs and alcohol; they're desperate. We'd have to send thousands to Canada to discover your values, see democracy in action, learn your work methods. Once back, they'd be agents of change, which is what we need most."

I briefly explain Canada World Youth to the minister. He listens intently, with eyes beaming.

"Ah! wouldn't it be wonderful to set up such a program with young people from Canada and Albania? Do you think it's possible?

I'd like to say yes. I at least assure him that Canada is sensitive to the crisis affecting Albania, as well as other former communist countries.

"To build the future, we must start with young people!" concludes the minister.[1]

Since Ms. Whiting has no official appointments before Monday, she suggests a weekend in the country to visit historic sites. Moreover, hotels and restaurants are much cheaper outside Tirana.

We first return to Durres by an alternate route. Narrow, uneven, and littered with

---

1 Since that trip to Albania, the idea has made some headway: Canada World Youth organized special exchange programs with Hungary and Poland in 1994-1995. Another Eastern country, Estonia, joined the program in 1995-1996. And, no doubt, Albania will get its turn ...

trucks, old backfiring cars, bicycles, carts pulled by oxen or tiny horses, donkeys collapsing beneath enormous flour bags, herds of cows or sheep, not to mention geese, turkeys and dogs. We drive along, at thirty kilometres an hour most of the time, which allows us to casually admire the pleasant rolling scenery, hills covered in olive trees, quivering vineyards, fields of corn or tomatoes. Alas! the landscape is littered with pathetic and ridiculous pillboxes ...

Here and about, a sprinkling of abandoned factories and rusted derricks that testify to the miserable collapse of oil production. The villages are enchanting: small stone houses with red-tile roofs, surrounded by strange cone-shaped haystacks. We cross a wide river that divides the country in two very different regions, the north and south, where, an important Greek population lives near the border with Greece.

Lunch (tomato salad and cheese spaghetti) at the *Adriatika Hotel*, on the seashore. The communist regime had reserved this hotel for the very rare tourists (Austrians, Germans or Scandinavians) who vacation here at extremely good rates. We seem to recognize a few foreigners on the beach, the others obviously being Albanian. A third-rate hotel by our standards, but, for $4.50, the food is rather good.

In mid-afternoon, under a bright blue sky, we finally spot a high mountain covered in cypress and acacia. On top of it lies the ancient Ardenica monastery, our refuge for the next two days. Orthodox monks left the monastery long ago, but a local priest still takes care of the old Byzantine church located in the interior court. The monks' living quarters have been converted into an inn designed for those rare travellers who manage to hear about this paradisaical place. On all sides, a view of the fertile, checkerboard plain strewn with green-and-gold squares. Our rooms are enormous, modern, with bathrooms and hot water: like being at a Laurentian lodge ... except we pay only $25.00 a day!

The church, built in the eleventh century, is decorated with splendid frescoes and period icons. In short, we're in heaven!

We dine on a veranda caressed by an evening breeze, as the sun sets behind the hill, turning half the sky crimson. Ten or so Albanian diners are laughing and having a spirited discussion. Suddenly, a sinister-looking character with a moustache appears, carrying an imposing rifle. He sits down. The type you wouldn't want to meet in a deserted area ... He abruptly gets up and heads straight for our table, with rifle in one hand, and a beautiful melon in the other ... which he offers us with a wide grin revealing two gold incisors. We try to thank him in Albanian, which is no mean feat: "*Faleminderit*!" Non-formal language, however, saves the day. Each in turn, Ms. Whiting, Milos the driver and I smell the lovely round fruit, slightly exaggerating our olfactory delight. Our new friend is totally enraptured ...

We finally learn that the chap with the rifle is the night watchman, whose principle mission is to protect our car against thieves.

July 24

We rise rather late—as paradise would have it!—and leave our beautiful monastery in search of another, said to be the country's most significant Byzantine structure.

As well, we're to visit the recently excavated ruins of the Greco-Roman city of Apollonia. The small, rough roads put the embassy's car through the mill ...

The monastery is even more impressive than that of Ardenica. After the monks left, it was converted into a museum that houses, under stone archways, low reliefs and antique statues found in the nearby Apollonian ruins.

Apollonia dates back to 588 B.C. The city was built by Corinthian colonists, at the edge of the Aoos river which was navigable at the time, and gave access to the sea.

In the year 229, Apollonia fell under vassalage to Rome and became very prosperous. Cicero talks of it as a great and influential city: "*Magna urbis et gravis ...*" In the third century A.D., a powerful earthquake changed the course of the Aoos river, depriving Apollonia of its access to the Adriatic. This signalled the beginning of its downfall, which was consummated by the barbarian invasions. Archeologists only discovered the Apollonian ruins at the beginning of our century.

We spend a few wonderful hours seeking out excavated monuments: a Parthenon-like mausoleum, a tiny six hundred seat odeon, colonnaded promenades, etc. We'd heard about the fountain of Cephise. We'll look for it, in vain, for an hour, ending up on a neighbouring mountain which, to our surprise, is crammed with bunkers, underground passages and shelters capable of housing hundreds of people—another lasting accomplishment of the communist dictator, Enver Hodja. In a thousand years, perhaps, archeologists will rediscover these indestructible concrete-reinforced and ghastly creations; they'll be justifiably troubled by the congenital folly of humans throughout history.

July 25

Next stop: Berat, a small town which Unesco has classified as a historical monument belonging to the heritage of mankind, something that will ensure it's restored and conserved.

It may happen, when entering and leaving cities, that a policeman signals us to stop. With the greatest courtesy, he shakes hands with each of us. But as soon as Milos pronounces the magic formula: "*Diplomate Canada*," the officer allows us to resume our journey. He repeats the word "Canada" many times, with a sort of elation. In his opinion, Canada is a good and wonderful country. He ignores everything about our country's relative indifference to Albania, lost who knows where in the miserable Balkans.

Berat is a true marvel. Built on the banks of the Osum river, its beautiful houses with red-tile roofs are anchored to terraces on the flanks of a tall hill, on whose summit lies a fortress defended by about twenty square towers. A small road made of large cobble stones allows our car to reach one of the doors that cuts through the wall. Inside, beautiful stone houses are entangled in an unbelievable maze, where it's a pleasure getting lost. Lanes and passages are so narrow that, with arms outstretched, you can touch the walls of houses on either side. Our stroll takes us to small and beautiful churches from the Byzantine period, including the Holy Trinity Church that dates back to the thirteenth century. The Saint Nicholas Church has been converted into a museum filled with icons, silver liturgical objects of the Orthodox faith, and paintings by Onuphre, a famous Albanian religious painter from the sixteenth century. And, to top it all off, the church is a genuine masterpiece with its sculpted wooden altar and pulpit.

We slowly return to Tirana, taking a detour through Elbassan, a new and dismal city attached to a huge industrial complex built with aid from China. Rumour has it that it only functions at ten per cent capacity ... Hard to believe, since factories, oil refineries, steelworks, all lay motionless, rusted, dilapidated, as though dead.

From Elbassan to Tirana, the road meanders through high mountains typical of Albania. Some reach two thousand metres. Scenery that leaves you breathless.

July 26

While Ms. Whiting attends to embassy business, I walk for hours through Tirana streets. Of course, sidewalks are pockmarked, roughcast crumbles off houses, and even government buildings look abandoned. Nonetheless, the city has its charms, likely due to magnificent trees filled with birds; they adequately cover the destitution of dwellings.

The only stores that existed under the communist regime were state-run. The first signs of the new, free-enterprise religion: numerous tiny shops have sprung out everywhere. A shed is converted into a shoe store (I count a dozen pairs, made in Egypt), a kiosk is transformed into a café where beer and soft drinks from Greece are sold. *Coca Cola*, both genuine and ersatz, is sold here. From a distance, a bottle of fake *Coke* looks like the real thing, since the red-and-white logo has been imitated so well. Looking a little closer, I notice that the maker, at once careful and spiritual, calls his product *Joy Cola*; *Coke's* famous trademark has become *Joke*.

This is watermelon season: heaps of them are stacked on street corners. But fruits and vegetables, which ought to be abundant in midsummer, are scarce: pallid tomatoes, tiny onions, potatoes, eggplants and peaches. Small piles of oranges imported from Greece and bananas from distant Colombia are spread on a sheet covering the sidewalk.

A hole in the wall: looking through, I come face to face with a cigarette vendor: she sells them by the pack or individually ...

A lovely, tree-lined street with well-kept houses. In one of them, somebody is playing Beethoven's *Moonlight Sonata*. A magnificent abandoned house trimmed with a plaque indicating that, in 1942, this was a meeting place for partisans fighting the fascist regime imposed by Italian invaders.

I stumble on a bookstore in the middle of the park: thirty or so used books neatly stacked on the grass. The works of Albanian authors, as well as translations of foreign books, including Molier's *Mizantropi*, the *Odiseja* by a certain Homeri and, a little closer to home, Viktor Hygo's *Tëmjerët* ...

13.
India

1996

Prime Minister Jean Chrétien chatting with Canadian and Indian participants in Mumbai (January, 1996).

January 10

As soon as I'd heard Prime Minister Chrétien was thinking of organizing a Team Canada visit to India to promote trade and investment, I got the daring idea of scheduling a meeting between the delegation's dozen eminent politicians ... and a group of modest Canada World Youth participants! As luck would have it, we had groups in three villages of Maharashtra, the state where Bombay[1] is located, which is on the first leg of the Team Canada Mission.

The prime minister immediately welcomed the idea. He was even ready to visit one of the villages, if possible. Alas! we had to give up on the idea after studying the enormous logistical problems the trip would have caused, and considering the two-day program in Bombay-Mumbai was already very heavy. However, if participants could make it to Bombay, the prime minister would be very pleased to meet them. Okay, if the mountain doesn't come to Muhammad ...

Again thanks to the prime minister's kindness, I was able to accompany him to Bombay aboard the Team Canada plane, allowing me to foist my modest propaganda on the seven provincial premiers taking part in the trip: if they weren't familiar with Canada World Youth, they now would be until the end of their days! But I didn't have to convince Nova Scotia Premier John Savage; his daughter, Sheilagh, had been a participant with the Malaysian program in 1977.

"The experience completely changed her," he told me.

"And for the better!" added Mrs. Savage with a smile.

In fact, since her time with Canada World Youth, Sheilagh Savage has been involved in various community and international-development causes. She'd been a project leader in numerous countries, and was very recently appointed Canada World Youth's regional director for the Atlantic provinces.

At 9:00 a.m., I take part in a briefing for the official delegation. Since the meeting with Canada World Youth participants will take place at 10:00 a.m. in the hotel garden, I'm invited to provide a few details to the ladies and gentlemen in attendance.

So I explain that the twenty-five Indian participants and their twenty-five Canadian counterparts left their three villages in the interior of Maharashtra, happily enduring an eight-hour bus trip over bad roads, to participate in this "historic" meeting. After living and working together for over three months in three British Columbia communities (Premier Harcourt displays a wide grin), participants have just spent three months in their Maharashtra villages, living with families and integrating admirably into the communities, while completing the community project assigned to them.

---

1 Those who insist on being "politically correct," should say Mumbai, which was Bombay's real name when the British arrived ... Although they have wonderful qualities, they don't have a knack for languages! And since they were unable to pronounce Mumbai, they decreed it be dubbed Bombay. The mistake was corrected last January 1, but had lasted over two centuries ... and will endure for some time yet!

Over the last few days, each of the three groups of sixteen participants prepared a small "presentation," to illustrate the program's principal elements through pantomimes, skits and songs: co-operation between both counterparts—Indian and Canadian—living with families, the work experience, development-education days, etc.

This should last about fifteen minutes. I stress that the most important part of the event should be the personal discussions premiers will have with participants from their province. As is the rule, all regions of Canada, if not all provinces, are represented in this group. Unfortunately, since fate doesn't always do things perfectly, there are no participants from Prince Edward Island, Newfoundland or Manitoba. I apologize for this to premiers Catherine Callbeck, Gary Filmon and Clyde Wells ... who promised to take care of participants from the three provinces whose premiers didn't see fit to join Team Canada, i.e., Alberta, Saskatchewan and Quebec. As for Prime Minister Chrétien, choosing will be his only difficulty!

"During your stay in India," I dare say in concluding, "You'll meet lots of important people, work towards the signing of hundreds of millions of dollars worth of contracts, visit the Taj Mahal, the Qutad Minar, the Red Fort and who knows what else. However, I'm convinced this simple meeting with Canada World Youth participants will remain one of your fondest memories."

Amen!

Ten o'clock approaches. I have a few butterflies in my stomach. No doubt the effect of a ten-hour time change! Why should I worry about the quality of the participants' "presentation?" I've seen several dozen during my life and have never been let down. Besides, Canadian co-ordinator Robert Tudhope, an old hand, reassured me earlier this morning: "Everything should be fine!" he said with a confident smile.

With Prime Minister Chrétien in the lead, we finally reach the garden, where a small stage has been set up. A superb view of the Arabian Sea. We're greeted by Lieutenant General Mohan, director general of the National Cadet Corps (NCC), our counterpart in India. In full uniform, his chest festooned with medals. I congratulate him for this. "I have more," he says laughing, "but don't have enough space!"

Numerous guests are already there, including Roy MacLaren, the minister for international trade, and Raymond Chan, the secretary of state for Asia and the Pacific. The latter has been a steadfast friend of Canada World Youth since he visited a group in a Thai village last year.

Finally, I happily meet up with two colleagues from the Liberal Caucus, our two only MPs of Indian extraction: Gurbax Singh Malhi, from Toronto, a Sikh who always makes quite an impression with his magnificent turban (red, naturally!), and my cheerful accomplice from the memorable parliamentary delegation to Cuba, Herb Dhaliwal, from Vancouver.

Participants are decked-out for the occasion: the boys sport ties, while the girls wear Sunday saris (Indian "mothers" often lent theirs to Canadian daughters). They await us with flower garlands, placing them around our necks according to the wonderful local custom. Yanked out of the simple life in their villages since yesterday, they're obviously somewhat intimidated by all these good folks from the city.

Very brief speeches by Lieutenant General Mohan and the founding president.

And the feast begins! As expected, each of the three groups performs its number with infectious enthusiasm. I observe the gazes of the prime minister, premiers and other ministers: they appear delighted and, occasionally, touched, especially when the final scene occurs, where each participant places a hand on the globe (a humble thing borrowed from the school in one of the villages). At length, the earth almost disappears beneath a tangle of white and brown hands, as fifty youths from Canada and India sing about peace and friendship between peoples.

Besides, this will be the theme of Prime Minister Chrétien's brief address.

The ice is broken and participants surround each guest, often the premier of their province. I stand aside, knowing I'll later get to chat at length with participants during a luncheon organized for that purpose. Press photographers and cameramen are having a field day. Young Mathieu Trépanier, from Robertval, Quebec, who now speaks fluent English, is doing television interviews with both Radio-Canada and CBC.

The Indian press will surely mention the event ... which is perhaps more important for Canada-India relations than this afternoon's signing of contracts worth $444 million!

What about the Canadian press? Perhaps news editors will say "Good news is no news," since they'll have to choose between a photo of Mr. Chrétien speaking to the Indian prime minister, and the former in the midst of an animated conversation with Mario Losier, a young Acadian from Tracadie.

I discretely move from one group to the next. Mike Harris jokes with the five Ontario participants. He says to me, laughing: "Five more voters for the next election!"

Frank McKenna seems to be really enjoying himself with the two Acadian participants from New Brunswick.

Naturally, Prime Minister Chrétien is surrounded by a good crowd. At one point, he asks a young official from the Department of Foreign Affairs, Keith Fountain, what he thinks about Canada World Youth. I can't help from intervening ... perhaps to score yet another point.

"Mr. Prime Minister, I have to warn you that this young man can't provide an objective answer.

"Really?

"Keith is himself a former Canada World Youth participant! No doubt his experience in Sri Lanka, when he was barely twenty years old, helped him choose a career in diplomacy. Since Canada World Youth's world is small, I met up with him three years ago in Islamabad, where he was third secretary at the Canadian High Commission and, more recently, at our embassy in Warsaw, where he helped me set up a first youth-exchange program with Poland."

Never miss an opportunity! Thanks, Keith.

In short, as could've been expected, our participants perfectly executed this improvised operation aimed at charming the powers that be. Thanks to them, we now have new friends among the most important political figures in the country. All of them told me, with insistence, they were delighted by this encounter ... and that I'd been right to claim (with some temerity!) that this moment would likely be among the most moving recollections of their trip to Asia.

The day's program was very full and the event wasn't scheduled to last more than an hour. We finally had to take leave of one another after an *hour and a half*. Last to set off were Minister Chan, Premier Savage (for good reason!) and Minister Roy McLaren, who has the reputation of being stern and closer to businessmen than to exuberant young people. This mustn't be true, since his remarks were among the most praiseworthy I heard today:

"Jacques, this encounter was a wonderful idea. Trade between two countries is fine; but what Canada World Youth is doing to bring India and Canada closer together, in human terms, is perhaps better. These two endeavours obviously complement each other admirably. And your participants are wonderful!"

I give heartfelt congratulations to our co-ordinator, Robert Tudhope, a veteran I've known for a long time. I'd first met him fifteen years ago, when he was a participant in Sri Lanka. I saw him again here in India in 1991, when he was a project leader. He was still in the same country in 1992, and then headed to Egypt in 1993.

In the wake of the last hours' emotions, still dazed by a lack of sleep and the effects of jet lag, I follow Robert like a robot through Bombay's infernal streets: we walk to a neighbourhood restaurant, where we join participants, still astounded by the events they've just experienced. I eat one helping at a table, carry my plate to another, and so on until I've exchanged a few words with each participant.

Alas! I must leave after an hour to take part in Team Canada's program ... of which I'll be a member for a few more hours!

At 1:45 p.m., the signing ceremony for the noted $444 million worth of contracts.

At 2:45 p.m., a meeting with staff from the Canadian Consulate in Bombay.

At 4:20 p.m., the departure for Brabourne Stadium, where Prime Minister Chrétien will make an important speech before several hundred Indian and Canadian businessmen. Preceded by unavoidable motorcycle policemen, the delegation leaves the hotel in *fourteen* limousines, the first obviously being that of the prime minister. I climb into the eleventh ...

In the evening, I have another two-hour work session with our co-ordinator, Robert Tudhope, followed by another with our Indian counterpart, Lieutenant General Mohan.

One heck of a day!

January 12

Over the next days, I'll visit the other Canada World Youth team in the state of Karnataka, further south.

Another gruelling day in the works. I rise at 3:30 a.m. and leave Bombay for Bangladore at 6:30 a.m. Greeted at the airport by local NCC representatives around 8:00 a.m. We then hit the road for Mysore. Our official car, equipped with a powerful police siren, cuts a path through city streets teeming with vehicles, each more incredible than the next. From enormous trucks that belch thick black smoke, to the tiny three-wheeled taxis and countless bicycles that often give way under huge bags of rice or several dozen live chickens. And through it all, goats, stray dogs, sacred cows, and pedestrians often as heavily laden as the cyclists. Our siren doesn't impress overmuch ... Nearly four hours on bumpy roads, complete with a flat in the middle of the wilderness.

The two co-ordinators awaited us in Mysore: Scott Beveridge and his Indian counterpart, Sudhir Dautam. Given the brevity of my stay in Karnataka, we'll visit the Kadakola group today. Fortunately, the village is nearby.

Participants line up for the traditional welcoming ceremony. An Indian girl decorates me with a beautiful garland of jasmines and red roses. A Canadian participant, Erin Davidge, from Ottawa, marks my forehead with *Tilak*, a blood-red paste, and then sprinkles flower petals onto my bald head ... which sorely needs protection from the midday sun!

Following a routine briefing concerning the village of Kadakola and participant activities, the entire group lunches with the host family of Julie Landry, an Acadian from Petit-Rocher, New Brunswick, and her Indian counterpart, Manasi Majumder, from East Bengal. This house was selected because it's the only one with a room large enough to accommodate a group of twenty or so people. We sit on mats of braided rattan. A freshly picked banana leaf is placed in front of each guest, serving as a plate for the numerous vegetable helpings placed in small, multicolored clumps. It looks like a large painter's palette. We eat with the right hand, using caution with the smallest clumps, which are always dreadfully spiced.

To liven up the meal, participants sing a few ballads for me. First, an Acadian song in French, *Le monde a bien changé*, then another in English, *The Lion Sleeps Tonight* and, naturally, one in Hindi, *Chalte, Chalte*.

A tour of the village. Each Canadian participant and his counterpart take me into their family and introduce me to their "father" (*aja*) and "mother" (*ama*), not to mention their numerous brothers and sisters. To underscore India's religious diversity, the NCC has selected Muslim, Christian, Hindu and Jainist families.

Close links between members of the host family and the two participants are seen everywhere. This is particularly evident in the Muslim family, that of Jo-Annick Proulx from Saint-Agapit, Quebec, and his counterpart, Montoo, who's from the distant state of Gujarat. The family is in deep mourning following the recent and accidental death of a son who was the same age as participants. Out of consideration for the bereaved, organizers momentarily thought of finding another host family for Jo-Annick and Montoo; however, the *aja* and *ama* insisted on keeping their two adopted sons, who therefore experienced the family tragedy in all its intensity. This ordeal helped bring the two participants even closer; they tell me they've become friends for life. Jo-Annick writes letters to Montoo's parents, whom he's never met and, in turn, Montoo writes to Jo-Annick's parents. Both are still in contact with their host family from Blenheim, Ontario. "Even before returning to my own family in Saint-Agapit," Jo-Annick says, "I'll call on my Blenheim family. This will be easier since we'll return through Toronto. When I left them last October, my "parents" gave me a key to the house, indicating I could return whenever I pleased."

Kadakola participants are justifiably proud of their community project, which consists of building a new classroom for the village school. We go over to admire the humble concrete building that's to be completed within a week.

Besides this group activity and the development-education days, each participant has to perform a so-called individual work project, usually with a local craftsman. For example, Bill Spensely from Victoria, and his counterpart, Narender Khatri, from the state of Upper Pradesh, worked with a family that weaves mats using reeds from the river. They admit it takes them ten times as long to weave one on a crude loom made from wooden pieces planted in the ground. "I wove my first mat with great difficulty," Bill admits, "but it was sold in the market with the others."

Barbara Gravel from Desbiens, Quebec, and Sandhya Shetty, from neighbouring Maharashtra, work in the village's tiny bakery (eight metres square), which produces between six hundred and one thousand rolls every day.

Finally, the whole group meets for a long question-and-answer session: the moment of truth! Unfortunately, due to a lack of sleep and the continuing effect of jet lag, I'm nearly exhausted. But how can I fail to answer the pressing questions of participants? How can I not be moved by their spontaneous testimonies which, for the thousandth time, prove that Canada World Youth is worth all the effort, and most certainly all the money invested into it?

Peter Ruttan, from Stoney Creek, Ontario, says: "Canada World Youth changed me. My point of view and plans for the future have changed. And I owe much of this to discussions with my counterpart, Praveen. I now want to take action and use all I learned during the program. I have so many more options!"

For his part, Praveen says without hesitation: "Canada World Youth gave me self-confidence. It taught me patience. I previously didn't listen to others very much, but do now. I listen and understand others better: this is part of my new lifestyle."

When he arrived in this village, Travis Anderson from Regina, Saskatchewan, was completely staggered by the destitution, the poverty of the people who, in his opinion, lacked everything. "I then understood there are different ways of living. I discovered beauty in the simplest things. The children, especially, were a constant inspiration to me; I understood they were happy in their way."

Praveen adds that his stay in Blenheim, Ontario, helped him understand his own country better: "I returned to India with a desire to appreciate our extremely rich culture even more. As a result of Canada World Youth, I became prouder of my country, its culture, traditions and values."

I've left some out, likely some better ones, since I have a great deal of difficulty concentrating and listening as much as I should to these boys and girls who have so much to say.

I leave this beautiful group with some disappointment, knowing that lack of time—as well as that damned jet lag!—prevented me from doing justice to it.

Return to Mysore at about 6:00 p.m. I dream only of the large canopy bed that awaits me in the amazing hotel where my NCC hosts have lodged me, against my most earnest objections. It happens to be one of the Maharajah of Mysore's former palaces, dating from the still-recent time when, thanks to the complicity of their British masters, a plethora of sultans, maharajahs and other rajahs pretended to reign.

But our NCC friends had planned a grand dinner for me in another Mysore hotel.

They wanted to introduce a few notables to me, including the university's vice-dean, Mr. Madaiah, a great friend of Canada World Youth who's done us a thousand favours.

I admit it took superhuman effort to play my role during this wonderful dinner. It was served in a garden bursting with flowers, bougainvillaeas and, of course, palm trees whose crazy hairdo carved the nearly black sky into fine strands.

January 13

In the morning, we head to Palhalli, a village less than an hour from Mysore. A traditional welcome from the group, led by Claire Rochefort from Toronto and her counterpart, Sandhya.

At first, a brief cultural performance is given for me, no doubt excerpts from the more important production held before the community barely a few days ago, which attracted thousands of people, i.e., practically the whole population.

Two francophone participants, Geneviève Soucy from Cap-Chat, Quebec, and Pierre Chrétien from Gaspé, describe life in the village with a French song, whose lyrics they've written. Each Canadian participant and his Indian counterpart then speak about their host family and work project.

Dave Thompson from Timmins, Ontario, who's as skinny as a rake (he's lost fifteen pounds!), and his counterpart, Srijeet, enthusiastically describe their work project: building the small library which the village sorely needed. "We're really proud of our library," says Dave. "It's not the Taj Mahal, but we built it with our hands. All that wonderful concrete passed through our fingers ..."

A train of skits and pantomimes that describe all aspects of the program is next. To demonstrate their ability to learn languages, the group sings four songs, each in a different language: English, French, Hindi (India's national language) and Kannada (the local language).

A visit through the village guided by Meghan Masterson from Montreal: she informs me she lives in my neighbourhood, a few streets from my house! We first drop by the famous library, to be inaugurated in a few days, before the group departs. Through the bars of a window, waiting to be affixed to an exterior wall, lies a marble plaque engraved with the names of all the Indian and Canadian participants who helped with construction.

We visit host families at random as we stroll through small and dusty dirt streets, flooded with bright sunshine. Tea perfumed with cardamom and cookies. Participants introduce me to their *aja* and *ama*, often to a grandmother and, always, to swarms of beautiful, laughing children. Pierre Chrétien shows me the small room he shares with his counterpart, Francis, a boy from Tamil Nadu. They sleep on braided reed mats like everybody. Their only window looks out onto an interior court, where the family's three cows feed all day.

To visit some work projects, we must use an NCC truck. I happily pile into it with participants, sitting on the hard seat, to the greater despair of local NCC officials who'd prefer I ride in their official car. A discreet way of saying that participants count first and foremost at Canada World Youth. Everything else: staff, managers, field personnel, board members: exists only to ensure the unique experience offered to participants is made possible.

At some distance from the village, we stop before a crude installation where juice from locally grown sugar cane is extracted with a ramshackle machine ... no doubt in use for the last century or two. This work project is assigned to Michael Bendszak from Toronto and his counterpart, Mehrai Dube, from Madhya Pradesh. They show me the huge cauldrons where cane juice boils for hours. The dark-brown syrup is then poured into wooden moulds. The cakes of unrefined sugar thereby obtained are placed in large jute bags and shipped to a refinery.

Next stop: a poultry farm containing over a thousand cackling chickens, lovingly tended by Dave and Srijeet. Then come Cheryl Loeb from Comox Valley, British Columbia, and her counterpart, Niyati, from Gujarat; they introduce the wood sculptor they work with—when they can get away from building the library. This craftsman specializes in sculpting low reliefs on rosewood, and carves extremely beautiful doors and lintels. Both participants show me the small low reliefs they sculpted with their master's basic tools: an astonishing success for beginners.

We return to the centre of the village and stop at the tiny bakery, where the oppressive heat doesn't prevent Geneviève and Archana from working many hours a day.

Following this exhausting half-day we all end up in a corner of paradise: a bird sanctuary located a few kilometres from Palahalli. Luxuriant vegetation, with groves of enormous bamboos that burst out, now and again. Adorable little monkeys play hide-and-seek in the banyans, whose large, twisted branches look like the muscles of green giants.

Under the cool shade of a gazebo, we devour a picnic prepared by the seven host families, who each provided one dish. Neither variety nor spiciness are lacking! To help us digest, we take a rowboat ride on the river that crosses this tranquil bird kingdom. They fill the sky and hundreds are perched in trees on both banks. Here, a mango tree whose flowers are long-necked, white birds arriving from Siberia (who can blame them!). There, enormous trees whose branches are heavy with large brown fruits: giant bats, hanging by their feet. Their bodies dangle, huddled beneath hairy wings, as though eiderdown.

Here and there, on rocks that are awash, crocodiles warm themselves in the sun with open mouths. Easy to see why we'd been warned not to soak our fingers in the water.

Back to the gazebo. Participants and I exchange words that are lighthearted or serious. Their testimonies naturally remind me of similar ones, heard yesterday in Kadakola, or last year ... or twenty years ago!

Yet, I can't help being moved when hearing tall Dave declare before all his colleagues: "Never in my life have I made friends like these!" And his sympathetic gaze sweeps across the gazebo.

Niyati, Cheryl's counterpart, adds:

"Since we came to this village, Cheryl and I have shared absolutely everything: from belongings to ideas. We often talk during the day but, when night falls, we can't get to sleep without talking more ... until exhaustion overcomes us! Otherwise, we can't fall asleep!"

Lakshmi from Keral, counterpart to Winnipeg's Caithlin McArton: "I finally learned to take my responsibilities."

Menraj, Michael's counterpart: "I acquired maturity. Oh! and I learned English!"

He's not alone, if we're to believe our flamboyant Geneviève from Cap-Chat: "When I joined Canada World Youth, I didn't know a bloody word of English. And now, I think I speak it pretty well!" she concludes, bursting into laughter.

The cup runneth over.

"Still," I inquire, "there must be something you don't like about the program."

Following a protracted silence, towering Dave unfolds his gaunt carcass and answers: "Yes, there is and it hurts me: repeatedly having to tear ourselves away from those we love. First from our Canadian host families. Then, in five days, from my Palhalli family and our friends in the village. And I'll have to leave this group in a few weeks in Toronto. That's extremely difficult ..."

January 14

Kennalu, 5,500 inhabitants: last village before I return to Canada.

"A village wealthier than the others," explains Leela Acharya from Toronto, the group leader. "The villagers all own plots of land and grow sugar cane, rice, coconut."

Awaiting us at the village entrance are the mayor of Keenalu, the member of the legislative assembly for the state of Karnataka and other notables. A small musical ensemble makes a lot of noise: two flutists, whose strange instruments cry out for joy, somewhat jarringly, accompanied by a drum which pounds us with marvellous enthusiasm.

A female participant places a flower garland around my neck; its powerful bouquet makes my head spin somewhat. The sun blazes. Not the time to faint! Here again, the *Tilak* ceremony, which is religiously inspired, is entrusted to the tall and beautiful Terri Sundin, from Thunder Bay, Ontario. Draped in the sari of a princess, she prepares the red paste. She marks my forehead and sticks a few grains of rice to it, while her counterpart, Shubhra, dangles a small oil lamp in front of my face, its smoke blending with the scent of jasmine.

The village chief signals the musicians, who must lead our procession to the new library built by participants (with help from the villagers). It glimmers in the distance, at the end of main street, having been freshly painted lemon yellow. I'll have the honour of inaugurating it officially (look out for the paint: the last brush stroke was given last night!).

In front of the small building's door, a woman performs an extremely complex religious ceremony—needed to forever dispel bad spirits and attract good ones. She waters down three small and differently coloured clumps of powder placed on a banana leaf on the ground. She soaks a finger in the paste and draws a series of parallel bars at the base of the door. Evil spirits should henceforth beware. To ensure this, the woman smashes a coconut on the concrete threshold. In one half, she places a piece of camphor which burns as she twirls this unusual lamp. She then ignites a large fistful of incense sticks, whose fragrant smoke goes right into my nostrils, at the very moment I was getting used to the heavy perfumes of my buttercup-and-jasmine garland.

Evil spirits dispelled, the representative from Karnataka hands me a pair of scissors and beckons me to cut the two ribbons, one red, the other green, which block the door. Snip! Snip! The crowd, now including several hundred villagers, brings down the house. I'm then invited to visit the building: three rooms of concrete where, of course, there still isn't a single book.

There wasn't enough time to install the commemorative plaque, but we're able to read the following inscription:

DEDICATED TO THE PEOPLE OF KENNALU
FOR THEIR LOVE AND CO-OPERATION FOR
THE INDO-CANADIAN YOUTH EXCHANGE
PROGRAM BY SENATOR JACQUES HÉBERT

As well, the names of all Indian and Canadian participants are engraved in the marble for posterity.

The time for speaking to participants still hasn't come: this wouldn't be a proper inauguration without emotive speeches from the village chief, the district, state and NCC representatives, not to mention the member of the legislative assembly. We therefore sit beneath a huge, warmly coloured awning, installed at great cost for the occasion. A row of chairs is reserved for notables and, of course, the two microphones work only sporadically. The master of ceremonies is Shridnar Reddy, an Indian participant from Tamil Nadu, and counterpart to Hon Lu, a Torontonian of Vietnamese extraction.

I'd expected to speak last, which would've given me time to prepare my brief address. But the wretched Shridnar called me up first! I manage as best I can; the translation of each phrase into Kannada, the local language, allows me to think about the next one. My speech was very brief: a good example not followed by the other speakers, who wanted to give their money's worth to the hundreds of villagers squeezed together under the canopy, seated on mats on the ground. In any event, small metal chairs for members of our host families are placed on either side of the row of notables. Here and there, we recognize our male participants with their white shirts and Sunday ties. This is more difficult in the case of female participants, since they wear saris, like all the village women.

The star of the day will unquestionably be Anabelle Boulanger, from Laval, Quebec. With the quiet confidence of someone who's inaugurated libraries all her life, she approaches the microphone, beautiful in her gold-trimmed, burgundy sari. Her speech, many pages long, is written in the local language! The people appear to understand it, since they applaud repeatedly. She then repeats it in English (with a few French words thrown in for my benefit) for those who don't understand Kannada, including the Indian participants who, however, all speak at least three languages: English, Hindi, and the language of their respective state.

Anabelle then invites each Canadian and Indian participant to place a garland of flowers on their "father" and "mother," proudly seated in the first row.

The long ceremony completed, participants drag me down to the house inhabited by Christopher Chapman from Halifax and his counterpart, Sushil Rai, who's from the distant Northeast Territories, the poorest region of India.

Participants sit Indian-style before table mats made from tree leaves, on which portions of numerous vegetarian dishes are placed. Seated beside me, Christopher explains the composition of each with precision and authority.

We then have tea with the family of Vivien Lo from Saskatoon and her counterpart, Meenakshi Vekatesan, from Tamil Nadu. They show me their tiny room: "We're privileged," says Vivien, laughing. She opens the shutters of the little window which looks out on ... the library! "We were able to relax until the last minute ... As soon as we'd see Leela (the group leader) heading towards the construction site, we just had to cross the street to get there before she did!"

We set out in small groups to explore the village, followed by a swarm of children who call participants by name, since they're now old friends. We stop time and again. Here, to visit a host family; there, to see a craftsman who taught the basics of his skill to two participants.

Ghyslain Plourde from Saint-Hubert, Quebec, suddenly tells me: "I'm absolutely certain I'll return to this village, one day, to see my 'parents' and friends. And I'll look at the library with pride, knowing I had a small part in its construction ..."

The more formal meeting with all participants takes place in a school room. As is fitting, they sing a few songs, a small sample from the cultural performance they gave before the public two days ago which, by popular demand, they'll repeat tonight.

Their big hit was a song whose lyrics they wrote. It's very topical and concerns the bitter fight opposing the entire population of Karnataka and that of Tamil Nadu, the neighbouring state which suffers from a sever water shortage. The latter gets some of its water from the Cauvery River which flows through the village. The river usually swells during the Monsoon season and Karnataka, which controls the source, then allows the surplus to flow towards Tamil Nadu. However, rain was scarce this year and the river level fell dangerously, which convinced state authorities to stop supplying Tamil Nadu. "Charity begins at home ..." Thus began an epic dispute between the two neighbours. Threatened by draught, Tamil Nadu appealed to the central government in Delhi, which rendered a decision in its favour. The party of Prime Minister Rao will pay dearly for this, since Karnataka's entire population is outraged. There's even been violence.

The participants' song obviously sided with *their* state, which explains their success the other night. The audience even clamoured for an encore!

Participants take turns describing their experience. It's fascinating to observe what's happened to the hearts and minds of these young people in less than seven months. I have reams of notes I'll occasionally re-read. But, to save a few trees, I'll settle on quoting only four out of fourteen participants. May the others forgive me!

Anabelle Boulanger, from Laval, Quebec: "Our group is radically different from the way it was at the beginning. We've come a very long way ... We finally learned to co-operate and work together. As well, I developed leadership skills, learned English and a little Kannada, the village language. My plans for the future have changed: I was thinking of becoming a doctor, but am now attracted to journalism, or by the more creative sciences. Today, I realize *everything* is possible; I can change the world!"

Shalaka Patkar, from Maharashtra, Anabelle's counterpart: "I learned to respect differences. And, believe me, I found it hard to adapt to this village, since I'd always lived in a large city. In fact, I had fewer problems adapting to life in Canada! Thanks to Canada World Youth, I finally discovered how Indians in our villages live (seventy-five per cent of the population!). This changed my way of seeing and my horizons have broadened infinitely ..."

Leigh Manikel, from Winnipeg: "As a Westerner, I had preconceptions about Quebeckers, especially because of the referendum. During the program, I was able to speak in all frankness and friendship with francophones in my group. I realized that people in my province often lack tolerance and don't properly judge our compatriots from the rest of Canada."

Christopher Chapman, from Halifax: "I was frankly disappointed when I learned the Canadian part of the program would take place in Ontario. The worst province to be in! I've changed my mind. I lived in Strathroy with a first-generation Iranian family. My 'parents' questioned me more about life in Canada, than they did my counterpart about his country! It was a challenge, but very rewarding as well."

And that's how, thanks to Iran, Christopher reconciled himself with Ontario!

Let's give the last word to Shalaka Patkar, Anabelle's counterpart:

"We finally understood that the world is small. I'd previously considered Canada as part of the world. But it wasn't *our* world. Following the experience I've just been through, I now realize Canada is part of *my* world."

Index of names

L

M

N

O

P

R

S

T

PRINTED AND BOUND
IN BOUCHERVILLE, QUEBEC, CANADA,
BY MARC VEILLEUX INC.
IN APRIL, 1996